WRETCHED
SISTERS

PETER LANG
New York • Bern • Frankfurt • Berlin
Brussels • Vienna • Oxford • Warsaw

MARY WELEK ATWELL

WRETCHED SISTERS

Examining Gender
and Capital Punishment

SECOND EDITION

PETER LANG
New York • Bern • Frankfurt • Berlin
Brussels • Vienna • Oxford • Warsaw

Library of Congress Cataloging-in-Publication Data
Atwell, Mary Welek, author.
Wretched sisters: examining gender and capital punishment /
Mary Welek Atwell. — 2nd edition.
pages cm. — (Studies in crime and punishment; vol. 20)
Includes bibliographical references.
1. Trials (Murder)—United States. 2. Female offenders—Legal status, laws, etc.—United.
3. Capital punishment—United States. I. Title.
KF221.M8A98   364.66092'520973—dc23   2014024885
ISBN 978-1-4331-2234-7 (paperback)
ISBN 978-1-4539-1418-2 (e-book)
ISSN 1529-2444

Bibliographic information published by **Die Deutsche Nationalbibliothek**.
Die Deutsche Nationalbibliothek lists this publication in the "Deutsche
Nationalbibliografie"; detailed bibliographic data are available
on the Internet at http://dnb.d-nb.de/.

The paper in this book meets the guidelines for permanence and durability
of the Committee on Production Guidelines for Book Longevity
of the Council of Library Resources.

CONTENTS

ACKNOWLEDGMENTS

This book has been both a labor of love and labor of pain. At times the sadness of the lives and deaths of the wretched sisters and the failures of the system were almost overwhelming. But I hope I repressed the anger and sadness to tell their stories in an honest and respectful way.

I have been extremely fortunate to work with some wonderful graduate students who helped with research, read drafts of the manuscript, and discussed the death penalty at great length. I am especially grateful to Mindy Griffith, Donna Hale, Bakir Poljac, Brandi Sanders Mullins, and Katherine Miller.

My daughter, Polly Atwell, is, as always my confidant and most valuable intellectual colleague.

ACKNOWLEDGMENTS (2014)

I have additional thanks to offer as the second edition of *Wretched Sisters* is completed. Abby Smith and Hollie Fitzgerald assisted enthusiastically with research. Graduate students in several seminars on Capital Punishment asked interesting questions and helped to clarify the discussion of how gender impacts the administration of the death penalty. I will miss conversations about these issues with many wonderful students.

David has offered immeasurable support as well as the opportunity to spend some time in Texas, an excellent place to learn about capital punishment.

INTRODUCTION TO THE
SECOND EDITION

2001 - 2007. 6 F. (4w +2B)

2008- 2014: 295 executions
4 female
2 black, 2 white
Victims: all male
except Kimberly McCarthy (b)
killed w.F.

2015 - 2016: - 98
2017: 6
Jan -4, Mar -2

2015: 1 (w)

When *Wretched Sisters* was first published in 2007, I hoped there would never be a need for a second edition, that no more women would be executed in the United States. After the execution of Frances Newton in 2005, five years passed before another woman, Teresa Lewis, was put to death in Virginia. Then in 2013 and 2014, Texas executed Kimberly McCarthy and Suzanne Basso. With three recent executions, it seems there is a reason to update this work. The second edition offers a chance to see what has changed and what has remained the same.

Most observers would agree that the climate surrounding capital punishment is different from the atmosphere of the late twentieth century, even from the atmosphere of seven years ago. Although the death penalty still has many strong supporters, there is also more vigorous and widespread opposition. Statistics bear this out. Since 2007, five states—New Jersey, New Mexico, Illinois, Connecticut, and Maryland—have abolished capital punishment. New York's highest court found its capital statute unconstitutional and that state's death row has been demolished. Governors of Oregon and Washington have each declared a moratorium on executions. Perhaps even more revealing of changes in attitude toward capital punishment, the number of death sentences per year has decreased from over 300 in the late 1990s to

80 in 2013. Likewise the number of executions carried out has declined from 98 in 1999 to 39 in 2013.

Public support for capital punishment as measured by opinion polls has decreased in the twenty-first century. While in 1994, 80% stated that they favored the death penalty for murder, in 2013 the number had declined to 61%. When offered options including life without parole, only 33% expressed support for capital punishment.[1] Scholars and commentators have offered a number of reasons to explain the decline in support for the death penalty. Some have suggested that the stories of innocent people on death row—some exonerated, some apparently not—have led many people to question the use of the death penalty. The availability of life without parole as an alternative sentence in all death penalty states may also contribute to its declining popularity. Greater awareness that a death sentence costs the state many times more than a sentence of life in prison may also have changed some minds, especially among fiscal conservatives. Some have noted that the rise of libertarian sentiments may lead those who believe government's power should be limited to question whether any government should have the power to take the lives of its citizens.

In addition, the United States stands virtually alone among modern industrial democracies in its use of capital punishment. The European Union nations oppose the death penalty and follow policies intended to curb its use. For this reason, a number of European drug companies have refused to sell preparations used in lethal injections to the U.S. Thus, the states who wish to continue to execute their citizens have found themselves either seeking new drugs from unregulated pharmaceutical companies or experimenting with novel combinations of drugs. The gruesome executions that have resulted from these procedures have raised further questions about the future of the death penalty.

But even as some things have shifted, other things have changed very little—at least in the states that have retained the death penalty. Respected non-partisan organizations, such as the American Bar Association and The Constitution Project, have issued major reports outlining problems with the way capital punishment is administered.[2] To no one's surprise these studies document some persistent issues: incompetent and underfunded defense lawyers; wide prosecutorial discretion; problems with jury selection; geographical inconsistencies; elected judges for whom capital cases may determine their political future; inadequate policies for dealing with mental disabilities and mental illness among defendants; racial disparities. Death sentences continue to be largely a feature of states in the South. Texas is still performing approximately one-third of all executions in the nation.

This new edition of *Wretched Sisters* demonstrates a number of those themes. Of the three new cases, all took place in southern states two of them in Texas, one from Dallas and one from Houston. These conform to the geographical pattern of where capital sentences are most likely to occur. Likewise, all the women executed since 2007 had inadequate assistance from their court-appointed attorneys. One of them had indications of mental retardation, one was mentally ill, and the third was addicted to drugs. There are clear issues of racial bias in Kimberly McCarthy's case. And, as this book seeks to illustrate, gender played a role in each case. In ways subtle and overt, all three of the most recently executed women were convicted—at least in part—based on their failures to measure up to the social expectations for women.

Endnotes

1. Death Penalty Information Center, *Facts about the Death Penalty* (May 12, 2014) at www.deathpenaltyinfo.org
2. American Bar Association, *Texas Capital Punishment Assessment Report: An Analysis of Texas Death Penalty Laws* (American Bar Association, 2013).

INTRODUCTION TO THE
FIRST EDITION

Since 2004 when I began researching and writing this book, I have found a common response among friends, students, and colleagues when I explain its subject. Of the fourteen women executed in the last thirty years, most people recognize only the names of Karla Faye Tucker and Aileen Wuornos. The others are anonymous. They were poor, often uneducated, not particularly attractive women, who, in most cases led difficult lives. When we talk about the small number of women who have been put to death for murder, people usually assume there are so few because the criminal justice system is reluctant to execute women, that they receive some sort of special treatment based on their sex. Many see this as part of a historic attitude of chivalry.

I posed the question to my students, "Suppose Lizzie Borden had been Larry Borden. How would the story be different?" We were discussing the 1892 ax murders of Andrew Borden and his wife Abigail. Thirty-two year-old Lizzie, a spinster who lived at home, was arrested and charged a week after the murders. Although she never gave a coherent account of her activities on the morning of the deaths and although no other suspect was ever identified, Lizzie was found "not guilty" of the two bloody killings.

The students answered immediately that "Larry" would have been denied the special favoritism, the "chivalry" that acquitted Lizzie of the murder of her father and stepmother. They agreed with the general popular sentiment that the legal system treated Miss Borden more leniently in part because the male lawyers, male judge, and all-male jury could not face the prospect of convicting a female of a violent ax murder. As a respectable, middle-class "lady," Lizzie Borden reminded those in court of their wives and daughters, a comparison drawn overtly by the defense attorneys and the presiding judge and acknowledged even by the prosecutor. The defendant herself seemed to exploit these gendered assumptions by carrying flowers into the courtroom and weeping when the proceedings offended her feminine delicacy. Yet the simple conclusion that Lizzie Borden walked free just because she was a woman and that her experience in some way typified that of other women accused of murder ignores the larger context of gender and its relation to the legal system.

As Carol Smart has noted, law not only acts on gendered subjects, law is part of the continual reproduction of gender differentiation. In other words, Lizzie Borden's fate was influenced by the man-made legal system under which she lived, and, at the same time, her experience became a factor in the way others would see and interpret the law. As a woman in the 1890s, Lizzie Borden's life was circumscribed by her sex. She was expected to be a dutiful daughter and to live "a life consisting mainly of things that didn't happen."[2] Had the fictional Larry Borden existed, his life would have been different long before he ever set foot in the courtroom. Larry and other men like him would have had a voice in the laws under which they lived and a chance to participate in interpreting them. Even on trial for murder, Lizzie was held to a system of laws which *no* woman had helped to formulate. She lived within a patriarchal structure in which power and privilege were unequally distributed, where maleness was the standard for full citizenship. Yet her acquittal has been interpreted as evidence of privilege and deference accorded to women—or more properly to "ladies," for class was surely a significant factor in Lizzie Borden's case. Those who sat in judgment of her were mindful of her respectability and of her family's position in the community. Equally important was the competent legal representation her money was able to secure. Had she been a poor woman or a woman of "questionable virtue" on trial for murder, her failure to meet the class-based definition of femininity would have undermined her claim of innocence.

The point of this exercise is not to plead that Lizzie Borden should not have been accountable for murder, if she was actually guilty. Rather in looking at the story of Lizzie Borden or of any other person accused of a crime, gender and class are inextricably linked with the circumstances of the case. Our real concern is why, if Lizzie had been Larry and if Larry/Lizzie had been a marginal member of the community, the outcome would have been different. To demonstrate that such considerations are not just idle speculation, one might compare the story of Lizzie Borden with that of a notorious female ax murderer of the late twentieth century, Karla Faye Tucker. Totally lacking the privileges of class, social status, and conventional femininity, Tucker found that a modern jury could easily believe that a woman like her was capable of murdering two people with a pickax.

Formal Equality

An examination of the women, including Tucker, who ended up on death row in the contemporary era reveals both similarities to and differences from the Borden example. Today governments and private individuals are prohibited from discriminating on the basis of sex. Women are thus promised formal equality with men. But merely setting up a male standard of justice, demanding that women be treated as if they were men, does not address the complex issues of gender and law.

The title of this book comes from an article by legal scholar Elizabeth Rapaport in which she notes that some efforts to substitute formal equality for gender bias in the application of the death penalty could result in a "campaign to exterminate a few more wretched sisters."[3] Rapaport's comment is a useful starting place for this inquiry. From one perspective, women have been underrepresented in the history of capital punishment in the United States. We know that since capital punishment was reinstated in 1976, women have made up less than 2% of those sentenced to death and only 1.1% of those were actually executed. We know that at the end of 2006, 58 women and more than 3000 men reside on the death rows of the 38 states that have capital punishment. It is a fact that when three women, all in Oklahoma, were given lethal injections in 2001 (a year when 63 men were put to death), it was the largest number of female executions in a single year since 1863 when Virginia hanged six slave women. Two women were executed in 2002 and none were put to death in 2003 or 2004. Many were surprised when Texas executed one woman, Frances Newton, in 2005. By comparison, the numbers for men were 70, 65, 59, and 59, respectively. Thus Rapaport's rueful comment makes sense. A certain interpretation of gender equity would demand the execution of more women. The reality of capital punishment tells us that they would be among our more wretched sisters.

But simply reiterating the "maleness" of death row is old news.[4] Counting the number of women sentenced to death and comparing it to the number of men is just the smallest segment of the story of gender and capital punishment. It comes as no surprise to anyone conversant with the criminal justice system that death house residents are mostly men, just as men far outnumber women throughout prisons and jails. Nor is it any surprise that the 9:1 ratio of males to females in the corrections system reflects a distribution that crosses jurisdictions and that has persisted for as long as anyone has calculated patterns of crime and punishment. During the last several decades, influenced by a maturing feminist scholarship, criminologists have finally devoted some serious attention to questions raised by the disparities correlated with sex and gender. We now have some valuable work that addresses the twofold puzzle: why do so few women commit crime and why do those few do so? The work of feminist criminology is one element within the scope of this book.

Theory, Law, and Practice

One might begin by noting that because the gap in criminal behavior between men and women is consistent across time and space, gender itself must be part of the explanation.[5] Nothing else seems to account for why such disparities persist, especially when it comes to the most violent crimes. In general, serious offenses by women are more likely to be "situationally induced," embedded within an abusive relationship rather than part of a criminal lifestyle. When one examines the stories of women sentenced to death, prior relationships with the victims, often enmeshed within a history of abuse, are common factual similarities. The first chapter will explore what feminist criminological theory offers to explain the links between victimization and deviance, especially as these factors exist within a patriarchal society. In addition to examining the patriarchal structures that value victims so unequally, the chapter will also look at the ways in which the system continues to hold men and women to different standards. It will support the argument that with respect to gender, the capital punishment regime is *especially* arbitrary and capricious in a way that disadvantages women as offenders and as victims.

Chapter two places the issue of gender and capital punishment in the context of relevant decisions by the United States Supreme Court. Although the Court has never directly addressed the question of sex discrimination in the application of the death penalty, its decisions with respect to equal protection for women and their general death penalty jurisprudence offer a foundation for placing the issue within a legal framework. Many argue that the edifice of law created around capital punishment in the recent past has made its application more "arbitrary and capricious" than it was when it was temporarily outlawed in 1972.[6]

Chapters three through nine focus on the eleven women who have been put to death in the recent past. Each has a story, and the stories place the women within the framework developed by feminist criminology. Their stories include terrible crimes, and honesty is not served by pretending otherwise. Yet every one of the executed women experienced a flawed criminal justice system. This work examines their cases—not simply from the perspective of the crime but also from the perspective of how fallible human beings operated the "machinery of death."[7]

The final chapter is an effort to synthesize what can be learned about crime and punishment in a patriarchal society by looking at the issues of gender and the death penalty. Some would argue that such a small number of cases do not afford enough examples from which to draw conclusions. But if the few women who face death at the hands of the state have life experiences common to significant numbers of other women, their stories can contribute to our understanding of systemic gender inequities. They may also afford further evidence of the impossibility of creating flawless and unerring policies for determining who lives and who dies.

Psychiatrist Dorothy Otnow Lewis poses a question that captures the perspective of this book. When you read about the trials and executions of witches, she asks, do you identify with the woman accused of witchcraft or do you identify with the crowd calling for her death?[8] Like Lewis, I realized, I empathize with the "witch." I can see myself in her shoes—condemned to death by a system where the rules were written and applied by people who knew little about my life and who were unwilling or unable to hear my story.

A similar approach, seeing the fourteen executed women who are its subjects through the prism of their own experience, is my goal for this book. Each of these women was found guilty of murder. In most cases, there is little doubt that she actually "did the crime." Yet I would argue that an empathetic probing into each of these stories may offer a useful way to address the basic question posed by these fourteen death cases. How do we explain the role this woman played in the crime and why, out of all the murders committed in the United States, was she selected for the death penalty? As I read about each one of these cases, I tried to imagine what her life was like before the killing. Where did she live? How did she survive and earn a living? Who were the people around her? Did she have friends? What was going on in the days immediately before the murder? How did things get to the point of desperation where killing someone seemed to make sense?

I also wanted to imagine what each of the women felt as she sat in the courtroom and listened to the prosecutor describe her as a "monster," a "black widow spider," an "unnatural mother," or any one of dozens of dehumanizing terms the state will use to persuade a jury that someone does not deserve to live. Perhaps readers of this book will put themselves in the place of some of these offenders as they heard their own lawyers offer truncated or inadequate defenses that left out the critical events in the accused women's lives.

This book is not an extended argument that the fourteen executed women were "innocent," although I believe there is strong evidence that Frances Newton was wrongly convicted. But perhaps because there are only fourteen cases to examine and therefore it is possible to flesh out their lives and deaths, it offers an extraordinary chance to confront the structural factors that determine the application of capital punishment in the United States and to raise questions about the arguments that support that application.

Justice Thurgood Marshall claimed that if Americans understood the injustices that characterize the workings of the capital punishment system, they would reject it. This book is an effort to expand that understanding.

Endnotes

1. Carol Smart, *Law, Crime, and Sexuality* (London: Sage, 1995), 2–3.
2. Ann Jones, *Women Who Kill* (Boston: Beacon Press, 1996), 237.
3. Elizabeth Rapaport, "The Death Penalty and Gender Discrimination," *Law and Society Review* 25 (1991), 368.
4. Joan W. Howarth, "Executing White Masculinities: Learning from Karla Faye Tucker," *Oregon Law Review* 81 (Spring 2002), 210.
5. Darrell Steffensmeier and Lisa Brody, "Explaining in Female Offending," in *Women, Crime, and Criminal Justice*, ed. Claire M. Renzetti and Lynne Goodstein (Los Angeles: Roxbury, 2001), 111–112.
6. *Furman v. Georgia*, 408 U.S. 238 (1972).
7. *Callins v. Collins*, 510 U.S. 1141 (1994).
8. Dorothy Otnow Lewis, *Guilty by Reason of Insanity* (New York: Fawcett Columbine, 1998), 9–10.

· 1 ·

WHY SO FEW AND WHY THESE FEW?
GENDER AND CRIMINOLOGY

It is a cliché to state that mainstream criminological theory does not adequately address issues relating to women's criminality. Much empirical research examines the delinquent behavior of young males and, until the fairly recent contributions of feminist theory, most researchers failed to consider the two big questions regarding gender and crime. Why do women consistently commit many fewer crimes than men? And, why do a small number of women commit serious offenses? It is beyond the scope of this study to attempt general answers to those questions. However, a vital part of this inquiry involves an effort to find the themes in criminological theory that help to explain the crimes committed by the fourteen executed women and to address why they evoked the most extreme response. As Chesney-Lind and Pasko note, feminist criminology is concerned with "how gender matters," not only in explaining the pathways into and out of crime but also regarding how the criminal justice system responds to offenders. Those issues are at the heart of this work.

Historically, explanations of female crime have fallen into two major categories. On the one hand, biological and psychological approaches argued that women offenders were more "masculine" than law-abiding women, that their crime was anomalous and attributable to some unnatural male-like qualities. Another more sociological perspective claims that males and females are influenced by the same social forces and that the findings of criminological theory transcend gender. In other words, those taking such a position would argue that the factors that explain male offending work just as well to explain female offending.[2]

Partly because the total number of serious crimes by women is so small, there continues to be a tendency to explain those offenses by examining individual pathology and neglecting larger social and structural concerns. Individualized explanations have a "strong foothold" in the study of female crime. But such theories leave out the importance of social and structural influences.[3] For example, most of the women included in this study experienced some form of physical and/or sexual abuse. But, while acknowledging the events of their lives, we cannot focus our discussion only on their personal stories without placing those experiences of abuse within a larger social—patriarchal—framework. Likewise, if their reactions to that abuse took the form of violence, the social context in which other responses were unavailable may provide some explanations for that behavior. If within a patriarchal framework, a Christina Riggs or a Betty Lou Beets or a Velma Barfield believed she had no legitimate recourse against an abusive sibling, spouse, or parent, how did gendered social structures channel their behavior?

According to Steffensmeier and Broidy, three elements should inform an inquiry into female offending and the gender gap in crime: how the organization of gender either deters or shapes female deviance but encourages male deviance; the different contexts of male and female offending; and how women's routes or pathways into crime differ from men's. The last element involves such social realities as the blurring of lines between victimization and offending by women; how women are excluded from the most lucrative criminal opportunities; the exploitation of women's sexuality; the consequences of motherhood and child care; the centrality of relationships for women; and women's frequent need for protection from exploitive, predatory males. Those factors influence why and how women come to engage in criminal behavior.[4]

Those authors argue that broad social forces have a general impact on both male and female crime. For example, social disorganization (environments that lack strong conventional institutions) and differential association (the influence of deviant associates on learned criminal behavior) may increase the propensity toward crime by both men and women. But those forces are mediated by gendered structures and dynamics at both the social and individual level and therefore they play out differently in women's lives than they do in men's. Steffensmeier and Broidy claim that although general causal explanations may apply to the context of both male and female offending, the pathways into criminality are different, especially for serious crime.[5]

It Takes a Lot to Make a Girl Go Wrong

Giardino and Rockwell develop a similar theme. Their research found that "high-end" female offending (serious crime) was best explained by an extreme form of differential association theory. In typical families, if there is one deviant parent—generally the father—his influence may be balanced by a conforming mother. But in Giardino and Rockwell's study, serious female offenders came from homes engulfed in deviance. Girls from such families experienced "total immersion" in antisocial behavior with little or no access to conforming individuals.[6] Among the executed women, this pattern is particularly applicable to the lives of Karla Faye Tucker, Aileen Wuornos, and Suzanne Basso, arguably the most violent of the "wretched sisters." In Giardino and Rockwell's sample, the subjects experienced both indirect and direct opportunities to learn criminal behavior. The indirect messages came through exposure to drugs, sexual abuse, and violence and the direct through actual instruction in deviance.//The encouragement to engage in deviant behavior was accompanied by the absence of sanctions for failure to conform.// Thus in the lives of these women, dropping out of school, for example, was not treated negatively by the "responsible" adults. Instead, such parents forced autonomy on their daughters when they were too young to handle it. Abuse plus neglect plus exposure to violence, stealing, prostitution, and drug and alcohol abuse led to involvement in those behaviors.[7] What makes Giardino and Rockwell's theory gender-specific is their conclusion that the exceptionally high level of exposure to deviance and the almost total lack of negative response to it correlate with "high-end" female offending/Presumably serious offending by males can be connected with much lower levels of immersion in deviance during the formative years.

When Nothing Goes Right

General Strain Theory (GST) offers another possible approach to understanding female criminality. Strain theory posits that crime and deviance occur when socially approved goals and socially approved means are out of alignment. For example, if material wealth has a high social value, but many people find the legitimate routes to gaining wealth are blocked for them, they may turn to crime to achieve their goal. General Strain Theory expands the possible sources of strain beyond the failure to achieve financial success. Proponents of GST suggest also that different responses to strain may be correlated with gender. Broidy and Agnew argue that strain among men is more likely connected with financial disappointments. For women, relationships, family, and friends are more important measures of success and therefore greater sources of strain. In GST, crime is linked to strain via the negative emotions, especially anger, produced by the stressful experience. Men and women typically deal differently with anger. Where men may respond with violence, women are inclined to repress anger into depression, guilt, or anxiety. These different ways of coping, plus differences in social support, opportunity, social control and disposition lead to different responses to strain. Thus Broidy and Agnew assert gender differences both in the sources of strain and in the responses to it.[8] They argue further that for women and girls strain is exacerbated when the failure to achieve expectations is perceived as unfair, as the result of discrimination. Strain may also result from the loss of positively valued stimuli, e.g., the death of friends or family members or the lack of opportunity to take on desired social roles. Or strain may be caused by negatively valued stimuli, particularly victimization. According to GST, women's criminality can be correlated with failure to achieve goals, including financial well-being and interpersonal relationships, with unfair treatment, with the loss of positive ties, and with control and restrictions on behavior. Crime will become more likely when non-deviant coping strategies (e,g., self-medication), are not available.[9]

Others, such as Owen, cast GST in the form of pathways or life-course theory. Owen examined women in prison and found that their lives before incarceration had been shaped by multiple types of abuse, disrupted personal relationships, and drug use. These experiences (strains) contributed to spiraling marginality and eventually to criminality in their lives.[10] Katz also subscribes to a revised version of strain theory. She argues that the victimization of girls and women predicts criminal involvement over the life course. Women who are victims of abuse at an early age have often been socialized to conform to male wishes and to silence their own voices, but eventually they may react to those negative stimuli through criminal behavior.[11] Many of the women in Katz's study first dealt with their abuse by turning in on themselves and, in some cases, self-medicating with prescription drugs, alcohol, illegal drugs, or promiscuity. Velma Barfield, Betty Lou Beets, Marilyn Plantz, Christina Riggs, Karla Faye Tucker, Aileen Wuornos, Teresa Lewis—all to some degree fit this model.

The Victim/Offender Continuum

Legal scholars, although not addressing criminological theory directly, also discuss the link between victimization and female crime. As Keitner points out, for many women criminality and victimization are not separate statuses. Rather victimization and criminality form a continuum of experience. The problem is a system that treats a crime as a "snapshot," a separate event in which one must be *either* victim or offender but cannot be both. Such a perspective (which is clear in the trial of every woman in this study) neglects to address the reality where women have experienced victimization either by individuals and/or by the action or inaction of the state.[12]

Keitner argues further that judicial determinations about violence by women should consider the pre-existing gender-power imbalance and the failure of state institutions to redress those inequities.[13] In the cases detailed in this book, such considerations were totally absent from the criminal justice process. That process tended to reflect "sex-based differences in norms and expectations."[14] The executed women acted aggressively. They did not, as women are expected to do, persist in internalizing their personal traumas. Instead, they externalized responses to trauma in violent ways. As GST predicts, they responded to strain by violence because non-deviant coping strategies were not available.

The criminal justice system, particularly the courts, have not seen women's violence that comes at the end of a long history of battering or abuse as either a form of self-defense or as part of the continuum of victimization/ criminality. Rather such women are often said to suffer from "borderline personality disorder." Kendall and Pollack call that disorder a "wastebasket diagnosis" given to troublesome patients, a new name for "disorderly women." They argue instead that victims of chronic abuse actually experience a form of Post Traumatic Stress Disorder (PTSD).[15]

Many feminists, however, caution against placing a psychological onus on battered women who kill. Schneider sees pathologizing such women as one of many misconceptions that prevent the justice system from perceiving the issues of gender inequality associated with domestic violence. Seeing victims of abuse simply as damaged individuals distracts attention from structural inequities that allow the abuse to occur. Another misconception is that battered women who kill are "monsters." Traditionally killing a husband or male partner has been treated as more serious than killing a wife because, in a patriarchal society, violence by a woman toward her husband struck at the heart of the civil order. It upset the social hierarchy and was therefore especially "monstrous."[16] Yet as Leonard notes, women who kill often do so out of mortal fear, while husbands often do so out of rage. The irony is that courts too often believe the man was "goaded into it" and treat him leniently, while treating a battered woman as more pathological than her batterer.[17] In Wilson's view this double standard toward violence by men and women serves to maintain the patriarchal structure.[18]

An Integrated Approach

For the purposes of analyzing the fourteen cases included in this study, an integrated criminological theory seems the most useful. Ogle, Maier-Katkin, and Bernard are critical of the utility of most theories of female criminality in explaining homicide. They raise six main criticisms of such approaches: most are based on studies of less serious crimes; many theories look at individual pathologies, not social structure; some associate crime and violence with women's liberation, yet most offenders are more traditional than liberated; some theories, such as studies of battered women who kill, apply to only one setting; many blur the line between criminological theory and strategies for legal defense; they do not adequately explain the similarities between those who kill spouses and those who kill their children.[19] Ogle et al. have an ambitious objective—to explain the low rates of violence among women, "punctuated by very infrequent and almost random instances of extreme violence."[20] In other words, they attempt to answer the two major questions of feminist criminological theory—"why so few?" and "why these few?" Their solution is to explain homicides committed by women by integrating General Strain Theory developed by Agnew with Megargie's notion of the overcontrolled personality and Bernard's thesis about chronic high arousal among the truly disadvantaged.

As with those who rely exclusively on GST, the integrated theory looks at sources of strain for women. Ogle et al. describe a number of gendered factors contributing to stress: lower social status; lower-paying jobs; few opportunities for advancement; dependence on men; internalizing the social devaluation of femaleness; a negative self-image connected with one's appearance; low self-esteem and the lack of self-confidence. Those who seek intimacy outside of traditional marriage (in this study, Barfield, Allen, Plantz, Tucker, Riggs, Wuornos, Block, Lewis) are seen as violating social norms. At the same time, most tend to evaluate themselves through the success of their relationships, conventional or not. Because standing alone is hard, women with less autonomy and especially those with disabilities work hard to preserve any valued relationship. Rather than lose a relationship, they often internalize the anger and hurt caused by many things, present and past.[21]

As women, they have been socialized to control the expression of anger but according to Megargie's work, the overcontrolled personality tends to explode if and when it overcomes its high level of inhibitions. The other side of repressing anger is a lack of experience in expressing it in harmless ways. Someone may commit no violence for a long period of time—or never—and then erupt like a volcano. Most women in this study had no history of violence, no criminal record, yet each apparently burst out into the most extreme form of violence, homicide.

Ogle et al. also consider situational stresses especially among the truly disadvantaged that can contribute to a sense of insecurity and threat, a state of psychological arousal. Among these stresses are abuse, postpartum depression, a low social position with few resources, discrimination, and isolation from conventional social supports. The failures of the criminal justice and social service systems may also be sources of stress, but these institutions are seldom available as targets for frustration. Instead, the women who experience the strains, who have few strategies for dealing with anger, and who feel a sense of threat erupt and strike out at targets that are nearby and vulnerable—very often family members.[22]

This integrated approach seems to offer the best framework for merging theoretical explanations about women and crime with the specific facts of the fourteen cases examined here. The emphasis on the gendered nature of the stressors and the socially conditioned response to them provides a useful extension to the principles of General Strain Theory. It allows for the consideration of environmental factors, such as low income, low status, and isolation. It offers a way to assimilate the experience of abuse into a larger theoretical framework. In addition, it offers a persuasive explanation of why these women, most of whom never before ran afoul of the law, became involved in taking human life. Subsequent chapters will test the application of Ogle et al.'s integrated theory to each specific case.

From Killing to Being Killed

If an analysis of gender is crucial to understanding why a small number of women commit murder, it is also crucial to explaining why an even smaller number of women are executed by the state. In the modern era, less than 2% of those put to death in the United States have been women. The disparity in the number of capital sentences and executions has several possible explanations. Perhaps the criminal justice system treats women who kill leniently based on a notion of chivalry. Some have claimed that prosecutors, judges, and juries shy away from inflicting a death sentence on someone who evokes their sympathy because she is a member of the "gentler sex," a mother, wife, or daughter. This view posits that there is a "lingering paternalism" in the justice system and for that reason, except in the most extreme cases, prosecutors are unwilling to ask for death when a women is on trial.[23] There are several flaws in this reasoning. First of all, women who are charged with murder seldom carry the social status likely to inspire a paternalistic or chivalrous attitude. The few prominent cases that come to mind—Jean Harris, Susan Smith, Casey Anthony—did not lead to capital sentences. On the other hand, a poor, uneducated woman with a history of drug use is not an especially good candidate for masculine protection. Secondly, an examination of the fourteen examples included in this book raises doubts about whether these were truly the "most extreme cases." In virtually every instance, the prosecutor's decision to ask for the death penalty had more to do with political calculations than with the extremity of the offense, and those political calculations often included weighing the pros and cons of charging a woman with a capital offense and estimating whether a judge or jury and the community would empathize with the defendant.

One cannot argue that the sex of the defendant is an irrelevant consideration in death penalty cases or that damaging stereotypes do not persist and influence the workings of the criminal justice system. In fact, gender stereotypes are quite powerful, and a death sentence may be the result when the state argues successfully that a particular defendant is not a "real" woman (who would deserve sympathy or chivalry) but a Monster, an Evil Woman, a Temptress, or an Unnatural Mother. These individuals are portrayed by the prosecution and often by the media as having deviated so far from feminine norms that they forfeit any claim to humanity, much less to respect for being female.[24] In a study of press coverage of the executions of women, Shipman notes how the media described female defendants with particular attention to their clothes, their weight (many articles commented on Christina Riggs and Suzanne Basso's obesity), and their "girlish" qualities (Tucker's hair) or lack thereof (Wanda Jean Allen's supposed masculinity). He also pointed out the tendency of newspapers to use female defendants' first names when discussing their cases, while typically using surnames for men.[25] Surely referring to an adult woman as Velma or Betty suggests a lack of respect.

Schmall suggests that a woman's culpability may be proportionate to the social value placed upon her victim or on the type of relationship she was supposed to maintain with the victim.[26] Thus women accused of killing husbands (who have higher status in a patriarchal society) or children (whom they are expected to nurture) have deviated further from feminine norms than men who kill wives or children have deviated from masculine norms. In Kopec's view, women who commit murder in the context of their caretaking role are seen to have actually "forfeited their femininity." They can be treated like men. A death sentence for such offenders would not violate the notion that only men should be sent to death row, for these offenders no longer deserved the deference due to women.[27] In a country where many would not be comfortable putting mothers or grandmothers to death (eleven of the executed women were mothers; six were grandmothers), supporters of their sentences could ease their consciences by imagining that they were the worst of the worst, too dangerous even to spend their lives in prison, because they had committed "unspeakable crimes."[28]

It could be argued that executing anyone, male or female, requires seeing that person as "other," not really human like you and me. But the process is more extreme for women. Civilized societies tend to accept certain situations where men kill men (e.g., during wartime) as normal. But what about a situation when all the power that men have vested in the state is brought to bear to kill a woman? Such an occurrence requires extraordinary justification. She must be the embodiment of evil, demonic, and most of all "unwomanly."[29]

Race, class, sexuality, and sexual orientation can contribute to marginalizing and alienating a woman from the protections extended to those whose behavior conforms to social norms. Two of the executed women were lesbians. In the cases of Wanda Jean Allen and Aileen Wuornos, prosecutors portrayed them as male "wannabees," man haters, or both. It was easier to defeminize a defendant who did not conform to the heterosexual standard.[30] Likewise, attorneys for the state could play up Marilyn Plantz's affair with a young black man, Wornos's prostitution, Betty Lou Beets's multiple marriages, Teresa Lewis's infidelity, or Karla Faye Tucker's comments about sexual pleasure to appeal to jurors' fears of a society out of control, one where women's sexuality ran amok. Although it requires a huge leap of logic, it seems juries were willing to believe that if a defendant transgressed sexual boundaries, she was capable of the most diabolical acts and should be punished accordingly. Gillespie claims that in addition to not portraying the expected gender roles, women who are executed fail to elicit a connection with their sentencers. That may be due to the offensiveness of the crime, but other circumstances may also factor in. An accomplice who testifies against her, wide publicity for the case, or even a derogatory nickname may predispose a jury to dehumanize the defendant.[31] Imagine how difficult it would be for jurors to be objective toward someone known as a "black widow," "the pickax murderer," or "Mean Nadean."

A wife who killed an abusive husband might evoke sympathy. Such a murder violates the gendered hierarchy, but a spousal abuser, especially if he comes from the working class, could also incur the community's wrath. But suppose that woman who claimed abuse profited financially from her husband or boyfriend's death? Then she loses her claim on public sympathy and becomes a greedy, grasping Black Widow. Her behavior could be viewed not as self-defense but as purely malevolent. She could strike fear in any man with a life insurance policy and a shaky marriage. Such was the theme prosecutors spun out in describing Betty Lou Beets, Velma Barfield, Judias Buenoano, and Teresa Lewis. Their victims occupied places higher on the gender hierarchy, and their crimes threatened existing power arrangements.

Prosecutors may have been especially effective in making monsters out of defendants when they were able to play upon the underlying fears of the community and the jury who represented it.[32] And the fears were of an expressly gendered type. Imagine a world where mothers do not protect their children but kill them instead; where heterosexual relationships and fidelity are optional; where husbands must fear the greed of their wives. Those pictures may well have been persuasive in overcoming any impulse to spare these women's lives. Instead they justified sending them to their deaths.

It seems, then, that the notion of chivalry is a two-edged sword. Their sex might mean that some defendants are spared death in some communities in some circumstances. But we have seen that others receive capital sentences when they are viewed as unnatural or monstrous women who have forfeited any claim to protection.

There are other explanations besides paternalism and chivalry to account for the small number of women on death row. One factor involves the way state laws, usually shaped by men, define capital crimes. In most states, the most common capital offenses are felony-murders, cases in which someone was killed during the commission of another serious crime, such as rape or robbery. Capital punishment is generally associated with "predatory" killings usually committed by male strangers. Women are more likely to kill in anger. They seldom commit predatory crimes against strangers. More men than women are also exposed to death sentences based on the amount of violence involved in the crime, its brutality, or the number of victims. But one scholar claims that the definition of capital crimes in favor of offenses against strangers and the undervaluing of domestic murder may be the most serious form of gender discrimination in death penalty law. In the eyes of the law, the consequences of violence toward women "belonging to others" are much more serious than for violence against "your own" woman.[33]

As Rapaport notes, "family life is notably absent from the states' universe of concerns."[34] Domestic killers are seldom considered eligible for the death penalty unless family murder is "transmuted by the alchemy of money," in which case it is considered as heinous as stranger killing.[35] But the vast majority of domestic murders are committed by men—not for pecuniary motives, because women seldom control the financial resources, but as part of an on-going power/control relationship. Yet the intimate killings that are viewed as "serious" enough to be eligible for a death sentence, where money is allegedly a motive, are more often committed by women. Her "greed," usually associated with a desire for an insurance benefit, is treated as if it were an aggravating factor. This pattern is a vivid reflection of patriarchal legal principles. It stands as a "dramatic symbol of the lesser dignity attached to the security and peace of the domestic sphere as compared with the realms of commerce and intercourse among non-intimates."[36] If the death penalty is seen as a measure of the social harm done by the criminal and of the social value of the victim, it seems clear that women killed by strangers and men killed by intimates are the valued victims.

According to Howarth, capital jurisprudence is a "hidden battleground of gender." Those in the legal profession often organize their ideas within dichotomies such as reason/emotion, distance/connection, or male/female. Dichotomies imply a hierarchy; one of the two is superior to the other. Within gendered dichotomies, the legal system privileges the male side. The greater penalty for stranger (distance) or stranger-like crimes compared to domestic (connection) crimes is an example. Howarth claims that dichotomies that privilege the male side operate in the capital sentencing decisions of juries.[37] An examination of the women sentenced to death and executed in the modern period reveals that the vast majority of their victims were male. Capital punishment is a statement of the state's use of power to punish those who are regarded as the greatest threats to social stability, those whose very existence jeopardizes the community's well-being. In these fourteen cases, they were women whose crimes so defied gendered expectations that they were deemed depraved and unpardonable.

Victor Streib, addressing the gendered quality of the death penalty, states that it is a "refuge for macho men." He claims that insecure middle-aged men use capital punishment more as a way of reassuring themselves about their manhood than as an instrument of justice, incapacity, or retribution. It serves as a symbolic way of vanquishing the toughest *male* opponents.[38] If Streib is correct, executing women does not serve that macho purpose, thus killing female offenders is both rare and controversial. Howarth makes a similar point. If the death penalty symbolically enacts the violence of men toward men (a violence often employed to avenge threats to "their" women), and the support of execution is identified with strength and manliness, that symbolism is distorted if capital punishment is used by men against women, especially if the women include an innocent-looking white female like Karla Faye Tucker. Thus, Howarth argues, the execution of women must be made to fit into a "dominant masculine script." If the person being killed is harmless, the executioner is not demonstrating power. Therefore the condemned woman must be deprived of her femininity and made into something dangerous.[39]

At the same time, laws in the United States formally prohibit discrimination on the basis of sex. It would seem then, that justice would demand that male and female murderers be treated the same and that women not be extended any "special treatment." Indeed, this is the position governors typically take when asked to offer clemency to a woman about to be executed. They claim, as George Bush liked to say, that the sex of the killer made no difference to the victim and that therefore they must treat all condemned persons alike. However, this formal equality is not really equal protection (it does not recognize the different circumstances of men's and women's lives nor the patriarchal social structure). Rather, formal equality consists of applying the same rules to men and women, regardless of whether those rules are appropriate in individual cases.[40]

The Supreme Court has said repeatedly in its "death is different" jurisprudence that individualized sentencing is constitutionally required, that each defendant must be judged as an entire person. How could sex and gender not matter? And more importantly, how could socially constructed notions about appropriate gendered behavior not matter? In other words, the evidence of all fourteen cases discussed here shows that gender definitions and their violation were invoked as elements in defining the seriousness of the crime. Yet, the same state officials would later argue that sex and gender were impermissible factors in considering clemency. Formal equality, alleging that sex and gender do not matter in the criminal justice system, is one of many explanations governors have used in the modern period to curtail their power to reduce death sentences. If the decline in use of clemency is tied to political agendas and to the perception that public opinion favors capital punishment, then George Bush's decision not to commute Karla Faye Tucker's sentence reinforced this practice. Bush suffered little or no negative political consequences for executing Tucker, despite the outspoken pleas of the Christian Right to spare her life. Other politicians could observe his experience and determine that they too could call on "formal equality," words that claimed a commitment to equal treatment of men and women as a justification for ignoring the reality of the lives of the women they put to death.

Endnotes

1. Meda Chesney-Lind and Lisa Pasko, eds. *Girls, Women, and Crime: Selected Readings.* (Thousand Oaks, California: Sage, 2004), 1.
2. Darrell Steffensmeier and Jennifer Schwartz, "Contemporary Explanations of Women's Crime," in *The Criminal Justice System and Women: Offenders, Prisoners, Victims, and Workers,* ed. Barbara Raffel Price and Natalie J. Sokoloff (New York: McGrawHill: 2004), 114–15.
3. Peggy C. Giardino and Sharon Mohler Rockwell, "Differential Association and Female Crime," in *Of Crime and Criminality: The Use of Theory in Everyday Life,* ed. Sally Simpson (Thousand Oaks, California: Pine Forge Press, 2000), 4–5.
4. Darrell Steffensmeier and Lisa Broidy, "Explaining Female Offending," in *Women, Crime, and Criminal Justice: Original Feminist Readings,* ed. Claire M. Renzetti and Lynne Goodstein (Los Angeles: Roxbury, 2001), 129.
5. Ibid., 124–27.
6. Giardino and Rockwell, "Differential Association and Female Crime," 11.
7. Ibid., 21–22.
8. Lisa Broidy and Robert Agnew, "Gender and Crime: A General Strain Theory Perspective," in *Girls, Women, and Crime,* ed. Chesney-Lind and Pasko, 9–11.
9. Ibid., 17–18.
10. Barbara Owen, "Differences with a Distinction: Women Offenders and Criminal Justice Practice," in *Gendered Justice: Addressing Female Offenders,* ed. Barbara E. Bloom (Durham, North Carolina: Carolina Academic Press, 2003), 30.
11. Rebecca S. Katz, "Explaining Girls' and Women's Crime and Desistance in the Context of their Victimization," in *Girls, Women, and Crime,* ed. Chesney-Lind and Pasko, 25.
12. Chimene I. Keitner, "Victim or Vamp? Images of Violent Women in the Criminal Justice System," *Columbia Journal of Gender and Law* 11 (2002), 78.
13. Ibid., 85.
14. Ibid., 84.
15. Kathleen Kendall and Shoshana Pollack, "Cognitive Behavioralism in Women's Prisons: A Critical Analysis of Therapeutic Assumptions and Practices," in *Gendered Justice,* ed. Bloom, 78.

16. Elizabeth M. Schneider, *Battered Women and Feminist Lawmaking* (New Haven, CT: Yale University Press, 2000), 112–13.

17. Elizabeth Dermody Leonard, "Stages of Gendered Disadvantage in the Lives of Convicted Battered Women," in *Gendered Justice*, ed. Bloom, 116–17.

18. Nanci Koser Wilson, "Gendered Interaction in Criminal Homicide," in *Homicide: The Victim/Offender Connection*, ed. Anna Victoria Wilson (Cincinnati: Anderson, 1993), 56.

19. Robbin S. Ogle, Daniel Maier-Katkin, and Thomas J. Bernard, "A Theory of Homicidal Behavior Among Women," *Criminology* 33: 2 (1995), 174.

20. Ibid., 176.

21. Ibid., 177–80.

22. Ibid., 185–86.

23. Janice L. Kopec, "Avoiding a Death Sentence in the American Legal System: Get a Woman to Do It," *Washington and Lee School of Law Capital Defense Journal* 15 (Spring 2003), 357.

24. See for example, Ilene H. Nagel and John Hagan, "Gender and Crime: Offense Patterns and Criminal Court Sanctions," *Crime and Justice* 4 (1983), 135–56; Marlin Shipman, *The Penalty Is Death: U.S. Newspaper Coverage of Women's Executions* (Columbia, Missouri: University of Missouri Press, 2002; Elizabeth Rapaport, "Some Questions about Gender and the Death Penalty," *Golden Gate University Law Review* 20 (1990), 513.

25. Shipman, *Penalty Is Death*, 6–10.

26. Lorraine Schmall, "Forgiving Guin Garcia: Women, the Death Penalty, and Commutation," *Wisconsin Women's Law Journal* 11 (Fall 1996), 304.

27. Kopec, "Avoiding a Death Sentence," 363.

28. Schmall, "Forgiving Guin Garcia," 314.

29. Keitner, "Victim or Vamp?" 69–70.

30. Kathryn Ann Farr, "Defeminizing and Dehumanizing Female Murderers: Depictions of Lesbians on Death Row," in *The Criminal Justice System and Women*, ed. Price and Sokoloff, 251–52.

31. L. Kay Gillespie, *Dancehall Ladies: Executed Women of the Twentieth Century* (Lanham, Maryland: University Press of America, 2000), 125–27.

32. Sharon Lamb, "The Psychology of Condemnation: Underlying Emotions and Their Symbolic Expression in Condemning and Shaming," *Brooklyn Law Review* 68 (2002–03), 929–58.

33. Elizabeth Rapaport, "The Death Penalty and Gender Discrimination," *Law and Society Review* 25:2 (1991), 380–82.

34. Rapaport, "Some Questions about Gender," 558.

35. Ibid., 559.

36. Rapaport, "The Death Penalty and Gender Discrimination," 369.

37. Joan W. Howarth, "Deciding to Kill: Revealing the Gender in the Task Handed to Capital Juries," *Wisconsin Law Review* (June–July 1994), 1348–51.

38. Victor L. Streib, "Gendering the Death Penalty: Countering Sex Bias in a Masculine Sanctuary," *Ohio State Law Journal* 63 (2002), 18.

39. Joan W. Howarth, "Executing White Masculinities: Learning from Karla Faye Tucker," *Oregon Law Review* 81 (Spring 2002), 194–95.

40. Ibid., 207–12.

A CAPRICIOUSLY SELECTED RANDOM HANDFUL

The Supreme Court and the Death Penalty

Between 1632 when Jane Champion became the first female to be executed in America and 2014 when Texas put Suzanne Basso to death by lethal injection, 571 women and girls have been hanged, gassed, electrocuted, or injected with toxic drugs. Fifty-three of those deaths have occurred since 1900. However, only fourteen executions, those that are the subject of this book, have taken place since the United States Supreme Court began to scrutinize the administration of the death penalty to determine whether its use was consistent with the Constitution.

Under the leadership of Chief Justice Earl Warren in the 1950s and 1960s, the Court embarked on the process of incorporating the provisions of the Bill of Rights to the states. Included among the Court's rulings were decisions that required the states to adhere to the Eighth Amendment's ban on cruel and unusual punishment. Because the terms "cruel and unusual" are difficult to define objectively, the Court has had to provide concrete meanings for those words and to develop guidelines for punishments that conform to the Constitution. In *Trop v. Dulles*,[1] the Court ruled that if punitive measures violated "evolving standards of decency," those sanctions were unconstitutional.

Although not a death penalty case, in *Trop* the Court found that "the basic concept underlying the Eighth Amendment is the dignity of man."

The words "cruel and unusual" are not precise, "their scope is not static. The Amendment must draw its meaning from the evolving standards of decency that mark the progress of a maturing society."

In 1972, the Court first applied those standards to address the question of whether capital punishment itself was constitutional. Since that time the United States Supreme Court has developed a body of jurisprudence concerning the death penalty. Although few of those opinions make any mention of gender, the Court's rulings form the framework in which the fourteen capital cases were contested. During the same period when the Court was ruling on the constitutionality of the death penalty, they also examined the Fourteenth Amendment's guarantee of equal protection. In a series of decisions they determined that the Constitution prohibited governmental discrimination on the basis of sex. Thus one may see in the cases examined here the convergence of two themes in modern constitutional development—the complex series of decisions that have framed the use of capital punishment and another body of law that mandated an end to most overt legal manifestations of differential treatment based on sex.

Furman and Gregg: The Modern Foundation

Between 1967 and 1977, not one person was executed in the United States. It was generally known that the Supreme Court was likely to accept a case that raised the issue of the death penalty's constitutionality. In 1972, they heard three death penalty cases grouped under the name, *Furman v. Georgia.*[2] Furman, who was black, had shot a white home owner during a botched robbery. The murder was apparently an accident occurring while Furman tried to flee. The other two cases from Texas and Georgia involved African American men sentenced to death for allegedly raping white women. Neither victim had been injured, aside from the rape. These cases raised the question of whether the death penalty was unconstitutional as a violation of the Eighth Amendment's ban on cruel and unusual punishment. Each justice in *Furman* wrote a separate opinion, but five of the nine agreed that the death penalty as it was being administered was unconstitutional. Their reasoning differed, ranging from the view that capital punishment itself was unconstitutional to the position that the penalty is flawed when its use is random and discriminatory.

Justices William Brennan and Thurgood Marshall both held that the death penalty was inherently unconstitutional. Brennan emphasized that it violated human dignity. In taking lives, the state treated some people as less than human, "as objects to be toyed with and discarded." Furthermore, capital punishment served no legitimate purpose, it was unnecessarily severe, and there was strong evidence of its arbitrary and biased use. Justice Marshall wrote that if the American people were fully informed, if they knew the death penalty burdened the "poor, ignorant, and underprivileged and members of minority groups least able to make their complaints," the public would not tolerate the system. Marshall noted the disparities of both race and gender that characterized the application of capital punishment.

Justice William O. Douglas also commented on disparities. He believed that the death penalty persisted because those who faced execution were outcasts, members of unpopular groups "whom society is willing to see suffer though it would not countenance general application of the same penalty across the board." Justices Byron White and Potter Stewart focused more narrowly on the randomness with which death sentences were handed out. Stewart contended that the penalty was "wantonly and freakishly imposed," "cruel and unusual in the same way that being struck by lightning is cruel and unusual." His words came to characterize what was wrong with capital punishment.

The decision in *Furman* meant that the death penalty, as it was being applied, was unconstitutional. The five member majority of the Court agreed that the arbitrary way in which courts made their decisions about who would live and who would die did not meet the standards of decency that the Eighth Amendment required.

Most states responded to the ruling by rewriting their capital statutes in ways they hoped would conform with the *Furman* holding. They chose two major approaches to address the issue of arbitrary application of the death penalty—either the punishment could be made mandatory for every first-degree murder or courts could be provided with statutory guidelines that clearly defined the criteria regulating its use. The Court handed down rulings on both types of laws on the same day in 1976. In *Gregg v. Georgia*[3] and *Jurek v. Texas*[4] they upheld laws providing guided discretion. In *Woodson v. North Carolina*[5] they found the mandatory sentence for murder unconstitutional.

The Court addressed two questions in *Gregg*. Was the death penalty itself unconstitutional? The majority of the justices answered that it was not. They believed that it served two legitimate penal purposes, retribution and deterrence. Did the Georgia law provide sufficient guidance to judges and juries to prevent its arbitrary application to only a "capriciously selected random handful"? The majority believed that it did. Acknowledging that "death is different," and that the penalty required careful attention to its application, they endorsed several features of the Georgia law. These became models for other states' capital statutes. The trial was divided into two phases, one to determine guilt and one to decide on the sentence. During the latter phase, the state had the opportunity to present aggravating factors, while the defense could offer mitigating information that might help to explain the defendant's role in the crime. In addition to the bifurcated trial, the Court approved Georgia's specificity concerning which crimes qualified for capital punishment; the provision that the state Supreme Court would automatically review every death-sentence case; and the requirement that the state Supreme Court review all such cases for proportionality and consistency. *Gregg* asserted that the Georgia law and others like it successfully addressed the Court's concerns about arbitrariness. However, in a troubling statement, Justices White, Rehnquist, and Chief Justice Burger acknowledged that "mistakes will be made and discriminations will occur which will be difficult to explain." They seemed prepared to accept an undefined rate of error in death sentences as a collateral cost of maintaining the policy.

Justice Brennan in his dissent described a fundamental moral concept underlying the Eighth Amendment, "the State, even as it punishes, must treat its citizens in a manner consistent with their intrinsic worth as human beings." He found the "calculated killing of a human being by the State involves, by its very nature, a denial of the executed person's humanity." Rather than providing justice for an offense against society, he argued that the death penalty "adds instead a second defilement to the first." It did not so much even the score as create a second deficit. The other dissenter, Justice Thurgood Marshall, reiterated that the American people knew little about the realities of the death penalty, and that "the opinions of an informed public would differ significantly from those of a public unaware of the consequences and effects of the death penalty." He further took issue with the justification that some murderers "deserved" death. Such a rationale had "as its very basis the total denial of the wrongdoer's dignity and worth."

Brennan and Marshall raised difficult questions about dehumanizing offenders in the capital process—a practice commonly seen in the cases discussed in this book. In *Jurek v. Texas*, the Court upheld a different approach to guided discretion. The Texas law provided a fairly short list of offenses that would qualify as capital murder. However, the brief list included murder committed in the course of a felony and murder for remuneration. The Texas procedure for sentencing required the jury to answer three questions: Was the murder deliberate? Was it unprovoked? Was there a probability that the defendant would commit acts of violence in the future? The last element has been the most controversial, as juries are asked to predict "future dangerousness." It is with regard to that element that Texas courts have been accused of employing junk science and racial stereotypes.

In the aftermath of *Gregg v. Georgia*, the Court has never again considered the constitutionality of capital punishment itself. They have not revisited the question of whether all state-supported executions violate the Eighth Amendment. They have focused their attention instead on its application.

While the *Gregg* and *Jurek* majority upheld the Georgia and Texas procedures, in rejecting mandatory death sentences for capital murder in *Woodson*, the Court held that the "respect for human dignity underlying the Eighth Amendment requires consideration of aspects of the character of the individual offender and the circumstances of the particular offense as a constitutionally indispensable part of the process of imposing the ultimate punishment of death." The process proposed by North Carolina was faulty because it "treats all persons convicted of a designated offense not as uniquely individual human beings, but as members of a faceless, undifferentiated mass to be subjected to the blind infliction of the death penalty."[6] In the *Woodson* decision and especially in *Lockett v. Ohio*,[7] the Court suggests that the Constitution requires that sentencers be offered a full picture of the defendant. They should see him or her as a human being, not as "faceless," "subject to the blind infliction of the death penalty." Yet it may be argued that in a number of the fourteen cases discussed here, the failure of attorneys to present evidence in mitigation deprived juries of just such humanizing information about the woman on trial for her life. After *Gregg* and *Woodson*, it seemed that the Constitution demanded both individualized sentencing and consistency—a true challenge to courts.

Lockett and *Strickland*: Mitigation and Representation

Following the Court's approval of the bifurcated trial separating the determination of guilt from sentencing, it became clear that the conduct of the punishment phase was critically important. Here the offender could be presented as a human being rather than as a dehumanized killer. What evidence would a defendant be allowed to produce at this stage of the proceedings? What was a lawyer expected to do to save his or her client's life?

In *Lockett v. Ohio*,[8] the Court reviewed the Ohio law that limited the defendant's opportunity to present mitigating evidence to only three factors:

the victim was partially responsible; the offender was under duress; or the offender suffered from psychosis or mental deficiency. They held that the capital process should not preclude the sentencing judge or jury from considering "any aspect of a defendant's character or record and any of the circumstances of the offense that the defendant proffers as a basis for a sentence less than death." Unless the law allowed the sentencer to consider all aspects of the defendant's story there was a risk that death might be wrongly imposed. "When the choice is between life and death, such risk is unacceptable and incompatible with the commands of the Eighth and Fourteenth Amendments." The majority opinion repeats the claim that "death is different," and therefore "the need for treating each defendant in a capital case with the degree of respect due to the uniqueness of the individual is far more important than in noncapital cases."

Lockett seems to make it clear that the Constitution requires that death sentences be based on respect for the individual defendant and on assurances that the judge and jury know the accused person's full life story and circumstances. Yet the only way a jury will know anything positive about the defendant in a murder trial is if that person's attorney puts the information before them. The prosecution will have devoted its efforts to describing the horrors of the crime and the monstrosity of the person accused. If the jury has found him or her guilty during the first phase of the trial, the defense attorney must offer them a compelling humanizing story in the sentencing phase—or a death sentence will result. Thus the value of allowing evidence in mitigation is contingent on having an attorney with the ability, the will, and the competence to put that evidence before a jury. The Court addressed the issue of adequate representation in death cases in *Strickland v. Washington.*[9] It seemed they would permit almost unlimited latitude in attorney performance without finding a constitutional violation.

In *Strickland,* the defendant David Washington claimed he had been denied effective assistance of counsel when his court-appointed attorney failed to request a psychiatric evaluation, to investigate or to present any character witnesses at the sentencing phase. In other words, no mitigating evidence was introduced. Given the Court's *Lockett* ruling, that mitigating evidence was vitally important, it seems logical that attorneys would be expected to present such information. However, *Strickland* suggests otherwise.

According to what became known as the *Strickland* standard, there are several prongs to a claim of ineffective assistance of counsel. The defendant must show that the attorney's performance was deficient and that the deficient performance was so prejudicial that he or she was denied a fair trial. Given the Court's definitions, both prongs are difficult, perhaps virtually impossible, to prove. A deficient performance is one that "falls below an objective standard of unreasonableness," based on "counsel's perspective at the time." Did the lawyer think his defense was reasonable? Few attorneys would say they did not. Sleeping during the trial, arriving drunk at court, financial dealings that created a conflict of interest with the client's defense, never meeting with a client, telling her to plead guilty without a plea bargain, failing to question racial bias in jury selection—all could be rationalized. All were excused as "reasonable" in the cases detailed in this book.

Even defendants who could prove that an attorney failed to provide a "reasonably" adequate level of representation would then be required to demonstrate that it was this performance that led to the outcome of the trial. This prong of the test was also extremely difficult to prove. Was it the defense attorney's failures or the strength of the prosecution's case that led to the result? The Supreme Court held further that an appellate court could first determine whether the proceedings in general were fundamentally fair before evaluating the performance of defense counsel. In other words, they could decide that, in general, the trial was not too unfair, and if that was the case, the attorney's poor showing was irrelevant. *Strickland* and the cases that followed seemed to doom constitutional claims of ineffective assistance of counsel, even the exceptionally deficient work of defense lawyers in the cases of Betty Lou Beets, Wanda Jean Allen, Frances Newton, Teresa Lewis, and Kimberly McCarthy.

McCleskey: Statistical Evidence of Discrimination

Some would claim that although there remains evidence of racial bias in the administration of the death penalty, the small number of women sentenced to death suggests that if gender discrimination exists, it benefits rather than disadvantages women. *McCleskey v. Kemp*[10] was the major case in which the Court considered whether patterns of discrimination could raise questions concerning capital punishment and the Eighth and Fourteenth Amendments. McCleskey, who was African American, was sentenced to death for the murder of a white police officer in the course of a robbery. His appeal to the Supreme Court was based on the massive and highly regarded Baldus Study which showed statistical evidence of systematic bias in the way death sentences were imposed. The Baldus Study indicated that, for example, black offenders whose victims were white were four times more likely to be sentenced to death than other racial combinations. In a 5–4 decision, the Court rejected McCleskey's claim on the grounds that statistical evidence of discrimination did not prove that the defendant had experienced bias in his own case. McCleskey would need to prove that participants had demonstrated racial prejudice against him and that such sentiments had affected the outcome of his case. The majority of justices acknowledged that there were risks of racial and other prejudices influencing criminal trials, but they did not find such risks "constitutionally unacceptable." They further suggested that if bias was a problem in the capital punishment regime, those affected could use the legislative process to fix it. They noted that if McCleskey prevailed, defendants would question other discrepancies "correlating to membership in other minority groups, and *even to gender*" (italics added).

The four dissenters found the "risk that race influenced McCleskey's sentence intolerable." They objected that "we should not be willing to take a person's life if the chance that his death sentence was irrationally imposed is more likely than not." They rejected the suggestion that the victims of discrimination should be charged with correcting the problem. "Those whom we would banish from society or from the human community itself often speak in too faint a voice to be heard above society's demand for punishment. It is the particular role of courts to hear these voices, for the Constitution declares that the majoritarian chorus may not alone dictate the conditions of social life."

Since *Furman*, the Court has endeavored to ensure that the death penalty was not applied arbitrarily. But *McCleskey's* argument, that punishment is influenced improperly and arbitrarily by social attitudes and preconceptions about the defendant and the victim, is applicable to questions of gender as well as to race.[11] If prosecutors, judges, and juries apply preexisting stereotypes about blacks or about women, especially when they evaluate aggravating and mitigating circumstances, sex, like race, may impermissibly influence their decisions. However, the *McCleskey* majority held that not all discrepancies needed to be eliminated from the use of capital punishment and that a certain amount of prejudice was acceptable. The women sentenced to death surely experienced some of that "acceptable" prejudice.

Defendants with a Disadvantage:
Ford, Penry, and Atkins

Additional questions have been raised in the modern era concerning whether the Constitution prohibits capital punishment for certain categories of defendants. Do the evolving standards of decency reject the execution of the insane or the retarded? *Ford v. Wainwright*[12] concerned the constitutionality of putting an insane person to death. The issue of sanity may be critical at several stages in a criminal proceeding. Persons who are too mentally ill to assist in their own defense would be found incompetent to stand trial. Those found not guilty because they were insane at the time of the crime would be sent to a treatment facility rather than to prison. In a capital case, mental illness is typically considered a mitigating factor, but juries may or may not feel sympathy with a defendant who displays psychotic behavior, as in the case of Aileen Wuornos or perhaps in the case of Suzanne Basso. The Court has never ruled on whether a seriously mentally ill person may be condemned to death. They did, however, determine in *Ford v. Wainwright* that it was unconstitutional to put someone to death who was insane at the time of execution. They have not determined whether a state may medicate a person to make him or her sane enough to be put to death.

Justice Marshall wrote for the majority in *Ford v. Wainwright* that putting an insane person to death violated evolving standards of decency. It did not serve the purpose of retribution as the person executed would not understand his punishment. It did not serve as a deterrent to the competent. It offended basic notions of humanity. However, clarification of the level of insanity that would prohibit execution remained for the state courts to decide. As the discussion of the fourteen cases in this study reveals, the definition of insanity tends to be very basic—is the defendant aware of her impending execution and of the reason for it? Often the question comes down to "dueling psychiatrists." The state claims the person facing death is sane enough, the defense disagrees. Laypersons—usually judges—decide what is ultimately a question for mental health professionals.

On several occasions, the Court has addressed the matter of whether the Constitution permits the execution of those with mental disabilities. In *Penry v. Lynaugh*[13] the majority ruled that it was not unconstitutional to put a mentally disabled person to death. However, they did insist that Texas courts must allow juries to be told that mental retardation was a mitigating factor. In 2002, they reversed *Penry* in *Atkins v. Virginia*,[14] which held that execution of mentally retarded persons violated contemporary standards of decency and was therefore unconstitutional. They found that mentally disabled defendants were more likely to make false confessions, less likely to make "a pervasive showing of mitigation." They tend to be poor witnesses and frequently appear to lack remorse for their acts. Additionally, juries may often see mental retardation as contributing to future dangerousness, and therefore an aggravating rather than a mitigating factor. However, the Court left the definition of retardation and the method for determining whether someone qualified as retarded to the states.

At least two of the executed women—Wanda Jean Allen and Marilyn Plantz—might have had their lives spared if their cases had followed *Atkins*. Had Teresa Lewis's case been handled differently, and had she had a jury trial, her life might have been spared based on the *Atkins* ruling.

Herrera and AEDPA: The Issue of Innocence

What could possibly be accomplished if the state puts an innocent person to death? Retribution requires that the guilty person bear the price of his crime. Who would be deterred by watching the criminal justice system make a serious mistake and fail to do its job? Yet the Court's ruling in *Herrera v. Collins*[15] and the enactment of the 1993 Antiterrorism and Effective Death Penalty Act (AEDPA) makes it more difficult for innocent men or women to reopen capital cases.

Herrera was convicted in the killing of two Texas police officers and sentenced to death. After ten years he claimed to have new evidence that would prove him innocent. In a 6–3 decision, the Supreme Court refused to hear Herrera's appeal. They found that his initial trial had been fair, that the Texas law prohibiting the introduction of new evidence more than thirty days after sentencing did not deny him due process, and that he could take his claims of innocence to the governor and ask for clemency. Because the criminal justice system needs "finality," the Court held that a defendant must have a very persuasive claim of innocence to get judicial attention.

Three justices who signed onto the majority opinion, Justices O'Connor, Kennedy, and White, stated that the execution of an actually innocent person would be "constitutionally intolerable." But they also wrote that "at some point in time the State's interest in finality must outweigh the prisoner's interest in another round of litigation." Of course it is the state who determines that point. What if it arrives before the person has an opportunity to raise a proper claim of innocence? What if that point occurs sooner rather than later because the defendant was represented by an incompetent attorney? What if the state has destroyed the evidence the defendant needs to prove innocence? The latter may seem outrageous. It happened to Frances Newton.

The idea of putting an innocent person to death seemed not to bother Justices Scalia and Thomas. In *Herrera*, they claimed there was no constitutional right to "demand judicial consideration of newly discovered evidence of innocence brought forward after conviction." Their cavalier attitude seems to suggest that the occasional execution of an innocent person is less important than an efficient system.

The three justices who dissented in *Herrera* wrote a strong indictment of the implication that "finality" was more important that accuracy. "Just as an execution without adequate safeguards is unacceptable, so too is an execution when the condemned prisoner can prove he is innocent. The execution of such a person ... comes perilously close to simple murder." The dissenters also challenged the idea that the innocent could rely on executive clemency as a remedy for their wrongful convictions. Constitutional rights should not be dependent on the "unreviewable discretion of an executive officer or an administrative tribunal." Aside from the danger that "unreviewable discretion" is exactly what *Furman* tried to eliminate from the death penalty system, the likelihood of a governor actually granting clemency in the modern era is almost nonexistent. Most state executives have learned, as George Bush demonstrated in the Karla Faye Tucker case, that the long-term political benefits of being "tough on crime" far outweigh the short-term pressures to spare the convict's life. One can see that pattern played out in almost every case discussed in this book. Political considerations always seem to take precedence over questions of due process or over questions of innocence.

Three years after the Court handed down its decision in *Herrera*, Congress passed the Antiterrorism and Effective Death Penalty Act (AEDPA), which further curtailed the appeals process for those on death row. The law raised the standard for federal courts to consider claims of actual innocence from "clear and convincing evidence" to "probable" evidence of innocence. It also required that the federal courts of appeals show more deference to the decisions of state courts and it set a time limit for federal appeals. In effect, AEDPA reduces the docket of the federal appeals courts by cutting off the routes available to prisoners who have claims of actual innocence. It is especially damaging to those who are in that predicament because of incompetent or inadequate representation. Such persons are disadvantaged because their claims were not raised properly in the state courts and because their putative advocate failed to meet the deadlines for appeals. The cases of Frances Newton, Teresa Lewis, Kimberly McCarthy, and Suzanne Basso whose last appeals came after the passage of the AEDPA, suffered from those complications.

Equal Protection and Gender

As indicated, there have been no Supreme Court cases dealing directly with gender and capital punishment and only a few judicial comments on the subject. Thus in describing the gender element in the constitutional structure that framed the fourteen executions, one must extrapolate from several sources. In *McCleskey v. Kemp*, the Court held that statistical evidence of discrimination would not suffice to challenge a death sentence on equal protection grounds. They insisted that a defendant must show that his own case was tainted by racial prejudice, that he received a lesser form of justice than his white counterparts. With respect to gender and equal protection, the very definition of discrimination is problematic. It is in part the pretense that women are identical to men that creates problems in the administration of capital punishment.

The Fourteenth Amendment mandates that no state may deny a citizen the equal protection of the law. The Court has ruled that claims that one has been deprived of equal protection on the basis of sex be subject to intermediate scrutiny. In other words, if a state is to make a distinction based on sex they must have a compelling reason for doing so, and they must demonstrate that the remedy is tailored to achieve that purpose. Few overt distinctions related to sex can pass the intermediate scrutiny test. The problem comes with assuming that equal protection exists in the absence of open discrimination.

Prosecutors who charge female offenders, jurors under questioning, judges ruling in capital cases, governors asked to grant clemency—all claim that they are not considering the sex of the accused in making decisions. Is such "formal equality" possible? Is gender "an individual attribute that can and should be isolated and ignored"?[16] The law may say that men and women are equal, but in a patriarchal society there are tremendous differences between the lives of men and women, especially women of the less-advantaged classes from which death row inmates come. Several of the subjects of this book were abused by husbands; others endured sexual abuse as children; at least two worked as prostitutes. Most were condemned because they had failed in or betrayed their "womanly" responsibilities. How can one argue that gender is irrelevant to those realities? Yet, as Mary Ann Case wrote, when it comes to gender, the Court has "required ... not that the protection be equal, but that the rule be the same."[17]

Is it possible that courts can turn a "gender-blind eye" toward female offenders in capital cases? Can they separate their gendered identity from their criminal identity? The Supreme Court has ordered that because "death is different," each death penalty defendant should be seen as unique and should not be judged in comparison to others. Yet when women are on trial, prosecutors constantly hold up the defendant's behavior against a standard of appropriate womanly conduct. Out there are ideal mothers, perfect wives, and virtuous women. The woman on trial fails in comparison to them.

Gender-specific traits are especially salient when used as aggravating or mitigating circumstances. Socially constructed expectations for women are so pervasive that they do not need to be discussed explicitly. Because gendered references are likely to be implicit, it has been difficult to challenge them and to find legal relief. Many characteristics of death-eligible women, such as a lack of femininity (as defined by the prosecutor), aggressiveness, poor mothering skills, and sexual promiscuity are not the aggravating factors listed in the law. Yet the presence of those traits may well compound the heinousness of the crime in the eyes of the jury or the judge. Jurors were usually asked if they could ignore the defendant's sex in judging her. Most will say they did so. Yet the implicit use of gender stereotypes as aggravating circumstances may well have affected their decision. There is little redress in constitutional law for such subtle inequities. As Elizabeth Rapaport has noted, since *Furman*, counterbalancing developments in constitutional law—death penalty jurisprudence and equal protection decisions—have made gender discrimination in the administration of capital punishment both "more problematic and more impervious to challenge."[18]

Endnotes

1. *Trop v. Dulles*, 356 U.S. 86 (1958).
2. *Furman v. Georgia*, 408 U.S. 238 (1972).
3. *Gregg v. Georgia*, 428 U.S. 153 (1976).
4. *Jurek v. Texas*, 428 U.S. 262 (1976).
5. *Woodson v. North Carolina*, 428 U.S. 280 (1976).

6. Ibid.
7. *Lockett v. Ohio*, 438 U.S. 586 (1978).
8. Ibid.
9. *Strickland v. Washington*, 446 U.S. 668 (1984).
10. *McCleskey v. Kemp*, 481 U.S. 279 (1987).
11. Jenny E. Carroll, "Images of Women and Capital Sentencing among Female Offenders: Exploring the Outer Limits of the Eighth Amendment and Articulated Theories of Justice," *Texas Law Review* 75 (May 1997), 1446–48.
12. *Ford v. Wainwright*, 477 U.S. 399 (1986).
13. *Penry v. Lynaugh*, 492 U.S. 302 (1989).
14. *Atkins v. Virginia*, 536 U.S. 304 (2002).
15. *Herrera v. Collins*, 506 U.S. 390 (1993).
16. Joan W. Howarth, "Executing White Masculinities: Learning from Karla Faye Tucker," *Oregon Law Review* 81 (Spring 2002), 206.
17. Ibid., 207.
18. Elizabeth Rapaport, "Some Questions about Gender and the Death Penalty," *Golden Gate Law Review* 20 (1990), 505.

· 3 ·

SETTING PRECEDENT

Velma Barfield

On February 3, 1978, Stewart Taylor, a fifty-six-year-old tobacco farmer, died of acute arsenic poisoning at Southeastern General Hospital in Lumberton, North Carolina.[1] Had his family not requested an autopsy, Taylor's death might have been attributed to gastritis, consistent with his symptoms of nausea, vomiting, and diarrhea. Toxicological screenings showed an arsenic level of .13 to 1 milligram in Taylor's system. Normally the human body contains no arsenic. Velma Barfield, Taylor's live-in fiancée, had been preparing his meals. She was the only real suspect, although at first such suspicions seemed outrageous. Barfield had worked for the last several years as a home health assistant. Like many other poor and minimally educated women, she made her living doing domestic work, providing basic help for sick and elderly people. Killing someone she was looking after, especially the man she was planning to marry, seemed an impossible contradiction for a "professional" caregiver.

After her arrest, the world saw at least three additional images of Velma Barfield. According to the prosecutor's version, she was a cold-blooded "murdering witch" who enjoyed watching helpless victims die. Her defense attorney attempted to present a somewhat more sympathetic view. His "Velma" was drug-addled and hapless. Because she had developed an addition to "dope," she could not think straight and stumbled into murder.[2] To pious people who heard of her religious conversion in the Robeson County jail, Barfield became a "radiant witness" to the power of divine salvation.[3] The dubious notoriety of being the first woman facing execution after the reinstatement of the death penalty made discussion of who Velma Barfield *really* was and why she poisoned people especially intriguing.

She was a bespectacled mother and grandmother, a "matronly woman who shopped at the A&P and worked spinning yarn."[4] She was addicted to prescription drugs and the victim of physical and sexual abuse. And she was poor—not starving or homeless, but rarely able to pay all her bills. She was a member of the rural southern white working class. In the small communities where Velma Barfield always lived everyone knew everyone else. Yet she seemed to have few friends—if friends are people who provide support, in whom one can trust and confide. Ultimately, her life was circumscribed by gender, class, and geography.

The process and events that led her to be the first woman executed in the modern era reflect the words of Justice Stewart in *Furman v. Georgia.* They are cruel and unusual "in the same way being struck by lightning is cruel and unusual." Her sex, class, and the region where she lived help to account for why Velma Barfield was numbered among "the capriciously selected random handful upon whom the sentence of death has in fact been imposed."[5]

The Crime(s)

One can attempt to define the circumstances that played into the decision to execute Velma Barfield without minimizing the seriousness of her actions. Although she was tried for the murder of Stewart Taylor and her death sentence resulted from that crime, Barfield confessed to police that she had poisoned three other people—all of whom were in her care at the time. In every instance, she gave arsenic to her victims to hide an earlier offense. She had stolen money from them, either by forging checks on their account or in one case by taking out a loan. At one point, Barfield maintained that she only wanted to make the victims sick so she could have time to pay back the stolen money. Whether her intention was death or illness, (and it is doubtful she thought clearly about cause and effect), she needed funds to pay for doctors and drugs. Thus the prosecutor was able to present the image of a mercenary killer who wanted money. The full implications of her long-running addiction to multiple prescription drugs were never presented to the jury. Without such an alternative explanation for her actions, the state of North Carolina drew the picture of a greedy, cold-hearted, self-indulgent deceiver who preyed upon the weak. Not surprisingly, a jury found that version of "Velma" a suitable candidate for execution.

Velma Barfield had been widowed twice when she met Stewart Taylor in 1977 while she was working for his aunt, Dollie Edwards, as a live-in helper. Taylor, who had been married three times, drank heavily and was described as "volatile." He seemed an odd choice for Barfield who abhorred alcohol. Later she would claim "I never really cared for him.... Sometimes we're just lonely. Somebody to talk to."[6] Whatever her reasons, they became engaged and she moved into his house. During the winter of 1977–78, Barfield recalled that Taylor often treated her badly. She had minor breast surgery, a lumpectomy, and was unable to work at her minimum wage job. Desperate for her "medicine" (tranquilizers, antidepressants, sleeping pills), she forged two checks on Taylor's account. He was furious and threatened to turn her over to the police. On January 31, 1978, apparently short of money again, Barfield wrote another bad check. Fearing Taylor's reaction, she put ant and roach poison containing arsenic into his tea and beer. She told the police that she only meant to make him sick. Later Barfield wrote that the poison was "an antidote to the unbearable." She claimed that, at the time, she did not connect the arsenic with his suffering "as though I saw myself poisoning him, and yet it was as if someone else had done it. I had no control over my actions."[7]

Barfield appeared to care for Taylor as he suffered the effects of the poison. She took him to the hospital twice during the four days between the administration of the lethal dose and his death. When Taylor died, she agreed with the family and the attending physician that an autopsy was appropriate.

Between Taylor's death and the results of the autopsy, Barfield moved out of her former fiancé's house and took a job working the night shift at a nursing home. She described her routine as going "back to a solitary life, living for the time I got off work so that I could medicate myself. Once at work, I counted the hours until I would be home and could medicate myself again."[8]

That was Velma Barfield's condition when the police brought her in for questioning on March 10, 1978. The officers' recollections of the events differed from Barfield's in several ways. They produced a signed waiver of her rights, indicating that she was given the Miranda warnings and did not wish to be provided with a lawyer, although Barfield later claimed no memory of that procedure. During the first interview, the deputies apparently asked about checks forged on Taylor's account. They also informed Barfield that Taylor's death was caused by arsenic poisoning. She began to cry and denied any involvement, although she said, "You all think I put poison in his food."[9]

Barfield claimed in her memoir that after the first session with the police she contacted an attorney in Fayetteville and asked him to represent her. Oddly, given that she was being questioned about a murder, he put her off and told her to call him back if she was charged. She recalled that during her second interrogation she wished she had called him but did not mention her thoughts to the police.[10] The interviews with the police took place on March 10 and March 13. They formed the basis of the state's case against Velma Barfield. However, the circumstances of her interrogation raise a number of questions. Did she understand what it meant to waive her rights? Was she competent to make that decision? Had she technically engaged counsel by asking someone to represent her? The court accepted her written waivers and her statements, including extremely incriminating admissions that she had poisoned three other people prior to the murder of Stewart Taylor.

On March 13, it was actually Barfield's son Ronnie who persuaded his mother to return to the police station to "clear things up." On the one hand, he knew her fragile emotional condition and thought that being a suspect might be devastating for her. On the other hand, despite knowing that his mother had ingested her usual mixture of prescription drugs (Valium, Tylenol with codeine, Sinequan, Elevil),[11] he discouraged her from calling a lawyer, apparently believing she would just have a chat with detectives who were old friends. Whatever Barfield and Ronnie were thinking, the second round of questioning proved to be her undoing. She confessed not only to poisoning Taylor but also to the murders of Dollie Edwards, John Henry Lee, and Lillie Bullard. The former two were elderly people in her care, the latter was her mother. In every case, Barfield had put arsenic in the victim's food. In each case, she had purchased the poison and been aware of the label warning, "Can be fatal if swallowed."[12]

Why did Barfield confess to all these crimes? One explanation is that she was misled by the deputies to think they would go easier on her if she told them everything. In her own words, Barfield claimed that guilt pressed heavily on her "like a wire at the top of my head that kept getting tighter and tighter." She had felt wrong and guilty and dirty, unfit to be around other people, all her life. She despised herself.[13] Perhaps telling all would be a cleansing experience. Undoubtedly she was in no condition—given the drugs she had ingested and her long-term addiction—to make rational choices about waiving her rights. She also recalled that she could barely stay awake during the questioning, and that as soon as she had confessed and been booked, one of the deputies assured her, "We called your doctor. I'm going to the drugstore to get your prescription filled."[14] She slept constantly during the next few days.

Meanwhile, a young attorney, Bob Jacobson, heard of Velma Barfield's arrest on his car radio. He knew that North Carolina law provided that murder by poison was eligible for the death penalty because it involved premeditation. He also realized that under the state's rotating system for appointing counsel for indigent clients, it was his week to be assigned cases. Although he had never tried a capital case and had practiced law in North Carolina for less than four years, he met the criteria to defend in a capital case.[15] He would represent Velma Barfield in her murder trial. Joe Freeman Britt, known as "the world's deadliest prosecutor" for getting thirteen death penalty convictions in seventeen months, was his opponent.[16] Britt saw Barfield as his greatest challenge. He had never before asked a jury to sentence a woman to death. But he believed that some people were so irredeemable, there was no choice but to eliminate them. To persuade a jury of this, Britt wanted them to identify with the victim. If necessary, he would recreate the "savagery" of the murder in the courtroom. Jacobson and Velma were outmatched in resources and experience from the beginning.[17]

The Trial

On March 26, 1978, Barfield was indicted for the murder of Stewart Taylor. Although she had signed a statement confessing to three other murders, those killings had taken place before the current death penalty statute was passed. Therefore, she could not be charged with a capital offense for the murders of John Henry Lee, Dollie Edwards, and Lillie Bullard. She was arraigned on May 5 and pleaded "Not guilty by reason of insanity." Her defense attorney made several motions at that time. He asked for and was granted an independent psychiatric evaluation to determine whether Barfield was competent to stand trial. His motion for a change of venue because of pre-trial publicity was granted to the extent that the judge ordered the trial moved to a neighboring county. It was not moved to a different part of the state, as Jacobson had requested. The motion to sequester the jury to protect them from media influences during the trial and the most important motion to suppress Barfield's statements to the police on March 11 and 13 were denied.[18]

When a defendant is tried in a capital case, the jury must be "death qualified." They must be willing to impose the death penalty if the evidence merits it. There is substantial scholarship claiming that eliminating those who oppose capital punishment and even those who express strong ambivalence about it leaves a jury biased in favor of the prosecution and predisposed to vote for death. There is certainly a good argument that such a jury is not representative of the community, as it leaves out the 30% or more of the population who are anti-death penalty. In Barfield's case, the judge explained the bifurcated trial to the prospective jurors and advised them that if a defendant is found guilty of first-degree murder, capital punishment *may* be imposed. If they found Barfield guilty, they would hear aggravating and mitigating evidence before determining her sentence. Britt then told the potential jurors that he would ask them "Do you oppose capital punishment or do you feel it is a good and proper law, a necessary law?" Despite that loaded question—a choice between feeling and necessity—twelve of thirty-four potential jurors were excused based on their opposition. Over a third of those summoned to the venire either truly found capital punishment unacceptable or lied to be excused. Assuming that most took their responsibility seriously and told the truth, what conclusion can one draw if a person is tried for her life based on the decision of the two-thirds of citizens who are willing to vote for execution and eliminating the voice of the other third who would not?

The prosecutor asked several of the women in the jury pool "Would the sex of the defendant influence you? Would you try her just like a man?" The questions themselves imply the desired answers—no and yes. Jurors were being asked the impossible, to ignore one of the major, indisputable facts of the case: the defendant was a woman. When one prospect answered, "I would try her just like a person," she was excused. Voir dire revealed several other troubling points. A number of those questioned thought the death penalty was mandatory, even after the judge's explanation. Others did not grasp the meaning of aggravating and mitigating circumstances. Nonetheless, a panel of five women and seven men was finally seated.

Neither attorney made an opening statement. Britt apparently opted to have the witnesses unfold the story as they testified. Jacobson did not seem to have an alternative theory of the crime and perhaps hoped merely to raise reasonable doubt about Barfield's intentions. The prosecution's case included testimony from medical personnel who had treated Taylor in his final illness. They described his symptoms and his death, all consistent with arsenic poisoning. A particularly dramatic moment came when Britt asked John McPherson, the ambulance attendant, to replicate Taylor's desperate dying scream. McPherson threw back his head and howled, and although the defense objected, the objection was overruled. The prosecutor had apparently succeeded in recreating the savagery of the crime in the courtroom as he had predicted. During this phase of the questioning, Jacobson asked the doctors whether they would prescribe the mixture of drugs Velma Barfield was taking at the time. Although the strategy was an apparent effort to show that the combination of drugs was dangerous, that Barfield's competence was diminished, objections to introducing that evidence were sustained. Thus the jury heard the state's case that Taylor had died an agonizing death brought on by arsenic poisoning, but did not hear the defense's halfhearted attempt to explain Barfield's impaired mental state.

Other witnesses testified to Barfield's alleged motive—money. Taylor's daughter described her father's habit of carrying hundreds of dollars in his wallet. It contained only $2 when he died. Jacobson, the defense attorney did not object to the implication that Barfield had taken the money. The daughter also identified forged checks written on her father's account. And although Barfield was not on trial for the murders of Dollie Edwards, John Henry Lee, and Lillie Bullard, the prosecution was allowed to introduce evidence of forged checks on their accounts and their cause of death, and to argue that all four crimes followed a pattern. Barfield, the state contended, had stolen money and poisoned the victims to cover her thefts. If all episodes had a similar motive and modus operandi, the defendant obviously knew what she was doing. She could not be found "not guilty by reason of insanity."

Ordinarily, evidence of prior offenses is not admitted in a trial. The accused must be found guilty of *this* crime based on evidence beyond a reasonable doubt. However, as the judge explained to the jury, he admitted testimony about the other poisonings in Barfield's case only to show her intent, her knowledge of the effects of arsenic, and "the possible existence of a scheme or system." It would not be surprising if the explanation of the distinction between considering prior crimes as proof of guilt and considering them to show state of mind was lost on those of the jurors who did not understand the sophisticated rules of evidence.

The state called one of the officers who had questioned Velma Barfield in March. Deputy Wilbur Lovett told the court that the suspect had been properly Mirandized and waived her rights. In contrast to the version told by Barfield and her son, the deputy stated that no threats or promises had been made, other than a promise of medical attention after the second interview. He denied that anyone had urged her to confess so that things would go easier for her. But because the record of the first interview consisted not of a signed statement but only of Lovett's notes, it was hard to prove just exactly what was said. Finally, when asked if Barfield was "under the influence" of drugs, the deputy said she did not appear so to him, although she cried often during the sessions. Surely the word of a deputy sheriff that someone did not "appear" to be under the influence, although there was evidence that she had taken a handful of sedatives, antidepressants, barbiturates, and sleeping pills, should have been challenged. What expertise did he have to diagnose her medical condition? Yet Lovett's opinion went into the record as a description of Velma Barfield's competence to make a voluntary and legal confession.

The defense then called Barfield and her son Ronnie to describe her men-tal state at the time of the interrogation. She recounted her drug intake on March 13—two Sinequin, two Elavils, two Tylenol IIs, two Tranxenes, and three Valium—prescriptions gathered from at least four different doctors. She had taken four very sedating antidepressants, five antianxiety agents that are highly tranquilizing, and narcotics.[19] Surprisingly, Deputy Lovett said she was not "under the influence." Not surprisingly, Barfield claimed to have no rec-ollection of waiving her Miranda rights or of being told that she could call a lawyer. She also did not remember how many statements she had made or whether she had signed them. She did claim, however, to remember that the detectives promised to "go easier" on her if she cooperated. Why would Barfield remember clearly only one sentence out of hours of questioning? Possibly her son had told her what he remembered and she fixed on that point. Or perhaps she was lying. Perhaps "go easier" meant their promise to bring her prescriptions. Or perhaps during her trial she was still foggy, under the influence of drugs, although in the process of withdrawal.

Prosecuting attorney Britt treated her as if her statements were lies. He asked her repeatedly if she remembered events at the time of the crime and the interrogation. When she answered, "No," he shot further questions at her. How could she recall that she bought the poison at Eckerd's Drug Store but not remember the Miranda warnings? If she was so muddled at the police sta-tion, why was her signature clear and legible? Britt made Barfield very angry. She snapped back at him and became defensive.

Ronnie remembered that his mother sobbed uncontrollably at the police station during questioning. He recalled that on March 13, Lovett simply said "You still have your rights," rather than providing the entire Miranda warn-ing, and that the police promised "to go easier on her" if she made a statement.

The court's ruling that the confession was admissible was critical to the outcome of the trial. Had the defense been able to suppress the statements, there would be no evidence of Barfield's involvement in the other three murders. Had the court recognized her impaired mental state while she was questioned, it would have added credence to the argument that her drug addiction made her less responsible. The judge, however, chose to accept the deputy's diagnosis that "she didn't seem to be under the influence" rather than the evidence of multiple drug effects that the defense tried rather ineptly to present. Additional doubts about the integrity of the interrogation came later when another deputy, Al Parnell, recalled how Velma cried constantly during both sessions. He remembered her saying on the 13th that she did not intend to kill Taylor but just intended to make him sick. However that point did not appear in the statement written by Lovett and signed by Barfield. Why did the deputy leave out her explanation and why, if Barfield was fully rational, did she sign a statement that omitted her best defense? Without arguing that the police purposely framed Velma Barfield, it is possible to see that the entire interrogation process took advantage of her mental and emotional state, her ignorance of the legal system, and her poverty and failure to ask for a lawyer.

Once the prosecutor had the information about the prior murders in the record—even if only to show that Barfield knew what she was doing when she poisoned Taylor—he added the coup de grace. The daughter of Jennings Barfield, Velma's second husband, was brought in to testify to the circumstances of her father's death. Barfield had suffered from several serious conditions, including emphysema and a heart condition. His death was attributed to heart failure. Now Britt suggested that Velma had poisoned him also. His body was exhumed and arsenic found. Velma had inherited a car and a few thousand dollars at his death. Although Velma never confessed to Barfield's death, the state could paint the picture of a "black widow," a serial poisoner who killed those close to her for monetary gain. And she killed not strangers but—allegedly—a husband, a boyfriend, a mother, and two elderly sick people. What could be more despicable conduct for a woman?

Jacobson had his work cut out for him after the jury heard Britt's side of the case. Because the defense was trying to establish Barfield's inability to form the requisite intent for first-degree murder, the testimony of doctors who treated her and prescribed medication was critical. Dr. Arthur Douglas, the state-appointed psychiatrist who had met Velma once, provided a facile diagnosis. In his view, Barfield had suffered from circumstantial depression (she was in jail awaiting trial for murder at the time), she had a passive-dependent personality disorder which meant she coped poorly with stress, and she had a problem with multiple drug abuse. He did not ask her where or why she got the variety of medications, just as none of the other doctors had. Somehow the responsibility for her addiction was placed totally on her shoulders, although medical professionals had willingly provided a whole pharmacopoeia without looking into her other prescriptions. The best testimony Jacobson was able to elicit from Douglas was that the mixture of drugs Barfield took would "affect her mind." The prosecutor, on the other hand, minimized Barfield's condition, calling it "simply" depression. He drew out the information that the doctor saw no evidence of mental illness when he examined Barfield, and no evidence that she did not know right from wrong at the time of the crime. Jacobson did not re-cross Douglas, leaving the jury with the impression that Barfield was quite competent. Three other doctors testified that she had a passive, inadequate personality, that she used prescription drugs to excess, that she had a "passive-aggressive neurotic reaction," that she was either a "parasite or a destroyer." Although all were allegedly defense witnesses, none assisted with Velma's defense. Their descriptions of Barfield's condition made her less, rather than more, sympathetic. At the end of the psychiatric testimony, the defense had only Barfield herself to make its case.

Her attorney debated over whether to put his client on the stand. On the one hand, she tended to be prickly and defensive; she might lose her temper. On the other hand, if she cooperated, Barfield might come across as befuddled or as repentant. Either of those images might mitigate her guilt in the eyes of the jury. Under oath, Barfield admitted that she had forged checks and that she poisoned Taylor. She stated that she "never intended to kill anyone," that she only wanted to make the victims sick to cover up the bad checks used to pay for her "medicine." As for the medicine, Barfield testified that she had been under the care of at least four different doctors, all of whom prescribed psychotropic drugs. She had been given such prescriptions for the last decade and had been doubling and tripling the recommended dosages of the drugs. On at least three occasions, she had been hospitalized for overdoses. Missing from all of her medical treatment was any effort by the professionals who saw Barfield to find out *why* she suffered from anxiety, depression, insomnia, or drug dependence. Had she been more affluent and manifested the same symptoms, it is likely Barfield would have been sent to a therapist. For a poor woman in the rural south, mind-altering drugs seemed the only remedy.

Questioned by her attorney, Barfield also reiterated that she had been under heavy medication during the questioning by police. She was vague about the details, but stuck by her recollection that the deputies had promised to go easier on her if she told them everything.

Joe Freeman Britt verbally attacked Barfield, shooting hostile questions faster than she could answer them. He took her over and over the details of Taylor's last days, confusing her and causing her to become argumentative and defensive. He asked several times why she did not tell the hospital about the poison and thereby save Taylor's life. When Barfield replied that she was afraid, Britt alleged that she was afraid Taylor would live and that her thefts would be exposed. The prosecutor's questioning was designed to establish Barfield's motive—money—firmly in the jury's thinking. He raised the same point about the previous deaths, suggesting that she learned from experience that arsenic was tasteless and that her greed led her to use it repeatedly against helpless and innocent victims. Britt cut Barfield off in mid-answer so many times that the judge had to remind him to "let her finish." He wanted to know if she took medicine every day. Was she under the influence every day? If so, how could she negotiate the narrow drive-through lane at the bank and cash a forged check for $300, as she had the day before Taylor's death while he lay "moaning, groaning, and turning blue?" Britt was a skillful prosecutor who painted a picture of a hardened, deceitful woman, stealing money and indulging her taste for drugs. Even written transcripts of the trial convey his bullying techniques, but those tactics allowed him to plant his theory of the crime in the jurors' minds. Neither Barfield nor her lawyer were able to offer an alternative narrative, one that would make them see her side of the story.

After testimony was completed in the guilt phase of the trial, the judge ruled that the insanity defense would not be allowed. When someone accused of a crime claims to be "not guilty by reason of insanity," they are offering an affirmative defense. They must prove to the jury that they have met the state's definition of insanity. In North Carolina, defendants must establish that they suffered from a mental defect making them unable to understand what they were doing or unable to tell right from wrong.[20] None of the doctors called by the defense in Barfield's case was willing to say that she was legally insane. Thus the insanity plea would not be allowed.

The two sides had spent five days presenting the case. Before the jury retired to determine whether Velma Barfield was guilty, each attorney made a closing statement.

They offered opposing versions of stereotypical womanly qualities. Jacobson's remarks betrayed, at the very least, his inexperience. His frequent factual errors suggest that he failed to prepare adequately. Perhaps he thought the case was hopeless at that point; perhaps he felt obliged to provide only the formality of a minimal explanation of his client's behavior. He assumed that the jury would find her guilty and focused on the issue of intent, asking them to choose second-degree murder. The defendant, he said, was unable to form the requisite intent for first-degree murder because she was too intoxicated from her multiple drugs. The Velma Barfield portrayed by Jacobson was pathetic, a woman who "had problems" she could not handle. He described her drug use as so severe that even her own daughter did not trust her to babysit for fear she would be incapacitated. Barfield's defense attorney called her a drug abuser and a "passive-dependent, passive-neurotic personality." Could he have believed a jury would empathize with the person he described?

Britt, on the other hand, had prepared a closing statement about twice the length of Jacobson's. He began by explaining that murder by poison qualifies as first-degree murder and "that woman sitting right there is guilty." He offered proof by citing the other murders to which she had confessed (for which she was not on trial) and lingered over the death of Jennings Barfield (to which she had not confessed and for which there was no proof). He focused not only on the similarity of the causes of death but on Velma's alleged financial motives. No one could miss the implicit comparison of the two men in her life. Justice, he said, comes through the "hard experience of our forefathers," and it is based on the kind of common sense that says "someone who would commit these kinds of horrendous crimes over and over again knows precisely what she is doing every time she does it." She was a "cold-blooded deliberate murderer." Her demeanor proved it. "Did you see what she looked like?" he asked. She was a "cold, hard woman … calculating and cunning … [who] calmly chewed gum." He asked the jury to decide who they believed—the [male] authority figures, the deputies and doctors who had nothing to gain by their testimony—or Velma Barfield. Did they believe the deputies' account of her interrogation or Barfield's "fuss that her rights had been violated" because she was under the "influence of some sort of narcotic drug?" Granted she had some sort of "little personal problems" or "hang ups" but those could not provide a "license to start killing." The drugs, Britt argued, were "her hobby" and the motive for her thefts—"to satisfy her craving for what she wanted." Finally, the prosecutor alluded to the favorite metaphor for the woman who murders a male partner, the black widow. While Taylor was "puking his guts out and sick and hurting … she was standing there the whole time.... like the spider in the middle of the web, waiting, waiting, for Stewart Taylor to go on, to die." When the prosecutor finished his peroration, Barfield allegedly caught his eye and made a motion as if to applaud his performance.[21]

The Verdict and the Sentence

The images Jacobson and Britt laid before the jury are profoundly gendered. The only picture the defense drew was of a weak, incompetent woman, lacking discipline and rationality. At most she deserved pity. The prosecutor, on the other hand, offered a portrait that negated any positive feminine quality. Crass and cold blooded, like a deadly spider, Barfield plotted murders to indulge her own perverse "hobbies." Her addiction and her neuroses were made to seem trivial, even self-inflicted. As Britt portrayed her, Barfield deserved the jury's utmost contempt and the vengeance of the community.

The guilt phase was almost over. The judge instructed the jurors that if they found that Velma Barfield put poison in Stewart Taylor's food, if she intended to kill Taylor, and if the poison caused his death they should convict her of first-degree murder. If intent was lacking, they should find second-degree murder. In one hour and ten minutes, the jurors returned with a verdict—guilty of murder in the first degree. The brevity of the deliberations suggest that the jurors spent little time debating. It would be interesting to know how heavily they weighed the earlier deaths, whether they felt they were actually finding Barfield guilty of four or five poisonings rather than only the death of Taylor.

The second part of the trial, the sentencing phase, allowed the defense to introduce mitigating circumstances, facts to explain why the death penalty should not be imposed, while the state could offer aggravating circumstances to argue in favor of death. Again, Jacobson was severely outmatched. The case he put on was minimal. A friend who had known Barfield for more than ten years testified that Velma's addiction had begun after the death of her first husband, Thomas Burke. Her son, Ronald Burke, and her daughter Kim agreed that their mother's drug dependency dated back for a decade. Both acknowledged that they loved their mother. These statements were apparently designed to show the extent to which Barfield should not be held responsible for her actions and also that her death would be painful for her children. Britt made mincemeat of those claims.

He began with a focus on sympathy for the victim. Velma had "killed him dead." Taylor currently "lies out there in the cold damp sod wrapped in his shroud because of the callous, indifferent, malicious act of this woman." Britt encouraged the jury not to be preoccupied with the defendant's rights but to remember that no one had protected Taylor's rights on the night of his death while he writhed, clutched his stomach, vomited, and threw back his head and screamed. Taylor did not really get to confront his murderer, because she was sneaky—"doing a nefarious act in secret." The prosecutor waved a bottle of ant poison in the air and called it "a killer that causes excruciating pain."

As for Velma, the jury was reminded not to feel sympathy based on the testimony of her children. Britt suggested that she poisoned people to "get her kicks" because she had "done enough of it for a cheap enough price." Did he mean that because the monetary rewards were small, Barfield killed people for fun? He would also argue that her motive was financial gain. Would her conduct be more or less reprehensible if the amounts were greater? But the prosecutor was less concerned with the logic of his argument than with convincing the jury that Barfield was sufficiently evil to deserve death. He ended by showing how far Velma Barfield strayed from the image of female virtue. "[Taylor] lay there dying, knowing that his Florence Nightingale was there beside him but not knowing that his Florence Nightingale was in truth Lucretia Borgia."

The defense is allowed the last statement in the capital sentencing phase. Once again, Jacobson rested his argument on Barfield's personal inadequacies and her drug consumption. What could the defense gain by rehashing all the murders and forgeries? But Jacobson did so, saying there were "five cases, maybe six, maybe seven." He must have hoped to win some sympathy from the jurors by saying "It all goes back to the dope, more dope, more dope, more forgeries, more covering up, more poisonings." Why was she addicted? "She is an inadequate personality, passive-aggressive, unable to cope." Did he know what he was talking about? Did those terms mean anything or were they simply labels hung on a defendant who was not treated with respect, even by her own lawyer? The most desperate part of Jacobson's argument for mitigation was that if Barfield had been tried separately for five murders, she could be sentenced to prison for five life terms and never see the light of day. He was offering the jury the opportunity to come back and convict his client four more times if they would vote against the death penalty. Her own lawyer repeatedly confirmed the jury's belief that she was a serial murderer.

Jurors were given a verdict sheet that asked four questions. Did aggravating circumstances exist? Did mitigating circumstances exist? Did mitigating circumstances outweigh aggravating circumstances? Were aggravating factors sufficient for the death penalty? They answered that aggravating circumstances were sufficient and that no mitigating circumstances existed. Although the voir dire had revealed that many in the jury pool did not really grasp the idea of aggravators and mitigators, they nonetheless sentenced Velma Barfield to die. Her execution was originally set for February 9, 1979.

Looking back, Barfield remembered very little of her trial. Although her drug intake was controlled, she was still heavily medicated. She felt angry with Britt and angry with the whole world. Her son Ronnie believed that even if his mother was technically sane during those months, she was not competent to assist in her defense.[22] Her gesture of symbolic applause for the prosecutor seemed to confirm this. The issue of Barfield's fitness for trial and the competence of her court-appointed attorney would become issues raised in the appeals that ultimately delayed her death until November 2, 1984.

The Appeals

North Carolina law provides that death penalty cases automatically go to the state Supreme Court for review. The Court heard Barfield's first appeal in November of 1979. Bob Jacobson was required to represent her for one last time before he earned his total fee of $6500 from the state for what Joseph Ingle, the Director of the Southern Coalition on Prisons and Jails, called a "perfunctory defense."[23] All of the matters to which Jacobson had objected during the trial could be reviewed by the state Supreme Court. Those sixteen points fall into several categories.[24] Four concern the constitutionality of the state's death penalty law. The court found no errors in the law or in its application in Barfield's case. Nor did they find any problems with the jury selection process. Several of the objections dealt with the introduction of evidence of the other poisonings. Early in the proceedings against Barfield, Jacobson had asked for the assistance of additional counsel, as his client was suspected of four other murders. The North Carolina Supreme Court found that, although evidence of those crimes was introduced at the trial, the burden on the court-appointed attorney was "not excessive." The Court also noted that evidence of prior offenses is admissible if its probative value exceeds the "specter of unfair prejudice." In Barfield's case, they decided, the stories of the earlier deaths could "show that the defendant knew the probable consequences of her actions when she administered the poison to Stewart Taylor." They would also illustrate that she administered the fatal doses intentionally rather than accidentally, and show that she knew "full well the probable consequences of her actions." Additionally, in the court's eyes, all of the deaths came about for the same motivation, "pecuniary gain to the defendant." They also found that the crimes had common features demonstrating that they were "caused by a general plan." Not only did the court find that it was proper to admit all the evidence of the earlier poisonings, they approved Britt's discussion of them before the jury in his closing arguments. The prosecutor seemed to be allowed the best of both worlds in this instance. He did not need to prove beyond a reasonable doubt that

Barfield had committed the earlier murders. Her attorney was not given assistance to investigate them. Yet Britt was allowed to remind the jury repeatedly of those crimes, as if Barfield's guilt had been established.

The Supreme Court also declined to find prosecutorial misconduct or abuse of judicial discretion in Britt's request that the ambulance attendant mimic Taylor's final scream. They found that the episode met the definition of a "courtroom demonstration," corresponding "in all essential particulars with those existing at the time and place of the event" and necessary for the jury to "fully understand the facts and circumstances." Surely some essential particulars were different—the place, the person screaming, his condition (health) opposed to Taylor's (fatally ill). In fact, despite the court's ruling, it is difficult to see either a single "essential particular" that corresponded to the event or to show whether it increased the jurors' understanding or inflamed their emotions.

Barfield's mental state at the time of her questioning and the attempted insanity defense also came under review. With evidence from the police that Velma "did not appear to be under the influence of anything" compared to the testimony that she had consumed numerous drugs, the court agreed with the trial judge in accepting the deputies' version of the interrogation. They found no basis for an insanity plea, "no evidence that she did not know the nature and quality of her acts." Ultimately, the court found no errors in Barfield's trial or sentencing. "The manner in which death was inflicted and the way in which [the] defendant conducted herself after she administered the poison to Taylor lead us to conclude that the sentence of death is not excessive or disproportionate considering both the crime and the defendant." They did not specify what aspects of Barfield's conduct after the poisoning they found relevant. Perhaps they referred to her failure to tell the hospital about the poison or her "financial gain" of $300. They may have meant her failure to cry in court or her feisty replies to the prosecution's questions. When they decided that the sentence was appropriate for both "the crime and the defendant" did they mean the cold-blooded, deceiving, gum-chewing woman whose only defense was "voluntary intoxication," the image Joe Freeman Britt had presented in his courtroom?

Once the initial appeal had been completed, Jacobson was released from his service and Velma Barfield was without a lawyer. The state of North Carolina does not provide attorneys for indigent capital defendants once they have completed their trial and the first automatic appeal. As in many other states, men and women on death row must depend on the kindness of strangers, on the services of organizations who provide free legal service in death penalty cases. The American Civil Liberties Union (ACLU) found Richard Burr of the Southern Prisoners' Defense Committee to represent Barfield. Local attorney Jimmy Little who was licensed in North Carolina joined the defense team. Unlike Jacobson, in whom Barfield never really had confidence, Burr clicked with her immediately. He recalled that at their first meeting, they liked each other a great deal. Burr found it inconceivable that the "kind, sensitive, and loving" woman he met could have committed several murders. He concluded that her mental and emotional states must have been "seriously altered." Burr and Little decided that at the next appeal stage—a full evidentiary hearing to request a new trial—they would present a different psychiatric profile to challenge the picture of the "cold-blooded murderess" who had emerged from the original trial record.[25] They would also need to show that Barfield's constitutional right to competent representation by an attorney had been violated.

The hearing began on November 11, 1980, and lasted for a week.[26] Joe Freeman Britt once again represented the state. This time he had to argue that his old adversary, Bob Jacobson, had done a decent job and that Barfield's trial had been fair. Britt did not hide his hostility to having an "outsider" question Robeson County justice and he objected to almost every point Burr and Little raised. Virtually every one of his objections was sustained by Judge Braswell, who seemed to share the prosecutor's feelings. Often during the hearing Burr simply asked that his witnesses' testimony be "for the record" even if not admitted as evidence. That way he could at least cite the information in later appeals.

Jacobson's testimony revealed two things. He had not been well prepared for either the trial or the post-conviction hearings, and he did not like Velma Barfield. Although the defense attorney had intended to use an insanity plea, he admitted to doing no reading on the effects of multiple drug addiction. The only doctors he consulted were those, hired by the state, who testified. His own belief was that Velma "couldn't cope" and that she went to doctors because of her "passive-dependent personality." He had made no efforts to find experts to explain her drug dependency beyond that facile "diagnosis," although he thought an insanity plea would put a "label" on her condition. Jacobson had little recollection of his conversations with his client, although he did assert that he had prepared her to testify. "I wanted her to look like somebody's mother. Here was this poor lady and look what she was going through and I wanted her to invoke sympathy." He wanted her to cry on the stand. Instead Barfield "made a spectacle of herself and I reprimanded her severely for it."

Jacobson was vague about the relationships among the victims and the names of Velma's immediate family. He admitted to omitting any information about her past life, her employment record, or her family history from the mitigating evidence in the sentencing phase of the trial. And Jacobson's knowledge of criminal procedure seemed shaky. He had failed to notice that Velma signed the waiver of her Miranda rights after, not before, the police questioned her. He was unfamiliar with major Supreme Court cases on the death penalty and unaware that groups such as the ACLU and the NAACP were available to assist in capital cases. With Britt's constant objections, much of Jacobson's testimony did not find its way into the official record, but it remains in the transcript as evidence of the flaws in Barfield's legal process.

Psychiatric testimony was critical to the appeal and to show that Jacobson had been ineffective in gathering and presenting evidence of Velma's mental condition. Dr. Selwyn Rose had examined Barfield two months before the evidentiary hearing. His report differed significantly from the state-appointed doctors who had testified at trial. Rose learned that Barfield's father had been abusive. She mentioned an attempted sexual assault and described a family who lived in constant fear of his violent rages. She also explained how she resented her mother for permitting the abuse. Rose diagnosed a "psychopathic deviation," characterized by paranoia and schizophrenia. In his view, Barfield had not been legally sane at the time of the crimes. Her thought processes had been impaired by depression and drug abuse. She had low impulse control and could not, at that time, conform her behavior to the law. Rose concluded that Barfield was not passive and dependent but hostile and aggressive when under the influence. At the very least, Rose's testimony presented an alternative explanation of Barfield's character; one that not merely labeled her but offered a reasonable context for explaining her behavior.

Burr and Little hoped to introduce expert witnesses to support the contention that Jacobson's defense had been inadequate. In response to Britt's objections, the judge ruled most of that line of argument inadmissible, although John Ackerman, Dean of the National College of Criminal Justice and Mary Ann Talley, a criminal defense attorney, were allowed to testify for the record. Britt treated both witnesses with contempt, calling them "Brother Ackerman" and "Madame Talley." He even accused Talley of developing a strategy to build constitutional errors into a trial as a way of providing grounds for appeal and preventing capital convictions. As no jury was present, his reasons for such a display of rudeness are not clear.

While Barfield's lawyers closed with a summation of their points, Britt used his final statement to accuse them of "Monday morning quarterbacking." It is fine to raise points of law, he noted, but "when you get down to real life and the mano-a-mano confrontation in the courtroom, it ain't quite that simple anymore." The judge's thirty-seven-page ruling, finding that Barfield's constitutional rights had not been denied or violated and denying her request for a new trial, surpassed Britt in its use of sports metaphors. The judge wrote "Parenthetically ... it is noted that on Sunday, November 16, the Pittsburgh Steelers and the Cleveland Browns played a football game that went down to the last six minutes before victory for the Steelers." He recounted, in his judicial opinion, the last three minutes when the Steelers twice failed to score and "Terry Bradshaw ... as good a professional quarterback as can be found in the business" could not get the ball into the end zone. "In the waning moments, with six seconds left, a second chance came when Bradshaw threw what proved to be the winning touchdown pass, as he found Swann free in the end zone." The judge's point? The "living room quarterbacks, the "Monday morning quarterbacks" had given up on the Steelers during the last three minutes. Actually in his eagerness to embrace Britt's metaphor, Judge Braswell misused the term. Monday morning quarterbacks wait until the final score to replay the game—they typically have all of Sunday night to second guess the players and coaches. Nonetheless, he pressed the point, "While football and a person's life are not to be equated in value, the perfect game in sports or life is yet to be played. Success—or failure—always look different in hindsight."

Incredibly, the court seemed to believe that those who conducted a trial that would deprive a human being of her life should be held to the same standard of accuracy and fair play as a football team playing a *game*.

After the North Carolina court rejected the request for a new trial, Velma Barfield's new attorneys, Jimmy Little and Dick Burr, pursued every avenue of appeal for their client. Meanwhile, many of those sentenced to death under the new post-*Gregg* statutes were getting closer to execution. By 1984, fifteen men had been put to death, including one in the neighboring state of Virginia. In March of that year, North Carolina administered a lethal injection to uneducated alcoholic James Hutchins for the murder of three police officers. With Barfield definitely next in line, her lawyers determined that a request to the governor for clemency was her best hope.[27]

Her supporters formed a clemency committee of anti-death penalty activists, ministers, and friends who produced a brochure called "A Shared Responsibility." It noted that Barfield had admitted her guilt, that she was now drug free and "painfully aware of the gravity of her actions." Velma had called out over her lifetime for help that never came from friends, family, or society. "There but for the grace of God go every one of us," the pamphlet asserted. No one was asking the state to free or to forgive her, just to spare her life.[28] The woman on death row was not the same person who had poisoned Stewart Taylor. She had experienced a religious conversion and was trying in every way to live a Christian life. The lawyers and the committee gathered testimony from people inside and outside the prison who cared for her and whom she had helped. Many of the women at the prison wrote letters saying they loved Barfield like a mother or a sister. They called her "Mama Margie." Perhaps as a symbol of her restored personality, she had reclaimed her original first name. Prison guards, whom Barfield called "the help," and Assistant Warden Jennie Lancaster entered pleas on her behalf. As Burr stated, Velma "grew where she was planted and sank deep roots in the prison and touched a lot of lives."[29] The committee produced a video for the governor showing Velma with her family, focusing on her connection with her grandchildren.

Burr sought additional psychiatric consultation to explain Barfield's crimes. He brought in Dr. Dorothy Otnow Lewis, an expert on the connections between neurologic impairment, psychopathology, and violence. She had examined many offenders whose history of childhood abuse had resulted in frontal lobe damage that influenced their inability to control violent actions. Those who knew Velma Barfield well believed that something was missing to explain the "anomalous behavior of this charming grandmother who had killed four people." Dr. Lewis offered a completely new diagnosis, bipolar mood disorder. She learned from Velma about a history of repeated sexual abuse by male members of her family and about patterns of manic episodes. Bipolar disorder explained how Barfield could swing from normality to psychosis. It also revealed how counterproductive and even dangerous most of the drugs prescribed for her had been.[30] Giving someone in a manic phase an antidepressant was like throwing gasoline on a fire.

Barfield's claim of sexual abuse stunned some members of her family who denied the truth of her story. On the other hand, Lewis was an expert in dealing with murderers and other violent offenders. She would not be easily fooled. In fact, it is likely that Barfield told Dr. Lewis even more startling facts about her history. In her 1998 book, Lewis wrote that to spare her family Velma had ordered her lawyer not to reveal "the most crucial psychiatric findings," information that might save her life.[31] Obviously, the psychiatrist was not referring to allegations of abuse or incest, as those had been made public. There was, apparently, something even more appalling.

While Barfield's advocates prepared her request for clemency, the victims' families began a counter-campaign. They made public statements expressing distrust of her conversion and fear that if she were not executed, she would be released and kill again. They wished she would be fed arsenic as a method of execution.[32]

The fall of 1984 when Velma Barfield was scheduled to die was election season in North Carolina. Democratic Governor Jim Hunt was involved in a Senate race against the incumbent Republican Jesse Helms. Hunt's early lead had diminished, perhaps as President Reagan's reelection coattails swept up the Helms campaign. In any case, the governor would have to decide about Barfield's clemency appeal in an atmosphere colored by his campaign against a strong advocate of the death penalty.

To his credit, Hunt took the petition seriously, setting aside two days to review the pleas. However, Barfield and her supporters believed that he did not respond to the real issue—that she was asking to spare her life because she had been rehabilitated.[33] Observers found the governor cool and detached and focused on the need for new evidence, not on whether Barfield, as she was in 1984, deserved death.[34] He thought the argument that she was a decent person, loved by many, was irrelevant.[35] Like many other politicians, Hunt claimed to believe that the death penalty was a deterrent. That goal would not be served if he were to intervene. He claimed that she had had a fair trial; that the jury had spoken; that she had been convicted of one murder, admitted to three more including her mother; and was suspected of a fifth killing. His choice not to grant clemency, Hunt declared, was consistent with the rule of law. He had "no idea" of the decision's effect on his campaign for the Senate.[36]

Many thought the fact that Barfield was a woman and no women had been executed since the reinstatement of the death penalty might sway the governor to be merciful. Before 1984, North Carolina had executed only two women in the entire twentieth century. Partisan politics, however, seem to have trumped chivalry. By the time Barfield was on death row, women in America had made many strides toward legal equality. To some jurists, such equality meant that men and women should be equally susceptible to the "forfeit of life for murders of extraordinary heinousness." Given that context and given that Barfield's execution was scheduled for two days before the election, Hunt probably perceived any concession to her sex as an electoral liability. Polls showed that 70% of North Carolinians supported the death penalty. Although Barfield's execution might keep a few liberals at home, clemency could anger a much larger proportion of voters who would see Hunt as weak and soft on crime.

He could not commute Barfield's sentence unless he was willing to pay a steep political price. Instead, as legal scholar Elizabeth Rapaport states, "chivalry and compassion ... were quelled by the compelling logic of equal justice."[37] Similar issues would arise when the next condemned woman, Karla Faye Tucker, sought clemency from Texas governor George W. Bush. Her case also raised the issue of redemption. If a person turned her life around through a religious conversion and service to others did she still deserve to die? Did redemption matter?

The Final Chapter

Governor Hunt denied clemency on September 27, 1984. Barfield's execution was scheduled for November 2. She was offered the choice between lethal injection and the gas chamber. As she had been told that "neither form causes pain," she decided on injection because it would be easier for her children to hear about and easier for the observers. She also wanted to donate her "usable parts" to a university hospital for research.[38] Barfield seemed resigned to death and even, given her faith, hopeful that she would soon be in heaven.

Her lawyers were not resigned. Burr hoped to raise one last issue on appeal—that Barfield was not competent at the time of her trial because she was in the midst of acute withdrawal. This plea could be seen as a new issue which the courts required to reopen the case. Knowledge of drug withdrawal was much more complete in 1984 and new medical testimony could be produced. Although her children were tired, discouraged, and extremely reluctant to go through another round of appeals, Barfield determined to try. She said she owed it to the others on death row not to give up. In the last days before the scheduled execution, Burr and Little argued for a stay so a new evidentiary hearing could be conducted. They appeared in the North Carolina Supreme Court on October 29, in Federal District Court on October 31, and in the Fourth Circuit Court of Appeals on November 1. Their appeal was rejected at each level.

Velma Barfield went to her death on November 2, 1984. Much was made of her last meal and her clothing. She rejected the dinner the prison provided (chicken livers, macaroni and cheese, beans, peas, pie, and cake) and chose to have a Coke and some cheese doodles from the vending machines instead. For the first woman executed by lethal injection, what to wear to her execution posed a problem. James Hutchins had been executed in his underwear. Barfield asked if she might wear a pair of pajamas, for modesty. Perhaps pajamas offered her a modicum of dignity as she went to her death before an audience. Press reports referred to a grandmother executed in pink pajamas and blue house slippers, making her sound like an eccentric old lady. None of those close to Velma Barfield concurred in that description.

Fourteen people—eight official witnesses, four members of the press, Jimmy Little, and Anne Lotz (the daughter of evangelist Billy Graham) observed the execution. Dick Burr was perplexed that Barfield appeared so serene as she drew nearer to her death. He thought a person being intentionally killed by the state would be clawing, scratching, and screaming in self-defense.[39] Instead, she had come to think of the room with the gurney as the "gateway to heaven." Her last words expressed remorse for the hurt she had caused her victims and their families and gratitude to her own family and supporters. According to Anne Lotz, "Velma Barfield, with peace and tranquility on her fact, her lips moving in silent prayer, closed her eyes in death at 2:15 AM on November 2, while opening them to the face of her beloved Savior and Lord for all eternity."[40] Others did not express such faith. Her two children waited in the warden's office for word of their mother's death. Ronnie said later that it was a "bizarre, state-sponsored circus in which the main act would be hidden from view, held in the dead of night to attract the least attention possible, as if the state were ashamed and embarrassed by it."[41] Many other commentators have questioned why, if the government believes that executions are noble and moral acts, they choose to perform them deep inside prisons in the dead of night.[42]

Outside the prison two groups congregated. One comprised opponents of capital punishment who lit candles and represented an "affirmation of the worth of Velma's life, regardless of what the state of North Carolina decided." On the other side were a boisterous bunch made up mostly of young men, calling out for Barfield's death and yelling "Kill the bitch." Velma's brother walked over and watched them for a while, wondering why they felt so much hate and spite for a woman they had never met.[43]

Why?

The overriding question remains "Why?" Why did Barfield poison four or five people and why, of all the murderers in the country, was she executed? How did gender and perceptions about gender affect her life and the legal process?

The connections between her life experiences and her drug addiction are clear. Although she told several different versions of abuse in her childhood home, undoubtedly Barfield grew up with violence and brutality, and with little moral and emotional support. She described her father beating her oldest brother with anything he found handy and her mother being intimidated. "Daddy didn't hit her, but he would grab her arm and twist it until she screamed from the pain. Sometimes he grabbed a finger and did the same thing. Mama never fought back."[44] Later, Barfield admitted how she resented her mother's passive acceptance of physical assaults on herself and her children. When she asked why her mother had not left her father, Lillie Bullard replied "Where would I go?" Today we know much more about the dynamics of domestic violence—that abusers are asserting power and control and that children in violent homes are victims, whether they are physically harmed or not. We also know that the best predictor of becoming a violent offender as an adult is to grow up in a violent home.

According to Velma, where she grew up, people did not talk about their problems. What happened at home stayed there. Victims blamed themselves. "I did the only thing I knew how to do, I kept it all inside me. Over the years the feelings got worse and worse." When she was thirteen, her father raped her. Velma did not know who to tell so she "pushed things deeper inside."[45] Although early on, she had been a good student, she began to act out at school and to steal things to impress her classmates. Her parents did not encourage education, often making her stay home to help with the younger children. With no sense of self-worth, she believed her family valued her only because she would work like a slave.[46]

It is not surprising that she jumped at the first chance to escape her family and eloped with her high school boyfriend Thomas Burke.[47] Both dropped out of school but for the first years of their marriage, both had decent jobs. They made a stable home for their two children. Thomas, she recalled, was nicer to her than anyone had ever been. Barfield later traced her first bout with depression to a car accident when she was in her early twenties. She also had anxiety attacks worrying about her children during her recovery. At thirty, she was advised to have a hysterectomy. Again, she suffered from "nerves" and anxiety. Doctors gave her little information about the hormonal consequences of a hysterectomy. She dealt with her mood swings by taking diet pills and by going on shopping binges. Meanwhile her husband's drinking brought strains to their marriage. Velma blamed herself. In 1968 she had a "nervous breakdown." Perhaps sedatives were the only known treatment for her condition, but it is not hard to believe that if Velma had been able to pay for private care she might have gotten a better diagnosis of her mental health. A year later Thomas Burke died in a fire at their home. Although some tried later to accuse Barfield of murdering him, Burke had a habit of smoking in bed and passing out. His death was consistent with that scenario.

The loss of Burke definitely drove Velma deeper into drug dependence. Between then and her arrest, she got prescriptions for Valium and other addictive drugs from more than two dozen different doctors. She self-medicated with barbiturates, narcotics, sleeping pills, stimulants, antidepressants—all were dangerous, especially if taken with Valium. She overdosed four or five times, was hospitalized, and released with more medication. Her whole life, she remembered, revolved around making sure she had enough pills available.

In 1970, she married Jennings Barfield "just to have someone to ease the emptiness" and regretted it almost immediately. He continued to smoke despite his emphysema and refused to watch his diet, although he had diabetes. About eight months after the wedding, Barfield was dead. The cause was listed as heart failure, apparently aggravated by his respiratory problems. Velma overdosed again and spent three weeks in a hospital. She remembered no treatment for her addiction and no attempt to discover its cause. After she was released, she stopped making payments on her house. She lost her job at Belk's department store. Homeless and broke, she was reduced to moving in with her parents, this time to help care for her ailing father. After his death, her drug use increased. Velma "functioned like a robot. I showed no emotions. I felt nothing. For days at a time I felt neither pain nor happiness. Nothing. The emotional part of my life had been taken out and stored away."[48]

Life with her mother was impossible, especially as Lillie Bullard kept saying to her daughter, "I wish we could go back to when you were thirteen or fourteen." Of course, that was the time when Velma was sexually assaulted—the worst experience buried the deepest. Emotional stress, coupled with a desperate need for money to buy her "medicine" led Barfield to take out a loan in her mother's name. Fear of discovery led her to give her mother poison to "make her sick" and to buy time to repay the money. It was the pattern of the later poisonings—John Henry Lee, Dollie Edwards, and Stewart Taylor. In each case, she was both a caregiver and a dependent. In each case, her drug addiction plus her poverty led to the irrational conclusion that poisoning someone would be a solution.

How is blame to be parceled out in such a case? Velma Barfield administered deadly chemicals. The court determined that she did not meet the legal definition of insanity. She was, however, mentally ill and addicted to prescription drugs. She was almost certainly under the influence of multiple

incompatible drugs when she was questioned and during her trial. Does anyone bear the responsibility for decades of misdiagnoses and casual dispensing
of psychotropic drugs?

Faith

Velma Barfield had considered herself a Christian since she joined the Baptist
church in high school. She had gone to services regularly, taught a few Bible
study classes, and volunteered to help with church activities. The evening
after she put ant and roach poison in Stewart Taylor's beer, the couple went
to a revival meeting and gospel sing. What is the meaning, then, of Barfield's
claim that she experienced a religious conversion while she was in the Rober-
son County jail awaiting trial for murder? Many people, including her victims'
families and the district attorney, believed her newfound Christianity was just
a sham. Others, such authorities as Billy Graham, his wife, and daughter considered her a "dearly beloved sister in Christ."[49] The question of conversion
seems impossible for ordinary humans to judge, although some who call themselves Christians are quite willing to disparage the possibility that others have
experienced similar redemption.

Barfield traced her religious rebirth to a night in her jail cell when she
happened to hear a radio broadcast on a gospel station. While Velma lay
on her bunk, deeply depressed about her situation and her own actions, she
heard a message from evangelist J. K. Kinkle. From her childhood until that
night, she had felt "unclean," that the message of salvation was just for "good
people," not for her. That night she realized that Jesus was willing to be her
friend and to listen to her, that she was included among those he saved.
"I would never be the same again," she said, although she also admitted that
really living the Christian message was difficult. It was easy, she wrote, to
follow the gospel teachings with words, harder with actions, and hardest of
all with attitude.[50] During her time in jail and prison, Barfield worked hard
on her new life. She read both the Bible and other inspirational literature,
corresponded with the Grahams and other evangelists, and talked regularly
with her spiritual advisors, a series of Pentecostal ministers. She believed that
she moved from a disregard for human life, her own and others, to grasping
the sanctity of every life. She wrote apologies to her victims' families, taking
responsibility for the hurt, sorrow, and pain she had brought them. (When,
after Barfield's execution, Anne Lotz drove several hours to deliver the letter

to Taylor's family, they refused to accept it.) Velma tried to understand the role of prescription drugs in her behavior. Although she blamed herself and not the addiction, she also said "I'm convinced I never would have poisoned anyone if I hadn't been under the influence of those medications."[51] Becoming drug free was a real test of her resolve to turn her life around, even if she was on death row. And she did—although it took a long, painful year, filled with nightmares, sleeplessness, and reliving every terrible part of her life.

Perhaps the greatest testimony to Velma Barfield's conversion is her positive influence on others within the women's prison, where she became "Mama Margie," beloved by both the staff and her fellow inmates.

Prison Life

Even in women's prisons which are generally more humane than male institutions, keeping one's dignity and self-respect is difficult. Barfield noted the lack of privacy that implied a lack of respect. One could argue that prison rules intentionally dehumanized the inmates, even in a facility where most of them were non-violent offenders. The "human cage" in which Velma Barfield lived was open to full view of those in the corridor. She was allowed to put up a sheet around the toilet to block the view, but those who designed the facility had not even provided for that minimal modesty. She was also disturbed by the shower room where one stood completely out in the open. There were intrusive searches and periodic de-lousings.[52] If one considers that a substantial percentage of the women in prison had previously been victims of physical and sexual abuse, these degrading and unnecessary practices seem especially counterproductive. It is likely that Barfield's resolve to maintain her dignity and her decency helped to make her a role model.

Despite the prison regimen, Barfield was fortunate to be in a facility where Jenny Lancaster served as the Assistant Superintendent. Lancaster felt she was under scrutiny, not only because she was a woman in a high administrative post but also because her superiors were concerned with how she would handle a prisoner condemned to death. She, on the other hand, wondered why there was so little concern for the human costs of capital punishment, especially the toll on the inmate's family. She wanted to support them through the "unbelievable stress and pressure they experienced because a person they loved lived on death row and faced execution."[53] Lancaster devoted herself especially to Velma's daughter Kim, talking with her and comforting her like a sister. She knew too how difficult the execution would be for the other inmates. On the day Barfield was killed, they were allowed to watch the television coverage and counselors were made available in every dormitory. Afterwards, the prison held a religious service as a memorial for Velma.

Lancaster also believed that Barfield's commitment to her faith made her a resource to the other prisoners. One of them was "Beth," a fifteen-year-old girl, sentenced to thirty years for being present at a murder. It was Beth who first used the name "Mama Margie." Lancaster placed the frightened girl in the cell next to Barfield's. They talked through the wall, cried, and prayed together. They helped each other, "She listened to me, returned my love, and made life much more bearable to me."[54] There were many others. On Velma's last birthday, dozens of inmates sent letters and a card over two feet high. They thanked her for being a substitute mother, for teaching them about God, for not giving up. Their testimony also became part of her clemency plea. Anne Lotz received many letters after Barfield's death, telling her how Velma's "witness continued to permeate the prison."[55] Richard Burr offered a metaphor to describe how many lives she had touched when he referred to the "tapestry of relationships Velma had knitted together." There were multitudes of "really fine folks…. It's the fabric in which we were woven together. Velma was the seamstress, the weaver. She was the weaver."[56]

Gender

Burr's description uses a traditional feminine metaphor. Indeed, gendered references occur throughout Barfield's case from the "black widow spider" image to the grandmother in fuzzy slippers, to the sports metaphors used by District Attorney Britt and Judge Braswell. Given the rarity with which governments decide to execute women, it makes sense that female offenders become death-eligible not simply based on their crime but on their failure to "conform to socio-gendered norms."[57] Poisoning victims is, on the one hand, traditionally a "woman's crime," primarily because women have generally prepared the meals in which the lethal substance was placed. Yet poisoning, because it is usually administered within the home seems to run especially contrary to the image of the wife and mother as the angel of the hearth. The caregiver becomes the exterminator. Even some modern scholars have taken up this point, arguing that the "history of female serial killers is littered" with examples of women who murder people who trusted them motivated by financial gain or as a means of personal empowerment. According to this view, such women predators are opportunists who pursue their goal with "single-minded determination."[58] And thus it was with the state's case against Velma Barfield. Repeatedly the prosecutor told how she had betrayed the trust of the people who relied on her to take care of them and how she had cold-bloodedly watched them die instead of helping them. Such a blatant failure to follow the prescribed female role as nurturer and nurse demands an explanation. In Barfield's case, it was the "dope." From the state's perspective, she craved drugs for pleasure. The defense claimed she was addicted because of her personal failures. She was either a fiend or a loser.

It is not surprising that the prosecutor focused on the crimes themselves rather than on the reasons for her addiction. However, when one examines those factors, her story becomes quite consistent with the experience of the typical female offender. She had suffered physical, emotional, and sexual abuse as a child. She self-medicated throughout her adult life, developing a ferocious multi-drug addiction. She lived on the edge of poverty with limited job opportunities because of her limited education. Each of her crimes occurred when she was a live-in caretaker for a sick person. It may have been the worst possible job for a person suffering from bi-polar disorder, but what job options were available for a woman like her in rural North Carolina in the 1970s? She tried them all—retail sales, factory work, and home health care. Neither her work nor her family circumstances afforded the opportunity to treat her root psychological problems or to support her addiction.

Barfield had the worst luck of all to be caught in the middle of a fierce political struggle. Her supporters argued not that she be spared because she was a woman but that she be spared because she was *this* woman—one whose life had value and whose crimes occurred under vastly different circumstances. But her petition for clemency, which surely had merit, was just one factor in the governor's calculation of his political future. Barfield's arguments that her sentence be commuted were subsumed in the pre-election competition, and she became a casualty as Hunt proved to Helms that he was too tough to back down.

The execution of Velma Barfield set the precedent that executing a woman did not violate contemporary standards of decency in the post-*Furman* era. Hunt was the first of several governors to call upon formal equality to justify a refusal to consider other issues raised by her petition for clemency. Barfield and most of the thirteen other women in this study did not ask for favors based on their sex. They asked that those who would condemn them look at the circumstances that had brought them to death row. Among the factors were the realities of a patriarchal society.

Endnotes

1. The official records of the case, including court transcripts, refer to the victim as Stewart Taylor. Books about the crime, specifically Velma Barfield, *Woman on Death Row* (Nashville, TN: Thomas Nelson, 1985) and Jerry Bledsoe, *Death Sentence: The True Story of Velma Barfield's Life, Crimes, and Execution* (New York: Dutton, 1998) call him Stuart. This chapter will conform to the official record and refer to him as "Stewart."
2. Accounts of Velma Barfield's trial are taken from *State of North Carolina v. Margie Velma Barfield*, Bladen County (1978).
3. Anne Graham Lotz, "Afterword," in Barfield, *Woman on Death Row*, 170.
4. Joe Ingle, *Last Rights: Thirteen Fatal Encounters with the State's Justice* (Nashville, TN: Abingdon Press, 1990), 234.
5. *Furman v. Georgia*, 408 U.S. 238 (1972).
6. Quoted in Bledsoe, *Death Sentence*, 107.
7. Barfield, *Woman on Death Row*, 90–91.
8. Ibid., 92.
9. *State of North Carolina v. Margie Velma Barfield* (259 S.E. 2d 510), 1979.
10. Barfield, *Woman on Death Row*, 10.
11. Valium is an anti-anxiety agent. Depression is a side effect, as is confusion. Sinequan and Elevil are highly sedating antidepressants. Confusion and disorientation are side effects. Tylenol with codeine is a narcotic that can cause agitation, disorientation, confusion, or anxiety.
12. *North Carolina v. Barfield* (1979).
13. Barfield, *Woman on Death Row*, 5.
14. Ibid., 12.
15. *State of North Carolina v. Margie Velma Barfield*, Robeson County (1980).
16. Ironically these convictions were under a North Carolina law that made the death penalty mandatory for certain crimes. That law was declared unconstitutional by the Supreme Court in *Woodson v. North Carolina*, 428 U.S. 280 (1976). Barfield was tried under a new death penalty statute.
17. Bledsoe, *Death Sentence*, 137–39.
18. Unless otherwise noted, the account of Velma Barfield's trial is taken from the official transcript, *State of North Carolina v. Margie Velma Barfield* (1978).
19. A useful glossary of Barfield's prescription drugs is included in *Woman on Death Row*, 173–75.
20. North Carolina uses the M'Naughton Rule, developed in the mid-nineteenth century, to define insanity.
21. Bledsoe, *Death Sentence*, 210.
22. Barfield, *Woman on Death Row*, 102.
23. Ingle, *Last Rights*, 234.
24. Unless otherwise noted, information about the appeal in the North Carolina Supreme Court is taken from *State of North Carolina v. Margie Bullard Barfield*, 259 S.E. 2nd 510 (1979).
25. Quoted in Ingle, *Last Rights*, 234–35.
26. Unless otherwise noted, information about the evidentiary hearing is taken from the official transcript, *State of North Carolina v. Margie Velma Barfield*, Superior Court of Robeson County, (1980).

27. Ingle, *Last Rights*, 238; Bledsoe, *Death Sentence*, 250.

28. Barfield, *Woman on Death Row*, 145.

29. Ingle, *Last Rights*, 238.

30. Quoted in Ibid., 239.

31. Dorothy Otnow Lewis, *Guilty by Reason of Insanity* (New York: Fawcett Columbine, 1998), 292.

32. Bledsoe, *Death Sentence*, 266–67, 278.

33. Barfield, *Woman on Death Row*, 160.

34. Ingle, *Last Rights*, 240–41.

35. Kathleen O'Shea, *Women and the Death Penalty in the United States* (Westport, CT: Praeger, 1999), 268.

36. Bledsoe, *Death Sentence*, 281.

37. Elizabeth Rapaport, "Equality of the Damned: The Execution of Women on the Cusp of the 21st Century," *Ohio Northern University Law Review* 26 (2000), 594.

38. Barfield, *Woman on Death Row*, 160–61.

39. Ingle, *Last Rights*, 245.

40. Lotz, "Afterword," 170–71.

41. Bledsoe, *Death Sentence*, 339.

42. See for example, Sister Helen Prejean, *Dead Man Walking: An Eyewitness Account of the Death Penalty in the United States* (New York: Vintage, 1994), 94–95.

43. Ingle, *Last Rights*, 245–46.

44. Barfield, *Woman on Death Row*, 26.

45. Ibid., 27.

46. Bledsoe, *Death Sentence*, 24.

47. Both Barfield and Bledsoe tell essentially the same story of her life before the Taylor murder as does Ann Jones, *Women Who Kill* (Boston: Beacon Press, 1996). Unless otherwise noted, those sources were used here.

48. Barfield, *Woman on Death Row*, 65.

49. Lotz, "Afterword," 170.

50. Barfield, *Woman on Death Row*, 96–97.

51. Ibid., 113–14.

52. Ibid., 106–7.

53. O'Shea, *Women and the Death Penalty*, 271.

54. Barfield, *Woman on Death Row*, 125.

55. Lotz, "Afterword," 170.

56. Quoted in Ingle, *Last Rights*, 246.

57. Jenny E. Carroll, "Images of Women and Capital Sentencing among Female Offenders: Exploring the Outer Limits of the Eighth Amendment and Articulated Theories of Justice," *Texas Law Review* 57 (May 1997), 1437.

58. Candice Skarper, "The Female Serial Killer: An Evolving Criminality," *Moving Targets: Women, Murder, and Representation*, ed. Helen Birch (Berkeley, CA: University of California Press, 1994), 251–60.

· 4 ·

SHE DIDN'T LOOK LIKE A KILLER

Karla Faye Tucker

Karla Faye Tucker humanized executions. Unlike the hundreds of other "insentient beings" whose names and faces do not matter to the general public, Tucker looked and spoke like someone TV audiences could relate to. People thought they "knew" Karla Faye Tucker and, at least briefly, they cared about her.[1] The photogenic woman, the second to be put to death after the reinstatement of capital punishment, was white, articulate, attractive, and Christian. She had the characteristics that should ordinarily afford protected status in America. The paradoxes this case presented—the horrific crime for which Tucker admitted guilt coexisting with her post-conviction, post-conversion persona—forced consideration of the purposes of capital punishment. Because Tucker was clearly a murderer but just as clearly an outstanding role model for rehabilitation, her case defied simple analysis. Even Governor George Bush, who rejected her petition for clemency, apparently felt he had to justify that decision. He claimed that he agonized over Tucker's case in ways he apparently did not in the other 151 executions over which he presided.

Fourteen years had passed since North Carolina put Velma Barfield to death in 1984. Until Texas executed Tucker, it was still possible that Barfield's case had been an aberration, explainable by the political context in which it occurred. Many of the questions raised about Barfield's execution were revisited in the Tucker case. There was the matter of breaking tradition. If Karla Faye Tucker was injected with lethal chemicals, she would be the first woman executed in Texas since before the Civil War. Would the public approve?

Like Barfield, Tucker posed no threat of future dangerousness. Rather, supporters of both women could reasonably claim that they showed great potential for making valuable social contributions. Thus the argument that putting them to death protected society was surely moot. Both Barfield and Tucker were devoted born-again Christians. Commuting their sentences had support from powerful leaders of the evangelical community. On the other hand, it could be argued that while Barfield was accused of a series of poisonings and convicted of one of them, her crime was neither as violent nor as sexualized as Tucker's. If someone, even a charismatic woman, who "picked" two people with an ax and boasted of sexual gratification from the crime was not a good candidate for the death penalty, then why have capital punishment and why claim that men and women were equal before the law? In Tucker's case as long as there were constant reminders of the crime itself and as long as these references asserted that "the killer's gender did not matter to the victims," other parts of her story could be relegated to secondary importance in the fight to save her. Once Tucker was found guilty and sentenced to death, from a legal standpoint anything she did to change her life was irrelevant. As David Dow describes the post-conviction process, it focuses on "what you did, not on whether your rights were violated. All they [the courts] know about you—all they care about knowing—is what you did that one night. What you are now does not interest them."[2]

Tucker's story did not begin with "that one night," but it is the place to start her legal odyssey.

The Crime

The Karla Faye Tucker who worked as a high-priced prostitute, used every drug in the pharmacopeia, loved fights and motorcycles, and cursed like a sailor could not have been more different from the person on death row described by her religious supporters as an angel, a compassionate friend, a "most beautiful Christian woman."[3] In 1983, however, one of the men who prosecuted Tucker stated, "Her attitude and the way she looked and everything about her was the personification of evil."[4] Certainly Tucker, along with her boyfriend bartender Danny Garrett and acquaintance Jimmy Leibrant, a methamphetamine manufacturer, seemed to embody evil when they committed a gruesome, pointless, double murder on June 13, 1983.

The three drove in Garrett's blue Ranchero, a half car-half truck, to the working-class apartment development where Jerry Lynn Dean lived. Tucker despised Dean and had once punched him in the face, breaking his glasses. He hated Tucker in return. Furious with her, he tore apart her photograph albums and poked holes in a treasured picture of her mother. Shortly before the murders, he allegedly threatened Karla by hiring someone to burn her face. In Tucker's subculture, one way to get back at a man you loathed was to interfere with his motorcycle. Dean was known to be building a Harley in his living room. In the days before the murder, Tucker and her friends talked often about stealing the parts or messing with Dean's bike. They considered those possibilities over a weekend while shooting crystal meth, drinking tequila, and "eating" pills for three days and nights. By late on Sunday, June 12, everyone had given up partying except Karla, Danny, and Jimmy Leibrant. As Tucker described it, "We were very wired and was looking for something to do."[5] They decided to go to Jerry Dean's apartment—to check it out, to mess up his motorcycle, to intimidate him—no one could explain the exact reason. Lowry says, "There was no *formal* plan to hurt anyone that night or steal anything." But Danny Garrett took a gun.[6]

Garrett had visited Dean and knew his way around the first-floor apartment even in the dark. He knew that Dean slept in the smaller bedroom. On this night, he was sharing his bed with Deborah Thornton, a woman he had met that day at a party. According to testimony, Tucker went into the room and woke Dean by sitting on his naked chest. He tried to plead with her to work out their differences. She told him to shut up and may or may not have cursed at him. They wrestled until, according to Karla, Danny Garrett stepped in and hit Dean on the head repeatedly with a ball-peen hammer. Wounded and unconscious, Dean apparently made a loud gurgling sound as blood and fluid flooded his lungs. The sound infuriated Tucker who was desperate to make him stop. "So I looked, I seen a pickax against the wall. I reached over and grabbed it and I swung it and hit him in the back with it ... four or five times."[7] While Tucker was striking Dean, Garrett and Leibrant moved the motorcycle parts from the living room to Garrett's truck. At some point, Leibrant looked into the bedroom, saw Tucker attacking Dean, and left. In his words, he "burned off."[8] All agreed that he participated only in the robbery, not in the murders. Danny, on the other hand, came in, flipped Dean over, struck him with the pickax and finished him off. Then he resumed stealing motorcycle parts.

After Garrett left the room, Tucker noticed a "body" under the covers. The body was the terrified Deborah Thornton, who began to fight for her life. She and Tucker struggled over the pickax. Thornton was wounded in several places when Danny returned. He kicked her in the head, took the weapon, and finally drove the ax into her chest. Tucker and Garrett picked up the frame used to hold Dean's motorcycle, put it in the vehicle, and the two drove off—Danny in his own truck, Tucker at the wheel of Dean's. About thirty minutes later, around 7 AM on Monday, a neighbor who planned to ride to work with Dean found the bodies. As he testified at Karla's trial, "I seen the girl with the pickax in her heart."[9]

The Back-story

Only in very bad fiction or in the arguments of prosecutors, does someone, for no reason at all, murder two people with a pickax and brag about it. In real life, there is always a "back-story," a probe into the killer's previous life for some sort of explanation. In Tucker's case, there was little pointing to the prospect of a "normal" life.

It is not an exaggeration to say that Karla Faye Tucker had no childhood. Nor is it an exaggeration to say that, with very few exceptions, she had never seen people treat each other with even minimal respect. She grew up admiring and emulating her mother's high-priced prostitution and drug addiction. It appears that for Tucker, most people and things served only for instant gratification; few had any inherent value. Sometime after her conviction, the details of Tucker's earlier life were revealed. Although born into a marginally middle-class family, she experienced only a few years of either material or emotional security. Karla was the offspring of one of her mother's extramarital affairs. It is not hard to imagine that the instability in her parents' relationship predated her birth. That instability meant a great deal of conflict, several separations, and finally a divorce in 1969 when Karla was ten years old. It is impossible to read of Tucker's early life without concluding that discipline, guidance, protection—the things that parents are expected to provide—were totally absent. She was introduced to marijuana by her sisters at about the age of eight. When Tucker's mother found out, she showed Karla how to roll a joint so she would do it properly. At ten, one of her sisters' boyfriends, took Karla out on his Harley, provided her with some heroin, and tried to molest her. From the age of fourteen until she was incarcerated after the murders of Dean and Thornton, Tucker was on drugs—pills, acid, speed, prescriptions, heroin, cocaine—experimenting, balancing the highs and lows, and seldom experiencing a sober moment. Tucker told her friend and biographer Beverly Lowry that she used drugs not as an escape, but because she liked the way they made her feel.[10]

But whether she admitted it or not, Karla Faye Tucker had plenty to escape from. After her parents' divorce, she lived briefly with her father. His job, however, involved long hours away from home. He finally conceded that he could not control his youngest daughter. Karla then joined her sisters in her mother's life "on the edge." Carolyn Tucker supported herself and her daughters by her day job as a secretary and her night job as a call girl. School was optional and many men would pay for sex with a very young girl. Money was easy; drugs were plentiful; life was like an extended party. At what point does a girl who had no meaningful adult supervision and no respectable role model become responsible for her own bad choices?

Tucker made several of those before the night when she participated in the murders. At thirteen she went on the road with the Allman Brothers band, riding in their bus and sleeping with one of the roadies and possibly with Greg Allman. At sixteen, she married Stephen Griffith, a carpenter. Griffith later recalled Karla as "a pretty good wife," which he defined as cooking his meals and getting him off to work on time. But he also remembered that they "fist fought a lot. I never had men hit me as hard as she did. Whenever I went into a bar, I didn't have to worry because she had my back covered. She was tough." So tough, they played tackle football without gear.[11] About four years into the marriage, Karla left Steve Griffith. Her mother had died from hepatitis at the age of 43 and Karla felt more rootless than ever. She lived in a series of apartments and houses, sometimes with her sister Kari, sometimes with her girlfriend Shawn. All worked as call girls. Karla went twice a year to set up shop in Midland, Texas, where oil field workers paid well for sex. Back in Houston, she met Danny Garrett in the waiting room of a doctor's office where both were waiting to get prescriptions for their recreational drugs. They moved in together. On the second weekend of June 1983, they partied for three days.

The Trial

Police did not immediately have any real leads in the murders of Jerry Dean and Deborah Thornton. The case broke five weeks later when Doug Garrett, Danny's brother, called the authorities to identify Danny and Karla as the killers.[12] They had bragged about the crime to Doug and Kari, Karla's sister. Supposedly "frightened for their lives," the two told their stories to the police. Doug agreed to wear a wire, to go to Danny and Karla's house, and try to get confessions on tape. The one-and-one-half-hour recording included their admissions that they had "picked" the victims, "offed" Dean, abandoned his truck, and thrown away most of the motorcycle parts. In other words, they admitted to the robbery as well as the killing. It was felony murder, a capital offense in Texas. One could argue, however, that by far the single most incriminating comment on Doug's tape and the point that would make Karla Faye Tucker a shoo-in for the death penalty was her remark that she had reached sexual climax with every stroke of the pickax.

Karla's trial was held in the Harris County courtroom where Judge Patricia Lykos presided. Lykos was a tough, no-nonsense Texas jurist. Her courtroom was highly disciplined. There were to be no theatrics. Attorneys stayed in their chairs and stood only with her permission. Everyone—witnesses for both sides, the defendant—was to be addressed as Mr., Mrs., or Miss. Calling the accused by her first name was not an option in Judge Lykos's court. Nonetheless, the prosecutor managed to annoy Karla by addressing her as "Mrs. Griffith," the name of her ex-husband. She had shed his name and resumed "Tucker" several years earlier. Although at one level, deciding which name to use could seem trivial in a case that deals with life and death, it was one instance of the state's assertion of power and patriarchy.

In Harris County, prosecutors led by District Attorney John B. Holmes were practiced at seeking the death penalty. They had the highest rate of capital convictions in the country and knew how to exploit every advantage that would persuade a jury. Holmes saw the death penalty as a sort of divine retribution for murder and remarked that "Backing off is not part of the culture" in Harris County. Joe Magliolo, who prosecuted Karla Faye Tucker, shared in the culture of the county and the DA's office.[13] Tucker had two court-appointed attorneys for her defense. Both Mack Arnold and Henry Oncken were experienced lawyers, but they too had earned most of their experience as prosecutors. Oncken later told Beverly Lowry that when he met his client, "I couldn't stand her. The drugs were still in her. She didn't care about anything. I didn't want to take the case."[14] Tucker's appellate attorneys would argue later that she was denied effective assistance of counsel.

Before trial, Karla was given two psychological examinations. The exams were critical if the defense hoped to prove the mitigating factor that Tucker suffered from temporarily insanity caused by intoxication at the time of the crime. The standard for temporary insanity is high. A defendant must show that she did not know her conduct was wrong or that she was incapable of conforming her conduct to the requirements of law. In this case, she would also need to demonstrate that the condition was caused by voluntary intoxication.

The psychological reports written in February 1984 recounted Tucker's extensive history of drug use. Every day for years she had used some combination of heroin, downers, valium, and "bandit reds" and mixed them with prescription drugs such as dilaudid, codeine, percodan, and speed. She described herself as "flippy in the head." Tucker admitted that she had a history of fist fights but asserted that she had never used weapons. To the defendant, her behavior did not seem bizarre but "normal." The doctor found no evidence of delusional thinking, hallucination, or psychosis. The second psychological examination also concluded there was no evidence that the defendant was "unable to tell the difference between right and wrong" during the period when the crime was committed. She appeared to be of sound mind despite her level of intoxication. However, examinations conducted seven or eight months later could only make a wild guess as to her level of intoxication or sanity on the night of the murders. She might not be hallucinating in February 1984, but who, aside from Karla herself, knew her state of mind in June 1983?

Karla remained in jail awaiting trial. Her attorneys argued before Judge Lykos that Tucker was unable to assist in her own defense because jail conditions deprived her of sleep. She was housed at first in a cell where the lights were left on all night "for security." When she complained of sleeplessness, she was moved to solitary confinement where it was totally dark. Finally, the court ordered that Tucker be put in a regular cell with regular lights. A few months into this incarceration, Karla began attending AA meetings. She also began Bible study with Chaplain Rebecca Lewis.

Once Tucker's case went to court, the jury selection process took a month. It involved questioning dozens of prospective jurors and revealed issues that colored the entire trial. The prosecutor asked whether the fact that the defendant was a woman was a problem, reminding them that "the law is blind to the sex of a person." He further inquired whether they could sentence a "female" to execution by answering "yes" to the special issues that determined a death sentence. Lawyers for both sides attempted to explain the process—the bifurcated trial, the meaning of reasonable doubt, the concept of "deliberate," how to access the guilt of an accomplice, the definition of corroboration. Prospective jurors often seemed confused, even confounded, by the law. Some were willing to vote for death for whoever "deserved" it. Others claimed they had never thought about the death penalty. "Future dangerousness," "intoxication," "special circumstances," seemed elusive concepts to many members of the jury pool. Finally, with all those who opposed capital punishment and those who seemed totally confused excluded, a panel of eight women and four men was seated.

Prosecutor Magliolo, in his opening statement, set out the chronology of the crimes and set up the state's version of events. He made repeated references to the allegation that Jimmy Leibrant had seen Karla with her foot on Dean's chest and a grin on her face. Although the defense objected to the introduction of some of the crime scene photos, the prosecution was allowed to show most of them to the jury, including those where the pickax was embedded in Deborah Thornton's chest. Thus the trial began with visual evidence of the brutality of the murders and an image of Tucker as a heartless killer.

Next, the medical examiner testified that the pickax wounds had been the cause of death for both Dean and Thornton. Meanwhile the defense attempted to elicit an admission that the head wounds, inflicted by Danny with a hammer, could have actually killed Dean. If that were so, Karla would have been an accessory rather than the murderer. The next prosecution witness was Sergeant J.C. Mosier, the officer with whom Doug Garrett and Kari had spoken. He testified that although both Doug and Kari had been accessories after the fact because they helped to dispose of property stolen from Dean, the police had made no deals with them. However, it is a fact that neither Doug nor Kari was ever charged with anything. They turned in their own siblings, perhaps to save themselves from charges. Perhaps they embellished the story along the way.

Jimmy Leibrant, the next state's witness, certainly had an interest in portraying Karla and Danny as the perpetrators. He had been indicted for burglary rather than the more serious charge of armed robbery in connection with the crime, but he swore that the prosecutors had made him no promises, no plea bargains, no reduced charges. He offered several pieces of evidence that were crucial to the state's case against Tucker. According to Leibrant, Karla was coherent when they went to Dean's house. She could walk, talk, and hold a normal conversation. Most damaging, he claimed that when he looked into the bedroom, he saw Karla with her foot on Dean's chest, swinging the pickax. When she spotted Leibrant in the doorway, she turned to him and grinned. "Will you ever forget the way she looked and smiled at you before she struck the blow?" asked Magliolo. The picture of Tucker, a smiling, merciless killer was to be implanted in the jury's, and the public's, minds. Leibrant also said that Karla had been so proud of the murders that he was afraid for his life. But despite that alleged fear, Leibrant helped his own sister move in with Danny and Karla after the crime and visited them frequently and voluntarily.

On cross-examination, although the defense tried to get Leibrant to explain why the state had not charged him with capital murder or why they had not chosen to enhance his burglary charges, he maintained there were no deals. Nor would he agree with the defense's attempt to characterize Karla's state of mind as intoxication. He insisted that she had only had a couple of joints and some Jack Daniels. He could not explain why if he would "never forget" Karla's grin with the raised pickax, he had neglected to mention that scene in his original statement to police.

Karla's sister Kari (who had by the time of the trial married Doug Garrett) was another vital link in the state's case. She added what was perhaps the single most damaging piece of evidence, the image that probably deprived Karla of any residual sympathy she might have because she was a woman. Kari stated that her sister had told her that each time she "picked" Dean, she "got a nut." In other words, Karla had reached sexual climax with every stroke of the ax. It could be argued that statement, more than any other accusation against Tucker, condemned her. In addition, Kari undermined the intoxication defense by claiming that people at their weekend party used only alcohol and marijuana. Finally, Kari, along with Doug Garrett, described how Karla and Danny had laughed at the television coverage of the crime and bragged "We're the pickax murderers."

Doug, who had worn a police wire and taped the statements of his brother and Tucker, reiterated Kari's assertion. As he told it, Karla had said "I picked him. I come with every stroke." Under cross-examination, Doug admitted that Karla had been stoned when he made the tape for the police. However, her foggy state of mind probably did little to distract from the shocking linkage of sex and violence.

Both Kari and Doug could have faced prison as they had assisted in disposing of Dean's wallet and the motorcycle parts. The police denied any connection between their testimony for the prosecution and the decision not to charge them.

The defense did not call a single witness in the guilt phase of the trial. Judge Lykos refused to allow them to introduce a statement that Leibrant had made a deal for his testimony. They offered nothing else. Mack Arnold, Tucker's attorney, conceded her guilt in his closing statement. After deliberating for only one hour and ten minutes, the jury agreed with him. Having admitted that their client was guilty, the defense then faced the challenge of persuading the jurors to spare her life.

The state argued that Karla should be sentenced to death because the crime met the special circumstances necessary to qualify for capital punishment. Jerry Lynn Dean and Deborah Thornton had been killed deliberately, and, according to the prosecutor, Karla Faye Tucker posed a threat of future dangerousness. Kari Garrett was the state's first witness. She testified that she was afraid Karla and Danny would kill her as they had threatened to murder others. Doug also stated that he feared for his life. His credibility may have been undermined somewhat when he claimed that Kari's ex-husband, Ronnie Burrell, was the devil. Nonetheless, the brother and sister of the killers seemed to convince the jury that Karla and Danny had a thirst for violence, that had they not been arrested, they would have killed again and that they would continue to pose a threat.

Karla Faye Tucker took the stand during the sentencing phase to tell her story.

She described her earlier life, her drug use, and her brief marriage to Stephen Griffith. She told how she and Griffith had taken care of a little girl whose drug-addicted parents had abandoned her. She explained how easy it was to get a "pill doctor" to write prescriptions for stimulants and sedatives. Tucker claimed that because of all the substances she had used, she had only vague memories of the days before the crime.

Most importantly, Tucker asserted that Danny had actually killed Dean with the hammer and that he had also stuck the blow that killed Deborah Thornton. Karla maintained that she had made up the sexual gratification to impress her friends. She concluded, "I've hurt a lot of people and I wish I could take the hurt out of everybody and put it on myself. I sometimes don't think enough could be done to me to really be justice."

Asserting control over Tucker, District Attorney Magliolo persisted in addressing her as "Mrs. Griffith." He annoyed her but did not crack her composure. He did succeed in his purpose of convincing the jury that Tucker knew that killing was wrong and did it anyway. He did not let them lose sight of her history of violence.

The defense also called a psychiatrist, Dr. Barbara Felkins, and several character witnesses. The doctor testified to Tucker's early exposure to drugs, her long history of addiction. At the time of the crime she had gone without sleep for three days. She was both drinking heavily and consuming a variety of drugs. Therefore, in Felkins's opinion, Tucker could have been in a drug-induced psychosis. That meant, she may not have known what she was doing or understood the effect of her actions. She also pointed out that it would take the artificial stimulation of speed for someone Karla's size to wield a pickax. Felkins addressed the matter of sexual climax, suggesting that Tucker was too high to feel gratification. Finally, she testified that Tucker would not be a threat to anyone in prison.

The District Attorney struck at the credibility of everything Tucker had told Felkins. The doctor admitted that Tucker could have manipulated her and lied to her. Magliolo referred to the drugs the defendant was "supposedly" taking. If the drugs were absent, there was no basis to question the deliberateness of the killings. He also elicited the opinion from Felkins that it was possible for some people to get sexual satisfaction from "perverse things."

A second psychiatrist, Dr. James Hayden, also defined drug-induced psychosis and the links between speed, paranoia, and psychotic behavior. Again, Magliolo drew out the opinion that Tucker could be lying about the drugs she had used. Dr. Hayden admitted he could not be certain that *this* defendant did not know right from wrong on the night of the crime.

In addition to the experts, the defense offered several character witnesses: Karla's grandmother, her father, a real estate developer friend who claimed she was not violent, and a deputy from the jail who described her good behavior. Rebecca Lewis, the chaplain at the women's jail told of Tucker's involvement in Bible study, and the jail's drug and alcohol counselor vouched for her participation in the 12-step program.

The defense and prosecuting attorneys made final arguments in their efforts to convince the jury of the appropriate sentence. Arnold's closing was characteristically loose and lacking in substance. He began by declaring that he would rather be anywhere else in the world than in that courtroom. Perhaps that was a ploy to make the jurors like him, but it surely did nothing to arouse sympathy for his client. He admitted they might have the feeling that Karla deserved death, another concession. He gave short shrift to the first special circumstance, whether the crime was committed deliberately. That was, he claimed weakly, "tied in with her drug use ... but I certainly understand there is evidence to the contrary." Yet the jury was asked to find that drug use made Karla temporarily insane and therefore incapable of forming the requisite intent. He essentially argued against his own client.

Incredibly in asserting that Tucker was not a continuing threat, he began by congratulating Doug Garrett for turning her in, acknowledging that she was dangerous. He also agreed that the substance of Kari's testimony was true. Even more incredibly, he thanked Doug, Kari, and the police for putting Karla in jail so she could get sober. He asked the jury to make an "educated guess" that a drug-free Tucker, in a structured institutional environment would cease to be violent. It is a pathetic closing argument.

Magliolo seemed to have all the cards, and he played them well. He pointed out to the jury that they were not required to consider temporary insanity, even if they believed it described Tucker's condition on the night of the murders. Subtly, he reminded them that a life sentence might not really mean life; that its duration would be up to the Board of Pardons and Paroles. He assured them it would not be their fault, but Tucker's, if she were put to death. The prosecutor stated that deterrence was a fact—"if she had known she was going to be sitting right here before she swung that ax it never would have got swung. If she knew that she was going to receive death for killing those two people and taking their property, she would have never even gotten in that car and gone over to that apartment." Tucker's sole purpose was to "get another high, to enjoy what she was doing." The purpose of the death penalty is "to punish people for what they do and to deter others from doing it." Magliolo's argument rests on the premise that Tucker was fully competent but decided that the "high" from the killings was worth risking the death penalty. But if she were executed, others would calculate those choices differently. He countered the psychiatrists' testimony by turning it on its head and arguing that if a person had enough violence in her early life, it would warp her personality forever. The prosecutor detailed Tucker's offenses: she was a prostitute, she procured and used illegal drugs, she assaulted people and engaged in fights. According to Magliolo, she was not only sane the night of the crime, she orchestrated the whole thing. The "innocent" victim, asleep in his own bed was a good guy who had a dream to drive a Harley. Deborah Thornton was a mother who would never see her son play ball again.

Magliolo touched every nerve. He painted the victims as upstanding, regular folks and Tucker as unmitigated, perverted evil. Last of all, he replayed the portion of the tape where she responded that she "come" (sic) each time she struck Dean. "I think it says it all, ladies and gentlemen," the district attorney concluded.

The jury apparently thought so too. After three hours of deliberation, they found both of the special circumstances and sentenced Karla Faye Tucker to death. They saw a person who was, as Howarth described, frightening and easily dehumanized.

After the Trial

Tucker's jury found her eligible for death on the basis of two special circumstances. They concluded that her actions met the standard of deliberateness, and they accepted the probability of her future dangerousness. Most of her appeals were based on those two grounds. At trial, her attorneys had tried to establish that Tucker was temporarily insane due to voluntary intoxication, and that therefore she did not actually intend to kill Dean and Thornton. They also argued that Karla would not harm anyone as long as she was locked up in prison. Her appellate attorneys, who actually wanted to represent her and believed in the merits of her case, raised the issue of ineffective assistance by her original court-appointed lawyers. In the last stage of the appeals process, Tucker's request for clemency to Governor George W. Bush drew national attention to her case. The media focused on her religious conversion and her sex, but at least one of her appellate attorneys argues that the real legal dilemma resulted from a jury's attempt to predict a person's future conduct as a basis for executing him or her.[15]

George McCall Secrest, David L. Botsford, and Walter Long represented Karla in the many legal efforts to spare her life between her trial and her execution. When it was over, Long developed a list of reasons why those efforts failed and Texas killed Karla Faye Tucker. First was the crime itself. The other reasons were problems with the application of the death penalty.[16] Tucker's trial attorneys asked the jury to find her temporarily insane (a very high standard) rather than intoxicated. The jury was not able to consider whether the level of intoxication was enough to affect the rationality of her behavior but not enough to qualify her as insane. The appellate courts refused to either find her attorneys inadequate or to allow review of her state of mind at the time of the crime.[17] They called the faulty jury instructions "invited error," a strategic choice by the trial lawyers. In layperson's terms, the client was denied relief because the lawyers failed to do their job properly. A number of jurors were apparently confused both by the "intoxication" instructions and by the court's refusal to define the meaning of a life sentence. Texas did not, at the time, have a sentence of life without parole. Prosecutors like Magliolo purposely raised the specter of early release by reminding the jury that the Board of Pardons and Paroles had the discretion to determine the meaning of "life" in prison. Magliolo himself remained convinced that Tucker should be executed and even argued that point on television when her supporters asked for clemency.

Tucker's appellate attorneys tried to raise every possible claim for relief. The most thought-provoking had to do with her reformation, with gender equity, and with the flaws in the Texas clemency process. The Karla Faye Tucker who sat on death row in the late 1990s was not the woman who had been involved in the murders in 1983. She was, by all accounts, rehabilitated, reformed, and in every way a positive influence on those whose lives she touched. If one reason the jury found her death-eligible was her "future dangerousness," wouldn't that rationale disappear if she no longer posed a threat but instead served as a model of virtue? This argument is not about Tucker's religion per se but about the competing claims of retributive justice and restorative justice. For, if she was no longer dangerous, the only reason to kill Tucker was retribution. Sister Helen Prejean wrote that Karla "would have been a source of healing love to guards and prisoners for as long as she lived," but the "iron protocol of retributive justice demanded that she be put to death."[18] Of course, an argument over the meaning of justice does not carry weight in the courts. They must decide cases on the basis of their conformity with constitutions and state laws, even though the reformation issue may be folded into the claim of cruel and unusual punishment. Several Supreme Court justices, for example, have written that if the only purpose of the death penalty is retribution, a civilized society must reject it as barbaric, a denial of human dignity, and thus, by definition a violation of the Eighth Amendment's ban on cruel and unusual punishment.[19]

Tucker also appealed her sentence on the basis of gender equity, asserting that she would be executed *because* she was a woman. In support of the argument, her attorneys stated that equally situated men had been given clemency based on rehabilitation, but not one woman had received such relief; that the media had disseminated information prejudicial to Tucker, claiming that "equal justice" demanded her execution; that any differences in the sentences of men and women within the criminal justice system were attributed to differences in behavior, not to special treatment; and that there was evidence that violent female offenders received harsher sentences than their male counterparts. They noted that despite evidence that women were more likely to be rehabilitated, the only persons who had their sentences commuted for rehabilitation were men. The widespread public misinformation concerning bias *in favor of* women would actually work as bias *against* Tucker and deny her the equal protection of the law guaranteed by the Fourteenth Amendment to the Constitution.[20] Although the court rejected the Fourteenth Amendment claim along with all the others, it forces consideration of assumptions about gender bias. If women are seldom sentenced to death because they seldom commit capital murder and if the rarity of their presence on death row obscures real instances of invidious differential treatment, then equal protection is an issue.

Metamorphosis

While her appeals were brought before state and federal courts, Karla Faye Tucker remained in prison from 1984 to 1998. The evidence is irrefutable. During that time, she became a new woman, a different person from the "pickax killer." Two books describe Tucker's time on death row, Beverly Lowry's *Crossed Over* and *Karla Faye Tucker: Set Free* by missionary Linda Strom. The latter is all about faith and designed as inspirational literature. The main character is intended as a sort of spiritual guide. Even skeptical readers, however, may be impressed that Tucker had such an impact on her fellow believers. Her story, in effect, joined the pantheon of evangelical "lives of the saints."

Lowry interviewed Tucker many times. She offers some remarkable glimpses of how the four women awaiting execution (Tucker, Betty Lou Beets, Pam Perillo and Frances Newton) fashioned a life. For Karla Faye Tucker, it was the first time since childhood that she was without drugs, men, or violence. In the 1992 edition of her book Lowry wrote. "In March 1989, when I met her, Karla was twenty-nine. She seemed more like maybe thirteen, a transitional girl, and no wonder: Karla Faye missed out on adolescence. Prison has given her a chance to go back, and, like a learning disabled child, catch up on the steps she missed. She's up now to, I'd say, maybe fifteen." Perhaps by 1998, when she was put to death, Tucker had matured to legal adulthood. But whether one emphasizes her religious conversion or simply the process of growing up, Karla became a different person.

When Tucker was on death row, the women worked six hours a day making stuffed dolls called Parole Pals. Customers, who were mostly prison officials, ordered dolls with specific hair, skin, and eye color. In a variation on the Cabbage Patch dolls, each of these came with a parole certificate. Making the dolls gave a structure and order to the day—something Karla's life on the outside had lacked. The inmates were also permitted to take classes by correspondence. Tucker finished high school and earned credit for a number of college courses. The four women spent virtually all their days together. Besides working on the dolls, they all learned to crochet and made decorations for their day room. They figured out ways to cook "party food" to celebrate birthdays and holidays with things they ordered from the commissary. As Lowry describes it, the majority of recipes consisted mostly of cream cheese. Sadly, this limited and makeshift existence on death row was the closest thing to a stable, conventional life that Karla Faye Tucker ever experienced. In response to a question whether she would trade her death sentence for life without parole, Tucker told Lowry "You bet I would. I can make a life here. I *have* made a life."[21]

There was also Bible study and visits from the Christian missionaries, the only non-prison affiliated people allowed to visit death row. Tucker embraced the scriptural message of repentance and forgiveness. She believed that her conversion had "set her free" from the vices of her past life but that she would live her remaining time giving what she could to others. She wrote letters to teenagers through a Christian anti-drug program, and she talked to other women in the prison of the transformation her faith had brought. The warden believed she had helped to save two other inmates from suicide. Karla told an interviewer, "I love life now. Instead of taking lives, I just want to share the life in me."[22] In a way, Tucker shared that life with Chaplain Dana Brown, whom she met in 1992 and married in a proxy ceremony in 1995. Under Texas prison rules, death row prisoners were not allowed any physical contact with outsiders. So, after their marriage the couple never touched. They communicated through the screen and plexiglass that separated Karla from the rest of the world. Among other things, they prayed together for Karla's life.

Can one make a valid argument that a person whose life has undergone a spiritual transformation is not the same person who was sentenced to death? If the basis for her sentence is that she will pose a threat in the future, does it make sense to execute her after that threat has passed? Rapaport captures the difference in the killer Karla and the Karla about to be killed. At trial, Tucker was "fascinating and repellant." She later sobered up and became a devout evangelical Christian. When she appeared on *Sixty Minutes* and *Larry King Live* in the weeks before her execution, her "wan, pixieish good looks, youthfulness, wry, self-deprecating humor, her self-possession, articulateness and thoughtfulness captivated TV audiences."[23] Karla Faye Tucker as a media personality confronted Americans with the reality that capital punishment means that a real individual with a unique life history will have her life ended when the state places a needle in her arm and shoots a lethal substance through her veins. By the time Tucker became familiar to the public, her legal options were virtually at an end. The only realistic hope for saving her life—which millions of people hoped for—was that Texas Governor George

W. Bush would grant clemency. Tucker's case shone a national spotlight on Bush and on the clemency process over which he presided.

Clemency

The essential argument raised in Tucker's clemency petition did not refer to her sex or to her religious conversion; instead it focused on her rehabilitation. A great many people contributed support. Four guards from the women's prison where she had lived wrote a petition asserting that she was not a threat. Charley Davidson, the assistant district attorney from Harris County who had prosecuted Danny Garrett, wrote that he would welcome Karla into his home to meet his family. "If the purpose of the death penalty is to execute an individual solely for a crime they have committed, then Karla Faye Tucker should be executed. However, if the purpose is to execute a person for what they have done and what they are now, then Karla Faye Tucker should not die. She is no longer a threat to society."[24] The sister of Jerry Lynn Dean and Ron Carlson, the brother of Deborah Thornton, pleaded that Tucker's life should be spared. The prison psychiatrist stated that Karla used her time and energy to assist in the rehabilitation of others. She was, he said, a contributing, productive member of society. Billy Moore, a former resident of Georgia's death row and at the time a pastor, had a letter hand delivered to Alberto Gonzales, legal counsel to the governor. He appealed to Bush's professed status as a born again Christian. "Governor Bush, Sir, I know that you know Mercy and have this quality within your person ... I am sure that as you allow mercy to stand tall behind the walls of prison, that Karla's life will be that light in the darkness."[25] Members of the evangelical community were vocal in their encouragement that Bush exercise clemency. Pat Robertson, head of the Christian Coalition and usually an ally of the Governor, described Tucker as a "most beautiful Christian woman," sublime, a lovely spirit, absolutely radiant—a different person from the woman who killed Dean and Thornton. She was not a "wild-eyed hippie murderess but a sweet and gentle lady."[26] Tucker herself wrote a dignified letter to Governor Bush asking that her life be spared but recognizing that he might subscribe to the theory of retribution. "If my execution is the only thing, the final act that can fulfill the demand for justice and restitution, then I accept that."[27]

Tucker's petition did not persuade Bush, but it did persuade others that conversion is relevant to sentencing. Many are suspicious of post-conviction conversions, claiming they may not be sincere. Others believe that religion and spirituality have nothing to do with secular punishment. But there is a utilitarian argument, the position raised by Tucker's supporters—that conversion mitigates future dangerousness. Even a strict retributive advocate might wish to consider that conversion, atonement, and expiation involve a repudiation of the aspects of a person's character that generated criminal behavior. If a person does the spiritual "work" to transform herself, does she deserve a lesser punishment than the unrepentant?[28] There is nothing to prevent a governor from considering such a redemptive approach when faced with a decision about clemency. Historically, there are many cases where heads of state considered sincere repentance and rehabilitation when exercising their clemency power. By the late twentieth century, however, most governors seemed reluctant to make such a choice. As the *New York Times* noted immediately after Tucker's execution, "the quality of mercy varies from state to state and governor to governor, often proves to be quixotic, subject to political winds, and very strained."[29]

In Texas, the governor has the authority to commute a sentence for thirty days. An actual clemency decision requires a vote of the Board of Pardons and Paroles (BPP), theoretically separate from the governor but actually appointed by him. During his tenure, George W. Bush approved 152 executions and commuted one sentence. He and the BPP were in perfect accord. There were no rules guiding the BPP's decision-making process. They could meet or not, deliberate or not, read the petitions of the people on death row or throw them in the trash. In one of Tucker's appeals, she raised the point that the lack of any formal procedures for clemency decisions was a violation of due process.[30] The courts disagreed, but a 2003 article by Alan Berlow in *The Atlantic Monthly* reveals how casually Bush and his legal counsel Gonzalez made life or death decisions.[31] Typically on the day the execution was scheduled, Gonzalez gave the governor a three-to-seven page summary of the case. The summaries contained a detailed description of the crime, a paragraph on the appellant's background, and an assumption that if the courts had rejected appeals, there were no grounds for clemency. The summaries contained no discussion of legal issues, such as ineffective counsel, mitigating factors, or even evidence of innocence. Although he apparently read the two or three pages provided by Gonzalez, there is no evidence that Bush actually read any clemency petitions so laboriously prepared by the defendant's attorneys and supporters. On the day of an execution, Bush would usually meet with Gonzalez for about thirty minutes. His appointment book showed the notation "Al G.—execution."[32] For sixteen of the 152 executions, the governor was out of the state and simply left the last-minute decision (clemency or not) to the highest-ranking state official who happened to be available.[33]

According to Berlow, Tucker's case was one of the few which merited a more extensive discussion and where the governor considered things other than the three-page summary. Bush had indicated that he would never grant clemency unless a question of actual innocence was involved. Tucker's case did not meet that standard, but the great popular interest it generated clearly raised some political concerns. It was 1998, and the governor was looking ahead to a presidential bid. This decision was under scrutiny from supporters and opponents alike. Calls to spare her life came from all over the world, including from Pope John Paul II. Disingenuously, Bush told the pope and others who championed Karla's case that he lacked the power to intervene with the Board of Pardons and Paroles (BPP).

Exactly what and how the governor communicated to the BPP is not known as that body operated with no set of rules or procedures. They generally "met" only by fax. There is no evidence they looked at the petitions submitted to them.[34] Perhaps they read Karla's letter to them that stated, "Fourteen years ago I was part of the problem, now I'm part of the solution." But even if they studied it and all the supporting documents, the BPP chair concluded that Tucker had shown no reason why her sentence should be set aside.[35] Ultimately, the fate of Karla Faye Tucker like that of all the other inmates on Texas death row was left in the hands of a board that never had to account for its decisions and a governor who believed he could never be seen as too tough on crime.

Justice Thurgood Marshall's statement in *Evans v. Murray* seems an apt comment for the way Texas handled Tucker's case. Marshall wrote that if a state cannot figure out how to accommodate post-sentencing evidence casting doubt on someone's future dangerousness, it is not right that the petitioner bear the burden. If the system cannot accommodate *all* evidence, no matter when the evidence is disclosed, the "system, not the man [sic] sentenced to death, should be dispatched."[36] Here it seemed not that the state could not accommodate that evidence, but that it would not.

How could anyone see Karla Faye Tucker as an ongoing threat? In her last days, she was as Elizabeth Rapaport describes, a "woman of breathtaking ordinariness." She was neither a drugged-up, two-fisted bad girl nor a pitiable husk of a person asking for pity. She was now well within the moral mainstream. Her perspective on the world was similar to theirs. One must emphasize that she never asked that her life be spared because she was a woman or a born-again Christian. Her letter to Governor Bush made two arguments. She asserted that any truly repentant person on death row should have his or her sentence commuted. She also appealed to Bush's avowed pro-life beliefs, noting that she shared his opposition to abortion and euthanasia and asking that the lives of all the human beings on death row be spared.[37] Tucker herself disregarded the arguments associated with sex and religion, but the majority of commentators persisted in focusing on those factors.

O'Neil, for example, contends that if "born again" men were executed, born again women should be executed also. She also points out that Tucker got the death penalty because she was "cold, outrageous, boastful, and because her claim that killing the victims gave her orgasm was too heinous a crime for a woman to commit." Tucker's actions seemed like "male evil." In a sense, by her involvement in the pickax killings, Karla forfeited once and for all the protections available to other women. She became male-like in her behavior, apt to be violent, and acting of her own accord. She was "the type of woman society wants to punish and put to death. Her crime stripped her of her gender, took away her identity as a person, and placed her in a category of those deserving to die."[38] From this perspective, Tucker was doomed for two reasons. First, formal equality demanded that she be treated just like a man. Secondly, she had acted "male-like" in her crime, so her own behavior, coupled with the demands of formal equality, sealed her fate—no matter what might happen after June 13, 1983.

Columnist Bob Herbert in the *New York Times* wrote that Tucker's case illustrated the capriciousness of the death penalty. He described the calls for mercy because she was a woman as "chivalry in a cowboy hat." No respectable public figure would sympathize with a "guy" who committed double murder and got a sexual charge out of it, Herbert stated.[39] But public figures were not sympathizing with the pickax murderer, rather they cared about the new woman who lived on death row.

David Dow takes that point a step further noting that Tucker's race, Christian faith, and good looks "forced us to acknowledge she was human, not a feral beast." In his experience, most death row inmates who found religion were black males. Few were handsome and the majority found Mohammed rather than Jesus.[40] But the value of the Karla Faye Tucker phenomenon was that her qualities forced the issue of redemption into the public debate. If discussion of the death penalty could expand to include the question of whether it was purely an act of retribution based on past acts or an act of justice reflecting the present character of the condemned person, then Tucker's case could open the doors to a reevaluation of capital punishment. Did it?

Karla Faye Tucker was pronounced dead by lethal injection at 6:45 PM on February 3, 1998. There are several possible measures of the effect of her execution on the death penalty debate. Some took the view expressed by Dow, that she had raised questions by putting a "particularly human face" on condemned offenders. A Boston accountant told the *New York Times* that the case made it harder for him to support the death penalty. It would have been easier, he said, if she had died right away after the crime instead of "waiting fifteen years and changing her personality."[41] A poll by Pat Robertson's Christian Broadcast Network asked whether views on the death penalty had changed after hearing Tucker's story. Thirty-four percent of respondents said yes, while 39% said no.[42] A survey carried out by Scripps-Howard and the University of Texas showed that support for the death penalty among Texans decreased from 85% to 68% immediately after her execution.[43]

Others maintained that Tucker's death would be a deterrent to others because convicted persons would know that the ultimate punishment would be carried out, regardless of gender. Dianna Clements, a spokesperson for Justice for All, a "victims' rights" group in Houston, said the campaign to spare Karla Faye Tucker was "based on fraud, lies, ignorance, and sexism." Unfortunately for the consistency of that argument Karla's actual victims, family members of Jerry Lynn Dean and Deborah Thornton, had supported her pleas for clemency. Perhaps the claims of deterrence and retribution resonated with the rowdy crowd who stood outside the prison chanting "Na, na, na, na, hey, hey, hey, goodbye."[44] The rowdiness of the crowd may have had external causes. A group of scholars attempting to distribute surveys to the onlookers found "a substantial number of respondents appearing to be at least mildly intoxicated while a few were both drunk and belligerent."[45] Why they chose to be on hand for Tucker's execution remains unaccountable.

In some ways, Tucker's execution made little difference. Capital punishment remained the province of the poor, mostly male, disproportionately members of racial minority groups, most of whom would be killed without public notice. The case did not seem to interfere with Bush's political ambitions, although he did occasionally face questions about it. In a 1999 interview, the governor told reporter Tucker Carlson that although he did not meet with any of those who asked to speak with him regarding clemency for Karla, he did watch her interview on *Larry King Live*. When Carlson asked what she had said on television, this exchange followed. "'Please,' Bush whimpers, his lips pursed in mock desperation, 'don't kill me.' I must have looked shocked [Carlson wrote]—ridiculing the pleas of a condemned prisoner who has since been executed seems odd and cruel, even for someone as militantly anticrime as Bush—because he immediately stops smirking." Actually, Tucker had never asked that her life be spared during the Larry King interview.[46]

During the 2000 presidential debates, Bush responded to a question by reiterating his narrow grounds for considering clemency. "My job is to ask two questions. Is the person guilty of the crime? Did the person have full access to the courts of law? And I can tell you, looking at you right now, in all those cases the answers were affirmative."[47] He apparently remained comfortable with his retributive view of capital punishment, and, if Tucker had raised any doubts about rehabilitation and redemption, those doubts had been put to rest soon after she was pronounced dead.

Austin Sarat states that capital punishment is critical in maintaining the power structure. Governments and governors need to substantiate their claims to sovereign power. If the state is unable to execute those it condemns, it appears impotent. Clemency could be seen as an example of this impotence. Therefore, one executive prerogative, clemency, gives way to another, execution.[48] It is a patriarchal power structure that execution helps to maintain. By misstating the problem of Karla Faye Tucker as an issue of special privilege for women, real questions were ignored. Instead of debating either the deeply gendered assumptions at work in portraying the "old" Karla as a feral beast or the implications when a civilized society kills a harmless person, those interested in the case were presented with a false dilemma. Executing Tucker was not a step toward equality for women, nor did gender equality require it. But like George W. Bush, other governors could assert that they were bowing to the demands of formal equality and rejecting requests for special treatment. Under some skewed notion of fairness the execution of women was "normalized" and the patriarchal power structure remained in place. Governors in Oklahoma, Florida, Alabama, Arkansas, and Virginia would follow Bush's lead, asserting their prerogative to put women to death while claiming to do so in the name of formal equality.

Endnotes

1. David R. Dow, *Executed on a Technicality: Lethal Injustice on America's Death Row* (Boston: Beacon Press, 2005), 193.
2. Ibid., 197.
3. See Linda Strom, *Karla Faye Tucker Set Free: Life and Faith on Death Row* (Colorado Springs, Colorado: Water Brook Press, 2000) and Pat Robertson, "Religion's Role in the

Administration of the Death Penalty," *William and Mary Bill of Rights Journal* 9 (December 2000), 217.

4. Beverly Lowry, *Crossed Over: A Murder, a Memoir* (New York: Vintage Books, 2002), 13. Lowry's book is the essential source for the detailed story of Tucker's life. Tucker confided in Lowry over a period of years while she was in prison. Most other authors rely on Lowry's account as I have for much of the narrative.

5. The description of the crime may be found in Tucker's testimony at her trial, *State of Texas v. Karla Faye Tucker*, 263rd District (1984). It is also reviewed in the appellate cases. Beverly Lowry recounts the murders and notes where Tucker's account differed from others, including those of Lebrant, Doug Garrett, her sister Kari, and the police. See Lowry, *Crossed Over*, 42–62.

6. Ibid., 47.

7. Ibid., 58.

8. Ibid.

9. Ibid., 163.

10. Ibid., 117.

11. Quotations from Griffith are found in Strom, *Karla Faye Tucker Set Free*, 20. Strom's version of her story is intended to convey a religious message.

12. Information about the investigation and trial testimony may be found in the transcript of Tucker's trial, *State v. Tucker*, etc.

13. Mike Tolson, "A Deadly Distinction," *Houston Chronicle*, February 5, 2001.

14. Lowry, *Crossed Over*, 158.

15. Walter C. Long, "Karla Faye Tucker: A Case for Restorative Justice," *American Journal of Criminal Law* 27 (1999–2000) 121.

16. Ibid., 123–25.

17. *Tucker v. State*, 771 S.W. 2nd 523, 534 (1989). *Tucker v. Johnson*, 115 F. 3rd 276, 281, (1997).

18. Helen Prejean, *The Death of Innocents: An Eyewitness Account of Wrongful Executions* (New York: Random House, 2005), 250.

19. *Furman v. Georgia* 408 U.S. 238 (1972).

20. See *Ex Parte Tucker*, 973 S.W. 2nd 950 (1998).

21. Lowry, *Crossed Over*, 199. Italics in original.

22. Strom, *Karla Faye Tucker Set Free*. 130.

23. Elizabeth Rapaport, "Equality of the Damned: The Execution of Women on the Cusp of the 21st Century," *Ohio Northern University Law Review* 26 (2000), 591.

24. Quoted in Long, "Karla Faye Tucker," 121.

25. Quoted in Ibid., 122–23.

26. Robertson, "Religion's Role in the Administration of the Death Penalty," 217. Pat Robertson, "Sparing Cain: Executive Clemency in Capital Cases: The Importance of an 'Escape Valve' for Mercy." *Capital University Law Review* 28 (2000), 581.

27. Quoted in Allen R. Williamson, "Notes and Comments: Clemency in Texas—A Question of Mercy?" *Texas Wesleyan Law Review* 6 (Fall 1999), 138.

28. Michael O. Simons, "Born Again on Death Row: Retribution, Remorse, and Religion," *The Catholic Lawyer* 43 (Fall 2004). See also Austin Sarat, *Mercy on Trial: What It Means to Stop an Execution* (Princeton, New Jersey: Princeton University Press, 2005), 96.

29. Jan Hoffman, "Execution in Texas: Legal Debater; Seeking Clemency in a Labyrinth That Varies by State," *New York Times*, February 4, 1998.
30. *Ex Parte Tucker.*
31. Alan Berlow, "The Texas Clemency Memos," *Atlantic Monthly* (July/August 2003).
32. Ibid.
33. Jim Yardley, "Texas Board Denies Clemency for Woman, 62, on Death Row, *New York Times*, February 23, 2000.
34. Berlow, "Texas Clemency Memos."
35. Sam Howe Verhovek, "Texas, in First Time in 135 Years, Is Set to Execute Woman," *New York Times*, February 3, 1998.
36. *Evans v. Murray*, 498 US 927 (1990).
37. Rapaport, "Equality of the Damned," 599.
38. Melinda O'Neil, "The Gender Gap Argument: Exploring the Disparity of Sentencing Women to Death," *New England Journal of Criminal and Civil Confinement* 25 (Winter 1999), 223–24.
39. Bob Herbert, "Death Penalty Dilemma," *New York Times*, February 1, 1998.
40. Quoted in Irene Merker Rosenburg and Yale L. Rosenburg, "Lone Star Liberal Musings on 'Eye for Eye' and Death Penalty," *Utah Law Review* (1998), FN 4.
41. Sam Howe Verhovek, "Karla Tucker Is Now Gone but Several Debates Linger," *New York Times*, February 5, 1998.
42. *New York Times*, February 4, 1998.
43. *New York Times*, March 23, 1998.
44. Sam Howe Verhovek, "Execution in Texas: The Overview," *New York Times*, February 4, 1998.
45. Tana McCoy, Patti Ross Salinas, and W. Wesley Johnson, "The Execution of Karla Faye Tucker: An Examination of the Attitudes and Motivations," *Justice Professional* 12: 2 (September 1999), 212.
46. Tucker Carlson, "Devil May Care," *Talk Magazine*, September 1999, 106.
47. George Lardner, "Symposium: Forgiveness and the Law: Executive Clemency and the American System of Justice," *Capital University Law Review* 31 (2003), 183.
48. Sarat, *Mercy on Trial*, 19.

DOMESTIC OFFENSES

Judias Buenoano and Betty Lou Beets

Within months after Karla Faye Tucker was put to death, Florida executed its first woman in the modern era, Judias Buenoano. Less than two years later, Texas followed when Betty Lou Beets was subjected to lethal injection. Neither case attracted the public attention Tucker had. Governors Lawton Chiles of Florida and George Bush of Texas seemed confident that they would not lose votes over these deaths. As Rapoport describes, the governors were released from the dilemma of either "bowing to pressure" not to execute a woman or "appearing blood thirsty."[1] They could stand behind the banner of formal equality and claim that gender equality prohibited any choice but death. Despite those claims, gender does lie at the very center of the Buenoano and Beets cases. They became candidates for capital punishment in the first place because of past histories that occurred *because* they were women.

But unlike Tucker who had defied stereotypes about death row and seemed warm and likeable, Buenoano and Beets fit into an old gender stereotype of women who kill. According to the popular media, they were "black widows," husband killers. The term itself both trivializes their stories and dehumanizes the women. What they did is made analogous to the spider's instinct, removing any need for understanding, explanation, or motive. Categorizing Buenoano and Beets as "black widows" creates a "psychic distance" between them and ordinary people.[2] That distance makes it possible for the state to take their lives with little or no public objection.

Judias Buenoano

Among the executed women, Judias Buenoano was the only one convicted of several prior violent crimes. Although she was sentenced to death for the murder of her husband James Goodyear, she was earlier found guilty of the second-degree murder of her son Michael and the attempted murder of her fiancé, John Gentry. In addition, although not charged, she was considered a suspect in the death of her former boyfriend, Bobby Joe Morris. Like Velma Barfield, poison was allegedly her weapon of choice. Like Betty Lou Beets, Marilyn Plantz, and Teresa Lewis, her apparent motive was collecting insurance benefits.

The steps that led to the execution of Judias Buenoano on March 30, 1998, are winding and convoluted. When John Gentry, engaged to marry Judi, started his car on June 25, 1983, the vehicle exploded. Although he sustained head wounds and lacerations, Gentry survived. Investigators considered whether there might have been a drug connection, as car bombings are favored among such underworld figures. They also looked to Gentry's business associates to see whether anyone held a grudge because of a commercial dispute. But it seems from the first, the police chose to focus on the girl friend, Judias Buenoano. Gentry told the police that prior to the car incident, Judi, a former nurse, had been giving him capsules for a cold. She told him the pills were vitamins, but when the medicine seemed to make him sicker, Gentry became suspicious. He provided the police with several of the capsules. They were found to contain paraformaldehyde, a poison with no known medical uses. Gentry also informed investigators that he and Judi had $500,000 life insurance policies on each other.[3]

Although one must always be skeptical about the version of events put forward by "true crime" writers, Chris Anderson and Sharon McGehee the authors of *Bodies of Evidence* seem to suggest that the police and prosecutor were determined from the beginning to convict Buenoano for the attack on Gentry. Whether because the significant other is always a strong suspect or because Detective Ted Chamberlain found Judi arrogant and/ or seductive or because she seemed to be the dominant partner in the relationship with Gentry, the detective wanted to "get the bitch."[4] In the process of interviewing acquaintances about the attempt on Gentry's life,

Chamberlain probed into Judi's background and there found more grounds for suspicion.

There were conflicting stories about her life, her professional credentials, her income, and especially about the tragedies she had experienced. The investigators learned that Judias Buenoano, alias Judy or Judi Goodyear, alias Anna Schultz, alias Ann or Judias Welty had created a number of different biographies for herself.

The woman who lived in a suburb of Pensacola, Florida, and called herself Judias Buenoano was born in Quanah, Texas, in 1943 and named Anna Lou Welty, according to her family. She claimed that her mother was a full-blooded member of the Mesquite Apache tribe but no such tribe exists. She also insisted the name Judias was her mother's, although it appears that her mother's name was actually Mary. It is true her mother died when Judi was a small child and that she and her brother were sent to live with grandparents, while her older siblings were adopted. Buenoano told psychiatrists who examined her in 1990 that during her youth she had been sexually and physically abused as well as starved and neglected by foster parents and by her own father and stepmother. At fourteen, she retaliated and attacked her parents. During the melee, she threw hot grease on her stepmother. Judi was sentenced to sixty days in jail (apparently her parents were considered the victims and not charged). After serving her time, Judias opted to be sent to a girls' reformatory, the Foothills High School, rather than return to her parents' home. She remained there until she graduated in 1959.

After leaving the reformatory, Judias assumed the name Anna Schultz and worked as a nurses' aide. She became pregnant the following year and gave birth to a son, whose official name was Michael Schultz. The following year, Judi (sometimes also called Ann) married Air Force pilot James Goodyear. Their son James was born in 1966; their daughter Kimberly was born in 1967. Goodyear was transferred to Orlando, Florida, and subsequently assigned to a tour of duty in Vietnam. He returned in 1971 and died at the Naval Hospital in Orlando in September of that year.

The next year, Judy (Judi) Goodyear moved her children to Pensacola where she began a relationship with Bobby Joe Morris and subsequently followed him to Colorado. There she sometimes called herself his common-law wife, Judias (Judy or Judi) Morris. Bobby Joe Morris died in Trinidad, Colorado, on January 28, 1978. His cause of death was listed as cardiac arrest and metabolic acidosis. He was apparently an alcoholic. Five months later, Judias changed her name and her children's surnames to Buenoano (a Spanish version of Goodyear) and moved her family back to Pensacola.

Her son Michael had been a poor student and a discipline problem. After dropping out of high school, he enlisted in the Army in 1979. A few months later, Michael developed paralysis in his arms and legs. One day after his release from an Army hospital, he drowned while on a river-fishing expedition with his mother and half-brother James. Michael was wearing heavy leg braces and a hook on his hand when he fell into the river.

After Michael's death, Judi opened a hair and nail salon near Pensacola. Her careers had included practical nurse, child care provider, and salon owner. At various times, she falsely claimed to be a physician, the head of nursing at West Florida Hospital, and a PhD in both biochemistry and psychology.

In 1982, Judi began dating John Gentry, a businessman. They moved in together and later became engaged. In October 1982, they took out life insurance policies valued at a half million dollars on each other.[5]

Buenoano's life seemed quite eventful, but over the years she concocted many different versions of her experiences. It is difficult even now to sort fact from fiction. She told some friends that her first husband died in Vietnam, others that he had died from a disease he contracted there. A co-worker reported that Judi told her Gentry suffered from terminal cancer. She claimed to police that her annual income was $500,000, although she owned and operated a small beauty and nail salon. Exploring these contradictory stories after Gentry's car bombing, the police learned that Judi's former live-in boyfriend, Bobby Joe Morris, had died mysteriously in Colorado, leaving her as beneficiary of a large insurance settlement. She had also collected benefits from the deaths of James Goodyear and her son, Michael Goodyear. Additionally, all three deaths involved symptoms consistent with the presence of arsenic.

A Series of Charges

Judias Buenoano was arrested on December 1, 1982, and charged with the attempted murder of John Gentry. In addition to the "vitamin" capsules that the FBI laboratory found to contain poison, the police traced some of the dynamite used in the car bombing to an acquaintance of Judi's. They found blasting caps and wires similar to those used in the crime in the bedroom of her son, James Buenoano. The state's theory of the crime was that failing to kill Gentry by poisoning him, Judi had enlisted her son to blow up his car—all so she could collect the $500,000 in life insurance. While waiting to bring Buenoano to trial, District Attorney Russell Edgar began to refer to her, not very originally, as a "black widow." He also reopened an investigation into the drowning death of Michael Goodyear.

Michael was born in 1961 when Judi was working as a nurse's aide in Roswell, New Mexico. At that time, she was using the name Anna Schultz. The identity of his father is unknown, but the boy was christened Michael Schultz. After she married James Goodyear in 1962, he adopted Michael. By most accounts, the child had difficulty in school and also suffered from emotional problems. He was treated in a residential facility for military dependents during Goodyear's life and after his adoptive father's death Michael was placed in foster care for a time. He moved back into his mother's home in 1977, subsequently dropped out of high school, and joined the army in 1979. While in the service, Michael trained at Fort Leonard Wood, Missouri, as a water purification specialist. There, according to the Army, he came into contact with arsenic. After completing that training and before reporting for his next assignment at Fort Benning, Georgia, Michael visited his mother in Pensacola for several days. Shortly after he arrived at Fort Benning, the young man complained of numbness in his extremities. Six week later, the muscles in his forearms and lower legs had atrophied to the point that he lost the use of them. These were symptoms of a metal-based poisoning that could have been arsenic. He was treated, given physical therapy, and provided with braces weighing approximately 3 ½ pounds on each leg and a hook for his right arm. According to the Army doctor who treated him, Michael had a "severe impairment" and might never have regained function of his arms and legs.[6]

Judias Buenoano, her son James Buenoano, and her daughter Kimberly picked Michael up from the Army hospital on May 12, 1980. The next day, Judi, James, and Michael went fishing on the East River in a two-seater canoe with Michael in a folding lawn chair in the middle of the boat. He was wearing his seven pounds of leg braces, his two-pound hook, leather shoes, and, according to the family, a ski belt. About two hours into the outing the canoe capsized and Michael drowned in the river. Originally Judi, identified in the newspaper as Dr. Judias Buenoano, a clinical physician at an alcoholic treatment center,[7] and James claimed that the boat had hit a log, possibly after a snake fell into the canoe or after a fishing line had snagged in a tree. The Army and the local sheriff's department investigated the incident, and both concluded that the death was an accident.

In 1984, District Attorney Edgar probed again into Michael Goodyear's drowning. He believed Judias was responsible, and he was convinced that he had found her motive. She had collected more than $100,000 in insurance benefits from Michael's Army policy and from private companies where she had taken out several policies that provided double indemnity in the case of accidental death.[8] Edgar brought charges of capital murder against Buenoano in March 1984. In his opening statement, the prosecutor portrayed Judias as a liar and a very bad mother. She had "a peculiar relationship" with her son, characterized by "neglect, shame, embarrassment, and hatred." His mother hid Michael from her "male friends." She "diabolically executed" her son for his insurance so she could lead the life-style she wanted. As Edgar described it, Buenoano was in financial straits at the time of Michael's death. She had written a number of bad checks during the previous year, and her employment records showed that she earned $3.50 per hour as a licensed practical nurse. She could not maintain her "high living" under those conditions.

The defense argued that Buenoano had loved her son. He was not the awkward, inept, uncoordinated boy who embarrassed her as the state claimed. After all, her attorney James Johnston told the jury, Michael had been accepted by the Army. While Edgar presented evidence that Michael could have been fed arsenic while visiting his mother, the defense showed that he might have ingested the poison during training at Fort Leonard Wood. The state's case was circumstantial, based largely on Judi and James' contradictory stories of what had happened to make the canoe capsize, alternately a snake, a log, or a tangled fishing line. Judi also reported that the current in the river carried her downstream away from the accident, but a diver from the local rescue squad described the current as "very, very slow." Testimony that Michael was not wearing a life jacket or a ski belt and reports from neighbors and relatives that Judi had not loved her son surely contributed to the jury's finding of guilt. Edgar tried to introduce reports that Bobby Joe Morris and James Goodyear had been killed by arsenic poisoning and that James Gentry had been given poisoned capsules. He hoped to argue that because of the similarities among those crimes, the jury could conclude that Judias had also poisoned Michael with arsenic, causing his disability. The judge refused to allow that testimony. So, without the "black widow" image, Edgar fell back on the "bad mother." In his closing statement, the prosecutor repeatedly emphasized Judi's failings as a parent. After she was pulled out of the water by a passing fisherman, Judi drank a beer and changed her clothes. "Is that the way a mother acts when her boy drowns? They're looking for her firstborn, crippled child in the river and she's off changing her clothes." Her motives, Edgar said, were pride and greed. Pride made her reject Michael for not being "normal" and greed showed in the way she spent the "blood money," Michael's insurance. She spent it on "a motor home, a powerboat, new furniture, a Caribbean cruise. It was a life of fun, of Caribbean cruises and big fruit drinks."[9] Perhaps because they harbored some doubts about exactly how Michael had died, the jury rejected the death penalty and sentenced Judias to life in prison. The appellate court agreed that there was sufficient circumstantial evidence to support her conviction for first degree murder and theft from the Prudential Insurance Company.[10] To the end of her life, Judi claimed that Michael's death was an accident.

In October 1984, only seven months after the trial for Michael's murder, Buenoano was tried for the attempted murder of John Gentry. The state argued that the car bombing was the last of a series of attempts on Gentry's life plotted to collect the $500,000 insurance. Judi was not directly linked to the bombing. Her son James had previously been tried for that crime and found not guilty. Judi's trial focused on her alleged scheme to poison Gentry. The prosecution claimed that Judi had tried to murder him with the fake vitamin capsules containing the toxic substance paraformaldehyde. The pills were analyzed by FBI forensic chemist, Roger Martz, whose work would later be widely discredited. In addition, a doctor for the defense stated that to be fatal, a dose of paraformaldehyde would require more than 100 times the amount Gentry had taken. There seems to be reasonable doubt about whether there ever was a serious attempt to poison Gentry. Nonetheless, Judi was found guilty and sentenced to twelve years to be served consecutively with her life sentence.

Exhuming James Goodyear

The relentlessness of the Florida prosecutors led to opening a new investigation into the 1971 death of James Goodyear. As there is no statute of limitations on murder, no legal barriers prevented exhuming his body to look for evidence of foul play. Goodyear's remains were disinterred in March 1984 and examined by a forensic toxicologist. The results led to the second charge of murder against Judias Buenoano, this time for the death of her husband by arsenic poisoning.

The trial for Goodyear's murder was held from October 21 to November 1, 1985, in Orange County where Orlando is located.[11] The prosecutor was Assistant State Attorney Belvin Perry, who relied heavily on evidence supplied by Russell Edgar and his team. Buenoano was again defended by James Johnson. The state was required to prove that Goodyear had died as the result of a crime without introducing any evidence of collateral offenses. The defense hoped to raise reasonable doubt about the cause of Goodyear's death, which had originally been attributed to natural factors. If they could successfully suggest that Goodyear was killed by poison ingested in Vietnam or from the surrounding environment when citrus trees in the area were sprayed with a pesticide containing arsenic, there would be no corpus delicti (no criminal act). They also claimed that the amount of arsenic found in the victim's body was insufficient to cause death. However, the judge allowed the state to introduce evidence of the death of Bobby Joe Morris (for which Buenoano had not been charged, much less convicted) and evidence of the attempted poisoning of John Gentry. This ruling made the state's case easier to argue. They could lump the three incidents together and persuade the jury that Judi was in the habit of using toxic substances to remove men from her life, especially if they were well insured and named her as beneficiary.

Dr. R. C. Auchenbach who had treated Goodyear for nausea, vomiting, and diarrhea at the Naval Hospital in Orlando in 1971 testified that Goodyear told him he had been exposed to toxic and lead fumes at the Air Force base where he worked. The victim died on the third day of hospitalization after he had been given five quarts of IV fluid. The cause of death was listed as cardiovascular collapse and renal failure. Fluid overload may have also been a factor. Tests conducted at the time were inconclusive regarding the presence of lead. When Goodyear's body was exhumed and autopsied fourteen years later, a Florida state forensic toxicologist found the presence of arsenic, but admitted the amount may or may not have been fatal.

The medical evidence was followed by testimony that Buenoano had ample motive to kill her husband. Constance Lang, a friend of Judi's in the early 1970s, recalled that the two women had "joked" about putting poison in their husbands' food when they were having marital problems. Debra Sims, a sort of live-in babysitter at the Goodyear home, testified that Buenoano did not seem unhappy in her marriage to Goodyear. She did remember that Goodyear had hallucinated in the days before his last hospitalization. Hallucinations are consistent with arsenic poisoning. Robert Crawford who had an affair with Buenoano while her husband was in Vietnam had no memory of derogatory remarks about her husband. He was presumably put on the stand to illustrate the defendant's loose morals. Another female acquaintance, Mary Beverly Owens, said Judi had confessed to killing Goodyear and had suggested Owens kill her own husband with "fly bait" insecticide. The mother of Bobby Joe Morris also alleged that Judi had admitted to Goodyear's murder.

Thus far the state had tried to establish that Goodyear died of arsenic poisoning, planned and carried out by a cold and boastful Judi. They then introduced information that she had collected approximately $100,000 in insurance and veterans' benefits. The money provided the motive.

Points of similarity

After presenting the witnesses who established that Goodyear's body had contained arsenic and that Judi had presumptive motives, the prosecution began introducing evidence of collateral crimes. Although Buenoano's guilt in the death of Bobby Joe Morris was never legally proven, the state argued that an autopsy had shown arsenic to be the cause of Morris's death. Judias was living with Morris at the time of his death; therefore, she had the opportunity to poison him. She profited from his insurance, therefore, she had a motive. A jury unschooled in the law could certainly see the "black widow" pattern at work. Buenoano's attorney objected. "There are no cases which allow you to prove the collateral crime by other crimes and then use that collateral crime as proof one committed the crime for which he is on trial. If that were so, the state could always throw in all accusations of other crimes by a defendant without proof the defendant committed them." He claimed that the Morris case alone could never go to trial, yet it was used as proof that Judi murdered Goodyear.[12]

John Gentry, her next romantic partner, described the capsules containing paraformaldehyde which had made him ill. He also told of the $500,000 life insurance policy. The defense argued that Gentry's testimony should not have been admitted in the Goodyear trial, even as similar fact evidence. Eleven years passed between the two events, raising questions of timeliness and relevancy. They also questioned whether making someone sick with paraformaldehyde was truly similar to killing someone with arsenic. Similar fact evidence might be admitted to show a continuing course of conduct or be of such special character as to point to the defendant. Two poisonings, separated by more than a decade and involving different substances did not meet those criteria, according to the defense.

The appellate court disagreed with that point, finding that poisoning was a "particularly unusual modus operandi." They did find a clear pattern. All three victims formed a close relationship with Buenoano. Each became ill while living with her. Poison was a factor in each instance. Buenoano was the beneficiary of insurance and other benefits in all three cases. Therefore, the Florida Supreme Court found "these points of similarity pervade the compared factual situations and when taken as a whole are so unusual as to point to the defendant."[13]

Given the introduction of information about Morris and Gentry in the Goodyear trial, the state developed a picture of Judias Buenoano that perfectly embodied Edgar's description of her as the "black widow." She appeared to be sitting at the center of a web, heartlessly plotting the death of gullible, unwary men who fell under her thrall. After the jury found her guilty of first-degree murder, it would be difficult, if not impossible during the sentencing phase, to convince a jury to spare her life.

Mitigating and aggravating factors

The state's strategy was to connect the series of events from Gentry's injuries to Michael's drowning to Morris's death back to the death of James Goodyear. It seems they wanted the jury to consider Judi a serial killer, even as they skirted the usual procedures to present that image. Testimony during the sentencing phase from Russell Edgar who had prosecuted Judias for the Gentry incidents and for Michael's drowning fit perfectly with that plan. Edgar was allowed to summarize the testimony from the two prior trials and, the defense believed, to put his own spin on things. Normally, the state would simply inform the jury of the defendant's previous convictions. Adding details about the crimes, and perhaps editorializing about them, could surely influence the jury to a harsher view of the Goodyear case, perhaps to "tip the scales" in favor of the death penalty.

According to Buenoano's appellate brief, Edgar misrepresented testimony from the trial for Michael's death, when he stated that several witnesses had testified that Judias did not love her son. No such testimony was actually in the record. Additionally, he mentioned that Michael had white lines under his fingernails consistent with arsenic. That information had not been allowed before the jury at the earlier trial as no link had been established between Judias and any arsenic found in Michael's body. But the mention of arsenic could only serve to make the jurors see the connections the state wanted them to see.

Edgar claimed that at the time of Michael's death Judias was in dire financial straits. If that were true, the insurance motive was consistent in every case. To further that impression, he "recalled" that the only times Buenoano had called the hospital where Michael was recovering were calls about his benefits. Actually the doctor who testified about the phone conversations said one concerned Michael's medical and school history, the other discussed preparations for his return home. Perhaps Edgar's recall of so much testimony and of so much detail was simply faulty. However the defense believed that Edgar, as a prosecutor, was an especially powerful witness who painted a picture that Buenoano hated her son, that when he became crippled she planned a canoe trip so she could drown him. He portrayed a woman who took a paraplegic boy to a secluded river even though he was afraid of the water, hit him on the head, and tossed him out of the canoe. Her motive— insurance to pay the bills for her extravagant lifestyle. The defense believed Edgar's whole performance was "overkill," and that Buenoano should be pro- vided a new sentencing hearing where the jury would not be swayed by such biased and inflammatory testimony. The Florida Supreme Court found that even if Edgar's testimony amounted to "overkill," it was "harmless and did not result in prejudice to the defendant's case."[14]

Buenoano objected to the state's allegation that the murder of Goodyear was committed for pecuniary gain. That factor, if proven, would serve as an aggravating circumstance. Judias did collect life insurance after her husband's death. But it can be argued that receiving a financial benefit *after* Goodyear died does not show a motive. Perhaps, like Betty Lou Beets discussed later in this chapter, she did not even know the insurance existed. And if she did, surely every family member who collects on life insurance for a spouse or relative is not ipso facto a murder suspect. On the other hand, if the jury accepted the view that Buenoano made a habit of killing people to benefit from their insurance, they would assume pecuniary gain was the explanation for Goodyear's death.

Finally, was the murder of Goodyear "heinous, atrocious, or cruel?" The defense thought not but the Florida high court took the position that poisoning is "conscienceless and pitiless." They mentioned that "systematically poisoning one's husband over a period of time until it causes his death and witnessing the effects of the poison is an unusual manner and method of committing a homicide."[15] It is worth noting that the court apparently believed the nature of the relationship between the victim and the defendant, wife poisoning husband, contributed to the atrociousness of the crime.

New Counsel and New Insights

In 1989 Buenoano changed lawyers. Her appeals were taken over by death penalty experts, Capital Collateral Representatives (CCR). They raised some startling and troubling questions about her original lawyer, James Johnson. During the sentencing phase of her capital trial, Johnson had insisted that

Judi sign a contract giving him exclusive book and movie rights to her story. This arrangement meant that Johnson had a clear conflict of interest—if Judi were sentenced to death the profits would potentially be much greater than if she received a lesser sentence. Who would rush to buy a book about someone serving 25 years to life? The potential financial benefit of a death sentence could make a defense attorney less than zealous. In appellate pleadings, the CCR lawyers argued that Buenoano had received inadequate assistance of counsel.[16] They asked for a fact-finding hearing to determine the extent of Johnson's conflict of interest. Here Buenoano's case was stymied by a true Catch-22 situation. Johnson had been disciplined by the Florida Bar Association for his conduct in the Buenoano case, but those proceedings were sealed and not available to her new defense team. Therefore they could not provide the appellate court with the particulars of the situation. They could only argue that such a conflict of interest precluded Johnson from acting in the client's best interest. The CCR lawyers cited his errors in Buenoano's trial as evidence of the inadequacy of her defense.

A major issue was Johnson's total failure to provide the sentencing jury with mitigating information. He knew there were issues of Judi's mental health to investigate but totally failed to do so. Her brother Gerald Welty contacted Johnson and offered to tell his sister's story. The attorney did not respond. Her father likewise stated that he would have testified but was not asked. If Gerald Welty and Jessie Welty had been called they would have described Judi's miserable childhood. Her mother died of tuberculosis when Anna Lou Welty (as her family called her) was three years old. The court removed the children from their father who was disabled. Judi was sent to a variety of relatives and foster homes. In her brother's words, she experienced "no love" as a child.

The new defense team arranged for Buenoano to be examined by psychologists Dr. Pat Fleming and Dr. Robert Phillips.[17] Both concluded that she was severely mentally ill. At last there was an explanation for her erratic behavior and for her seeming tendency to lie about almost everything. Fleming wrote a lengthy report which described a terribly unstable childhood marked by physical, psychological, and sexual abuse at the hands of foster parents and even her own father and stepmother. In one home, the "mother" forced her to sit on her lap and nurse, even though Judi was four or five years old. The child was punished by being put out in the woods at night where she was told the devil would get her. When returned to her father's custody in a tiny trailer with five or six other people, she was forced to steal food, and she was beaten regularly. Thus it was not an irrational decision when Judi chose to go to the girls' reform school rather than returning to that environment. At least at the reformatory she was fed and clothed.

Fleming found that Judi's "grandiosity," her habit of exaggerating her successes, was consistent with mental illness. She had a short attention span and fragmented thought processes, and she suffered from insomnia and agitation. The doctor diagnosed Judi with a right hemisphere impairment and a severe emotional disorder consistent with a schizoid personality disorder. The mental illness accounted for her "pervasive patterns of indifference to social relationships." Fleming described how a history of abuse such as Judi experienced would impair someone's ability for attachment. It would contribute to emotional isolation and a fear of being overwhelmed by others. The doctor noted that Buenoano had suffered brain damage, a point reiterated by Dr. Phillips. She had sufficient cerebral dysfunction to significantly disrupt her thought process. That physical damage to her brain plus severe psychological problems made her "incapable of adequate judgment." Dr. Fleming stated the Buenoano could not conform her conduct to the law (a definition of legal insanity in some states). Dr. Phillips agreed. Her mental impairment resulting from injury, plus a personality disorder caused by significant developmental deprivation, plus longstanding drug and alcohol abuse, plus her psychological condition (bipolar disorder) made any expectation of conforming her behavior to social norms unlikely.

Both mental health experts found Judi either legally insane or at least severely mentally ill. But the jury in her trial did not hear a word about her terrible childhood or about her current condition. Johnson, her attorney, may have well been counting the profits from his book deal rather than searching diligently for mitigating evidence. The CCR argued that this constituted inadequate assistance of counsel.

One of the few witnesses Johnson called in the sentencing phase was Professor Michael Radelet, a death penalty scholar and contributor to the Innocence Project that investigates wrongful convictions. When Johnson contacted Radelet, the latter agreed to testify but asked to meet with the attorney to prepare so he could make the best use of his expertise. Radelet suggested that Johnson find out everything he could about Judi's background and even offered to help with those efforts. Johnson never followed up on Radelet's offer, meeting with him only over lunch on the day of his testimony. The professor wrote that he had never, in testifying in 25 capital cases, felt so unprepared to take the stand. Knowing nothing about Buenoano, he was only able to offer the most general comments on the relative dangerousness of women compared to men.

Johnson's inadequate representation showed up in several other areas, according to the CCR. He failed to ask that lesser charges be included in the jury's deliberation. They might have found her guilty of manslaughter or second-degree murder which would have spared her life. Johnson chose to go for "all or nothing." Again, one could argue that either all (a death sentence) or nothing (a not guilty verdict) would be better material for his story than a lesser sentence.

The new lawyers included in their appeal the argument that Judi was tried under an ex post facto law, which is prohibited by the Constitution. She was tried in 1985 under a law passed in 1973 for a crime committed in 1971. They also alleged that the jury was prejudiced by seeing her wearing leg irons throughout the trial. They argued too that the jurors had been given several improper instructions—that they should feel no sympathy for the defendant; that they were not really responsible for putting her to death; and that a sentence of life would require a majority vote (actually a tie would result in a life sentence). The CCR attorneys could claim that an adequate defense attorney would have properly objected to these things at the time of trial.

Of course if a less than able defense attorney fails to raise claims in a timely way, the claims will generally be procedurally defaulted. The defendant is made to pay the price because her attorney made mistakes or acted with bad judgment.

The Florida Supreme Court disagreed with every one of those claims. They found "no evidence to support the contention that counsel's performance, even if perceived as deficient, prejudiced the outcome of the proceedings." As appellate courts often do, these justices could proclaim with confidence that no matter how much information the jury had about Judi's life, even if they had known her to be diagnosed with a serious mental illness, the outcome would have been the same. How could they possibly be so sure?

The Electric Chair

The penultimate set of appeals in Judias Buenoano's case concerned the use of the electric chair as Florida's only method of execution. Her death was scheduled for June 19, 1990. Shortly before that date, her new lawyers filed papers alleging that use of the "present system for carrying out a state-sanctioned execution in Florida would violate the Eighth and Fourteenth Amendments."[18] It would, in other words, literally amount to cruel and unusual punishment. Buenoano claimed that Florida's one electric chair was defective; that Department of Corrections (DOC) personnel were incompetent to carry out an execution properly; and that these problems were known to DOC administrators who refused to correct them.

On May 4, 1990, a month before Buenoano's scheduled execution, Jesse Tafero was burned to death in the Florida electric chair. Observers reported fire and smoke coming from the top of his head while he continued to breathe. When the first jolt of electricity did not appear to kill Tafero, a second jolt was administered. This time flames shot six inches above his head while his chest pushed against the leather straps. Smoke reached the ceiling of the chamber. A third surge of electricity finally killed Tafero, after eleven minutes of smoke, burning flesh, and struggles to breathe. Journalists reported the gruesome details. Governor Bob Martinez asked for an investigation calling it an "unfortunate incident." But ever mindful of the politics of execution, he went on to say "It is far more unfortunate that it took 14 years to bring to justice a man who killed two police officers." Aside from the fact that someone else later confessed to the murder for which Tafero was executed, the governor's priorities are clear and would be applied to Buenoano as well. He seemed to be saying that a malfunctioning electric chair that tortures a human being is "unfortunate," but a process that provides convicted inmates with numerous appeals and delays retribution is "far more unfortunate."

The DOC did investigate Tafero's execution and found problems were caused by a sponge. They insisted that, all appearances to the contrary, Tafero had died instantly, but that the fire had been caused by the substitution of a synthetic sponge for the worn-out natural sponge used in previous executions. In fact, the sponge on Tafero's head was the normal kitchen variety, purchased at a local store by a DOC employee who never considered whether the composition of the sponge might have an effect on conducting the electric currant. To test whether the synthetic sponge had been at fault, the DOC investigators cut a piece from it, put it in a regular toaster, and noticed that after five seconds it began to smoke and to produce a noxious odor. If those responsible for working the electric chair could close the investigation by blaming a sponge, the DOC would be vindicated and executions could continue as planned. This approach assumed no one would pursue the question of why the protocols for capital punishment were so casual that one could make the mistake of purchasing a vital part of the lethal equipment from the local K-Mart. If one accepted Governor Martinez's position that retribution was more important that guarding against torture, carelessness about the equipment was inconsequential.

Buenoano's appeal asked for an evidentiary hearing to examine the entire process—the poor or broken electrical connections that were the real probable cause of burning Tafero; the poor qualifications of the DOC personnel who maintained the chair (there was no licensed electrician on the staff); the general negligence of the DOC in taking care of the equipment. A particularly shocking piece of testimony came from Fred Leutcher who had constructed most of the extant electric chairs in the country. He told how a Florida DOC official, on learning that repairs to the chair would cost over $3000, chose instead to fix the problem by fashioning a leg electrode from an old army boot.

Buenoano's pleadings also contained testimony from Dr. Robert Kirschner, an eminent medical examiner known for documenting torture and human rights violations. Kirschner claimed that Tafero was not dead until the third jolt, and that he "experienced conscious pain and suffering during his execution." If Kirschner's conclusion is correct, Tafero was tortured, and anyone subject to the same execution system might well be tortured too. Buenoano's appeal concluded "This Honorable Court should not allow a woman to be dispatched to her death when there exists every likelihood that she will be burned, abused, and tortured during that execution.... If as a sovereign people we have decided that the lives of certain people should be forfeited for their crimes, at the very least we must ensure that the process by which we extinguish life is consistent with the humanity that we are supposedly seeking to protect. The Eighth Amendment demands no less."[19]

Although Buenoano was given a stay of execution while the courts considered her request for an evidentiary hearing on Florida's method of execution, her plea was eventually rejected by the state and federal courts. The Florida court found that "the State is not required to employ the most modern state of the art technology in implementing the death penalty or to foresee and meet every problem which could conceivably arise during an execution."[20] The United States Supreme Court agreed, upholding a ruling from the Eleventh Circuit that Florida's electric chair was "sufficient to cause painless termination of life." The lower courts based this conclusion on "expert testimony." A test carried out by a professor of engineering using a "makeshift inmate" constructed with a metal colander for a head, a rubber tub of saline solution for a body, and a pipe for a leg found that the chair worked just fine.[21] The way was cleared for more electrocutions.

The Last Appeal

One more line of appeal remained before Buenoano was put to death. When Judi was tried for the attempted murder of John Gentry, the state had called an FBI scientist, Roger Martz, to testify that the capsules she gave Gentry contained a toxic substance. In her trial for the murder of Goodyear, this evidence had been presented to the jury. However, an investigation of the FBI Chemistry-Toxicology lab in 1997 had come to the conclusion that "Roger Martz lacks the credibility and judgment that are essential for a unit chief, particularly one who should be evaluating a range of forensic disciplines." Martz lacked credibility because "he failed to perform adequate analyses to support his conclusions and did not accurately or persuasively describe his work." The report continued, "If Martz continues to work as an examiner we suggest that he be supervised by a scientist qualified to review his work substantively and that he be counseled on the importance of testifying directly, clearly, and objectively, on the role of protocols in the Laboratory's forensics work, and on the need for adequate case documentation. Finally, we recommend that another qualified examiner review any analytical work by Martz that is to be used as a basis for further testimony."[22]

Buenoano alleged there was a risk that Martz had testified erroneously at the Gentry trial and that misinformation had contributed to the outcome in the Goodyear trial. The appellate court found that Buenoano could have had the capsules tested herself at any time before they were destroyed in 1992. In their view, she had essentially forfeited her right to challenge Martz's testimony. Not surprisingly, the court found that even if the questions about Martz's competence had been raised at the Goodyear trial "it is not of such a nature that would produce a different result." Here too the appellate court determined that additional or different information about the defendant's past would make no difference to the jury. On March 29, 1998, the federal court also rejected Buenoano's final habeas petition based on the Martz evidence.

Her appeals exhausted, Buenoano's execution took place on March 30, 1998.

According to press reports, she visited with her two children and other family members on the day before her death.[23] Several hours before going to the chair, her head was shaved to reduce the chance of catching fire. Her last meal included healthy fruits and vegetables—strawberries, asparagus, and broccoli. She was escorted into the death chamber and seated in the electric chair at 7 AM. She had no last words before the voltage was turned on at 7:08.

She was pronounced dead at 7:13. A small puff of white smoke or steam curled up from her right leg. Tests of electrocution conducted in England have found that steam is generated when bodily fluids have been heated to the boiling point.[24] Based on that research, Judias Buenoano's blood was actually boiling when she died.

Buenoano never attracted positive publicity as Karla Faye Tucker had. Her thirteen years on death row were spent quietly for the most part. She wrote letters and crocheted blankets and baby clothes. She reportedly taught Bible study to some inmates. At a point, Buenoano described herself as a "devout Catholic." She allegedly requested a rosary shortly before her death. There are no reports about whether she received any medication or therapy for her mental illness.

Until the end of her life, Buenoano claimed that she was innocent. On the other hand, she was convicted on the basis of circumstantial evidence that points strongly to her guilt. Yet one can also argue that those who tracked and prosecuted Judias Buenoano bootstrapped their way to an execution. They built their ultimate case not on a firm evidentiary foundation but piled assumption loosely upon assumption, so that the verdict against her seemed based as much on supposition as on legal proof. It is ironic that Buenoano's adversaries, the state of Florida prosecutors, asked juries to trust them as they talked their way into a conviction. Their approach was the mirror image of Buenoano's life. Until the attempt on Gentry, Judias Buenoano had been able to talk and bootstrap her own way from a miserable, destitute beginning to a respectable middle-class life in a pleasant suburban community.

Betty Lou Beets

Betty Lou Beets was a sixty-two-year-old great grandmother when she was put to death in Huntsville, Texas, on February 25, 2000. She was convicted and sentenced for the murder of her husband, Jimmy Don Beets. It was execution number 121 for Governor George W. Bush, who was in the midst of his first presidential campaign. In a silent but ironic statement on the reality of gender difference, the tiny woman was placed on a man-sized gurney to receive her lethal injection. She was so short that if her head lay at the top of the gurney, the cross-panel designed to be at shoulder height came to her waist. To make her arm accessible to the needle, the guards moved her to the middle of the stretcher. There she looked "like a little old lady who had slid off her pillow to the middle of a hospital bed." Thick leather straps across her legs and stomach and between her breasts bound her to the gurney. "She was completely helpless."[25]

Competing narratives offer explanations of how Betty Lou Beets came to end her life in that death row chamber. One version, the story propounded by the state of Texas and such sources as the execrable "true" crime book *Buried Memories* portray her as a wild, sexy, greedy manipulator who killed several model citizens and terrorized others.[26] An alternative telling of her story includes a history of abuse and neglect from early childhood, hearing loss, leaning disabilities, a series of relationships with controlling men who battered her physically and psychologically, and finally a death sentence largely attributable to a lawyer who betrayed her interests for his own personal gain. Betty Lou Beets was not simply a victim, but she was surely a casualty of a criminal justice system incapable of correcting its own mistakes and, in its patriarchal structure, unwilling to understand the dynamics of domestic violence.

Betty Lou Dunevant was born on March 12, 1937.[27] Her early life bears some striking similarities to Velma Barfield's. Both were children of the Great Depression, born in poverty-stricken rural North Carolina. Both had violent alcoholic fathers. Whereas Velma's mother was weak, Betty's mother was mentally ill. Betty's family were sharecroppers on a tobacco farm. They lived in a shack that lacked running water, screens or glass on the windows, plumbing, and electricity. Like other impoverished farm families, most of the time they ate a diet of salt pork, flour, and corn meal. The children almost never had milk, fresh eggs, vegetables, or fruit. It is not surprising that such poor nutrition meant a lifetime of health problems. After the Dunevants moved to Danville, Virginia, to look for work in the textile mills, Betty contracted measles encephalitis when she was about six years old. She ran a fever of over 105 degrees for several days and suffered permanent brain damage and hearing loss.

Those disabilities, coupled with her parents' inability to afford medical treatment, doomed Betty to failure in school. She could not hear the lessons nor, due to her learning disability, could she learn to read or to work math problems. She was frustrated, isolated, and confused. From the time Betty was about 12 years old, her mother suffered intermittent "nervous breakdowns" resulting in several stays in state mental hospitals. The mother's illness meant that Betty as the eldest daughter was expected to be in charge of the house—cooking, washing, cleaning, and taking care of her younger siblings. Her father veered back and forth between alcoholic stupors and uncontrollable rage. He was wildly jealous of Betty's contacts with anyone outside the family and beat her often when he suspected her of disobeying. At 13, Betty was hospitalized for five days because of an injury to her left eye, the result of one of her father's beatings, probably with a belt buckle. Around the same time, she began to suffer from migraine headaches—most likely a result of stress and anxiety. When she was 14, Betty's weight was recorded as 82 pounds, putting her in the lowest percentile of girls her age. The next year, Betty dropped out of school permanently and, at her mother's urging, married Robert Branson. She was 15 and her husband was 18. They became parents a year later.

Branson began to hit Betty within a few months of their marriage. This, like her subsequent relationships, was a classic battering situation. Because of her disabilities her lack of education, and her inability to support herself, Betty relied totally on her husband. The six children born to her and Branson increased her dependence. When he decided to move the family to Texas for better work opportunities, she had no choice about leaving familiar places to accompany him. When, in 1958, he threw her out of the house in a jealous rage, forced her to pack her bags and put her on a bus to Virginia without the children, Betty tried to commit suicide by overdosing on sleeping pills. After 17 years of a tempestuous marriage, Robert Branson demanded a divorce because he wanted to marry a younger woman. Betty was left with six children under the age of 15, no skills, no job, and a promise of $350 per month in child support.

Betty had managed as a homemaker with limited occasions to interact with the outside world. After Branson left her, she had no reliable income as he soon stopped paying child support. A brief job as a grocery clerk was a disaster. Betty could not read the labels or hear questions from customers. She could not hold an office position that would require answering the telephone or working with written communication. A low-paying job in a warehouse was her only possible work. In desperation, Betty sent two of her children, Robbie and Phyllis, to live with Branson and his new wife.

At that point, Bill Lane, an old friend, proposed marriage. Although he was kind and attentive during their courtship, Lane had a history of drunkenness and of battering his former wife. After he and Betty married, Lane began his attacks on her. He punched, kicked, and slapped her, and threw her against the wall. As one of her daughters described it, Lane "beat her senseless." She sent the children away to escape his brutality. However, even when Betty divorced Lane, she was unable to avoid him. Students of domestic violence describe "separation assault," a behavior that occurs when an abuser refuses to relinquish control over his victim and escalates the violence when she tries to leave. Lane was a textbook case. He ignored protective orders, broke into

Betty's home, threw a large piece of concrete through a window onto her bed, threatened verbally to kill her, and destroyed her property. Betty was terrified and depressed. She was prescribed antidepressants, and she self-medicated with alcohol. Finally, about six months after their divorce, Lane called and threatened to kill Betty and her children. She shot and wounded him slightly as he tried to come through the back door. This was the incident used by prosecutors to argue that Betty had a history of violence. Totally without context, they told the jury that she had shot her former husband.

Betty still had no resources to take care of her family. She moved them back to Virginia for a brief time, but Lane followed her there. He pleaded with Betty to remarry and return to Texas with him. He promised to treat her well and never to hit her again. Out of desperation or out of foolish optimism, Betty believed him. Instead, he abused her for four more years before throwing her out of the house. What was left of Betty Lou? She had been abused, humiliated, and treated like dirt. Not surprisingly, she continued to drink heavily and to look for a man to "take care of her." She married another alcoholic abuser, Ronnie Threlkeld. Once he choked her in a bar because she danced with another man. Ronnie told an onlooker that Betty was his wife and "he could beat her if he wanted to."[28]

She divorced Threlkeld and the next year married Doyle Wayne Barker. The cycle continued. Barker was a drunk and a bully. He had terrorized his former wives, and he terrorized Betty. He hit her in the face and, according to her son, every few weeks Barker would "beat the holy shit out of her."[29] She ran away from him, he pursued and threatened her. Betty drank and took diet pills, and she divorced Barker in 1980. He stalked her, assaulted, and raped her. According to her son-in-law's affidavit, Barker beat Betty the day before he disappeared. "She had a bruised chin, bruises all up on her chest, both eyes were black, there were dark black and blue choke marks on her neck, and her arms were covered with big black bruises…. I've never seen anybody so beat up."[30]

Barker disappeared in 1981. Betty claimed that he had simply left. Although her immediate tormentor was gone, Betty was a wreck. Years of abuse aggravated her disabilities. She still could not support herself adequately. She had been betrayed by every man who promised to love and take care of her. She suffered from migraines and nightmares. Beer and diet pills became her daily regimen. Then, while she was working as a waitress at a club, she met Jimmy Don Beets, a fire fighter. Like all the others, Beets courted her and treated her well at first. But like the others, he was an alcoholic. He packed his cooler with beer and whiskey when he left for work in the morning and returned with it empty. But in the final triumph of hope over experience, she married Beets in 1982. His son and her son Robbie moved in with them. By all accounts, there was a lot of conflict and arguing in their trailer home at Cedar Creek Lake.

Crime and Punishment

Jimmy Don Beets disappeared on August 6, 1983. Betty claimed he had gone fishing and had not returned. Although the boat was found with his pills for a heart condition scattered in the bottom, a three-week search by the Henderson County Sheriff's Department, members of the Dallas Fire Department, and the Texas Parks and Wildlife Service failed to discover a body in the lake. Two years later, acting on an anonymous tip, the local police dug up a planter shaped like a wishing well in the Beets front yard. Under it, wrapped in a sleeping bag, they found Jimmy Don Beets's body. They uncovered a second body, that of Doyle Wayne Barker, wrapped in a similar sleeping bag and buried under a shed in the back yard. Both had been shot with a .38 caliber revolver. Later that day, Betty and her daughter Shirley Stegner were arrested and charged with capital murder. Betty was tried, convicted, and executed. Shirley, who testified against her mother, had charges against her dropped.

To anyone who knew of Betty's life story, a charge of capital murder seems outrageous. How could a victim of chronic abuse merit the death penalty? Why wouldn't she claim self-defense which would involve a lesser charge? The state argued that Betty had killed Beets for his insurance benefits. The prosecution alleged that constituted a "murder for remuneration" and was thus a capital offense. The nature of that charge is one of the controversial issues in the Beets case. Betty always claimed that she had not known of her husband's pension or insurance, that she had only learned of those benefits a year after Beets was dead when she visited an attorney, E. Ray Andrews, about a fire insurance claim. Andrews informed Betty that she might be the beneficiary for Beets' insurance and pension and that she should look into those things. If she did not know about the financial payoffs until one year *after* Beets was dead, how could Betty have killed him to get those benefits? The only person who could testify that she was unaware of the financial implications of Beets's death was Andrews. But because he became Betty's defense attorney in the murder trial, he could not testify that she did not know about Beets's finances. Andrews agreed to represent Betty Lou Beets in return for the rights to a book and movie about her case. He had every financial incentive to see her case sensationalized and to follow it through to death row. He had no financial incentive to tell the truth about her motivation. So Betty Lou Beets went to trial for the murder of Jimmy Don Beets with physical and mental disabilities, a life history as a battered woman, a string of failed marriages, and a lawyer who had powerful monetary reasons to see her convicted and executed.[31]

The trial opened in Henderson County, Texas, on October 8, 1985.[32] One of the state's key witnesses was Robbie Branson, Betty's son who had lived with her and Beets. He testified that his mother told him of her plan to kill Beets and that he had helped her with the burial of the body. At her direction, he had driven Beets's boat and set it adrift on the lake. He claimed that after Beets was buried under the wishing well, he saw his mother plant flowers there. It was one of those images, like Karla Faye Tucker grinning as she attacked Jerry Dean, that suggested callousness toward the victim. It was meant to stick in the jurors' minds as evidence of the killer's hardheartedness. She buried husbands in the yard and with blatant hypocrisy, pretended to be tending flowers. In addition, Robbie's testimony was offered as proof that Betty had instigated and planned the murder. The prosecution did not want the jury to see her as an abused, disabled victim but as a crafty, greedy, sexually hungry woman who involved even her own children in her carefully crafted plot to murder men for money. It could not have been more inaccurate, but with a defense attorney like E. Ray Andrews, the state had a huge advantage.

Andrews's handling of Robbie Branson was an example of the quality of Betty's defense. He made not a single objection when the prosecutor asked Robbie leading questions that incriminated his client. Barely literate, Andrews asked questions such as "You was not indicted for nothing?" Several times, he addressed Robbie as "Bobby," the name of another of Betty's sons. There was a legitimate issue with respect to Robbie's testimony as well as that of his sister Shirley. If both had participated in the murder as accessories after the fact, why was neither charged? Had the state promised to drop felony charges against them in exchange for their testimony against their mother? But Andrews's inept questions failed to highlight that point.

Shirley Stegner, Betty's daughter, told how her mother had outlined a plan to kill Beets several months before his "disappearance." She also stated that Betty had planned to kill Barker because he beat her and that Shirley had helped dispose of Barker's body. The daughter aided the prosecution's case in two ways—she established that the killing of Beets had been premeditated, and she got the information about Barker's murder before the jury. The court allowed the state to introduce evidence about Barker, even though Betty was on trial only for the murder of Beets. The judge ruled that it showed a design or pattern by the defendant. As in the cases of Velma Barfield and Judias Buenoano, permitting the jury to hear about prior killings, even when the accused had never been found guilty of them in court, created the image of a serial murderer. It would seem virtually impossible for such inflammatory data not to influence their finding of guilt and their determination of punishment.

The case for the defense was pitiable. Andrews called another of Betty's daughters, Faye Lane, who offered the information that her mother had never talked about murder and that her sister Shirley drank. A second defense witness, Ray Bone, who had lived at Betty's house in some undisclosed capacity after Beets' death, testified that Betty had treated him "decent," and that he "didn't know nothing about a murder." Finally, Andrews called Betty Lou Beets to the stand. Her story was that Robbie had shot Beets after a fight between the two men. She had helped her son bury the body, rather than the other way around. She claimed she knew nothing about her former husband's insurance. Of course, no one but Andrews could support her on that point, and he chose to "represent" Betty rather than to provide the crucial evidence that she did not kill Beets for "remuneration." When the district attorney cross-examined Betty, her answers were often unresponsive. Had the court been aware of her deafness, they might have made allowances for her hearing loss. As her lawyer never mentioned Betty's disability, her rambling responses to questions seemed like she was avoiding the truth. It is unlikely that having her take the stand accomplished anything for her case, but it was consistent with the inept representation she received.

Likewise, the closing statements offered more heat than light on Betty's real story and offered contradictory accounts of when she had learned about the insurance money. Billy Bandy, the district attorney, discussed inconsistencies by the defense. He noted that Betty had not cried or seemed upset when Beets went missing. He claimed that she was impressed when the Fire Department chaplain told her about her husband's insurance, although that point seems to undermine the state's case that she killed him for those benefits. If Betty learned about the insurance from the chaplain, it was several days *after* Beets's death and could not have been a motive for his murder. Perhaps because of the weak evidence supporting monetary gain as a motive, Bandy took care to draw a picture of the "black widow" as serial killer. Although she was on trial only for the murder of Beets, Bandy described the similarities in the deaths of Barker and Beets. "Now I don't doubt that you're as appalled as I am, this picturesque site out here on Cedar Creek Lake to be turned into a killing ground. Two men buried in the yard. With the common denominator, both were married to Betty Beets. And who looked after the yard? She did. Who planted the flowers and mowed the grass? Betty Lou Beets."

The prosecutor tried to make her into a criminal mastermind who calculated and killed husbands and coerced her children into aiding and abetting her crimes. Betty Lou Beets was, in the picture he drew, the quintessential Evil Woman who threatened the order of the patriarchal society. She was, in Bandy's words, a "domineering woman," a "forceful personality." And she had a heart of stone. After Beets was shot she "put him in a sleeping bag, pushed him in the wishing well," and went shopping in Dallas the next day. "Cold. Cold as a well chain throughout it all." She tried to say that her son Robbie had killed Beets. But, Bundy asked, "What kind of a mother would seek to pin a murder on her own child? The female of the species protects the young, above all, above her own life." By comparison, Jimmy Don Beets's loving family deserved "justice." At the end, the prosecutor appealed to the jury to find her guilty of capital murder. "It's tragic. It's horrifying. Certainly, it's shocking. Such a crime could occur in our county. Such a person could commit a crime like that, could reside among the God-fearing, law-abiding citizens of Henderson County, Texas." The defendant, the husband-killer and unnatural mother, was not like those good people and therefore, her life was expendable.

Andrews, the defense attorney, offered a rambling, incoherent closing statement. It later became known that he had been drinking heavily during the trial, and after reading the "argument" he made to the jury one can easily believe that charge. Essentially, Andrews offered no sensible alternative explanation of Beets's death. He tried to assert that Robbie had been the killer and that Betty had covered up for her son, but he had no proof. Instead, he pointed to Robbie's behavior in the courtroom. Robbie had waved and smiled. "He's a macho man. He's a tough boy." Betty, on the other hand, took the witness stand, "to protect macho man, the liar." At another point, Andrews seemed to be arguing that if Betty had just wanted to kill Beets, she could have done it while they were on a vacation shortly before he died. "If she had wanted to kill him—they went through Oregon—well, maybe they went through Virginia but they came through a bunch of states. They slept then and the whole bit. If she had wanted to kill him, I believe she could have done it then." Of course claiming that Robbie had been the actual killer also ruled out any arguments of self-defense or any discussion of the domestic violence that would have put Betty's story into its true context.

He tried to discredit some of the state's expert witnesses, calling them "doctors and city people, you know, the insurance people and the whole bit and that lawyer from Tyler, sure, you can believe them…. I wouldn't buy a used car from him, I guarantee you. Huh-uh. Certainly wouldn't do that." The "him" selling the car remained unspecified.

Although Andrews's summation was both colorful and incomprehensible, it omitted two crucial points. He was the only person who could testify that Betty did not know about the insurance benefits, and he chose not to be a witness in her behalf. His information would have eliminated the grounds for capital murder, remuneration, or monetary gain. But with all his vociferating, Andrews chose not to save his client. Secondly, aside from putting his own financial interests before the life of his client, the defense attorney simply acted incompetently in failing to do any investigation or to provide any evidence of Betty's lifelong victimization by violent men. Six and a half hours later, the jury returned a guilty verdict.

During the sentencing phase, the state argued that the shooting of Jimmy Don Beets was deliberate with a reasonable expectation of death. He had been shot twice, once in the head. They claimed Betty had planned the murder, discussed the plot with her daughter, Shirley, and arranged a place to dispose of the body. They further claimed that Betty had killed Wayne Barker with similar planning and deliberateness. The second special issue concerned future dangerousness. She had shot Bill Lane; she had killed before, the prosecutor argued; she could kill again. If the jurors believed Betty had deliberately killed Beets and that she would pose a threat in the future, they should sentence her to death.

Rather than offer any mitigating evidence, Andrews seemed to want the jury to reconsider the evidence of guilt. In any event, he offered them no reason to spare Betty's life. They chose to sentence her to death.

Appeals

The incompetent Andrews remained Betty's lawyer during the first round of appeals in 1986. There were several grounds to challenge the outcome of her case. Perhaps the most significant argument was that the prosecutor had misapplied the notion of murder for remuneration. If it could be determined that the language of the statute defined murder for remuneration as murder for hire, then the very grounds for charging Betty with a capital offense would be removed. She obviously did not profit from Beets' death in the way a hired gunman would, she merely stood to experience some financial gain. But that could be said of many spouses of victims. It did not mean that money was the motive for the death. This point becomes especially salient if Betty was not aware of Beets' pension and insurance benefits. A number of other points were raised in the first appeal, but the State Court of Criminal Appeals found that the trial court had misinterpreted the meaning of remuneration and reversed her conviction. "The state failed to prove beyond a reasonable doubt that the appellant caused the death of Beets *for remuneration*. The facts did not establish that this was a 'murder for hire' case."[33] Unfortunately for Betty Lou Beets, when the full Court of Criminal Appeals reheard the case the next year, they reversed the earlier ruling and reinstated her conviction and sentence.

Outside the regular appeals process, Betty Lou Beets wrote a letter from prison to Judge Teague of the Court of Criminal Appeals. It is a forlorn document, the work of a confused person. She points out that although the court was frequently reminded that Beets was her fifth husband, no one mentioned that she was his fourth wife. Nonetheless, she calls him a "good family man" and claims that she helped control his drinking by keeping him out of bars. As for her own reputation, Betty claimed that she never worked as a barmaid, but as a cashier, that she was never on welfare but had $40,000 in the bank. Thus she did not need or know about Beets's benefits. In fact, she claims that the Fire Department chaplain did not talk with her about insurance at all. He must have spoken to her sister-in-law, Betty Beets, by mistake.[34] She disputes the description of the "wishing well" in her yard, arguing that it was a planter not a well. Finally, in perhaps the most accurate statement in the letter, she asks for the judge's compassion, as she was 65% deaf and suffered from arthritis.[35]

Of course her plea was as ineffective as those Andrews brought forth. Finally, in 1990 she filed a petition for state habeas corpus with able advocates, free from any conflict of interest. Her habeas corpus brief provided an array of arguments for reconsidering her case. Several involved tactics used by the prosecution, such as the use of characteristics of the victim (he was a fireman for 26 years) as a reason for convicting and sentencing his killer to death. Properly such findings should be based on the strength of the evidence and the circumstances of the crime, not on the victim's alleged value to the community. Likewise, the judge had permitted relatives of the victim to testify to the impact of the murder on their lives, even though the Supreme Court ruled that Victim Impact Statements were unconstitutional in 1987.[36] The most important points in Betty Lou Beets's habeas petition, however, concerned her lawyer's ineffective assistance and the failure to offer the mitigating evidence of her history of abuse. A court was finally informed of Andrews's egregious failure to provide his client with an adequate defense. From the time she was arrested in June and tried in October, 1985, neither Andrews nor his associate visited her. They "prepared" for trial without a single conversation with their client.[37] Further, Andrews violated American Bar Association rules by trading his services for the literary and media rights to her case. In the middle of the trial, Andrews produced a contract whereby Betty signed over those rights. When she was at her most vulnerable, he persuaded her that she would be left without representation if she did not agree. Because his financial interests were tied to seeing the trial through and telling a sensational story, Andrews did not communicate to his client that the prosecution had offered a life sentence for a guilty plea. If Betty had taken the plea, her case would have been uneventful, "not unlike the vast majority of homicides in Texas" and the rest of the United States.[38] There would be no windfall for Andrews. Therefore he not only risked her life by not withdrawing to testify that she did not know about the insurance, he actually forfeited her life by not communicating the plea offer so he could make money. If anyone committed murder for remuneration in this case, Andrews was the killer and Betty Lou Beets was the victim.

The other huge failing in Betty's original trial was her attorney's failure to investigate her background and to introduce her history of domestic abuse as mitigating evidence. For the habeas pleading, her attorneys commissioned a report from Dr. Lenore Walker, at the time the nation's leading expert on domestic violence.[39] Walker interviewed Betty in 1990 and took her life history—all the stories of battering, disabilities, head injuries, and substance abuse. The report is substantiated with medical records and the testimony of witnesses. It makes appalling reading. At the end, Walker concluded that Betty Lou Beets was "a severely battered woman and suffered from battered woman syndrome, rape trauma syndrome, and Post Traumatic Stress Disorder." She had developed "learned helplessness," by which she tried to protect herself from abuse by a heightened sensitivity to danger. The arguments with Beets and between him and Robbie increased her level of fear. "Thus, the emotional, cognitive, and behavioral components of battered woman syndrome, rape trauma syndrome, and PTSD significantly interact with the organic brain dysfunction, the hearing impairment, the substance abuse, and the deficits from the impoverished childhood and affect every area of Betty Lou Beets' life. They have profound implications for her behavior and cognitive functioning. These multiple disabilities impacted on Betty Lou Beets' state of mind at the time of Jimmy Don Beets's death and subsequently, on her ability to assist her attorney or to comprehend her attorney's inability to competently prepare her defense."[40]

In 1989, in *Penry v. Lenaugh*[41] the Supreme Court found that the Texas capital sentencing process was flawed because it did not give adequate consideration to mitigating circumstances. In Betty's case, her attorney had failed to introduce any of the information about her life, the history of battering that would put the killing of Jimmy Don Beets into a different context. No mitigation was offered by the defense, therefore the jury had no such evidence to consider. Thus the attorneys in her habeas appeal argued that she had been denied due process, she had never had a meaningful day in court. The Appeals court found that Betty had not shown that either Andrews's testimony about the insurance or the evidence of domestic violence would have changed the outcome of the trial. They applied the *Strickland* standard, where the defendant has the almost impossible task of proving that without the lawyer's mistakes the trial would have had a different result. If the defendant cannot convince the court of that, any malfeasance by an attorney is simply "harmless" error.[42]

After her habeas petitions were rejected by the courts, the Fifth Circuit Court of Appeals also turned down her final appeals. Although numerous questions had been raised about Betty's knowledge of Jimmy Beets's pension and insurance, the judges reaffirmed that she had been "appropriately sentenced to death for her crime" of murder for remuneration.[43] One other possibility to save her life was a new Texas law that required the Board of Pardons and Paroles (BPP) to review for clemency all cases where the offender was a victim of spousal abuse. The BPP refused to apply the law to Betty Lou Beets and the Fifth Circuit upheld their decision. According to the federal court, there were several reasons why the provision did not apply. The legislature had excluded capital crimes from the mandatory review, and Betty had been found guilty of murder "with the specific intent of pecuniary gain." According to the Fifth Circuit there was no evidence she had been abused by the victim. "On the contrary, at trial, she blamed his death on her son, denied mistreatment by Mr. Beets, and professed her love for him."[44] So, in the eyes of the federal judges, Betty was not a victim of domestic violence. Her attorney's failure to offer evidence that would challenge the monetary motive, his failure to help her develop a plausible explanation for the murder of Beets, left a brain-damaged, terrorized woman, who could hear only 35% of what went on around her, to fend for herself.

The Final Days

The days leading up to the death of Betty Lou Beets were, in many ways, similar to the time before other executions. Her attorneys, Joseph Margulis and John Blume filed last-minute appeals, her supporters spoke to the press, and Governor George Bush and the Texas Board of Pardons and Paroles claimed to consider whether she should be granted clemency. The BPP was faced with two issues and two separate petitions in this case. First, was Beets entitled to a reprieve and review under Texas law because the crime involved domestic violence? The second petition asked for clemency largely on the basis of the denial of due process. The Board voted 13–5 not to grant the review and 18–0 against clemency. Once again, Bush had to make a decision. His record at the time, granting only one stay and approving 119 executions, suggested that the governor, deeply involved in his presidential campaign, was unlikely to show mercy toward Beets. Nonetheless, her supporters hoped that heightened awareness of domestic violence and its importance as an issue among women voters might influence him in her favor. Amnesty International, the National Coalition Against Domestic Violence, and anti-domestic violence groups from fifteen states wrote an open letter to Bush urging commutation. "We ask the Governor to act on his stated concern for the victims of domestic violence and demonstrate his compassion…. Texas failed to protect Betty Lou Beets when she was being beaten by an abusive spouse. It will be a terrible miscarriage of justice if Texas executes this battered woman without hearing her story."[45] The president of the European Parliament also wrote to Bush citing "a profound sense of unease in the conscience of Europeans and the world at large" at the use of the "archaic and morally unacceptable" death penalty.[46]

Another view came from Pam Perillo, one of Beets's fellow residents on Texas death row. Perillo suggested that the state was rushing to execute Beets before she could generate the sort of publicity Karla Faye Tucker had. "They don't want the people of Texas to see another human face. After all this is a 62 year old grandmother with a very sweet smile. Remember this is the time for elections and no one wants to make Governor Bush look bad again by seeing he is about to kill Bettie (sic) Beets…. Bettie is a reflection of a lot of you people out there who have gone through a lot of the same things she went through and you may still be going through them right now. When you look in the mirror you could be seeing her face along with your own."[47] Perillo may have been right about the speedy execution. The press and public never did warm to the Beets story as they had to Tucker. Her story of abuse and domestic violence did not generate the same empathy as Tucker's radiant conversion.

Editorials in the *Washington Post* and the *Florida Times Union* called upon Governor Bush to spare Beets' life, because she was a victim of domestic abuse, because her lawyer was venal and incompetent, and because killing Betty Lou Beets would do nothing to make Texas a safer place.[48] According to his office, Bush received more than 2000 phone calls opposing the execution and only 57 in support. They also acknowledged receipt of 1100 letters in favor of clemency and two against. Nonetheless, the governor insisted upon viewing the decision to execute Betty Lou Beets as a simple matter of formal equality. With a striking lack of originality, his spokeswoman said that Bush had "upheld the laws fairly and evenly for all the people in Texas, including women facing the death penalty…. The gender of the killer didn't make any difference to the victim."[49] But of course it did. The victim would not have been abusing Betty Lou Beets if she had been a man.

Witnesses reported that Beets "coughed twice, then gasped before lapsing into unconsciousness as the chemicals pumped into her arms took effect."[50] Her attorney Joseph Margulis provided more vivid details, far worse than a cough. "In that instant I realized what all those straps are for. They have nothing to do with security for a sixty-two-year-old grandmother. Had Betty not been strapped down, she would have lurched off the gurney. Her head and shoulders raised up and strained against the straps across her breast? Her last breath exploded from somewhere deep within her. A line of spittle flew out of her mouth and landed on her chin. Her eyes opened wide, like discs, and she looked terrified, as though someone had struck her violently from behind, and she knew in that instant that she would die."[51]

Beets made no final statement, although in a letter she wrote the day before, she thanked her supporters and expressed the belief that she would "rest in the arms of my Heavenly Father inside his pearly gates." She hoped that her case would help other battered women and urged her friends to "Heal the lost, impaired, disabled, battered, and for all who are in need, stick by the banner and carry it on."[52]

The son of Jimmy Don Beets and the son of Doyle Barker attended the execution, the latter wearing a black cowboy hat. Both James Beets and Barker denied that their fathers had been abusers. Beets claimed that Betty had "tarnished" his father's good name. Barker told the press that "The state of Texas did the right thing tonight by putting Betty Lou Beets to death. I want the world to know there is always going to be a death penalty in the state of

Texas and they need to use it."[53] There was little doubt that Texas was using the death penalty. An average of two people were being executed there each week. Betty Lou Beets was the ninth person put to death in that state in the first two months of 2000.

Why, when there was strong mitigating evidence and a clear record of irregularities throughout her case, did Betty Lou Beets become the fourth woman executed in the modern period? Her appellate attorney Joseph Margulis says that her case "casts an uneasy light" on "the abysmal representation provided for poor people charged with capital crime." Few would argue with Margulis that E. Ray Andrews was among the worst of the worst lawyers. And, one cannot deny the saliency of the "black widow" image. If a woman kills her spouse and if there are any insurance benefits, a prosecutor may get an easy conviction based on the argument that she did it for financial gain. The very credibility of that charge reveals gender inequalities. It is easy for a jury to believe a woman (who has no resources or legacy of her own) would kill a man, the rightful owner of the family property. Elizabeth Leonard contends that domestic violence may actually make things worse for such a woman, as the state can claim that revenge for abuse provides a second motive in addition to greed.[54] The prosecutor also defined Betty Lou Beets as a thoroughly perverse mother, a "corrupter of the home" who persuaded her children to hide her husbands' bodies. Only the most evil woman would use motherhood, the ultimate feminine power, to implicate her children in her own wrongdoing.[55]

Leonard concludes that the official harshness of the legal system toward Beets served to reinforce the patriarchal structure. In a sexist society, a woman is expected to stay in her place—a message conveyed by both the abuser and the courts, each of whom exerts power and control over her. A woman who uses force in response to male domination is sentenced to prison and death, another assertion of patriarchal supremacy over her life.[56]

Black Widows?

There are remarkable similarities between these two executed women dubbed "black widows." Both experienced childhood abuse and deprivation in a home with a sickly mother and an alcoholic father. Both had multiple partners in adult life, never finding a healthy sustainable relationship with a spouse. Both suffered from poor mental health, likely attributable to an early life where love and security were totally absent. But even more amazing are the comparisons of their experiences with the justice system. In each case the state argued that the motive for murder was financial, in the form of insurance and pension benefits. Prosecutors professed outrage that a woman would kill her husband to get control of money. For Betty Lou Beets, there is little evidence that she was aware of the benefits. Her acts were much more likely motivated by a long history of abuse. But juries seemed to be satisfied with the image of a grasping woman who killed out of greed. They found that story plausible, at least in part because the picture of a man who controlled the family finances and a dependent wife with no money of her own was so familiar. In such a scenario, the woman used murder to get the financial security she could get no other way. In other words, prosecutors assumed that jurors worked within the context of patriarchal assumptions and used those assumptions to convince them of the defendants' motives.

Then there were the lawyers. Both Johnson and Andrews were disciplined by their respective bar associations, but arguably two women lost their lives because of their lawyers' greed. Judias Buenoano and Betty Lou Beets were executed when each was found guilty of killing a man for financial gain. James Johnson and Ray Andrews were each complicit in seeing a woman put to death. They received reprimands.

Endnotes

1. Elizabeth Rapaport, "Equality of the Damned: The Execution of Women on the Cusp of the 21ˢᵗ Century," *Ohio Northern University Law Review* 26 (2000), 596.
2. Ibid., 600.
3. For the details of Buenoano's alleged crimes see Chris Anderson and Sharon McGehee, *Bodies of Evidence: The Shocking True Story of America's Most Chilling Murderess … From Crime Scene to Courtroom to Electric Chair* (New York: St. Martin's Press, 1992); Marlin Shipman, *"The Penalty Is Death": U.S. Newspaper Coverage of Women's Executions* (Columbia, Missouri: University of Missouri Press, 2002); Kathleen A. O'Shea. *Women and the Death Penalty in the United States, 1900–1998* (Westport, Connecticut: Praeger, 1999); "Judias Buenoano," Bad Girls Do It at www.francesfarmersrevenge.com; "Judias Buenoano," available at www.clarkprosecutor.org
4. Anderson and McGehee, *Bodies of Evidence*, 77.
5. Versions of these events are found in Anderson and McGehee, *Bodies of Evidence*, Shipman, *"The Penalty Is Death,"* and O'Shea, *Women and the Death Penalty.*
6. *Judias Buenoano v. State of Florida*, 478 So. 2ⁿᵈ 387, October 29, 1985.
7. Anderson and McGehee, *Bodies of Evidence*, 98.
8. *Buenoano v. Florida*, 1985.
9. Quoted in Anderson and McGehee, *Bodies of Evidence*, 250–51.
10. Ibid.

11. Much of the information about the Goodyear trial is taken from the appellant's brief and the decision of the Florida Supreme Court, *Judias V. Buenoano aka Judy Ann Goodyear v. State of Florida* , 527 So. 2d 194 (Fla. 1988).

12. Ibid.

13. Ibid.

14. Ibid.

15. Ibid.

16. Appellant's brief in *Buenoano v. Dugger* and *Buenoano v. State of Florida*, 559 So. 2d 1116 (Fla 1990).

17. Ibid. The psychologists' reports are quoted at length in the appellant's brief.

18. Appellant's brief in *Buenoano v. State of Florida*, 565 So 2nd 309 (Fla 1990).

19. Ibid.

20. Deborah W. Denno, "Is Electrocution an Unconstitutional Method of Execution? The Engineering of Death over the Century," *William and Mary Law Review* 35 (Winter 1994), 663.

21. Ibid., 654.

22. *Buenoano v. State of Florida*, 708 So 2nd 941 (Fla 1998).

23. Accounts of Buenoano's death may be found at e.g., "Judias (Judi) Buenoano: Florida's Black Widow" at www.geocities.com

24. Denno, "Is Electrocution Unconstitutional?" 637.

25. Joseph Margulis, "Memories of an Execution," *Law and Inequality* 20 (Winter 2002), 126.

26. Irene Pence, *Buried Memories: The Chilling True Story of Betty Lou Beets the Texas Black Widow* (New York: Pinnacle Books, 2001).

27. Her early life, with appropriate documentation, is described in *Ex Parte Betty Lou Beets*, Texas Court of Criminal Appeals, April 6, 1990.

28. Lenore Walker, Psychological Report included in *Ex Parte Betty Lou Beets*.

29. *Ex Parte Betty Lou Beets*.

30. Ibid.

31. Information about Andrews and his conflict of interest may be found in Margulis, *Memories of an Execution*.

32. The account of the trial comes from *The State of Texas v. Betty Lou Beets*, 173rd Judicial District Court, Texas State Archives.

33. *Betty Lou Beets v. Texas*, Texas Court of Criminal Appeals, November 12, 1987. Italics in the original.

34. No one else called Betty Beets appears anywhere in the case.

35. Letter from Betty Lou Beets to Judge Teague, February 2, 1989, Texas State Archives.

36. The Court found Victim Impact Statements unconstitutional in 1987 in *Booth v. Maryland*, 482 U.S. 496 (1987). They reversed that holding in *Payne v. Tennessee*, 501 U.S. 808 (1991).

37. *Ex Parte Betty Lou Beets*.

38. Ibid.

39. See psychological report by Lenore Walker in Ibid.

40. Ibid.

41. *Penry v. Lenaugh*, 492 U.S. 302 (1989).

42. *Strickland v. Washington.* 446 U.S. 668 (1984).

43. *Beets v. Johnson,* 98-41482, US5th, June 28, 1999.

44. *Beets v. Texas Board of Pardons and Paroles et al.,* 00-50133, US 5th, February 24, 2000.

45. *Houston Chronicle,* February 25, 2000.

46. Nicole Fontaine to George W. Bush, February 24, 2000. ccadp.org/EU-bushplea

47. Pam Perillo's Page ccadp.org/pamelabettie

48. *Washington Post,* February 23, 2000; *Florida Times Union,* February 23, 2000 ccadp.org/beetsnewsupdates

49. Jim Yardley, "Texas Board Denies Clemency for Woman, 62, on Death Row," *New York Times,* February 23, 2000.

50. Reuters News Service, "Betty Lou Beets Executed in Texas," February 25, 2000, ccadp.org/beetsnewsupdates

51. Margulis, *Memories of an Execution,* 127.

52. Farewell letter from Bettie (sic) Beets, February 24, 2000, ccadp.org/finalbettie

53. Reuters New Service, February 25, 2000.

54. Elizabeth Dermody Leonard, "Stages of Gendered Disadvantage in the Lives of Convicted Battered Women," in *Gendered Justice: Addressing Female Offenders,* Barbara Bloom, ed. (Durham, North Carolina: Carolina Academic Press, 2003), 119.

55. Janice Kopec, "Avoiding a Death Sentence in the American Legal System: Get a Woman to Do It," *Washington and Lee University School of Law Capital Defense Journal* 15 (Spring 2003), 361.

56. Leonard, "Stages of Gendered Disadvantage," 131.

· 6 ·

THE OKLAHOMA THREE

Wanda Jean Allen, Marilyn Plantz, Lois Nadean Smith

In 2001, the state of Oklahoma executed three women. It was the greatest number of female executions in America in one year since the Civil War. Researching these stories is a challenge. Unlike other states where trial records of capital cases are available at the State Supreme Court, the State Court of Criminal Appeals, or the State Archives, in Oklahoma transcripts are sent back to the district courts where the case was tried. District court clerks seem overwhelmed with daily responsibilities and less focused on maintaining the historical documents. In each of these cases, the "record" consisted of one or two boxes of the type that holds paper for copiers. The boxes contained whatever someone happened to put into them—subpoenas for prospective jurors, appeals filings, and in one case, ten copies of the death warrant. What was missing was the complete transcript of the trial—voir dire, witness testimony, closing statements, rulings by the judge. Thus Wanda Jean Allen, Marilyn Plantz, Nadean Smith, and presumably all the other people put to death in Oklahoma are at a special disadvantage when their stories are reexamined. The historian must try to explain what happened to them without having a full range of resources. This chapter represents my best effort to understand why they were among the fourteen wretched sisters.

These three women represented milestones. Allen was the first woman executed in Oklahoma since it became a state. She was also the first African

American woman put to death since capital punishment was reinstated in 1976. Plantz is one of only two of the fourteen who was convicted not as the killer but as a conspirator in the death of her husband. But if Allen and Plantz represented statistical oddities, they, along with Smith, found themselves caught up in a wave of executions that swept their state in the last years of the twentieth century. Between 1973 and 1999, 294 death sentences were handed down in Oklahoma, the highest per-capita rate in the nation. The state also posted the highest rate of executions per capita between 1998 and 2001, the very time when Allen's, Plantz's, and Smith's cases reached the end of their appeals process. The larger number of executions in Texas drew national attention, but with a significantly smaller population than its neighbor, Oklahoma was sentencing and putting people to death at a faster pace.

How does one explain Oklahoma's propensity to engage in capital punishment and the relatively high number of women included? Earlier chapters in this book have noted that when women commit homicide their victims are more likely to be intimates or persons with whom they had prior relationships. When men kill, the victims are more likely to be strangers. Men who end up on death row are most often involved in another felony along with a murder. In Oklahoma, however, more than 25% of all the men and women on death row had killed a relative or someone with a previous family relationship. Many of the killers had been victims of abuse or domestic violence. The willingness to treat such crimes as capital offenses doubtless meant that more women found themselves charged accordingly.

A 2001 report by Amnesty International called the state's death penalty a "lethal lottery," that involved juveniles and the mentally impaired among those selected for execution. The system was characterized by inexperienced defense lawyers operating without adequate resources. They either did not look for or missed exculpatory or mitigating evidence. On the other side there were prosecutors and police officers who engaged in a variety of misconduct, including the suppression or misrepresentation of evidence.[1] During the time when Allen, Plantz, and Smith made their way through the capital system, three individuals also had a major impact on the outcome of those cases and other Oklahoma death sentences. Governor Frank Keating (1995–2003); Robert Macy, the district attorney of Oklahoma County, who prosecuted Allen and Plantz; and Joyce Gilchrist, director of the Oklahoma County Crime Laboratory, all put their unique stamps on the cases.

Keating, often described as an "ardent" supporter of the death penalty, also considers himself a "devout" Catholic. He took issue, however, with the

Church's position on capital punishment. He proclaimed that Pope John Paul II was wrong to condemn the death penalty. In Keating's mind, no matter what the pope or the Conference of Bishops said, Catholic theology supported capital punishment. Although George W. Bush of Texas oversaw the highest number of executions of any governor, Keating's administration competed to carry them out at a faster pace. As in Texas, the governor cannot offer clemency without the recommendation of the Pardon and Parole Board. The Board, with three of five members appointed by the governor, does not recommend clemency. As Amnesty International noted, they do not seem to be persuaded by remorse, rehabilitation, mental impairment, arbitrariness, international law, morality, or inadequate legal representation.[2] Keating announced that he would never support clemency unless the person was actually innocent of murder and the board acquiesced. Thus, it was obvious that if errors, improprieties, or injustices occurred at earlier points in a case, there would be virtually no chance of those problems being corrected in its final stages by the executive.

In Oklahoma there was much potential for error at the lower levels of the capital process. State law listed eight "aggravators," factors that may, at the prosecutor's discretion, qualify a murder as a capital offense, eligible for the death penalty. The aggravators are: murder for hire; prior felony convictions; killing a law enforcement officer; a crime that was "heinous, atrocious, or cruel"; an offender who poses a continuing threat to society; murder committed to escape prosecution; murder occurring while the offender was serving a conviction for felony; or a crime that created a great risk of death to more than one person. A prosecutor, such as Macy in Oklahoma County, could use these factors, especially the thoroughly subjective "heinous, atrocious, or cruel" description to raise virtually any homicide to a capital offense—at his discretion. Is not every murder by definition "cruel"? Macy would claim that his real criterion when asking for the death penalty was whether the defendant was likely to kill again.[3] A jury faced with that question cannot foresee the future; they can only look at the past. Those who kill intimates and family members are the least likely to commit additional murders. And yet, arguably all three of the women executed in 2001 fell into that category. Marilyn Plantz and Nadean Smith had never before been charged with a crime, but prosecutors argued successfully that those women were continuing threats.

Macy's actual Oklahoma County constituency was the area that included the state capital, Oklahoma City and its suburbs, but his influence extended well beyond his district. His career was linked to a rise in violent crime in the state (and in much of the nation) in the 1980s. Macy promised that if the death penalty were used more often, crime would decrease. During his twenty-one years as district attorney, Macy sent seventy-three people to death row. His own popularity as a "crime fighter" with what he described as "the best capital litigation team in the country," his leverage over elected judges (endorsing some and campaigning against others), and his intimidation of defense attorneys made capital sentences commonplace occurrences during his tenure.[4] He "always had time for cops." Macy never prosecuted a police officer for excessive force or coercion. The only officers he ever charged were those involved in financial corruption.[5] In turn, the police went out of their way to help Macy make his cases. And, there was no doubt that Macy put on a great show. When a murder was reported the district attorney himself rushed to the crime scene and assured the public that he would find the killer and give him the death penalty. As former police officer Mark Fuhrman wrote, "The Oklahoma County Police Department would identify the suspect, the crime lab would link him to the crime, and the assistant DAs would do the heavy lifting at trial."[6]

The *Daily Oklahoman*, published in the state capitol, took an extremely pro-prosecution position. Not only did the paper never criticize Macy and always defend the discredited Joyce Gilchrist, it argued that if a crime was "heinous," public opinion should oppose funds for the defense. Sometimes, if a crime were truly horrible, the newspaper opined, capital punishment might be "too kind" to the offender.[7] Such views about funding and the bias in favor of the prosecution were reflected in the cases studied here as judges refused to allow money for the defense to carry out investigations or to conduct psychological examinations. Juries who were selected from the communities where Macy made countless public speeches and where the *Oklahoman* published its hard line stories and editorials were likely to be predisposed to accept the prosecution's version of events and to vote for death.

Once Macy actually entered the courtroom, his techniques remained questionable. Until the legislature passed a Life without Parole statute in 1987, the district attorney often told jurors that "life" meant an offender would serve only seven years. For a heinous crime, the jury might well believe that the only two choices were death or a "slap on the wrist." Although vengeance is not a legal basis for a sentence of death, Macy often argued that the defendant should not be allowed to live in prison with a nice bed, a color TV, and healthy food while the victim lay in a cold grave. Typically, the Oklahoma Court of Criminal Appeals found that such statements were impermissible but only "harmless error." Thus there were no real consequences for those breach-es of the rules. Amnesty International calls the use of such tactics a "super aggravator applicable in every death penalty case."[8] In other words, the state can always argue that if the victim is dead, the offender does not deserve to be better off, i.e., alive. That comparison takes the focus from the issue of guilt and responsibility for a specific crime to simple retribution and skirts around the legally prescribed list of aggravators.

Another of Macy's techniques, one he used during the trial of Wanda Jean Allen, was to minimize the jury's responsibility for the defendant's death. He assured jurors they were not being asked to kill anyone, "only to return a verdict of death." He compared the responsibility of jury duty to military service during wartime. Both protected their communities. Lest they feel anx-ious, jurors could rest assured they were "just a small piece of the machinery designed ... to put people on death row." Presumably, like soldiers, if they did participate in killing, it was in self-defense and therefore blameless.[9]

The 2001 Amnesty International report, "Old Habits Die Hard: The Death Penalty in Oklahoma," summarized complaints against Macy. He cheated, lied, spurned the rules of fair trial, and concealed evidence. He launched into improper and abusive arguments. Even the Oklahoma Court of Criminal Appeals found at times that he "skirted the border of impropriety or engaged in improper conduct." The 10th Circuit Court of Appeals noted Macy's "menda-cious and deceitful conduct."[10] Macy resigned as District Attorney the day after the Amnesty report was published. But those who were executed or who sat on death row because of his prosecutorial misconduct could take little solace in his retirement.

Often, some of the most powerful testimony at a murder trial comes from forensic scientists or criminalists. Juries tend to believe that those wit-nesses are objective; that they simply report what the evidence tells them. Unfortunately, Joyce Gilchrist, forensic chemist with the Oklahoma County Police Department crime lab and ultimately its director, had little problem with "enhancing" the meaning of the evidence or even with lying under oath. She testified about hair, fiber, blood, and DNA evidence that might or might not link a specific suspect to a crime. She was the lead forensic chemist in at least twenty-three death penalty cases, including the investigation of Marilyn Plantz.

Although defense attorneys frequently challenged Gilchrist's conclu-sions and often objected that she failed to share evidence in a timely way, her career had seemed to be on an upward trajectory until serious challenges to her work came from professionals within the forensics community. James Starrs, a professor at George Washington University, one of the nation's best forensic science departments, published an article in a scholarly journal in which he said that Gilchrist's work was "just awful." He described her as one of the worst forensic scientists he had ever seen and found her work on death penalty cases especially troubling.[11] John Wilson, a scientist with the Kansas City Crime Laboratory, charged that Gilchrist exaggerated the proof of hair evidence (she claimed positive identification where none was possible). He argued that she made "preposterous statements under oath," that she either didn't know what she was talking about or didn't care that she made claims at odds with the entire forensic community. Macy called such criticisms "nitpicking."[12]

However, persistent questions about Gilchrist's work led to an FBI review of her office and lab in 2001. The examiners found a shambles, "open boxes of evidence, sacks and envelopes strewn on the floor, files damaged by water, rot, and animal infestation, biohazard bags with seals broken." They further discovered that Gilchrist had no established procedures for lab work, safety, training, or evidence handling. Rape kits were often destroyed shortly after the suspect was tried, making it impossible to revisit the physical evidence on appeal. Gilchrist never allowed anyone to look at her work nor were there any procedures for peer review of tests from her lab.[13] Given those findings, the FBI recommended that all of Gilchrist's death cases be reviewed. But Oklahoma Attorney General Drew Edmondson decided to review only thirteen of her twenty-three capital cases. He then announced he was certain that "No innocent person had been executed."[14] How could he be sure? Neither Edmondson nor anyone else could ever know whether Gilchrist's misleading or actually false testimony had led a jury to choose death over a lesser sentence. Nor could subsequent or posthumous appeals ever get to the truth contained in lost, missing, or destroyed files and evidence. One can only wonder why, if the authorities in Oklahoma are so completely certain of the accuracy of their justice system, the records are so difficult to check.

Fuhrman states that his acquaintance with the shoddiness of the death penalty process in Oklahoma turned him from a supporter to an opponent. As many observers of capital punishment have noted, once it has begun, the process gains momentum and puts pressure on everyone from the investigating officers to the governor. After a DA announces a capital charge, it is hard to admit a mistake, to express a doubt, to point out problems, or to ask obvious questions when inconsistencies arise. Anything less than an execution may be seen as a "loss" for the state. When the stakes are so high for the prosecution, humility and a sense of fair play are likely to be in short supply. Yet the stakes are even higher for the accused.

The stories of Wanda Jean Allen, Marilyn Plantz, and Lois Nadean Smith reflect the flaws in the capital system in general and in Oklahoma in particular. Although Allen certainly committed homicide and the other two were involved (the extent of their involvement is debatable) in brutal murders, all were still entitled to a fair trial and an appropriate punishment. Yet the press demonized the three women, the prosecution played fast and loose with due process, and their poverty as well as their gender made them grist for the Oklahoma mill of death.

Wanda Jean Allen

Wanda Jean Allen is the only one of the three women executed in Oklahoma in 2001 whose case drew any national attention. Her death warrant, issued on June 6, 1989, stated that her trial had taken place from April 10 to April 18, 1989; that she and her attorney had been present at the trial; that on April 17, the jury found her guilty of murder in the first degree; and that on April 18, the jury had unanimously fixed her punishment at death "by continuous, intravenous administration of a lethal quality of an ultrashortacting barbiturate in combination with a chemical paralytic agent until death is pronounced by a licensed physician according to the accepted standards of medical practice or in any other manner that may be designated by the state of Oklahoma, within the walls of the place of incarceration."[15] By the time Allen was given that continuous intravenous administration of barbiturates and paralytic agents on January 11, 2001, her case had attracted a few representatives of the national media. Her supporters included the Reverend Jesse Jackson, who led a large protest outside the women's prison. An HBO filmmaker arranged to make a documentary called "The Execution of Wanda Jean." Many were shocked at the irregularities in Allen's case, and shocked that the agencies charged with "fixing" its legal problems had little will to do so.

Wanda Jean Allen was the second oldest of eight siblings in a family often described as "dirt poor."[16] Four brothers and sisters were either developmentally or mentally disabled. None of the eight graduated from high school. Her mother, who drank heavily, was usually considered "very slow" and expected Wanda Jean to take on the responsibility for household tasks and childcare. After dropping out of high school in the eleventh grade, Allen briefly attended a vocational school but did not complete the program. She was involved in several minor offenses as a juvenile and spent almost a year in a residential facility.[17] In 1981, during an argument, Allen shot and killed Detra Peters, a childhood friend. For that offense, she was sentenced to four years in prison for manslaughter. Before she was released in 1984, she met Gloria Leathers. The two moved in together several months later when Leathers left prison. Their relationship was tumultuous, mutually so. Both women apparently had short tempers. Gloria's mother recalled fistfights and even shots fired when the two argued.

The events that led to Allen's execution began at a grocery store on December 2, 1988, when she and Leathers got into an argument over a welfare check. The fracas was serious enough that someone at the store called the police. Two officers accompanied Leathers to the home and watched as she started to move her things from the house into her car. Leathers's mother arrived and observed that the two women continued bickering. When the officers were called away to another incident, Leathers and her mother apparently set off for the police station to file a complaint against Allen. Allen followed and shot Leathers on the steps in front of the station. While Gloria's mother witnessed the shooting, several officers heard the shot from inside the building.

Allen fled from the scene while Leathers was taken to the hospital. She died there on December 6, after identifying her former roommate as the shooter. Two hours earlier, Allen had been picked up by the police. They interrupted their questioning to tell Allen that Leathers had died. Allen sobbed inconsolably. Her grief is plain on the police interrogation tape. The tragic episode had all the characteristics of a domestic murder, a shooting of an intimate partner in the heat of passion. Yet unlike the vast majority of domestic killers, Allen was charged with first-degree murder on December 7.

Why would Macy's office decide to go for a capital charge in this case? Most killings where both suspect and victim were poor and African American would not be high-profile or high-priority cases. In his desire to accumulate publicity for death sentences did Macy anticipate that because the murder occurred within the context of a lesbian relationship it would draw media attention? In any event, the decision to charge Allen with capital murder took all who knew the principals by surprise—with tragic consequences for her defense.

Allen's family had engaged Robert Carpenter to represent her. Both the family and the attorney assumed that she would be charged with manslaughter and that she would be offered a plea bargain. They agreed on a fee of $5000.

As it turned out, Allen's family was only able to scrape together $800. That remained the total payment Carpenter received for representing Wanda Jean Allen in a capital trial, from her arrest to her death sentence. If Carpenter spent the usual 500 to 1000 hours preparing a capital case, he was reimbursed at the rate of $.80 to $1.60 per hour.

Once it became clear that the state intended to ask for the death penalty, Carpenter, who had no experience with capital cases, asked to be removed. Failing that, he asked that the court appoint an attorney to assist him. The prosecutor argued that Carpenter was obliged to remain as Allen's counsel to fulfill his contract with her family. Not surprisingly, the judge sided with District Attorney Macy. He not only refused to provide any legal assistance to the defense, he also refused to make any funds available for investigation. Thus Carpenter was forced to rely on Wanda Jean for information about her life experiences. Among the things she failed to mention to her attorney was the testing done when she was fifteen years old indicating that she was mentally retarded. Prosecutor Robert Macy went to trial against Allen with all the resources of Oklahoma County on his side against an inexperienced, underfunded attorney representing a client who was mentally handicapped. In addition, the state made much of Allen's sexual orientation—the fact that she and Gloria Leathers were "lesbian lovers." A defendant, whose lifestyle violated gender expectations in the Bible Belt of Oklahoma had yet another strike against her.[18] As Mogul notes, "The prosecutor's task is also greatly enhanced when a defendant belongs to a class stigmatized in society as abnormal, deviant, or pathological.[19]

Allen attempted to claim self-defense in the killing. Her story was that in the midst of the argument, Leathers had attacked her with a small garden rake and cut her face. She said Leathers had grabbed the rake again at the police station. Allen reported she ran back to her car, grabbed the gun, and shot Gloria in self-defense. Neither the police officers at the house nor Leathers' mother remembered an attack with the rake. Additionally, one police officer described putting the garden tool into the back seat of Leathers's car, where it was found after the shooting. Allen's story may have seemed implausible, but the prosecution suggested to the jury that it was the defendant's responsibility to prove self-defense. Actually, once self-defense is raised, the state must prove that the act was *not* self-defense.

The prosecutor's strategy was to shift focus from the events the day of the shooting. Instead, he tried to show Allen as a liar and as the aggressor by painting a picture of her as the "man" in the relationship. Macy minimized

Leathers's violent history, objecting to testimony that she had killed a woman ten years earlier. Yet the state introduced Allen's prior manslaughter conviction as proof of her violent character. They showed the jury several greeting cards Allen had sent to Leathers, claiming the cards constituted threats. One showed a fierce looking gorilla. Allen had signed it "Gene." At trial, Leathers's mother was permitted to offer her observations that Wanda Jean acted the male role, that she shot Gloria because the victim intended to end their relationship, and that Gloria was the passive partner. According to the Oklahoma Court of Criminal Appeals, this stereotyped description of a lesbian relationship helped the jury "understand why each party acted the way she did both during the events leading up to the shooting and the shooting itself."[20]

The jury seemed to accept the state's version of events and found Wanda Jean Allen guilty of first-degree murder on April 19, 1989. When it came time to decide her sentence, the prosecution offered two aggravating factors: Allen had a previous conviction for violence against a person and there was a probability that she would commit further violence and therefore remain a threat to society. To illustrate her violent nature, Macy showed the gorilla card again. He also stated, falsely, that Allen had shown no remorse after Gloria was killed. He employed his familiar tactic of minimizing the jury's responsibility, telling them "you do not kill Wanda Jean Allen. All you do is return a death verdict. You don't kill her and I don't kill her. All you do is return a death verdict. That's all you do."[21]

Carpenter was able to offer a long list of possible mitigating factors that should merit a sentence less than capital punishment. The mitigators included Wanda Jean's relationship with her family and her care for them, her good work habits, her nature and personality, her conduct in prison, her showing of remorse. He cited the crime, committed in the heat of passion, Allen's fear of Leathers, her emotional instability at the time of the shooting. Those factors should make the murder "not especially heinous." And although Carpenter mentioned that Wanda Jean had an emotionally deprived childhood, he did not know and could not mention that she had experienced a severe head trauma as the result of an auto accident and that she had tested as mentally retarded.

The jury took two hours to return a sentence of death. Wanda Jean Allen's appeals would not be exhausted for twelve years.

In a brief applying for post-conviction relief, Allen's appellate attorneys made four claims, two of which—ineffective assistance of counsel and mental competency— were interrelated. The development of those issues illustrates the sort of Catch-22 a disadvantaged person could face in the capital system. Allen's trial lawyer, Bob Carpenter, working on his $800 fee, had requested that the state pay for an investigator to look into Allen's history. When the court refused Carpenter's proposal, he had no resources to learn about her academic difficulties or her head injury. Therefore he did not specifically request a psychological evaluation at the time of trial. Without that, Allen could not effectively claim later that she had been incompetent to stand trial or to assist in her own defense. From the outset, Carpenter pleaded with the court for assistance, stating that he was in over his head on the case and that he could not handle a capital defense for $800. However, appellate courts use the *Strickland* standard to determine whether a defendant was denied effective assistance of counsel.[22] The defendant must prove that the lawyer's performance was defective and that counsel's failures affected the outcome of the trial. Carpenter himself admitted to his failures in representing Allen, but it is almost impossible to show that a different defense would have led the jury to reach a different verdict or a different sentence. A key piece of evidence in Allen's case before the appellate court was a psychological evaluation by clinical psychologist Dr. Dale Watson on December 1, 1995.[23] Her appeal argued that information would have influenced the jury's decision.

Watson spent fourteen hours with Wanda Jean Allen and examined all available records. Written reports revealed testing done when Allen was about fifteen years old showing her IQ as 69, the upper range of mental retardation. At the age of twelve, she had suffered a head trauma in an accident when she was hit by a truck. The injury left her unconscious for an undetermined time, at least 30 minutes, creating a definite possibility of permanent brain damage. At fourteen, Allen was stabbed in her left temple, probably accounting for persistent headaches on the left side. As early as 1975, Allen's diagnosis showed "slowness" and difficulty in academic work and an inability to cope in complex situations. Her parents were also described as "slow," her mother likely suffered from mental retardation as well as alcoholism. Several siblings manifested either retardation or developmental disabilities. She left school in the eleventh grade and worked at a variety of low-skilled jobs such as house-cleaning and restaurant service. Although Allen had enrolled in a medical assistant program, she had dropped out without completing the course. Allen's academic history became a matter of dispute because during her trial she had claimed to have a high school diploma and a certificate from the technical school. Official records showed that Allen lied on the witness stand about her education.

At the time of the 1995 examinations, Dr. Watson described Allen as "small, attractive, polite, helpful and well-groomed." Although she was attentive, "fully oriented," she was inarticulate in dealing with complex conversation and had difficulty following simple instructions. Watson found "*consistent and clear* evidence of cognitive and sensori-motor deficits and brain dysfunction" especially in the left hemisphere.[24] Allen's condition impaired her comprehension, her ability to express herself logically, her ability to analyze cause and effect. It would also affect her ability to monitor and effectively direct her behavior and to attend to visual details. Her intellectual abilities were "markedly impaired." In addition, Watson reported that Wanda Jean had little common knowledge, i.e., the name of the president, the number of weeks in a year. She could not place pictures in a sequence from left to right, but set them up from right to left. Her reading skills were in the first percentile and she had the language ability of an eight-year-old. All of those qualities were consistent with frontal lobe dysfunction.

Watson also administered an MMPI which showed Allen attempting to portray herself as unrealistically virtuous. Such responses were not abnormal among unsophisticated persons who try to create overly favorable impressions. Thus if Allen exaggerated her educational successes, such misrepresentation conformed to her test results. Rorschach tests further showed that Allen was vulnerable to becoming disorganized over everyday stressors and likely to lose control under pressure. Her thinking was disorganized, but not psychotic. Watson concluded that "*Her thinking is so overwhelmed by affect that very little organized perception or thought takes place.*" In the psychologist's view, Allen had less ability to inhibit her responses, less "free will" than the average person.

Dr. Watson claimed that the head injury and the accompanying period of unconsciousness during Allen's adolescence had been a critical factor in her psychological make-up. Such a trauma would impact a teenager's self-image and individuation, as well as the development of her psychological defenses and the management of her emotions and impulses. Some developmental options would be lost forever. Because Wanda Jean had exceptional responsibilities for her family, she enjoyed little assistance or understanding after her injury. Her parents and siblings expected her to return to "normal" and to look after them. Another child might have been provided with psychological and educational assistance after a head trauma. Wanda Jean Allen was expected to fend for herself.

All of these matters—surely mitigating factors—could have been discovered if Allen had been tested *before* her trial. Those tests would have influenced the relationship between Carpenter and his client. He would have known that Wanda Jean had difficulty in comprehending stressful situations. It is not at all unlikely that the progress and outcome of her trial would have been different. But because the trial court refused the money for testing or investigation, no jury ever heard Allen's full story.

Besides the ineffective assistance claim, Allen appealed on other grounds. The jury had not been informed that life without parole was an option. Secondly, when the state charged that her flight from the scene of the crime betrayed consciousness of guilt, they placed the burden of proving her innocence on the defendant. The state's allegation that Allen was a continuing threat to society was based on her illegal possession of a firearm, a conviction that was later overturned. The District Court denied all of Allen's claims. Their decision was affirmed by the Oklahoma Court of Criminal Appeals in December 1995.[25] The federal courts also denied her appeals.[26]

By late 2000, the only real prospect of saving Wanda Jean Allen's life was through a petition for clemency. In Oklahoma, such a request went to the five-member Pardon and Parole Board who made a recommendation to the governor. The hearing took place on December 15, 2000, at the Lexington Assessment and Rehabilitation Center. Four members of the Board were present in a room filled to capacity with 181 supporters of Allen and members of the victim's family.

The Reverend Jesse Jackson testified in favor of clemency. He emphasized that Allen suffered from a mental disability and that her offense had been a crime of passion. But he had little confidence in the openness of the process. "In that room, they heard my case [his arguments for relief] but they weren't [listening]. The politics were they had to kill her. She was sacrificed at the altar of their politics."[27] Allen's defense team also asked the Reverend Robin Meyers to argue in her behalf. They believed someone with moral authority, a minister who could "offer a second opinion when it comes to the prevailing religious assumptions," might appeal to the consciences of the Board members, all of whom were Christians. Meyers described the Sermon on the Mount where Jesus rejects "an eye for an eye" and the passages where He tells Christians to choose forgiveness seventy times seven, 490 times, over vengeance. The minister also argued that Wanda Jean had been denied due process because the jury did not hear about her mental retardation and brain injury.

Incredibly, the state of Oklahoma told the Board that Allen was *not* mentally retarded. Although they had official records to prove otherwise, they reminded the Board that during her trial Allen had claimed to have a high school diploma and a certificate as a medical assistant. How could she be retarded and brain injured if she had those credentials? The Pardon and Parole Board was faced with a choice—would they believe the defense, who argued Allen's mental disabilities, or the state, who maintained those claims were a lie? It may be that the Board members did not know that the state was misrepresenting the truth. Or it may be that they were in the habit of ignoring all evidence from a person on death row, no matter where the truth was found. One member of the Board, Currie Ballard, disposed of the claim that Allen was retarded by making a split-second diagnosis. He had a retarded brother and "I did not see those signs or any signs of mental retardation in Allen."[28]

In addition to arguing that Allen was not mentally retarded but a "fully functional adult," the state told the Board that she was a "hunter," who would kill again if she were not executed. Sandy Howard, the assistant attorney general belittled the idea that the killing was impulsive. "She is a cold-blooded murderer. She thought it out, she got the gun and she did it."

Wanda Jean Allen pleaded with the Board, "Please let me live. Please let me live." And although none of Leathers family members spoke formally in favor of execution, one of the victim's brothers piped up, "That's the same thing my sister said."[29]

With no debate or discussion among themselves, the Board members voted 3–1 to go ahead with the execution. Steve Presson, Allen's lawyer, called the Board a "kangaroo court; it's a joke." He found Ballard's comments, that poverty, race, sexual orientation, and mental retardation were not "excuses for murder," showed a "fundamental ignorance of the pardons process. If he does not think that race, poverty and mental status have a place in a clemency hearing, he has no business being on the clemency board."[30]

Although her attorneys filed a final appeal in federal court and Jesse Jackson met to plead with the governor, realistically Allen's execution was virtually certain after the Board's decision. On January 10 she was driven in secret from the Mabel Bassett Correctional Center for Women to the Oklahoma State Prison at McAlester where she was put in a holding cell next to the death chamber. At 9:15 PM on January 11, 2001, Wanda Jean Allen was pronounced dead. The "ultrashortacting barbiturate and chemical paralytic agent" had ended her life.

Why was this woman executed? She killed Gloria Leathers, but few would argue that it was the type of murder that typically results in a death sentence. She was poor. She was extraordinarily unfortunate in that the court refused to allow her adequate legal representation. They chose to accept the formality that she had an attorney, knowing full well that for $800 he could not put on an effective case. In 2003, in *Wiggins v. Smith,* the Supreme Court reversed a death sentence when court-appointed attorneys failed to conduct an investigation of their client's childhood history of abuse.[31] Perhaps if Allen had lived longer, the precedent in *Wiggins* might have made for a successful appeal.

Wanda Jean Allen was mentally retarded and that affected the outcome of her case in many ways. Not only did the state lie about her intellectual ability in the clemency hearing, but it is also unlikely that Allen was fully able to assist her attorney in developing her defense. She failed to tell him the truth about her life history. Perhaps she did not remember everything clearly or perhaps she was embarrassed to discuss her family and the injuries resulting from her accident. If Wanda Jean Allen had been on death row in 2002 when the Supreme Court held in *Atkins v. Virginia* that it was unconstitutional to execute a person with mental retardation, it is likely she would still be alive today.[32]

Oklahoma Attorney General Drew Edmondson told a reporter that "Gender is simply not relevant to the legal process." But he went on to say, "Whenever you have someone of a *different* gender or background, they do tend to draw more attention."[33] His usage suggests that women represent a gender that is "different" from the norm. If a characteristic stands out in such a way to merit the adjective "different," it must be noticeable and therefore it is unlikely to be ignored in the legal process. In Allen's case the state repeatedly used the image of Wanda Jean as the "man" in her relationship with Gloria Leathers. That hardly suggests that gender is irrelevant. Some would argue that the portrayal of the relationship and of Allen herself as "unnatural" was one of the prosecution's most effective tactics. They evoked a masculine image by claiming that Allen "hunted down" her victims. The state repeatedly produced the card signed "Gene" with the picture of the gorilla. The counter-image in the state's case was Gloria Leathers as the passive victim of Allen's violence—a picture even Leathers's mother contradicted. But as Reverend Meyers stated, "Given what we know about homophobia in this state, many people may not even consider that we are about to execute the first woman ever in Oklahoma—because they really think of her as a man."[34] Whether the jury saw Wanda Jean Allen as a man in a woman's body, or as an "unnatural" woman, or as a sinner, there is no doubt her sexual orientation had a bearing on her case. As Mogul argues, "the labeling of a woman as a lesbian often falsely brands her as a man hater, aggressive, and deviant, and thus more capable of committing a crime than a heterosexual woman."[35]

In a larger sense, gendered expectations had shaped many events in Allen's life. Because she was the eldest girl in a family beset with disadvantages, she was expected to take on responsibilities for the younger children. Given their special needs, she—despite her limitations—was thrust into an adult female role. After her head injury, instead of receiving therapy and medical treatment, because of her class and gender, she was required to carry on. Dr. Watson found that many of Allen's later problems with impulse control stemmed from that largely untreated brain injury.

The ACLU made the claim that race was also a factor in her sentencing. Citing references to Allen as aggressive and dominant, they found her trial permeated with stereotypes of both lesbians and African American women.[36] One could certainly find racial as well as gendered stereotyping in the gorilla image. Equating the defendant with a dangerous animal, whether a black widow spider, a snake, or a gorilla is often a way of dehumanizing the person and making it easier to take her life.

Shortly before her execution, Wanda Jean Allen told a reporter that many people think those on death row are monsters. Speaking of herself, Marilyn Plantz, and Lois Nadean Smith, Allen said, "We are humans. We care for other people. We feel what they are going through. Even if we are in a worse position than they are, we still focus on them." Her last words were "Father, forgive them. They know not what they do."[37]

Marilyn Kay Plantz

On August 26, 1988, at 5:15 AM, thirty-three-year-old James Earl Plantz was found dead in his pickup truck which had caught on fire at a secluded spot outside Oklahoma City. He had suffered burns and head injuries. His body was slumped behind the steering wheel. His left leg was outside the truck, with the foot flat on the ground. It appeared at first that Plantz, on his way home from working the night shift as a pressman at the *Daily Oklahoman*, had an accident. A closer look at the damage to his body suggested foul play. Police investigators determined that Plantz had been murdered and, typically, his wife Marilyn was a major suspect. She was arrested three days later.

At first, Marilyn Plantz denied she had anything to do with her husband's death. She affected shock, and even claimed they had a "perfect marriage."[38] Meanwhile, two eighteen-year-olds, William Clifford Bryson and Clinton McKimble were bragging to friends that they had killed Jim Plantz by beating him with baseball bats and setting his truck on fire. Stories that Marilyn

Plantz and Bryson had a romantic relationship gave rise to one type of theory of the crime—they had plotted to kill her husband to a) run away together; b) collect his life insurance; or c) both of the above. Although from the first, Bryson told the authorities that he had killed Plantz to punish him for abusing Marilyn, that part of the story was omitted from the prosecution's case. It was obvious that Marilyn had not physically killed her husband, but District Attorney Robert Macy chose to portray her as the mastermind, claiming she promised to pay the young men for the crime. As the state developed its case, she "engineered" or "orchestrated" the murder—not because she was the victim of abuse but for $300,000 in insurance money. This version of "murder for hire" meant that she, along with Bryson and McKimble, could be charged with capital murder. The case shows startling similarities to the case of Teresa Lewis in Virginia which the state also presented as murder for hire.

Although three people were charged with capital murder, only two were tried and sentenced to death. About two months after the arrests, McKimble pleaded guilty to murder and agreed to a life sentence. In exchange, he testified against Marilyn Plantz and Bryson. His testimony, along with statements from forensic chemist Joyce Gilchrist, became the essential case for the prosecution.

According to McKimble, Marilyn Plantz had approached him and Bryson, hoping to enlist their assistance in murdering her husband.[39] McKimble claimed that at first he rejected her offer of $45,000, but later reconsidered and agreed to participate. Several plans to kill Jim Plantz went awry. In fact, even the appellate court's dry account of the mishaps prior to the murder seems more like the Three Stooges than the Three Monsters. Bryson and McKimble stole a car, planning to bump Plantz's truck from behind and force him off the road. When the victim left his pickup, the two assailants would jump on him and beat him with baseball bats. That scheme failed when Bryson and McKimble lost Plantz in traffic. It is not clear why they did not try the plan on another night. A second plot involved shooting Plantz with a gun that Marilyn gave Bryson. However, Bryson pawned the gun instead. Several days later, Bryson and Marilyn Plantz allegedly enlisted an additional accomplice, Roderick Farris, to help them. (Farris had earlier turned down $45,000 to kill Plantz, but now agreed to do it for $10,000.) According to testimony, the four sat around the Plantz home, eating hamburgers and watching television, waiting to jump Jim Plantz when he got home from work. Someone (unidentified) came to the front door, McKimble picked up a knife and Bryson grabbed a hammer. When the person at the door turned out to be someone other than the targeted Plantz, apparently they gave up their plan for that evening. Farris was arrested later that night on an unrelated charge.

Two days later, Bryson and McKimble picked up Marilyn Plantz from work. She bought them some beer and cocaine, left them in her living room, and went to bed at 10:30 PM. Her two children were sleeping in their rooms. Bryson and McKimble fell asleep or passed out but were awakened when Jim Plantz came in whistling and carrying a bag of groceries. The two assailants hit him repeatedly, bashing in his head with baseball bats. They finally carried him outside and placed him near his truck. At that point, Marilyn came out with the keys to the pickup and allegedly commented that the injuries did not look like an accident. The men said she told them to "burn him." They loaded Plantz into the truck; McKimble followed in Marilyn's car to a deserted spot. There McKimble put a rag in the truck's gas tank and lit it. When the truck failed to catch on fire, Bryson poured gasoline over Plantz and around the pickup's cab, and then lit them on fire. When the men returned to her home, Marilyn was cleaning up the blood.

Did Marilyn Plantz commit capital murder? She apparently participated in several inept plots to take her husband's life. It is likely she knew the beating was taking place but kept her distance. McKimble testified that during the assault the victim called out to Marilyn for help but she did not respond. She did provide the keys and her car to help dispose of the body. She cleaned up blood in her home. Did she do these things because she wanted Plantz's insurance or because she wanted to escape from an abusive marriage? Like Betty Lou Beets, Marilyn Plantz claimed she was not aware that her husband had a sizeable life insurance policy. Like Karla Faye Tucker and Teresa Lewis, Marilyn Plantz was executed while an accomplice was able to trade his testimony for a plea bargain. It is impossible to deny that Jim Plantz died a painful and gruesome death. It is possible to look beyond greed and lust to find an explanation for Marilyn Plantz's role in the crime. But like each of the women in this study, Plantz's story is made up of a series of specific factors that came together and resulted in her execution.

Robert Macy charged capital murder on the grounds that Bryson and Plantz killed for monetary gain and that the crime was "heinous, atrocious, and cruel." Plantz was poor and needed to rely on an underpaid and underresourced court-appointed lawyer. Her husband had worked for the *Daily Oklahoman*, the media outlet most uncritical in support of District Attorney Macy. She, a married white woman, had an affair with a young black man, William Bryson. All of those factors placed her in a vulnerable position when she was charged with killing a man who was portrayed by the prosecutor and the newspaper as the epitome of the hard-working, clean-living husband and father.

The state chose to try Marilyn Plantz and William Clifford Bryson together, although the attorneys for both defendants objected. The court would not sever their trials unless the defenses were "mutually antagonistic and inconsistent."[40] Although Bryson claimed that Marilyn had lured him into the crime and she claimed she was uninvolved, apparently the court did not find those claims sufficiently contradictory. The accused faced the impossible task of proving that their joint trial prejudiced the outcome. How could anyone ever know whether it had or not? One could, however, imagine that simply by looking over at the defense table, the jurors were constantly reminded that a white woman in her late twenties had a romantic and sexual relationship with a much younger black man. During voir dire, Bryson's attorney had raised that issue himself by asking potential jurors, "Doesn't it make you wonder what she's doing with an 18-year old black kid?" If one of the factors that sets women sufficiently apart to be condemned to death is a failure to meet gendered expectations, the prosecution placed Plantz on display in that position. She was guilty of infidelity and she crossed racial and age boundaries in the process.

Her attorney was denied funds to conduct an investigation or to engage a mental health expert to evaluate Plantz. As in Wanda Jean Allen's case, the trial court seemed to make every effort to insure a victory for the prosecution by providing no resources to the defense. And, as in Allen's case, a variety of mitigating evidence surfaced during the appellate process. As Allen might not have volunteered information about her mental deficiencies, Plantz did not volunteer information about her earlier experiences of physical, sexual, and psychological abuse. When it came to light that Marilyn had been molested by her brother, beaten and intimidated by her father, and raped by Jim Plantz at the age of fifteen, the courts determined that these events were "remote and insufficient mitigating evidence." Her attorney's failure to disclose those facts at trial was judged to have no effect on the outcome. Yet, would not the fact that Jim Plantz initiated his relationship with Marilyn by raping her have substantiated her claims of ongoing abuse in their marriage and called into question the picture of him as the perfect husband?

Psychologist Dr. Pamela Fisher examined Marilyn Plantz in 1995, seven years after the murder of Jim Plantz. Dr. Fisher found that Marilyn had an IQ of 76, "borderline intelligence" with limited intellectual functioning. Because of those deficiencies, along with Marilyn's submissive, dependent personality and her disorganized thought processes, it was unlikely that she could have "engineered" a scheme to murder her husband. In addition, because Jim Plantz dominated his wife and considered her "stupid and inferior," it was unlikely that he shared details of his life insurance with her. Dr. Fisher's analysis directly contradicted the prosecution's version of events. Rather than the ideal family, Fisher uncovered a patriarchal home where Marilyn occupied a distinctly subordinate position. Yet the psychologist's report was never allowed into the official record, as the appellate courts determined that it was "contrary to the weight of the evidence." The weight of the evidence was mostly the testimony of McKimble, who traded Bryson's and Marilyn Plantz's lives to save his own.

There were also issues about the jury who found Plantz and Bryson guilty and sentenced them to death. Ordinarily in Oklahoma, a defendant would be permitted nine peremptory challenges to prospective jurors. He or she could have nine possibly unsympathetic persons excused without giving a reason. Plantz and Bryson requested nine peremptories each. The court required them to share the nine challenges—apparently giving each one the opportunity to remove 4 ½ jurors. In addition, the judge rejected a request to excuse one juror who expressed the opinion that the state was too lax with the death penalty and another who had formerly worked with the judge's sister. Plantz and Bryson were forced to use one of their peremptory challenges to excuse a juror who had formerly worked with the victim's father and who had attended Jim Plantz's funeral "out of respect for his father." The judge had refused to excuse that juror for cause, apparently believing that she was unprejudiced.

Joyce Gilchrist made an appearance at Marilyn Plantz's trial. Although later when she was under fire, the state would minimize the importance of her testimony, Gilchrist offered evidence that the blood and fibers found on Jim Plantz's body could be connected with evidence in the Plantz home. The prosecution argued that such evidence, along with her attempt to clean up the blood in the hallway, proved Marilyn's complicity in the crime. In fact it had little to do with her actual role in the events.

The jury took only three hours to find Marilyn Plantz and William Bryson guilty of murder. They spent a bit longer, five hours, deciding to sentence both to death, along with 125 years in prison for conspiracy and 15 years for burning the truck. They could have served a longer sentence for damaging a vehicle than McKimble did for his part in the murder.

All of Marilyn Plantz's appeals to state and federal courts failed. In mid-April 2001, she pleaded with the State Pardon and Parole Board to spare her life. Earlier Plantz had indicated that she would forego the plea for clemency and accept her execution. However, in the year before she was put to death, Marilyn reconciled with her daughter Trina and reestablished contact with her son Chris. They apparently gave her the will to fight for her life. Plantz told a reporter that her time with her daughter was given over to recalling their lives together. "My heart aches for my children. I want them to have the most successful life they deserve. Both me and their father want them to have that. I'm very proud of them and always have been. And their dad would be proud."

Marilyn expressed regret that she had left high school without graduating and married too young. She encouraged other women prisoners to get an education. "I ... never had the opportunity to know who I am or what I wanted in life." Plantz said she accepted responsibility for her actions, "A tragedy took place in my life and I'm not trying to excuse that or justify that in any way. I had an association with bad people. You don't have to be a bad person to wind up in this situation." She cited her own lack of maturity, "I started out young and that may have had a lot to do with it. Everyone has problems in their marriage but you don't realize a lot of things or miss it until it's gone."

The statements are actually rather ambiguous. Perhaps Marilyn meant if she had more options she would not have married Plantz but could have been more independent. If he was an abuser, as she and her sisters testified, surely he was part of the tragedy and one of the bad people. But she should have realized that there were other ways than sex, drugs, and murder to move her life forward. Or perhaps she was indicating that everything would have been fine if she had not gotten involved with Bryson and McKimble.

While in prison, Plantz converted to Christianity and, along with Wanda Jean Allen and Nadean Smith, she was baptized in 2000. "It's only by the grace of God I've made it this far. I cannot make people forgive me. But you have to ask for forgiveness to be forgiven."[41]

Her testimony before the Board focused on her wish to live for her children. "Now I have a reason to live," Plantz said. She said she was truly sorry for what she had done and pleaded with the governor to spare her life. Her daughter, Trina Plantz Wells sobbed throughout the hearing. Trina had videotaped a statement which was played for the Board, "My father's gone and we need a mom, whether or not she is in prison. We need to have a relationship with her. I really don't want my mom to die—that is my hope. I've had thirteen years to think about it."[42] Although Chris Plantz did not speak at Marilyn's hearing, his sister indicated that he was ready to forgive his mother.[43] Plantz's appellate attorney Scott Braden also urged that she be allowed to live to continue the healing process with her family. "The best interest in this for the children is to let Marilyn Plantz live." He also noted that she had been a model prisoner and had embraced Christianity. Braden raised the question of what purpose her execution would serve. For its part, the state focused on the crime itself, calling it "calculated." Jim Plantz's sister and brother called for Marilyn's execution. "Did she show any mercy when he was broken and being beaten senseless on the floor?"[44]

Marilyn's supporters also asked that Governor Keating suspend the execution because Joyce Gilchrist had provided some of the evidence against her. As Plantz's date with the death chamber approached, questions about Gilchrist's investigations led the state to suspend the execution dates of twelve inmates because she had testified in their cases. But the governor claimed to be confident that the eleven other people executed partly on Gilchrist's evidence, including Marilyn Plantz, were not innocent. A spokesman for the governor said Keating demanded "legal and moral certainty" of guilt before allowing an execution. In the case of Marilyn Plantz, that certainty was based on the word of an accomplice who bargained for his own life and Plantz's apology.[45] By apologizing to Plantz's family, Marilyn, in effect, gave the governor an excuse for killing her.

Marilyn Plantz was put to death on May 1, 2001. Each "side" chose representatives to observe her execution. Three of her cousins, several spiritual advisors, her attorney and an investigator were Marilyn's witnesses. She spoke before the fatal injection. "I want to tell all of my family that I love them very much, especially Trina and Chris. What God has given me is love and I have overcome the world." Her children were not present to see their mother make "several snorting sounds and then [fall] quiet." After Marilyn "fell quiet," Jim Plantz's sister said she was feeling better, "because now we can get closure and get this behind us." His brother expressed sympathy for Trina and Chris but said "what had to be done, had to be done." He seemed surprised that Chris, who had recently visited with his mother for the first time in thirteen years, was "taking it pretty hard."[46]

Two weeks before Marilyn Plantz was executed a woman in Payne County, Oklahoma, was given ten years in prison for conspiring with her boyfriend who shot her husband in their home. What accounts for the inconsistency, the arbitrary decisions, and the capriciousness that sentences one person to lethal injection and another to a decade of incarceration? Why was Marilyn Plantz one of the "wretched sisters" chosen for capital punishment?

She had the bad luck of living in Bob Macy's jurisdiction and of being involved in the murder of a man who worked for the avidly pro-prosecution

Daily Oklahoman. The paper did its best to insure that its former employee's killers were punished to the fullest extent of the law. An article published in October 1996 entitled "Deadly Betrayal: Suburban Housewife Led a Sordid Double Life" provides an example of the *Oklahoman*'s version of the story.[47] In this narrative, Marilyn was totally evil—manipulative, greedy, deceitful, and sexually insatiable—the absolute reverse of a woman deserving of respect and sympathy. Jim, on the other hand, was the perfectly innocent victim. Max Haines, the article's author, describes the Plantes' "pleasant, comfortable lifestyle," in a middle-class suburb where Jim flipped burgers on the grill and cavorted with the children. Jim's mistake was trusting his wife implicitly because she was "one of those rare individuals without conscience or feelings" who lived only for herself. In the author's account, when Jim drove off to work in his pickup, Marilyn dumped her children with a babysitter and headed off to a park "where young black boys hung out and crack cocaine was the drug of choice." No one suspected that she was out to find youthful sex in sleazy motels with "trim young men," to whom she gave cash and drugs. According to Haines, once Marilyn had chosen "Cliff" Bryson, she and the youth drove around in her sporty Camaro. She provided him with money, "enough rock cocaine to keep him high most of the time and all the sex he could handle." Although she also slept with Clint McKimble, she and Bryson plotted to murder Jim Plantz so they could run away to Texas for more sex and crack.

In this version of events, Marilyn "hatched a diabolical scheme" but lived a double life as a loving wife and mother. On the night when Plantz was killed, Haines reported that she bought drugs for both men and had sex with both while waiting for her husband to come home. When he arrived, Marilyn "the housewife who was so considerate of her husband, extracted two baseball bats from the hall closet and gave them to her accomplices." As they hit him thirty times with bats, Jim's bloody key ring flew out of his hand. Although "sensitive Marilyn" hid in the bedroom during the attack, after the boys left (to follow her instructions and burn her husband), she tossed the key ring into a drawer under her lingerie.

Perhaps the most imaginative part of the article describes Plantz's death. "As the flames engulfed him, Jim managed to open the door of the vehicle before slumping back onto the seat. The two young men looked on entranced and then drove away in the Camero." If readers believed that description, it is no wonder they found the murder "heinous, atrocious, and cruel." But even McKimble's statement—the only actual reference to seeing Plantz appear to "rise up in his seat"—is inconsistent with the horror of the *Oklahoman*'s depiction.

Marilyn, meanwhile, had been a "busy girl" cleaning the carpet where Plantz had been assaulted. At 6:30 AM she reported her husband missing and at 9:00 AM she went to Wal-Mart and bought a throw rug for $44.96 to cover the bloodstains. The exactness of such a trivial piece of information gives the article an appearance of accuracy, even though major details, such as the circumstances of Plantz's death or the abusive nature of his relationship with Marilyn are distorted or omitted. The article mentions that detectives returned with a warrant, searched the Plantz home and found the bloodstains and the bloody key ring. It does not mention that Joyce Gilchrist matched them with the victim.

Clearly this is one of the newspaper's more colorful efforts to demonize persons on death row. Marilyn Plantz appears to be a sex-crazed, hard-hearted, money-hungry, irresponsible, deceitful, bad mother. It is almost impossible to think of a portrait less likely to draw sympathy to a woman. And as students of the death penalty know, demonizing and dehumanizing the person to be executed makes taking their life seem beneficial to the community.

Completely absent from the *Oklahoman* is the testimony of Marilyn Plantz's sisters and psychologist about the abuse she suffered during her marriage. Bryson repeatedly stated that the reason he killed Plantz was because he beat Marilyn, because Bryson hated to see her with the black eyes her husband gave her. Jim Plantz allegedly raped Marilyn when she was underage—hardly a foundation on which to build a life together.

There were two versions then of the Plantz family with a "double life." The newspaper claimed that Marilyn trolled for men and drugs. Marilyn's supporters described her as a victim of abuse. It is impossible to know exactly what went on behind the façade of that "perfect marriage." It is likely, however, that if Marilyn had decent representation, a psychological examination at the time of her trial, and an investigation into her history, the allegations of abuse could have been raised as part of a coherent defense strategy.

What went wrong for Marilyn Plantz? Why did the state of Oklahoma end her life with a lethal dose of drugs? Most likely, she was involved to some extent with the plans to kill her husband. The state was not able to prove, but only to assert a motive, that she was implicated because she was interested in his insurance benefits. A competent defense lawyer would have raised the issue of domestic abuse, both as an alternative motive for the crime (thus removing the aggravator, murder for remuneration), and as a mitigating factor. An alternative theory of the crime, coupled with testimony from experts who understood battered women, could have had a major impact on the outcome.

But Marilyn had a cut-rate trial, and was forced to split it with Bryson. It was to the state's advantage to try them together—not only did it save money for the taxpayers, it was possible for District Attorney Macy constantly to remind the jury, without words, that Marilyn Plantz had transgressed racial boundaries. Any sympathy that might have related to her gender was nullified by the violation of her marital vows with a young, black man. Given the flare for the dramatic in Oklahoma City criminal trials, it is quite feasible that Macy got much more mileage out of putting Marilyn Plantz and Clifford Bryson on trial than if he had tried the two real killers, Bryson and McKimble. The latter, who actually beat and burned Jim Plantz, was rewarded by a sentence of life with the possibility of parole.

Marilyn Plantz had the misfortune of being charged with murder while the state of Oklahoma was swept up in a frenzy of capital punishment. The state had never executed a woman until 2001, but it sent Plantz to the death chamber only four and a half months after Wanda Jean Allen died there. Lois Nadean Smith followed six months later.

Lois Nadean Smith

Press reports of Smith's case inevitably included a reference to a nickname she allegedly "earned" in high school, "Mean Nadean." Oddly enough, not a single article indicated how she "earned" the name. One might suggest that it was the same process—rhyming—by which people became known as "Tall Paul" or "Fat Pat." But in the newspapers, before and after her trial, Lois Nadean Smith was dubbed "mean." Such a designation hardly made her a sympathetic defendant.

Like Wanda Jean Allen and Marilyn Plantz, Nadean Smith was involved in some way in a brutal murder. Cindy Baillee, a former girlfriend and presumptive drug-dealing colleague of Smith's son Greg, was choked, stabbed, and shot. Both mother and son participated in the crime. According to the state of Oklahoma, Nadean Smith was the "mastermind" and the trigger woman. She was sentenced to death. Greg received life in prison.

Smith was not tried in Oklahoma City but at Sallisaw in Sequoyah County, a small town in the vast rural eastern part of the state. Although Robert Macy was not the prosecutor, her case has several elements in common with the others in Oklahoma. The all-purpose aggravator "heinous, atrocious, and cruel" was raised to justify a charge of capital murder. Kenneth Ede, a chemist employed by the state, lied about his qualifications and testified falsely about blood splatters that placed Nadean Smith as the shooter. Although his errors were later revealed and admitted by the state, appeals courts found there was sufficient evidence to find Smith guilty without Ede's testimony. In fact, his statements and testimony by Teresa Baker, the person Smith claimed was the actual killer, were the major elements in the prosecution's case.

On July 4, 1982, Teresa Baker, Nadean, and Greg Smith drove to a motel in Tahlequah, Oklahoma, where they picked up Cindy Baillee, who had been dropped off there the night before by Greg Smith.[48] Rumors had reached Nadean that Baillee was involved in a plot to kill her son, either because of a bad drug deal or out of jealousy. Several nights without sleep, as well as heavy indulgence in alcohol and a variety of drugs probably fueled Nadean's paranoia. In the car when Baillee denied any threats to Greg, Nadean grabbed her around the neck, choked her, and stabbed her in the neck with a knife from Baillee's purse. Greg, who was driving, had retrieved the knife from the purse and also pulled a gun on Baillee and told her not to lie to his mother. He said if she hurt his mother, he would shoot her and think nothing about it. For some reason, the group drove to the home where Jim Smith, Nadean's former husband and Greg's father lived with his current wife, Robyn. Greg carried the gun into the house. Apparently anticipating bloodshed, he asked Robyn to get a garbage bag for dirty clothes and informed her that Jim would not be involved in killing Baillee. Witnesses claimed that Nadean forced Baillee to sit in a recliner chair and taunted her with the gun. She then fired a shot close to the victim's head, followed by several other shots that caused Baillee to fall to the floor. While Greg reloaded the gun, Smith allegedly "jumped on the victim's neck," then fired five more shots into the victim's body after her son told her to "finish it off." The autopsy showed that Baillee had been shot five times in the chest, twice in the head, and once in the back.

Robyn stated that she left the house soon after the others arrived. Jim Smith said he was in the bathroom and stayed there after Nadean threatened him with the gun. Teresa Baker claimed she was in a back room with Greg most of the time, except, apparently, when Greg left to reload the gun. Why none of them attempted to call the police or to help Cindy Baillee is never mentioned. At one point, two neighbor men drove up and asked for Jim. Greg answered the door and said Jim was out to "divert attention from what was transpiring inside the house." Someone did call the police to report a disturbance, but Jim sent the officers away, saying everything had been settled. Police returned later in the morning after another call from a neighbor. They found the house clean and quiet, with no one inside except the victim's body.[49] Lois Nadean Smith and Greg Smith were arrested. Soon after, both were charged with murder.

Monte Strout, an attorney with less than two years' experience, had never handled a capital case. Nadean Smith hired him to represent her. Why? Because he had represented Greg previously and because both of the men liked horses. The judge later appointed Strout to defend Greg as well. The two Smiths were tried separately, with Nadean's trial first. Although Strout contacted John Q. Adams, a Sallisaw attorney who had been in practice for over thirty years to serve as co-counsel, the older lawyer's expertise was never used at trial. According to Adams, Strout met with Nadean for only one two-hour session before her trial, he had no alternative theory of the crime to challenge the prosecution's narrative, and he made no effort to educate himself on the subject of blood evidence. In Smith's appellate brief, Adams listed other things Strout did *not* do. He made no effort to check on a prior relationship between the witness Teresa Baker and Donny Baker, who worked in the prosecutor's office; no effort to learn of any deals in exchange for Teresa Baker's testimony; no motion for a change of venue; no evaluation of Nadean Smith's psychological or mental health; no strategy for the sentencing phase; no effort to get a continuance, although the trial began two weeks before Christmas and the jury was sequestered; no effort to find out the prosecution's strategy for the sentencing phase; no preparation of mitigating evidence; no effort to "humanize Nadean."[50]

Strout intended to but forgot to file a motion for a change of venue, although there was a heated contest for district attorney of Sequoyah County in the fall of 1982 and a great deal of pretrial publicity as Nadean's trial approached. When 79 prospective jurors were questioned, 63 had knowledge of the case, 35—including 6 of those actually seated—knew one or more of the participants. Strout remembered to file for a change of venue in Greg's trial. It was moved fifty miles away to Muskogee.

In her appeals, Smith argued that she had been denied effective assistance of counsel at trial because Strout had a conflict of interest in representing both her and Greg. She claimed that Strout failed to develop the idea that Greg manipulated her maternal instincts to get her to kill Baillee. Her lawyer did not offer any evidence to suggest Greg's culpability, therefore allowing the state to assert that Smith was "the embodiment of maniacal evil."[51] Nadean argued that Strout knew she would sacrifice her life to protect Greg, and therefore made her the "fall guy" by his inept defense. Six months later at Greg's trial, Strout told the jury that Nadean alone had planned and carried out the murder. He described his former client, the woman whom he had "defended" when her life was at stake, as maniacal and aggressive, a person of hatred who was popping pills and "became the devil herself." Strout provided the sort of caricature that prosecutors love. Nadean could be viewed as inhuman, a devil, and therefore someone who ought not to live.[52]

While the prosecution made every effort to portray "mean Nadean" as a heartless murderer, her lawyer had failed to develop an alternative theory of the crime. Avoiding the idea that Greg was an architect of the murder, at trial Smith claimed that Teresa Baker had been the killer. Baker, who had made a deal with the prosecution in exchange for her testimony, placed all the blame on Nadean. Strout, in his closing statement, left his client high and dry. Teresa didn't do it, he argued. Nadean didn't do it. Drugs did it. By leaving Nadean without a motive (protecting her son), she could fit the prosecution's description—a demon who didn't need a reason to kill and could be executed without a qualm.

The prosecutor's closing argument made just such a point through the heavy-handed use of a series of denials. The state, District Attorney Michael Daffin stated, was not trying to say that Smith was "not a fit mother, we are not contending that she should not have had her children, we are not contending that she is a drunk or that she frequents bars, we are not contending that she is evil or wicked because James Gregory Smith dropped out of school in the ninth grade."[53] Emphasizing that Nadean was not a typical compliant woman but aggressive and controlling, he said she "got on a rampage." No one helped Cindy Baillee that morning because "what Nadine (sic) wants, Nadine gets. Nobody interferes with Nadine." Daffin accomplished exactly what prosecutors seeking the death penalty against a female defendant try to do—he made her an "unnatural" woman. Stripped of her maternal role and empathy for others, she became a raging tyrant who forced cowering friends and family to conform to her evil designs. Her own defense attorney, choosing not to explain that she was protecting her son, blamed the crime on the demons rum and drugs. Not surprisingly, the jury chose to punish the "demon" Nadean.

In addition to the failures of her trial counsel, in her initial appeal Smith was assigned an appellate attorney by the state of Oklahoma. This assignment is critical, because issues must be raised in the initial appeal or, generally, they cannot be brought up in later pleadings. Elaine Meek, months out of law school, was Smith's new lawyer. Meek was based in Oklahoma City. She was given no time or money to visit Sallisaw, the town where the trial took place, no money for long-distance phone calls, and no resources other than the trial record to build arguments for the appeal. Her hands were tied by her employer, the state of Oklahoma, which wanted Smith's conviction and sentence upheld. They succeeded. On October 28, 1986, the Oklahoma Court of Criminal Appeals denied Smith's inadequate appeal put together with the skimpy resources allotted to Meeks.[54] It was not until Gregory Piche from Denver, Colorado, took over Smith's post-conviction appeals that she had a proper advocate. By then, of course, it was too late to save her life.

With an eerie similarity to the story of Joyce Gilchrist's faulty forensic evidence in Oklahoma City, Kenneth Ede, an unqualified chemist from the Oklahoma State Bureau of Investigation (OSBI), testified that blood stains on a blouse proved that Nadean Smith shot Cindy Baillee. His version of events bolstered Teresa Baker's story, but it contained outright factual errors. The most egregious falsity was that blood on the back of Smith's blouse had soaked through from the front. Other experts who examined the garment found that the blood would have splattered onto someone standing *next to or behind* the victim. If that were true, Nadean Smith could not have shot Cindy Baillee head on and the entire prosecution story, related by Teresa Baker could not be true. In her post-conviction appeal, Smith alleged that the state knew that Ede was unqualified, that they should have known that he lied about his credentials, and that therefore, the prosecution was responsible for the errors in his testimony. Incredibly but not surprisingly, the Tenth Circuit Court of Appeals found that Ede's testimony was "harmless error," and that the jury would have found Smith guilty anyway. But the other evidence that she killed Baillee came from Teresa Baker, who said Smith shot the victim from the front. If the shirt contradicted that, where was the proof that Smith committed the murder?

There seems little doubt that Smith was deeply involved in the abduction and death of Cindy Baillee. Several things are doubtful, however. Who "orchestrated" the crime and why? Who actually fired the fatal shots? Did Lois Nadean Smith receive a fair trial and an appropriate sentence?

Although there are no definite answers to the first two questions, it seems that Greg Smith was at least as guilty as his mother. If, as she testified in her statement to the police, Teresa Baker knew that Baillee had arranged to have both Baker and Greg Smith killed, the two of them had a motive to eliminate her. After her deal with the prosecutor, Baker testified in court that she didn't know of any plot to kill them. That change in the story made the crime seem motiveless and Nadean's actions all the more "heinous, atrocious, and cruel." In his trial, the state charged that Greg had the gun in the car and brought it into the house. He told his mother to "Finish her off." But Nadean told her attorney "above all else, you've got to save Greg."[55] Apparently, Strout took that advice to heart and saved Greg, while sacrificing Nadean.

Her trial was marked by questionable strategy, unfortunate rulings, and bad decisions. She hired Strout to represent her. The judge then appointed him to represent Greg as well. There is clear evidence of a conflict of interest. Ede's testimony had the status of scientific "truth." Juries often believe that the forensic evidence does not lie. But, of course, forensic experts can and sometimes do lie—as Ede did in Smith's case. In the sentencing phase of the trial, Strout did not present evidence that Smith was impaired by drugs and alcohol. He later defended that decision by saying that Nadean did not want her parents, who were in the courtroom, to hear about her substance abuse. Yet information about her drinking and drugs had already been mentioned in the guilt phase of the trial. It is unlikely her parents would have been shocked to hear it raised in mitigation. Nor did her attorney tell the jury that Smith had suffered an organic brain injury from an automobile accident in 1964. A psychological examination conducted after Smith's conviction indicated that the injury correlated with impulsivity and the inability to restrain behavior in adverse circumstances. According to the medical examination, Smith's reactions were "not the same as a normal person." Her records showed an unstable, insecure woman, not a violent beast.[56]

Contrary to the prosecutor's statement at trial, Smith's maternal instincts may have been misguided, but they were intensely powerful. It seems incontrovertible that whatever her role in the murder of Cindy Baillee, it was motivated by a desire to protect her son. Her interpretation of her role as a mother took over her life and led to her downfall. And, opposite to the prosecutor's portrayal of Smith as controlling and dominant, she had a history as a victim of domestic abuse. While she was married to Jim Smith, Nadean worked full time and provided for the children. Jim was an alcoholic and hit her often, once even breaking her leg during a beating.[57] Without domestic violence, financial struggles, brain damage, and alcohol, would Lois Nadean Smith have interpreted her maternal responsibilities to include participating in murderous revenge against a young woman who threatened her son? Why, as the National Coalition to Abolish the Death Penalty asked, did the state of Oklahoma rush to execute a sixty-one- year-old woman who posed so little threat to society?[58] As Smith argued in her post-conviction appeal, it was intolerable to execute someone "convicted and sentenced through foul play by state officers, [and] affirmed on appeal due to the inexperience and inadequate training of her appellate public defender."[59] And, one might add, subject to the geographical and chronological lottery of being in a state where the machinery of death was operating at peak efficiency.

Three in 2001

Were Wanda Jean Allen, Marilyn Plantz, and Nadean Smith the "worst of the worst"? Were they people who threatened society so much that the only safeguard was to put them to death? Or were they women who lacked the resources to afford a level playing field when prosecutors charged them with capital murder? It could be argued that not one of them had a fair trial—Allen with her $800 defense, Plantz with her shared jury, and Smith with her shared lawyer. All were targets of ambitious prosecutors and two were convicted partly on bogus scientific evidence. In each case significant mitigating factors were hidden or ignored. Allen suffered from mental retardation as did Plantz, Smith had suffered a major head injury. All three women engaged in disorganized thinking. Yet prosecutors portrayed them as "masterminds," as cold-blooded, premeditated murderers who might well kill again. Both Smith and Plantz had lived for years in abusive marriages, yet the failure of the state to provide psychological evaluations before trial meant this experience would not be factored in when they were judged. None of the Oklahoma Three fit the rigid mold of the ideal woman. Allen was a lesbian, Plantz had an affair with a younger man of a different race, and Smith carried her maternal protectiveness far beyond social expectations. Juries apparently believed the caricatures—Allen the gorilla, Plantz the greedy slut, and "mean Nadean," the demon. The lives of gorillas, sluts, and devils are expendable.

Endnotes

1. Amnesty International, "Old Habits Die Hard: The Death Penalty in Oklahoma," April 26, 2001, at www.amnesty.org/library
2. Ibid.
3. Mark Fuhrman, *Death and Justice: An Expose of Oklahoma's Death Row Machine* (New York: Harper Collins, 2003), 235.
4. Ibid., 251.
5. Ibid., 31.
6. Ibid., 29.
7. Ibid., 59.
8. Amnesty International, "Old Habits Die Hard."
9. Ibid., Fuhrman, *Death and Justice*, 81.
10. Amnesty International, "Old Habits Die Hard."
11. Fuhrman, *Death and Justice*, 88.
12. Ibid., 94–101.
13. Ibid., 103, 109.

14. Ibid., 216.
15. Unless otherwise noted, documents concerning the case of Wanda Jean Allen were located at the Oklahoma County District Court, Oklahoma City, Oklahoma.
16. Much of Allen's personal history is contained in a report by psychiatrist Dale J. Watson in January 1995.
17. Kathleen A. O'Shea, *Women and the Death Penalty in the United States, 1900–1998* (Westport, Connecticut: Praeger, 1999), 296.
18. See American Civil Liberties Union, *The Forgotten Population: A Look at Death Row in the United States through the Experiences of Women* (Washington, D.C.: 2004), 22–23 for a summary of Allen's case. See also Janice L. Kopec, "Avoiding a Death Sentence in the American Legal System: Get a Woman to Do It," *Washington and Lee Capital Defense Journal* 15 (Spring 2003), 362.
19. Joey L. Mogul, "Equality: The Dykier, the Butcher, the Better: The State's Use of Homophobia and Sexism to Execute Women in the United States," *New York City Law Review* 8:2 (Fall 2005), 475.
20. *Allen v. State*, February 15, 1994.
21. Amnesty International, "Old Habits Die Hard."
22. *Strickland v. Washington*, 466 US 668 (1984).
23. Dr. Watson's report is included with the brief for post-conviction relief, filed January 20, 1995. Denied December 27, 1995.
24. Italics in original.
25. *Allen v. State*, 1995 OK CR 78, 909 P. 2nd. 836.
26. *Allen v. Massie*, 2000 10 Cir 43, 236 F. 3rd. 1243.
27. Jesse L. Jackson, Sr., Jesse L. Jackson, Jr., and Bruce Shapiro, *Legal Lynching: The Death Penalty and America's Future* (New York: The New Press, 2001), xi–xii. Peter Hartlaub, "Real Life Drama on Death Row," *San Francisco Chronicle*, March 16, 2002.
28. APB News at www.ccadp.org/wandajeanallen-new
29. *The Oklahoman*, quoted at Ibid.
30. APB News at Ibid.
31. *Wiggins v. Smith*, 539 U.S. 510 (2003).
32. *Atkins v. Virginia*, 536 U.S. 304 (2002).
33. Tamie Ross, "Oklahoma May Soon Execute Woman for Killing," *The Daily Oklahoman*, February 2, 1999.
34. Draft sermon at Mayflower Church, December 3, 2000, at www.ccadp.org/wandajeanallen-killing
35. Mogul, "Equality: The Dykier, the Butcher, the Better," 484.
36. Letter from American Civil Liberties Union to Pardon and Parole Board, January 3, 2001, at www.aclu.org.news
37. Barbara Hoberock, "Woman's Execution Nears," *Tulsa World*, October 22, 2000, at www.ccadp.org/wandajeanallen-killing ; Lynn Sissons and Robert Peebles, "Wanda Allen Executed January 11, 2001 at www.dpio.org
38. "Marilyn Plantz," at www.dpio.org/inmates/Plantz,Marilyn
39. Much of the account of the plot to kill Jim Plantz comes from the facts related in Bryson's appeal 1944 OK CR 32, 876 P 2nd. 240.

40. In the absence of transcripts, most of the information about Plantz's trial comes from the opinion of the 10th Circuit Court of Appeals, *Plantz v. Massie*, 2000 10 Cir 731, 216 F. 3d 1088. See also Marilyn Plantz Clemency Letter, April 19, 2001, at www.aclu.org/news

41. Ginnie Graham, "Killer Feels Sad for Children," *Tulsa World*, April 30, 2001.

42. Robert Peebles, "Marilyn Plantz," www.dpio.org/inmates/Plantz_Marilyn

43. Ginnie Graham, "Woman's Clemency Plea Denied," *Tulsa World*, April 18, 2001.

44. Thomas Mullen, "Board Denies Request for Clemency." Associated Press, April 17, 2001.

45. Kevin Johnson, "Justice Department Investigates Police Scientist's Work. Eleven Executed after Convictions Based Partly on Her Testimony," Gannett Company, May 3, 2001.

46. Danny M. Boyc, "Woman Executed for Husband's 1988 Murder," Associated Press, May 1, 2001.

47. Max Haines, "Deadly Betrayal: Suburban Housewife Led a Sordid Double Life," *Daily Oklahoman*, October 17, 1996.

48. Most of the information about the facts and the trial are taken from *Smith v. Massey*, 2000 10 Cir 1518, 232 F. 3d 1342 and from Smith's 1992 application for post-conviction relief.

49. O'Shea, *Women and the Death Penalty*, 295.

50. Lois Nadean Smith, Application for post-conviction relief, 1992.

51. *Smith v. Massey*.

52. Smith, Application for post-conviction relief, 1992.

53. *State v. Smith*, December, 1986. Partial trial transcripts, pp. 1201, 1326.

54. *Smith v. State*, 1986 OK CR 158, 727 P 2d 1366.

55. *Smith v. State*, 1996 OK CR 13, 915 P. 2d 927.

56. *Smith v. Massey*, David J. Rubin, "Brain Damage Made Mom Murder," *The Forensic Echo*, July 17, 2001.

57. *Smith v. Massey*.

58. NCADP statement, December 4, 2001 at www.clarkprosecutor.org

59. Appellate brief, *Smith v. Massey*.

AGGRAVATING CIRCUMSTANCES: KILLING CHILDREN AND COPS

Christina Riggs and Lynda Lyon

Christina Riggs and Lynda Lyon were sentenced to death for crimes that are often considered the worst of the worst. Riggs murdered her two preschool-age children. Lyon was involved in an incident in which a police officer was shot. Public opinion tends to support the position that those offenses merit the most severe punishment. But to determine whether Riggs and Lyon deserved to die, there is more to consider than the general description of the murders. One might examine the factors that brought these two women to the scene of their crimes. In both cases the killings occurred at the end of a string of events that could have ended differently. Riggs might have had help in dealing with her depression. Lyon might have stopped to use a telephone at some other location. It is quite possible that higher courts would have found error in their trials. One could argue that both women showed evidence of mental illness. However, for different reasons, both women refused to appeal their death sentences. Riggs, who had tried to commit suicide when she killed her children, clearly wanted the state of Arkansas to end her life. Lyon, an anti-government activist, claimed Alabama had no jurisdiction to try her and sentence her. Therefore, she did not recognize the state's authority to execute her and, on that ground, chose not to fight it.

Before settling for the simple conclusion that when someone kills innocent children or police officers, that individual, regardless of sex or circumstance, deserves death at the hands of the state, consider the stories of Christina Riggs and Lynda Lyon.

Christina Riggs

In 1997, Christina Riggs was a single mother, a licensed practical nurse working double shifts in a futile effort to keep up with her bills. She was a severely depressed woman taking Elavil and feeling she was at the end of her rope. From death row Riggs described her life before the crime, "the grind, daycare, getting up before the sun to pack not just lunches, but everything toddlers need for the day ... then ten hour shifts with sick people; I was too shy and inhibited to make friends. Maybe too much rejection ... then pick up my babies and home to take care some more. If I could have gotten a back rub, someone to touch me, anything ... but we aren't set up like that; and to show a need is weakness. Children are even taken from us if we expose our depression, our illness. We aren't 'fit.' It is all so scary, and so illness progresses."[1] Even on the day before her execution, when she wrote that letter Christina Riggs could recall vividly her overwhelming exhaustion and hopelessness at the time she murdered her children and attempted to kill herself.

Riggs had spent most of her life in Oklahoma City where her experiences growing up reprised many of the themes in the lives of other death row women. From the age of about seven until she entered her teens, Christina was sexually abused by a stepbrother. At thirteen, she was raped by an adult neighbor. She kept information about the molestations to herself, but lost trust in her family's ability to protect her. That was probably a reasonable conclusion as both of her parents were involved in a series of marriages and relationships and paid little attention to Christina. Instead she looked to a wild group of peers to be her support system. She began drinking and using marijuana. "I felt no boy liked me because of my weight, so I became sexually promiscuous because I thought that was the only way I could have a boyfriend."[2] By the age of 16, Riggs had become pregnant although she hid her condition from her family until the seventh month. She gave birth to a biracial baby boy and, at her mother's insistence, gave him up for adoption. Riggs finished high school and went on to get her license as a practical nurse. Although there were always jobs for someone with her training, typically they paid poorly. Often Riggs held both a full-time and a part-time job just to keep up with basic expenses.

Christina dated a number of men and entered a relationship with Timothy Thompson, a serviceman stationed at Tinker Air Force Base. The day before Thompson was discharged, Riggs told him she was pregnant. Thompson was reluctant to admit paternity. Instead, he left Christina and returned to his parents' home in Minnesota. After Thompson's departure and before the birth of Justin in 1992, Christina took up with another old boyfriend, Jon Riggs, whom she eventually married in 1993 and who was the father of Shelby, born in 1994. The relationship with Riggs was stormy. Christina often felt depressed and suicidal, which she blamed on birth control pills. A doctor then prescribed Prozac, but she stopped taking the anti-depressant when she began to feel better. Both of her children had health problems—Shelby had serious ear infections while Justin suffered from hyperactivity and attention deficit disorder. Christina claimed that she was assigned to a triage unit at the Oklahoma City Federal Building after it was bombed by Timothy McVeigh in April 1995. She attributed some of her emotional difficulties to post-traumatic stress disorder resulting from dealing with the victims. However, although she was an employee of the Veterans Hospital in Oklahoma City at the time, there is no record that the hospital sent Riggs to the bomb site.

Nonetheless, her private life was fraught with problems. She and Jon Riggs moved to Sherwood, Arkansas, to be near her mother, Carol Thomas. The marriage floundered and ended in divorce not long after Jon punched Justin in the stomach so hard that the child needed medical attention. Christina's financial situation became progressively worse. Wages from her position at the Arkansas Heart Hospital and from part-time jobs were not enough for expenses. The more she worked, the more she had to pay for child care. Support payments from the children's fathers were erratic and insufficient. Riggs later told an interviewer, "I started out in a boat with a small hole. But the hole kept getting bigger, and no matter how hard you bail, you keep sinking. I was tired and I gave up. Suicide seemed like the only thing."[3]

On November 4, 1997, Christina Riggs tried to commit suicide. Rather than leave her two children motherless, she determined to kill them first and then to kill herself. Before leaving her job that day, Riggs smuggled doses of the anti-depressant Elavil, morphine, and potassium chloride from the hospital. At about 10 PM, she gave each of the children a drink containing Elavil to make them sleepy. After they had gone to sleep, Christina injected potassium chloride, the drug used to execute people by lethal injection, into Justin's arm. Riggs was unaware that unless potassium chloride was diluted it would cause severe burning of the skin. Justin woke up crying in pain. Christina also began to cry, and then injected her son with morphine to stop his pain. When he continued to scream, she smothered him with a pillow. Rather than hurting Shelby with the injection, Riggs held a pillow over the two-year-old's face until the child suffocated. The mother then placed her children side by side on her own bed and covered them with a blanket.

Christina Riggs next wrote suicide notes to her mother, her ex-husband Jon Riggs, and her sister Rosanna Pickett. She swallowed 28 Elavil tablets, ordinarily more than enough for a lethal dose, and injected herself with an amount of potassium chloride that could have executed five people. In a stupor, Riggs fell to the floor at the foot of the bed where the children lay while the potassium chloride burned a hole about an inch in diameter in her arm.[4] The prosecutor would later claim that her suicide attempt was a fake.

When Riggs failed to appear at work the next day, the hospital contacted her mother. Carol Thomas tried to reach Christina by phone and then drove to her house about 4 PM. There she found her grandchildren dead on the bed and her daughter, apparently dead, on the floor. Thomas called 911 and the paramedics found that Riggs was barely alive. She was taken the hospital where her stomach was pumped and her condition stabilized. Christina Riggs had been unconscious for more than eighteen hours.

Meanwhile, the police had searched Riggs's home where they found her suicide notes, the drugs, and the syringes used for the injections. Although she was in the intensive care unit, officers guarded Riggs's room at the hospital. Her family had arrived but the police denied them access, claiming that Christina was in no condition to talk with them. The relatives then retained attorney John Wesley Hall to represent Christina. Hall contacted the police and told them not to question his client unless he was present. Nonetheless, early the next morning about fourteen hours after she had been found comatose, two police detectives questioned Christina Riggs without her attorney and elicited a confession from her. Riggs had not seen her family, she was interrogated without legal counsel, and she told the story of the murder/suicide incoherently. That eight-minute confession became the heart of the state's case against her. Its admissibility was a critical issue in her defense.

Detectives Charles Jones and Cheryl Williams read Riggs the Miranda warnings and questioned her about the deaths of her children and her own suicide attempt. They did not tell her that her family had retained an attorney, although it is doubtful that information would have penetrated Riggs's confused state of mind. As the detectives asked questions, Riggs alternately cried uncontrollably, talked fairly rationally, could not say what day it was, and hallucinated. She admitted that she killed the children with medicine taken from the hospital and that she tried to kill herself about twenty minutes later, after smoking a cigarette and writing the suicide notes. When asked why, Riggs replied "Because I wanted to die. But I didn't want to die and leave my kids behind or for them to be a burden to somebody else. I didn't want them to think I didn't love them and I didn't want them to grow up separately because they have two different Daddy's (sic). And I knew if I passed away they would be fighting my mother for custody and I didn't want that for nobody."[5]

The explanation of her motive was the most lucid part of the interview. According to the transcript, at times Riggs's responses were inaudible, at other times she was crying and unable to answer. Asked about how she took the drugs, she gave the garbled answer, "And I know I should have thought better ... had somebody rinsing with me, but ... they were just what came home in my pockets." She talked about old people who looked like Detective Jones' mother (whom she had never seen) and described escalators (there were none) in the hospital.[6] Two minutes after the statement was finished, a doctor found Riggs unconscious, still suffering from the effects of the drug overdose. Nonetheless, shortly thereafter she was charged with capital murder and moved to the county jail.[7] She pleaded not guilty by reason of mental disease or defect. At the jail, Riggs was placed under suicide watch. The court ordered the state hospital to expedite her mental examination.

In pre-trial motions, Riggs's attorney asked the court to suppress her statement to the police on the grounds that it was involuntary due to her disoriented mental condition and also because she had not been allowed access to counsel. Although her family had retained Hall the night before the questioning and although he had told the detective in charge of the case not to allow an interrogation of his client, the officers on the scene went ahead with the interview. The judge denied the motions and found no indication in the transcript of the statement that Riggs had been hallucinating. He determined that she was "sufficiently coherent" and her statement was "voluntary."[8] That statement taken at the hospital provided the state with much of the basis to charge two counts of capital murder. They argued that Christina Riggs was fully competent and that she had planned to kill the children for weeks because they were an inconvenience to her. They further claimed that Riggs's suicide attempt was meant to fail, that she was trying to win sympathy for herself. The prosecution had the evidence of two dead children and a mother who admitted killing them. They merely had to convince a jury that a woman who would commit such an unnatural act would also be capable of any deception to save her own selfish, unmaternal life.

The Trial

Riggs's trial began with jury selection on June 23, 1997.[9] A number of potential jurors (about one-third of those questioned) were excused as they were not "death qualified." Quite a few others had seen and heard extensive coverage of the case in the local media, and several said they could not be impartial due to the nature of the crime. One woman lived across the street from Riggs and had spoken to the newspapers. She was quoted as saying that Riggs' home was not "child friendly." However, she did not mention that incident to the court. She was chosen as a member of the jury. Prosecutors Larry Jegley and Melody Piazza tried to elicit responses indicating that the potential jurors believed everyone should be accountable for their actions and that the standard of guilt should be the same for capital punishment as it was for lesser crimes. Hall, the defense attorney, asked questions to clarify their understanding of depression as a "real mental illness" and the standard of proof for a mental defect as "preponderance of the evidence" rather than "beyond a reasonable doubt." A jury was seated after two days of questioning.

The prosecution opened on a dramatic note, asking the jurors to imagine going into a house where they heard children laughing happily. That innocence was interrupted by a lady with vials of poison—that lady was their mother, Christina Riggs. Jegley went on to describe her as a selfish woman who liked to sing karaoke in bars, who locked up her children, who showed no remorse. Her friends, he said, had seen no signs of the alleged depression, and why should Riggs be depressed? She had a "great job," no money problems. The fathers of the children paid child support. She had simply planned the vicious murder for weeks for her own self-centered reasons. The jury should be brave and hold her accountable.

As Riggs was pleading not guilty by reason of mental disease or defect, Hall painted a dramatically different picture. Christina Riggs had been found on the floor with a hole two inches in diameter in her arm from an injection of potassium chloride large enough to kill thirty people. He emphasized her own and her family's history of depression, the sexual abuse, abandonment by her father, pregnancy at fifteen. He told of her children's "deadbeat dads," her chronic debt, and desperate attempts to pay her bills. The defense claimed that Riggs had been contemplating suicide for more than a year and a half before her last attempt. She finally determined to "take the children with her" when she died. Wasn't that proof that she suffered from a mental defect or disease? "You would have to be crazy to kill your kids," Hall concluded.

The state's evidence involved police and paramedics' testimony about the cause of death and numerous photographs of the dead children. They had no pictures of the comatose Christina. Her "confession" taken at the hospital was a key element in the prosecution's case. In addition, they summoned co-workers who reported they did not think she was depressed, that she "sounded normal." Other alleged friends testified to Riggs's bad mothering. According to one, Christina had told her she "hated" Justin because of his hyperactive disorder. Another told that Christina went to bars to participate in karaoke contests, a story designed to convince the jury that she was out drinking and having fun when she should have been home with her children. In cross-examination and with their own witnesses, the defense tried to contradict the picture of Christina, to show that she was a good and caring mother, so unselfish that she pawned her VCR to give Justin a birthday party.

The major part of the defense's case was to show that Riggs was not responsible at the time of the killings and that her depression constituted a real mental disease. The emergency room doctor who treated her immediately after the crime testified that she was truly a suicide risk. When she was brought into the hospital (and presumably when she confessed), she suffered from delirium and drug overdoses. Dr. Bradley Diner, a defense psychiatrist who had interviewed Riggs for four hours at the jail explained that she saw killing her children as an "act of love." She wanted to take them with her rather than abandon them. He cited her long and serious depression, the effects of sexual abuse as a child, her humiliation, feelings of worthlessness, guilt, remorse, and rejection. In Dr. Diner's opinion, she suffered from a mental defect or disease. He believed she saw killing the children as an extension of her own death, not as a criminal act.

In response the prosecution hammered home their version of the story. Dr. Diner was duped by the manipulative, karaoke-singing, high-functioning, self-centered Riggs. The process was the same when the defense called two other doctors to testify to Riggs' mental illness. Dr. James Moneypenney, the psychological examiner from the Arkansas State Hospital, reached essentially the same conclusion as Dr. Diner. He even cited examples of slave mothers who killed their children and themselves as acts of mercy. He found Riggs a textbook example of Post Traumatic Stress Disorder (PTSD). The prosecutor also faulted Dr. Moneypenney for believing the stories Riggs told. The state preferred to argue that Riggs was another Susan Smith—a mother who wanted to get rid of her children to be with men.

All of the defense's character witnesses—co-workers, other friends, the children's pediatrician, Justin's kindergarten teacher, Riggs's sister—were asked questions to elicit examples of Christina's love for her children and of her shaky mental state. The suicide notes written to her mother, her sister, and Jon Riggs reflect the same themes. She feels overwhelmed by life and unable to leave Justin and Shelby.

In rebuttal, the prosecution called a psychiatrist and a psychologist. Both agreed that Riggs showed "maladaptive behavior," that she suffered from a personality disorder, but that, when they examined her after her arrest, she did not suffer from severe depression and was not mentally ill.

The state chose Melody Piazza to give the closing statement. Surely it was not an accident that a woman stood before the jury describing that most unwomanly of crimes, killing one's own children. Although a careful reading of the text reveals a number of inconsistencies, it is likely that Piazza's listeners followed the emotions rather than the logic of her argument. It is striking how many times the prosecutor used the word "little" in conjunction with the victims. It would have been difficult for jurors to miss the contrast between the small children and the large woman who smothered them. In the district attorney's words, that woman had "broke[n] the oldest and strongest bond known to man," the bond between mother and child. She "made a huge rip" in the human fabric, and she did so intentionally. As Piazza argued, Riggs's acquisition of the deadly drugs and her suicide notes were evidence of premeditation. Lest the jurors feel any sympathy for Riggs, the prosecutor claimed that her own attempted suicide attempt was irrelevant to her guilt. She was not mentally ill but simply a whiner who manipulated people to feel sorry for her because, "She was a single mother. She's written a hot check. The utilities had been cut off from time to time. She'd been stopped for expired tags. She'd been sexually abused as a child. Her parents divorced when she was young. Her little boy had ADHD. She had financial problems." In Piazza's eyes those points were balderdash. "She had a great job, a great salary. She had a car, a home, beautiful children that were mentally healthy, they were sound." So ... Riggs could not have been *really* depressed, she must have simply been so selfish she thought her children were an inconvenience. Riggs wanted to have boyfriends and to sing karaoke in bars instead of living up to the standard the prosecutor held out— "Mothers give up their lives for their children."

In an emotionally wrenching conclusion, Piazza pulled out all the stops. "Our civilization is based on the ability of women to bear children," she noted. Mothers are "the glue that makes everything stick ... unless we allow this defendant to tear away the one thing we know to be true more than anything else in the world, unless we allow her to rip away at the very belief ... that a mother would never harm her children." She asked them to remember little Justin as his "little life began seeping away in all his confusion … he cried out 'Mama, mama, mama.' And no one was there to protect him, to save him, to reach for him." But the jurors were his salvation, they could hear him and "reach back and answer those cries…. And you know how to do that."

Riggs the bad mother should not be allowed to claim depression, "the excuse of the nineties" as a mental disease. "There are people who are insane and then there are people who do insane things. And that's what you have here."

How could the defense offer an argument to counter the prosecution's paean to motherhood? Hall could only try to make Christina Riggs into a sympathetic figure and to remind the jury that their role was to seek justice not to wreak vengeance. For them to find her "Not guilty by reason of mental disease or defect" the defense would need to establish that at the time of the conduct she lacked the capacity either to appreciate the criminality of her act or to conform her conduct to the law. Such a determination should be based on the greater weight of the evidence, not on the number of witnesses.

Like the prosecutor, Hall began with the night of the murders, but he needed to make the jurors see things through Christina's eyes. When she was found, "her lips were dry. She'd urinated on herself. She was cold to the touch." Surely those facts described a real suicide attempt. When the police finally found a faint pulse in her neck, they brought her back to life. "And now the state wants to kill her again." If, in despair, she tried to end her own life along with that of her children because she saw no hope for any of them—only poverty, separation from one another, rejection—then she was a loving, but misguided, mother as opposed to the self-centered villain of the prosecution's version. Hall retraced her miserable life: abandonment by her real father, abuse by her stepbrother, separation from her sisters, pregnancy at fifteen, rejection by Justin's father who called her "a one night stand," Jon Riggs's abuse of Justin. Those things formed the background for her life when she killed the children. At that time, she was working twelve-hour shifts. Her babysitter had quit. Her utilities had been turned off several times. Her car insurance had been cancelled. She had written bad checks and borrowed up to the limit at a payday loan company. If he hoped to save his client, Hall needed to persuade the jury that although he shared their distress at the death of innocent children, his client should be seen as sufficiently damaged and desperate to believe she was doing the best thing for them.

In Riggs's case, depression was both chemical and genetic. Several relatives had committed suicide, her grandmother, mother, and sister had been hospitalized for depression. If the family predisposition was added to Christina's sense that her life was a failure, her mental disease could have made her incapable of conforming her conduct to the law. The defense needed to focus the jury on that interpretation, not on the picture of her as selfish and hard. Did she cry? Yes. Did she call a lot of people from the hospital and jail to tell her story? Yes. One of the state's doctors noted that if Riggs had been truly "severely super depressed" she would have been in a fetal position when he interviewed her. Hall pointed out that she had been strapped down with restraints at the time. Faced with dueling mental health experts, the defense could only plead with the jury to believe its doctors—that Riggs could not conform her conduct to the law, that she believed she was performing an act of love in taking her children's lives along with her own.

District Attorney Jegley had the last word for the state. He urged the jury to "follow the law" and "do the right thing," phrases he repeated like a mantra. They should remember that Christina was a "selfish manipulator." They should find her guilty of two counts of capital murder and, presumably, prove that they had avoided her manipulative wiles.

Within fifty-five minutes the seven women and five men on the jury returned with the verdict, guilty of capital murder. Surely it is possible that the jurors, especially the women, chose to distance themselves as far as possible from such a monstrous mother. It would have taken more than an hour to give careful consideration to both sides of the arguments about Riggs's culpability. One can only assume that the jury did just as the prosecutors had hoped and looked only at the act, not at the context. It was reported by the defense that during their brief deliberation, laughter was heard coming from the jury room.

In the sentencing phase which lasted approximately 15 minutes, the state put Jon Riggs on the stand to provide a victim impact statement. The absent father who had punched Justin so hard he needed medical attention told how Christina had "ripped my family from me." Only Christina spoke on her behalf. She asked for the death penalty. "I want to die. I want to be with my babies." The jury did as she asked, the judge concurred. Christina Riggs was sentenced to death by lethal injection. "Thank you," she told them.

After the Trial

Riggs would have chosen to go directly from the courtroom to the death chamber but almost two years passed between July 1998 when her death sentence
was handed down and her execution on May 3, 2000. She asked her attorney
to waive all appeals because she knew she wanted to die and did not wish to
prolong the outcome. But in the strange way the capital process works, the
state that had been insisting that Riggs had no mental disease or defect, now
insisted that she have a psychological evaluation to ensure that she was competent to waive her appeals. Meanwhile her lawyer filed a motion for a new
trial based on four grounds: that her confession should have been suppressed;
that the prosecution's opening statement quoting the dying children was prejudicial; that jury instructions were faulty; and that the jury who deliberated
for only fifty-five minutes and were heard laughing in the jury room could not
have properly considered all the evidence.

Although all motions for retrial were denied, the state continued to
try the case in the media. A month after the initial verdict and sentence,
Riggs's lawyer filed a motion to gag the prosecutor's team. He claimed they
continued to make "gratuitous comments" on television and to the press
calling Riggs a liar and manipulator. Prosecutors claimed that her desire
to waive all appeals was simply the latest of her master machinations—the
classic Catch-22. By asking to die, she would be found incompetent and her
life would be spared.

It did not turn out that way. In January 2000, the court granted Riggs's
motion to waive her post-conviction appeals. According to her attorney
Hall, at that time Riggs was alert and stable because she was taking antidepressants. She knowingly, intelligently, and willingly chose not to appeal, even though she knew she could be dead soon. Riggs wanted no more
prison. "It's been hell the last eighteen months," she stated. She had been
looking forward to her own death since November 1997, when Justin and
Shelby died.

During her confinement on death row, Riggs carried on a correspondence
with writer Jenny Furio. In those letters, she told her story in her own words
and expressed frustration with a system that did not provide adequate support
for those with mental illness. Riggs's tragic lack of self-esteem comes through
in a letter where she describes being overweight and abused and turning to
drinking and drugs in her teens. "Pain turned to illness.... I gave my love

to men, and rejection after rejection. I was not pretty, typically, but I was at least a vagina."[10] Riggs believed that at the time she killed her children and attempted to take her own life, her depression coupled with her reaction to antidepressants explained her violent behavior. "I was insane when I reached that point." However, as she sat on death row, Riggs acknowledged that killing her children haunted her constantly. "I'm not blessed with chronic insanity, freeing me from endless remorse.... I honestly can't wait to be dead. I can't stand this pain."[11] If Riggs were the manipulator the prosecution made her out to be, perhaps she finally manipulated the state into colluding in her suicide.

Christina Riggs was executed on May 3, 2000. It took almost 20 minutes for the technicians to find a suitable vein for the injection, probably because of Riggs's weight. Lying on the gurney, the condemned woman agreed that the lethal tubes could be inserted into her wrists instead of her upper arm. In her last statement, Christina Riggs said "There is no way no words (sic) can express how sorry I am for taking the lives of my babies. Now I can be with my babies, as I always intended. I love you my babies."[12]

Why Riggs?

Christina Riggs was executed for causing the death of her two children. At the same time, national attention turned to the case of Susan Smith, the South Carolina mother who also drowned her two little boys. Arguably, Riggs was the more sympathetic of the two. Her crimes came at the end of a continuously hard life and a history of depression. She had tried to take her own life along with the lives of her children. Smith, on the other hand, seemed much more in control of her crime and her life. Apparently she killed her children because her boyfriend did not want the responsibility for them. She then plotted to lie to the police and the public, claiming that a black man had carjacked them.

The prosecution in Riggs's case urged the jury not to believe the "Susan Smith defense" at the same time they tried to draw as many parallels as possible between the two women. Repeatedly they claimed, based on the skimpiest evidence, that Riggs viewed her children as an "inconvenience" because of her desire to live a fun-filled life singing karaoke in bars. The evidence of abuse in Susan Smith's childhood seemed to earn the jury's empathy. The state of Arkansas minimized Riggs's experience of sexual abuse and depression. Finally, Susan Smith's attractiveness may well have drawn media attention and public sympathy to her, while Riggs, morbidly overweight and working class, never had the same public appeal. Altogether, it seems quite likely that Christina Riggs suffered negatively because of the juxtaposition of her case with that of Susan Smith.

Michelle Oberman writes that the criminal justice system polarizes female defendants as either mad or bad. Because any violent crime, but especially infanticide, is inconsistent with stereotypical womanly behavior, the explanation must be found in the irrational or the pathological. "Madness" or diminished responsibility may provide an excuse to treat the offender leniently. "Badness" is often correlated with race and class.[13] As Oberman suggests, both madness and badness focus on individual pathology, neither places the mother's behavior into context. Such analysis seems especially relevant to the case of Christina Riggs. Her defense attempted to situate her actions within the framework of a life of abuse, rejection, and marginality and to explain the killing of her children as an act of "madness." The state told the story of her "badness." Perhaps because of her social status, perhaps because of her appearance, perhaps because of her history of relationships with a series of men, the women and men on the Arkansas jury believed that version and invoked the ultimate punishment.

Lynda Lyon[14]

Of the fourteen women put to death, Lynda Lyon's case is the only one with overtly political overtones. For the most part, the stories recounted in this book concern murders that developed within the context of personal relationships. But arguably Lyon and her common-law husband, George Sibley, would not have been involved in the shooting of Officer Roger Motley had it not been for their commitment to an extreme libertarian philosophy and rejection of government. And had Lyon been willing to be assisted by an attorney at trial and had she been willing to appeal her conviction and death sentence, the outcome may have been different. The sequence of events that ended with Lyon's execution on May 10, 2002, began with her attendance at a Libertarian Party meeting in Orlando, Florida, in 1991.

Lynda Cheryle Lyon grew up in the middle class. Her father, a businessman, died when she was a child. Her mother believed Lynda, who was "always very idealistic," tried to replace him by looking for a Prince Charming.[15] Her search led her to marry a retired military man, securities broker Karl Block who was twice her age. Block was also hoping to compensate for the loss of a loved one. At the age of 70, he wanted a child to take the place of his son who had been killed in an automobile accident. Lynda, 35 years old at the time, gave birth to Gordon in 1984, a year after their marriage. Although Block's older children thought Lynda Lyon was a gold digger, the marriage lasted eight years. During that time, Lynda's life was a model of conventionality. She was a Cub Scout den mother, a volunteer at the Humane Society and the public library. That changed when in 1991 she became fascinated with the ideas of the "patriot movement" and the Libertarian Party. Through that organization, she met George Sibley, a mechanic who converted cars into drag racers. The two joined forces to publish a militant magazine, *Libertatus*, and to engage in research intended to justify white supremacy, to uncover the "real" meaning of the Constitution and the malfeasances of current governments at the state, local, and national level. Along with many others of their political persuasion such as Timothy McVeigh, Lynda and Sibley became even more radicalized after the federal government's 1993 siege of the Branch Davidian compound in Waco, Texas. Lynda Lyon Block separated from her husband in 1991 and claimed she became George Sibley's common law wife at that time. However, in 1993 she and Karl Block were still involved in a legal struggle over their marital property. In August of that year, she and Sibley went to Block's home either to discuss a settlement (as Lyon and Sibley claimed) or to threaten the octogenarian (as Block claimed). In any event, there was a physical struggle and Block sustained a minor knife wound. He later charged Lynda and Sibley with assault and battery.

The two were arrested and, in Lyon's account, they were held for five days in jail without access to an attorney. She described being strip searched and locked in a cell with thirty other women, where she cringed in fear of lesbians and bullies. From start to finish, Lyon believed she and Sibley were mistreated because of their politics. She blamed the sheriff because in a recent radio interview she had accused him of embezzlement. He had, she claimed, shut down and padlocked the radio station immediately after her statements. As further proof of the conspiracy against them, she and Sibley believed their attorney "sold us out for a job with the county.... He had an evil, satisfied look on his face and I knew we had been set up." At the judge's urging, Lyon and Sibley pleaded "nolo contendere." They would likely serve a term of probation in the community.

However, before sentence was handed down, the two defendants pub-licly accused the judge of corruption. They and their friends sent dozens of faxes outlining the charges against him to the governor, the lieutenant governor, the attorney general, the chief judge of the Florida Supreme Court, and the sheriff. Convinced they would be sent to prison in retaliation, Lyon and Sibley did not appear for sentencing. When warrants were issued for their arrest, the two believed their home would be raided by a SWAT team. They thought that because they had made important people angry, the police would kill them "and then say [we] shot at them first." On September 10, 1993, Lyon and Sibley took her son Gordon Block, three handguns, two semi-automatic rifles, and an M-14 rifle and fled from Florida in her red Ford Mustang. Her worst fears would come true. The State of Alabama would kill her and Sibley and say they "shot at them first."[16]

The Crime

On October 4, 1993, Sibley pulled the car into a Wal-Mart parking lot in Opelika, Alabama.[17] Lynda wanted to use the outdoor pay-phone to call a friend in Florida. She left Sibley and her son in the car while she made the call. Meanwhile a woman passerby, Ramona Robertson, noticed the boy in the back seat of the Mustang. At trial she claimed he mouthed the words "Help me" to her. Robertson stopped Officer Roger Motley who happened to be in the shopping center buying supplies for the Sheriff's Department. He radioed his agency that he would check on the child, got into his patrol car, and drove it to a spot behind the car where Sibley and Gordon Block waited for Lynda. Sibley got out of the Mustang and Motley asked him for his driver's license. Sibley said he had no license and began to explain why he rejected any contact with illegitimate governmental agencies. He later claimed he offered to show Motley other identification, but that the officer put his hand on his service revolver. Immediately Sibley pulled out a pistol from a concealed holster and began shooting at Motley. The policeman ducked behind his vehicle and fired back. Hearing the shots, Lynda ran from the phone booth, pulled out a Glock 9mm pistol from her purse and fired it at Motley. She fired three or four times, the officer turned toward her "looking surprised," and she fired again. Motley managed to get into his car and radio the emergency message "Double zero." Lyon claimed she thought he was grabbing a rifle rather than the radio and fired several more shots into the back window of the police car. Motley was able to drive a short distance before he crashed. Meanwhile, Lyon and Sibley with Gordon Block in the back seat, drove off at a high rate of speed. Those facts of the crime are generally not in dispute.

Unfamiliar with the roads of Lee County, Alabama, Sibley led the police on a high-speed chase that ended at a roadblock in Auburn. There Gordon was immediately released to the officers, but Lyon and Sibley held them off for more than four hours before surrendering as daylight faded and a real SWAT team assembled. During the stand-off, Lyon sat in the front passenger seat with a loaded automatic rifle pointed upward between her feet. Lynda did inquire repeatedly about the officer who was shot and was reassured that he was "doing ok." She talked with a police negotiator, alternating between threatening that the two would commit suicide and trying to explain their patriot ideology and distrust of government. "Let's not have another Waco happen here," Lyon reportedly said. "What's Waco?" he asked.[18]

Sibley had a fairly minor wound in his arm from the shootout with Motley. He apparently took only a small part in the negotiations. At the last moment, however, he promised his common-law wife, "We will fight this to the end, and if they still execute us, we'll die knowing we fought for what was right."[19] When Lyon and Sibley surrendered, a search of their car revealed a number of firearms, quantities of ammunition, and several large knives.

Both Lynda Lyon and George Sibley were charged with the murder of Officer Roger Motley, a capital offense in Alabama, although it was never determined who fired the bullet that killed him.

After the Arrest

Once Lyon and Sibley were in police custody, Lyon's version of events contradicted the public record. According to evidence introduced at trial, both were advised of their Miranda rights and both made statements to the police. Lyon admitted to shooting at Motley several times with her 9mm Glock pistol loaded with Black Talon bullets and described Sibley's shots using a .762 Tokorev. She detailed their flight from the scene, the police chase, and the roadblock. At the time they drove off, according to Lyon, "we did not know we hurt the police officer. We thought he was okay. We only wanted him to leave us alone. I didn't intend to kill the police officer. I didn't want that.... I don't know if we would have turned ourselves in if we had known." In the same statement, Lyon explained that they had renounced their citizenship under the U.S. government.[20]

Meanwhile, Sibley was making a similar statement. He spoke at length about his grievances against the United States government, including the incident at Waco and the shoot-out between federal agents and militiaman

Randy Weaver in Idaho,[21] both of which were rallying points for radical "patriot" movements. He explained how he and Lynda had severed their ties with the government and had become "free Americans" no longer bound by laws they believed illegitimate. Instead of a license plate their car had a tag that read UCC1-207. It referred to a provision of that number in the Uniform Commercial Code that allows someone who has discovered fraud in a contractual agreement to revoke the contract. Sibley and Lyon had, they believed, discovered fraud in the government and were therefore revoking the social contract. Sibley claimed he was defending his life when he shot Motley and felt he had done nothing wrong. He insisted that if the government tried to "enslave" him or take his guns or rights, he would start a war. It must have been clear to the police that in Lyon and Sibley they were dealing with no ordinary criminals but with people who believed they had a mission.

Part of Lyon's mission was to tell her story of government oppression to like-minded activists. In the version of events she called "From Heaven to Hell," Lyon claimed that she and George were placed in solitary confinement without access to an attorney. Yet she testified at trial that she had been advised of her rights when she made a statement on the day of her arrest. Certainly given her expertise on the Constitution, when Mirandized she would have asked for a lawyer immediately or refused to speak to the police. Lyon described her cell as dirty and frigid. She said she had no blankets until the sixth day when she passed out from exhaustion and starvation on the cold cement floor. (One should keep in mind that it was Alabama in early October.) And why were they tortured? To force them to take *their* (the state's) lawyers, Lyon asserted. The "imperious" judge, the prosecutor, and the Sheriff all conspired to cut them off from their supporters. It seems clear from reading Lyon's account of the case that her political goals—discrediting the legal and judicial system—overshadowed her grasp of the reality of her predicament. She cast herself as a martyr, even telling her court-appointed attorney (before she fired him) that she wanted acquittal or nothing.[22]

Lyon represented herself at trial, despite the urging of the judge that a capital case required someone experienced in the criminal law and trained especially in the intricacies of the death penalty. But the defendant disagreed. "We were more knowledgeable than they; all they knew was what they were spoon-fed at law school. They knew nothing about the common law rights of self-defense, of the significance of 14th Amendment citizenship, of the right to resist unlawful arrest."[23] Those issues were themes Lyon would spell out repeatedly both in pre-trial motions and in her post-conviction filings. Those of her political persuasion believed, among other things, in a "true" Thirteenth Amendment to the Constitution that prohibited special privileges for public officials. Therefore a law making it a capital offense to kill a police officer was unconstitutional. This "missing" amendment also prohibited titles of nobility for public officials, making the term "Esquire" for attorneys another constitutional violation. The organizations that conferred these illegitimate titles, the American Bar Association and the state Bar Associations, were engaged in illegal monopolies. She also alleged that the Fourteenth Amendment to the Constitution had never been properly ratified, as the former Confederate states were coerced into accepting it. Therefore, she would not claim, as her attorneys had advised, that her due process rights were violated.

Lyon concluded that as her court-appointed attorney was either ignorant of those truths or he was cooperating in obscuring them. She determined to represent herself and, in the process, teach constitutional lessons. If the court failed to learn them, she would give her life for the patriot cause.

The Trial

Lyon's trial began on Monday, November 28, 1994, with a two-day jury selection process.[24] By the evening of Thursday, December 1, the verdict and sentence had been decided. All things considered, the trial was conducted with care and decorum. The judge permitted Lyon to ask some questions that would have been ruled out if posed by an attorney. He also advised her several times to object to a prosecution question or to look at a piece of evidence. However, the outcome was a foregone conclusion. There was little to dispute about the events at the Wal-Mart Plaza on October 4, 1993. Numerous witnesses had seen Sibley and Lyon shoot at Officer Motley. According to Alabama law, it was not necessary to determine which one had fired the fatal shot. As the prosecutor said, the "defendant and her accomplice" were both heavily armed and both acted in a way to intend to cause the officer's death.

Civilians who watched the gunfire, forensic scientists, investigators, and the medical examiner testified about Motley's wounds, about Lyon shooting out the back window of his car as he attempted to drive away, about the defendant's attempted flight, and about the four-hour standoff with police. Officers confiscated a veritable arsenal from Lyon's car—guns, ammunition, knives, and holsters. The state made a weak attempt to show that Lyon was an irresponsible mother to leave her son in a hot car while she used the phone but barely mentioned a mother who left her child in a car with filled with firearms.

Probably because the case against Lyon was so strong, there was little effort to make an issue of her "failures" as a woman. A jury did not need to be reminded of her lack of feminine virtues to decide that she had—for bizarre political reasons—shot a law enforcement officer trying to do his duty. As the district attorney said in his closing, she "comes into Lee County armed to the teeth and kills an Opelika Police officer in cold blood in the middle of the day in the middle of a parking lot." Such a scenario left the jury little room for debate.

Lyon did attempt to put on a defense to the extent her politics would allow her to work within the system she claimed was illegitimate. She questioned one of the arresting officers about her show of remorse when she found out Motley was dead. Most of her effort was devoted to eliciting from Sibley a rambling story about the Florida case and their political beliefs. He claimed their movement was non-violent. It was an attempt to restore the government to the Constitution and to get rid of "socialism." He claimed the press misled the public about their beliefs and about their weapons. He denied he possessed a "sniper rifle" or a gun so powerful that a bullet-proof vest would do no good. The judge was extraordinarily tolerant and allowed Lyon to go far afield from the crime itself during her questioning of Sibley. It is unlikely, however, that Sibley's rambling testimony aroused much sympathy among the jurors. Her last witness, even less focused than Sibley, was Lyon's former firearms instructor. He asserted that he had taught her to shoot responsibly. Presumably his statement supported her claim that killing Motley was justified.

The defendant's closing statement denied that they were radicals or "paramilitary type people." She asked the jurors to understand that she was not guilty of murder but was forced to choose who to defend. In other words when all the political rhetoric was removed, as Sibley did in his trial, she claimed self-defense.

Although it might seem the state had a "slam dunk" conviction, the district attorney reminded the jury that Lyon had caused Motley's death intentionally while he was on duty answering the call of a concerned citizen. She and Sibley were cold. They shot to kill and showed no remorse. Even without determining who had fired the fatal bullet, the jury knew that Lyon had fired five or six shots at "Roger's" back window while the officer was trying to drive away. A claim of self-defense could surely not be sustained.

Possibly because of the ambiguity about which bullet had killed Motley, during deliberations the jury asked the judge for definitions of capital murder, murder, and manslaughter. The judge sent in photocopies of the state statutes. Whether or not that served to clarify their understanding, they returned a verdict of guilty. Without breaking for dinner, the jurors elected to move directly into the sentencing phase. The state set out two aggravating factors: the shooting had put many lives at risk, and the crime was committed while the defendant was fleeing from a lawful arrest. Neither the prosecutor nor the defendant put on any new evidence. But the state reminded the jury that Lyon had shown Motley no mercy, nor had she shown any remorse for the danger she caused to innocent bystanders. The district attorney claimed he had never seen such a clear and convincing case for capital punishment.

The jury returned a death sentence by a vote of 10–2.

From Sentence to Execution

Lyon was entitled to an automatic appeal to Alabama's highest court, the Court of Criminal Appeals, and she was entitled to court-appointed counsel for the appeal. Not surprisingly she again refused an attorney. She demanded to be allowed a joint appeal with Sibley, and when that was refused, she filed a number of documents challenging her conviction. These were not technically appeals but papers challenging the constitutionality of the proceedings that had sent her to death row. Some were sent to Congress and other federal officials. They were also distributed to like-minded political allies. Lyon asked Congress to grant a writ of habeas corpus. She alleged that she had been charged under an unconstitutional statute (one that treated police officers preferentially); that the judge and the district attorney did not have valid law licenses (because they were members of the Alabama Bar Association); that the district attorney had not taken an oath of office and was therefore not allowed to prosecute; and that the American Bar Association and the Alabama Bar Association were unconstitutional monopolies. All of her claims rested on the validity of the "lost" Thirteenth Amendment.[25]

About six months after her trial, Lyon filed a document she labeled "Notice and Declaration of Status." It reiterated her position that she refused to have contact with government agencies, that she was not a citizen of the United States as defined in the "alleged" Fourteenth Amendment and that she therefore refused the protections afforded under that amendment. She was not, she claimed, a citizen of any corporate government entity or body politic but "I am non-resident and alien to the corporation in the District of Columbia and its subdivisions. I am an American inhabitant."[26] Like religious martyrs, Lyon denied that the government had any jurisdiction over her and claimed to be answering to a higher authority.

Meanwhile, in the courts that she refused to acknowledge, the clock was ticking on Lyon's appellate process. She declined to accept counsel for her appeal and chose not to file a brief with the Court of Criminal Appeals. The court would not allow her to withdraw from the mandatory appeal although they could not force her to file any pleadings. Instead, she wrote a statement explaining why she would not appeal. It included her repeated arguments that the Alabama courts lacked jurisdiction and that forcing an appeal was "a preposterous, unconstitutional attempt to impose involuntary servitude." She was a "natural person" (not an American citizen) and therefore could seek a proper court to hear her appeal. A proper court, in her view, was one that would admit her arguments about the "real" Constitution.[27]

In November 1995, Alabama filed its appellate brief. The state argued that there had been sufficient evidence to convict Lyon. Fifteen witnesses had positively identified her as shooting at Motley, who was in uniform. There was no testimony supporting a claim of self-defense. The state further claimed that a sentence of death was proper in the case as two aggravating factors—a risk of harm to many people and a crime for the purpose of avoiding arrest—had been demonstrated. However, the attorney general did recommend that Lyon's case be remanded to the trial court to review her waiver of counsel. A "thorough inquiry" especially in reference to her mental health would prevent the procedural default that could prejudice later appeals. In other words, the state was taking steps to insure that Lyon's decision to represent herself was examined by the court in case she needed to raise an issue of mental incompetence at a later time.[28]

Lyon responded in a letter to the attorney general stating that the person named in the state's case LYNDA LYON BLOCK (sic) was fictitious. She was Lynda Lyon Sibley and that person was not in the court's jurisdiction. She made the same point at the hearing to determine whether she had properly waived her right to appellate counsel. She claimed no names other than Lynda Cheryle Lyon Sibley and maintained that Lynda Lyon Block was a fictional corporate persona. Her statement continued "I, Lynda Cheryle Sibley am relying on the counsel of Jesus the Christ and my husband George Everette Sibley, Jr.... My law is God's law. I have not waived but reserved all rights. I have refused attorneys and I have refused the state's automatic appeal."

The Court of Criminal Appeals found that Lyon had "intelligently" waived her right to counsel and that the judge had done and said all he could to make her aware of the gravity of the situation. They found no errors in either her trial or her sentence.[29]

In response, Lyon wrote to Congress charging Justice Sue Bell Cobb who had signed the opinion and other members of the Alabama Court of Criminal Appeals with fraud and treason. The letter, written in October 1997, reiterated her view that there was no such entity as "Lynda Lyon Block" and that all members of the Alabama Bar Association belonged to an unconstitutional organization. They had forfeited their citizenship and therefore their judicial acts constituted treason. Congress did not act on her allegations.

The Significance of Lyon's Case

When Lynda Lyon was executed on May 10, 2002, she was the last person to be put to death in Alabama's electric chair, "Yellow Mama." Subsequent executions, including that of George Sibley, on August 23, 2005, were by lethal injection. Lyon was also only the second white woman to be executed in Alabama's history. When Lyon was moved to Holman Prison's death row, corrections authorities transferred her common-law husband to another facility, presumably to avoid any unnecessary emotional stress among the inmates.

In spite of those curious circumstances and the potential for media attention, there seemed to be little emotional drama as Lyon was put to death. She wore prison whites. Her head was shaved, and her face was covered by a black veil. One account mentioned that she wore light makeup, including mascara and pale pink lipstick.[30] She chose no last meal nor did she make a final statement. Unlike the other executed women, she did not evoke demonstrations asking that her life be spared. Lyon appeared to be less sympathetic than the other thirteen. Her political extremism may have made her a martyr to those who shared those views, but as she was no doubt aware, it alienated her from most others.

Ironically, Sibley seemed a bit less eager for martyrdom. Days after Lyon's execution, he filed an appeal. Although he had written to Lyon, "we want … Patrick Henry's 'Give me liberty or give me death!' he managed to delay his own death for more than three years.

What made Lyon into the sort of zealot she became? There is no real evidence that she experienced oppression at the hands of the government. Until she met Sibley in 1991, she lived a conventional life well within the law. She volunteered her time to work with books, children, and animals. There are no reports at the time that she felt the need to arm herself with military-style weapons. Her relationship with Sibley must have seemed to offer the Prince Charming her mother mentioned, her "soulmate"[31] who happened to see the world as a hostile place. He wrote, "I have been punished all my life, as you have, for adhering to principle, and being honest. I defended my principles to my own detriment. Everywhere I went, someone wanted me to yield to a situation, an ideal, or purpose that was wrong—or at least wrong for me—and I rebelled. This has cost me dearly throughout my life. Realizing this, I am still unwilling to forfeit that what I hold dearest—my integrity."[32] Without arguing that Sibley coerced Lyon into accepting his vision of reality, one could say that as she fell in love with him, she adopted his world view, his peculiar form of "idealism."

Tragically, it was a world view that transformed an ordinary police officer making a routine inquiry about a child in a car into the oppressive illegitimate corporate government depriving a free citizen of her liberty and forcing her to take up arms to protect her family.

Lyon's case is really the outlier in the fourteen executions considered here. One can find little evidence that gendered expectations were determining factors in carrying out her death sentence. Unlike the other women on trial, Lyon was subjected to little of the "evil woman" or "bad mother" imagery. Nor can one argue that she was coerced into killing Officer Motley or that her co-defendant sold her out in return for a lighter sentence for himself. Perhaps Lyon's case is the only instance where formal equality may be accurately applied. By casting the issues in terms of a political struggle between legitimate and illegitimate versions of the Constitution, Lyon herself effectively removed gender as a consideration.

Endnotes

1. Christina Riggs to Jennifer Furio, May 1, 2000. Jennifer Furio, *Letters from Prison: Voices of Women Murderers* (New York: Algora Publishing, 2001).
2. Michael Haddigan, "They Kill Women, Don't They?" *Arkansas Times Online* at www.clarkprosecutor.org. Furio also recounts Riggs' early life in *Letters from Prison*.
3. Haddigan, "They Kill Women."
4. The crime is described in the court proceedings, including *Riggs v. State of Arkansas*, 339 Ark 111, 3sw 3rd, 305 (1999).
5. Ibid.
6. Ibid.
7. Rita Sklar letter to Governor Mike Huckabee, April 28, 2000, ACLU of Arkansas.
8. *Riggs v. State.*
9. Unless otherwise noted the account of Christina Riggs's trial is from the transcript, *State of Arkansas v. Christina Marie Riggs*.
10. Furio, *Letters from Prison*, 148–49.

11. Ibid., 149–50.
12. Capital Punishment USA at www.clarkprosecutor.org.
13. Michelle Oberman, "Mothers Who Kill: Coming to Terms with Modern American Infanticide," in *American Criminal Law Review* 34 (Fall 1996), 43–50.
14. Many of the sources about this case refer to the main character as Lynda Lyon Block. However, during her trial and after, she repeatedly stated that she had legally changed her name back to Lyon after her divorce from Karl Block. In her later writings, Lyon claimed her legal name was Lynda Cheryle Lyon Sibley. For the sake of consistency, I will use her birth name, Lyon, unless otherwise noted.
15. Most of the information about Lyon's early life is included in Michael McLeod, "A Dangerous Game," *Orlando Sentinel*, May 9, 2002.
16. The account of the Block assault and its aftermath are included in Lynda Lyon, "From Heaven to Hell," at www.clarkprosecutor.org.
17. Most of the information about the crime and the trial may be found in the transcript, *Alabama v. Lynda Lyon Block* (sic), 37th Judicial District, 93–955.
18. McLeod, "A Dangerous Game."
19. Lyon, "From Heaven to Hell."
20. See *Alabama v. Block*.
21. Randy Weaver and his family were separatists who rejected American society and government. The FBI believed they were a white supremacist militia who were gathering illegal arms. On that basis, they raided the Weaver compound and after a siege killed several people. Antigovernment groups regarded Weaver et al. as martyrs.
22. Lyon, "From Heaven to Hell."
23. Ibid.
24. *Alabama v. Block*.
25. Lynda Lyon, Challenge to conviction, March 8, 1995. Included in the records at the Alabama Court of Criminal Appeals.
26. Lyon, Notice and Declaration of Status, May 11, 1995, Court of Criminal Appeals.
27. Lyon, Withdrawal of Appeal, July 5, 1995, Court of Criminal Appeals.
28. *Block v. State*, 744 So 2nd 404 (Ala. Crim. App. 1996).
29. Ibid.
30. Todd Kleffman, "State Executes Block," *Montgomery Advertiser*, May 10, 2002.
31. George Sibley to Lynda Lyon, Lee County Jail, 1993 at www.clarkprosecutor.org.
32. Ibid.

· 8 ·

THE "MONSTER"

Aileen Wuornos

Press coverage at the time of her 2002 execution noted that Aileen Wuornos, "the first female serial killer," had been the subject of three books, two made-for-TV movies, and an opera. Since then, Charlize Theron, as an uncanny look-alike for Wuornos, won an Academy Award for her performance in *Monster*. That motion picture, which effectively ended when the main character was arrested, attempted to portray the desperation that lay behind the murders of seven men along Florida highways between December 1989 and November 1990. Other productions and especially the "true crime" books emphasized the sensational aspects of the case. These examples from the media show that Aileen Wuornos attracted an extraordinary amount of publicity. The events were titillating. She was a prostitute who worked the interstates. The victims were her customers. Her partner helped the police to extract a confession. The very sordidness of the story seemed the source of its fascination. And during the 1990s, the media loved to feature stories about serial killers. The first woman to be put into that category provided a "fresh take" on the theme.[1]

At the time of Wornos's arrest, trials, and convictions, most of those who devoured the gruesome details expressed little sympathy for a woman who not only admitted to seven murders but who cursed in the courtroom, lashed out at her own attorneys, demonstrated no remorse, and showed no real disposition to help herself. Yet as psychiatrist Dorothy Otnow Lewis found in looking beneath the surface of sensational crimes, "the gruesomeness of the murder is directly proportional to the craziness of the murderer."[2] She further argued that paradoxically, the offenders with the greatest mental illness often generate the least sympathy from the public or from the legal system.

With all the interest in the saga of Aileen Wuornos, few really tried to understand why this woman who had lived most of her life on the margins became a killer. The focus on her as a "damsel of death," a lesbian man-hater, or a sex-crazed prostitute obscured rational inquiry into what was responsible for her "craziness." It may be argued, however, that both her craziness and the popular fascination with Aileen Wuornos are expressions of the gendered structures in American society and the gendered nature of the administration of justice.

The Murders

On December 13, 1989, two men hunting for scrap metal found the body of Richard Mallory, proprietor of an electronics store, under a scrap of carpet in the woods near Daytona Beach. Police said the body was fully clothed. Mallory was shot three times in the back with a 22-caliber pistol. His abandoned Cadillac had been found about twelve days earlier by a Volusia County deputy. As Mallory was unmarried and frequently closed his business while traveling out of town, his disappearance had not caused anyone concern and had not been reported. The original suspects were two strippers whom Mallory had paid for sex by giving them items left for repair at his electronics store. Charges against them were dropped in mid-1990 for lack of evidence.[3]

Meanwhile, a truck belonging to construction worker David Spears was found on May 20, 1990. All personal property was missing. A torn prophylactic wrapper was left on the floor of the truck. Two weeks later Spears's body was discovered north of Tampa. He was nude except for a baseball cap. Spears had been shot six times in the torso with a 22-caliber pistol.

Within a week, the nude body of Charles Carskaddon was located about 30 miles south of where Spears was found. Carskaddon, who had been shot nine times with a 22-caliber handgun, was covered with a green electric blanket. When his car was recovered the next day, all of his personal possessions were missing.

A 65-year-old missionary, Peter Seims, disappeared in June 1990, headed from Jupiter, Florida, to Arkansas. His body has never been located, but his

Pontiac Sunbird was found on July 4, 1990. Two women, one taller and blond, the other shorter and dark haired, were seen near Seims's car after wrecking and abandoning it along a wooded roadside. From witnesses to the accident, police sketch artists were able to create composite drawings of the two suspects. License tags and keys were removed from the Pontiac, but Budweiser and Busch beer cans and Marlboro cigarettes had been left behind. Investigators also pulled a bottle of Windex from under the passenger seat. It had an Eckerd Drugs price tag from a store in Atlanta, Georgia. The store manager recalled *two* women who had purchased cosmetics and a package of Trojan prophylactics. They matched the police composites.

Troy Burress did not finish his deliveries for the Gilcrest Sausage Company on July 30, 1990. His employers initiated a search and found his truck the next day. Burress's body, shot twice with a 22, was discovered on August 4. All of his cash receipts were gone.

On September 12, police located the fully clothed body of Charles Humphreys with seven 22-caliber gunshot wounds, not far from where Spears's and Carskaddon's cars had been. Humphreys was retired from the Air Force. He had served as a police chief in Alabama and at the time of his death was a Florida state investigator dealing with abused and neglected children. A week later his car turned up behind an abandoned service station. License plates, keys, and bumper stickers had been removed. Officers did find a can of Budweiser and a convenience store cash register receipt dated the day of Humphreys's disappearance. The clerk could not identify a picture of Humphreys but did recognize composite drawings of *two* women she believed to be prostitutes.

Two months later, on November 18, Walter Antonio's body was discovered. He was nude except for a pair of tube socks. Antonio had been shot four times with a 22-caliber pistol. A gold and silver ring set with diamonds, a gift from his fiancée, was missing. After five days his car was found, tags and keys gone, bumper stickers removed. His personal possessions were not in the car, which was surrounded by empty Budweiser cans.

All of the men were middle aged, between 40- and 65-years-old. All six whose bodies were found had been shot with a 22-caliber handgun near a highway in central Florida. All had been robbed.

On November 30, 1990, the police released the composite pictures of the two women suspected in the series of murders. Within three weeks they had received over 900 "leads." At least four phone calls identified the short dark woman as Tyria Moore and the other as Lee Blahovec/Lori Grody/Cammie Green/Aileen Wuornos.

In 1990, Tyria Moore spent Thanksgiving in Ohio with her family. She returned briefly to Florida to pack up her things before boarding a northbound Greyhound bus and leaving Wuornos for good. She would later admit to knowledge of the murders. She was also aware that the pictures of the two suspects were circulating in newspapers and on television. Without her partner, Wornos's life became increasingly disorganized. All she owned was in one suitcase and in some boxes in a storage locker. She had pawned all the valuables from the victims, including Walter Antonio's diamond ring. A fingerprint required as identification on that pawn ticket led the police to positively establish the identity of one of their suspects as Aileen (Lee) Wuornos.

Wuornos, homeless and desperate, spent her last night of freedom sleeping on an abandoned car seat under a metal awning at the Last Resort biker bar. The next day, January 9, 1991, she was arrested outside the bar by Volusia County Officers Bernie Buscher and Larry Horzepa. They told her they were executing an outstanding warrant for a 1984 forgery charge. She was wearing a key on a chain around her neck and carrying a card from Jack's Mini-Warehouse, a storage facility. When police opened that locker they found personal property belonging to the murder victims.

Who Was Aileen Wuornos?

As Stacey L. Shipley and Bruce A. Arrigo note, Aileen Wuornos was not a reliable source for her own history.[4] Yet even if one acknowledges factual contradictions in her accounts of her upbringing, it is a story of almost unmitigated abandonment, abuse, neglect, and horror. Witnesses and public records substantiate the general truth of that picture.

From her first breath in Troy, Michigan, Aileen Wuornos was a member of a small demographic minority. She was born on Leap Year Day, February 29, 1956.[5] Her mother, Diane Wuornos, was sixteen at the time. Her father, Lee Pittman, had already deserted his family. Perhaps it was just as well because Pittman was by all accounts a violent man, later convicted of child rape and kidnapping. He hanged himself in a prison cell. Diane abandoned Aileen and her older brother Keith to her own parents. One night she announced she was going out to dinner. Instead she left town and, for all intents and purposes, her children's lives.

For about ten years, Aileen believed her grandparents were her real parents and that her aunt and uncle were her sister and brother. Someone revealed the truth, leaving the child with a sense of betrayal and abandonment. Those feelings might have been lessened had the grandparents created a warm and loving home. Both, however, were alcoholics—the grandfather abusive, the grandmother helpless. The pattern here mirrors the childhoods of Velma Barfield, Betty Lou Beets, and Judias Buenoano. All suffered harsh treatment at the hands of their male guardians, and all observed chronic weakness on the part of their female guardians. To those who hold that gender roles are learned and that learning begins in the home, these women saw two options for role models—either become the victim of a brutal man or take on the offensive role. In their childhood homes, none of them saw anything resembling healthy relationships.

Wuornos claimed that her grandfather beat her regularly, often using a belt buckle to maximize her pain. Her sister recalled that although the other children received Christmas presents, Aileen was not given any. Another story described her grandfather forcing her to watch him kill her pet kitten. Wuornos was not a bad student in elementary school, but around the time she learned about her real parentage she began to have problems. School officials administered mild tranquilizers. They also requested that her "parents" take her for counseling and that they tend to her problems with vision and hearing. None of these suggestions was followed. Aileen's problems, like those of Wanda Jean Allen, were ignored by the adults who should have been her caregivers.

In addition to the physical and verbal brutality of her grandfather and her family's neglect of her physical and psychological needs, Wuornos sometimes claimed that she had been sexually abused by her grandfather, brother, and her older brother-uncle. At other times, she claimed the sexual abuse did not occur at home. However, it did happen somewhere because at thirteen Aileen Wuornos was pregnant. The person who did that would today, if caught, be considered a "sexual predator." His name would appear on the sex offenders' websites for the rest of his life. Not so the man who sexually abused Wuornos. She said he was a friend of the family who offered her a ride home. He drove her into the woods instead and threatened her life. After that incident, Aileen hid her pregnancy as long as she could. When her grandparents found out, they made no effort to find the rapist but sent her, alone, to the Florence Crittenden Unwed Mothers' Home where she gave birth to a baby boy whom she never saw. The story of Wornos's pregnancy was verified by her friends and family members as well as the public record. It is typical of her upbringing that instead of sympathy or support, she was blamed for having a baby while she was barely more than a child herself. Her sister-aunt Lori said Aileen always hated men after that. She believed they used women and she was very angry.[6]

Wornos's reactions—anger and promiscuity—are not at all surprising for someone who experienced the traumas of rape and pregnancy, abuse and neglect as she did. Most observers reported that as a teenager she was loud, belligerent, impulsive, and vulgar. She was often rejected or humiliated by her classmates. She became known as a "cigarette slut" who would have sex for money or even for a few cigarettes. She also began to drink regularly and according to some, to experiment with drugs.

Clearly, her grandparents made little effort to control her behavior or even to understand it, although the caseworker at the Crittenden Home informed them that she was immature, impulsive, and had no conceptualization of the future. Those qualities are not unusual among adolescents, but in Wuornos they seemed especially prominent. It could be argued that those same traits continued to characterize her behavior long after her teenage years. Yet instead of professional help, Aileen experienced more rejection. Her grandmother died of cirrhosis of the liver when Wuornos was fifteen. Her grandfather, apparently blaming Aileen for his wife's death, kicked her out of the house for good. She lived in abandoned cars, slept in the woods, and occasionally stayed with her only friend, Dawn Botkins. Not one single adult stepped forward to help her, although neighbors knew she was homeless.

Wuornos told a reporter in 1999, "I was going on 16 ... when I hit the road ... and I was on the road ever since all throughout my life off and on everywhere, except for Daytona. I settled down there a while when I was in my twenties."[7] Settling down is a relative term. It was during that time that Wuornos made her living as a roadside prostitute and during that time that she killed seven men. In between leaving Michigan and the 1989–90 murders, Wuornos was arrested five times for a variety of offenses including disorderly conduct, driving under the influence, simple assault, and armed robbery. She had stolen several drivers' licenses and used the aliases Susan Blahovec and Lori Grody. She was married very briefly at the age of twenty to a seventy-year-old man. The marriage was annulled when the groom claimed Wuornos had physically attacked him.

Aileen Wuornos was living the life of a drifter on the edge of the law, supporting herself with prostitution when she met Tyria Moore at a gay bar in Daytona Beach. Wuornos fell in love with Moore immediately and the two began a four-and-a-half-year relationship. They started as lovers and remained roommates and, some would say, partners in crime until 1991 when the police took Wuornos into custody at the Last Resort.

Those investigating the murders along Florida highways were looking for two female suspects. After arresting Wuornos, they also located Tyria Moore who was staying with a sister in Pennsylvania. Detectives found her there, in possession of a briefcase and a radio belonging to Charles Humphreys. They persuaded her to return to Florida and to work with them to get information from Wuornos. Although Moore had been connected with a number of the crimes and she retained property stolen from victims, the police never charged her. Moore claimed not to have been given immunity nor to have plea bargained, but she did agree to testify against Wuornos. She also allegedly entered into a profitable contract, along with two of the detectives, to sell her story for a television movie.

After returning to Florida, with police officers at her elbow taping the calls, Moore had eleven telephone conversations with Wuornos during a four-day period. By crying and pretending to be afraid of arrest, Moore persuaded Wuornos to confess. She even threatened suicide to manipulate Wuornos into taking full blame for the crimes. The defense would later claim that Moore "exploited" the relationship and Wornos's "tremendous love" for her to get the confession.[8]

On January 16, 1991, Aileen Wuornos spent more than three hours telling her story to officers Lawrence Horzepa and Bruce Munster. Her confession, which is extremely disjointed and rambling, was recorded on audio and videotape and released to the press before the trial. Clearly Wornos's main goal was to explain that Tyria Moore had nothing to do with the murders. Over and over, she implicates herself in an effort to show Moore as a sweet, innocent angel. As one author notes, the police tried to put Wuornos at her ease. "They plied her with coffee and cigarettes, and gave her a warm jacket to wear in the chilly office. With such attention, linked to her need to protect her former lover, her only true love in an otherwise loveless life, and seemingly a desire to find favor with the Lord ... Lee's confession poured from her like a torrent."[9]

Wuornos admitted to seven killings, but claimed all were in self-defense. "[W]hen they started getting rough with me, I went ... I just opened up and fired at them. Then I thought to myself, Why are you giving me such hell for when I just ... I'm trying to make my money ... and you're giving me a hassle."[10] Wuornos had a public defender with her but rejected his urging that she keep quiet. Alternately crying and angry, she described how she had once wanted to be a nun, how she had been with "a hundred thousand guys" but unless the clients threatened her, she left them alone.

The statement is almost incoherent in parts. Wuornos did not seem to remember the details of the murders, or when she did remember them she mixed them up. She frequently asserted that she was drunk during each of the encounters and did not even know the victims' names. But, she claimed to be telling the truth. "I mean I can't be any truthfuller."[11] Two things stand out in Wornos's statement—she was obsessed with protecting Moore and she had a very poor grasp of the specifics of the crimes. Her tendency to conflate the murders might be taken as evidence that she was a sociopath who had no respect for human life, as the state would portray her. It might also be evidence of some truth to her claim that she believed she killed the men in self-defense if each incident triggered a type of Post Traumatic Stress Disorder where she felt threatened and struck out.[12] Each of the murders happened during a sexual encounter in or around a car parked in the woods. If one can believe her story of the rape by an older man when she was thirteen, the circumstances are remarkably similar.

But the notion of PTSD got little credence at the time of Wornos's arrest. To most observers, certainly to the police and the popular media, she was a vicious, predatory, sexually hungry woman, who had embarked on a killing "spree." She was the "First Female Serial Killer." That theory lay at the foundation of the case against her for the murder of Richard Mallory. It also sold newspapers, books, and movies.

The Mallory Trial

Themes of lesbianism, man-hating, deceitfulness, greed, deviance, and manipulativeness characterize Wornos's trial in the Mallory case. As Chimene Keitner argues, both the prosecution and the defense used sex-role stereotypes to develop a narrative that would persuade the jury.[13] For the state, Wuornos was a predator, motivated by greed and a desire to dominate. Prosecutor John Tanner said as much in his opening statement. "She was no longer satisfied with $10, $20, $40. She wanted it all. And she had to take it. And she did. And she used a gun to take it. And she shot him to keep it…. Aileen Carol Wuornos liked control. She had been exercising control for years over men. Tremendous power that she had through prostitution. She had devised a plan now and carried it out to have the ultimate control."[14] It appears that Tanner intended to persuade the jury that at least part of Wornos's crime was her desire for control. Perhaps that would aggravate her crime because it would be a subversion of the natural order of male dominance and therefore unnatural as well as dangerous.

Meanwhile the defense hoped to show that Wuornos was a victim herself. The "feminine, articulate public defender" Tricia Jenkins opened with a description of how "Lee" lived a frightening life on the road. "Existence for Lee was getting to be very dangerous… Time after time she was raped. Time after time she was beaten up and she wasn't paid." The fear and the experience of physical violence explained why Wuornos carried a gun. According to the defense, Tyria Moore was a real villain. She cooperated with the police and turned on "her friend, her love" in exchange for what the police gave her—a motel room, "whatever she wanted, beer, cigarettes, shopping." To the defense, Moore could be characterized as the greedy, opportunistic one.

The prosecutor reiterated the old stereotype that a prostitute could not be raped. He also contended that Wuornos chose to earn her living by prostitution because she "loved the guys, she loved the money, she loved the penis."[15] Such an image would contradict the defense argument that she feared her clients as potential rapists. By claiming that Wuornos herself was the aggressor, sexually and physically, she could be seen as doubly deviant and therefore undeserving of sympathy. The defense had to acknowledge Wornos's acts but had to convince jurors that she labored under the burden of a unique dysfunction. She was "not like us," but it wasn't her fault. She merited consideration despite her lifestyle. In killing Mallory, however, she "did what anyone would do, she defended herself."[16] In other words, Wuornos was outside the mainstream in her way of life, but she shared the human instinct for self-preservation.

The defense put Wuornos on the stand during the guilt phase of the trial to tell her version of the encounter with Mallory. Unfortunately for the case, this horrifying story differed from the earlier accounts in her confession. This time Wuornos claimed that the two had driven to an isolated spot where they drank beer and vodka for more than five hours. Wuornos said she was "drunk royal."[17] She described telling Mallory there would be no sex if he did not pay and that when she began to get dressed he wrapped a cord around her neck. He threatened to kill her "like the other sluts I've done," then tied her hands to the steering wheel and raped her vaginally and anally. She claimed he took pleasure when she cried out in pain. After Mallory cleaned himself with rubbing alcohol, he squirted some of the alcohol into her vagina and rectum where she was bleeding. Mallory eventually untied Wuornos and she feared he would rape her again. After a struggle, she was able to get the gun from her purse and when Mallory came toward her, she shot him. Wuornos admitted she had stolen and pawned some of Mallory's property.[18]

The prosecutor seemed delighted to have a chance to expose the contradictions in Wornos's stories. The defendant claimed her desire to protect Tyria Moore explained why she was too rattled to tell the truth in her statement to police which contained no reference to the gruesome rape described in court. She alleged that Moore knew Mallory was killed in self-defense but lied about it because she wanted to make money from book and movie deals about a serial killer. Wuornos, who no doubt found the whole trial process incomprehensible, ranted on the stand about her treatment in jail. She claimed they kept her sedated, in solitary confinement, with nothing to read. But the longer she was on the stand, the more she rambled and the more her frustration showed as the district attorney tried to get her to talk about the other murders. Most observers thought Wuornos did not help herself by taking the stand.

The state had been allowed to introduce evidence of the other murders, even though Wuornos had not been convicted of any of them. As in the case of Judias Buenoano, Florida law allowed testimony about collateral offenses that would show a pattern or a plan of criminal conduct. The state used the "similar crimes evidence" to rebut Wornos's argument that she killed Mallory in self-defense. Her lawyers objected to the use of that information as they claimed it prejudiced the jury, making them unable to reach a fair verdict in the Mallory case. The state spent two days of the trial on testimony about the Mallory murder and four days discussing the other killings. Most of the prosecutor's closing statement was devoted to "six men's murders," including charts to show that Wuornos had a "common scheme or plan to use her status as a prostitute to lure and trap men in isolated areas" to rob and kill them with a 22-caliber pistol. The defense objected that using later killings did not prove that the murder of Mallory—the first to happen—was part of a plan. It was equally logical that the first murder, in self-defense, provoked the others. However, the Florida Supreme Court upheld the prosecution. They found that the crimes showed a "pattern of similarities" and that "relevance outweighed prejudice."[19]

Another defense issue regarding the state's use of the similar crimes evidence was the tendency of the prosecution to "canonize" the victims and to assassinate Wornos's character. This was particularly troublesome as between the trial and the appeal, Michelle Gillen, a reporter on *Dateline NBC* revealed that Mallory had once served a ten-year sentence for violent rape.

Neither the prosecution nor the defense had found that information at the time of her trial. Gillen discovered the conviction by simply checking Mallory's name through the FBI's computer network—something any police officer could have done. The reporter commented that Wuornos was a "sick woman who blew those men away. But that's no reason for the state to say, 'She's confessed to killing men, we don't have to do our homework.'"[20] And, although Mallory's criminal history would have added some credibility to Wornos's claim of rape, the higher courts found it insufficient to reverse the verdict or sentence.

Aggravating and Mitigating Factors

On January 28, 1992, after the jury found Aileen Wuornos guilty of the first-degree murder and armed robbery of Richard Mallory, the penalty phase allowed the state to argue for death and the defense to argue against it. The defendant had hardly helped herself when, hearing the verdict of guilty, she screamed at the jury, "I'm innocent. I was raped. I hope you are raped, you sons-of-bitches and scumbags of America."[21]

In the sentencing phase, both sides produced psychological experts to testify to Wornos's mental health or lack thereof. The three defense psychologists, Drs. McMahon, Krop, and Toomer all agreed that she suffered from borderline personality disorder both at the time of the crime and through the rest of her life. That condition resulted in extreme mental and/or emotional disturbance, which *dominated her functioning* (italics mine). Dr. Krop noted a pattern of unstable relationships, manic-depressive behavior, self-destructive actions, a lack of impulse control, identity disturbance, and impaired cognition. McMahon stated that "Ms. Wuornos is probably one of the most primitive people I've seen outside an institution." Most of her time, he observed, was devoted to meeting her basic needs for food, shelter, clothing, and security. For Dr. Toomer, who described the defendant's background, Wuornos was "constantly hypervigilant." Her past abuse made her fearful. She perceived Mallory as a threat and acted accordingly. He explained the abandonment by her mother, the abuse and neglect by her grandparents, her vision and hearing problems, her alcohol use—all while she was still a juvenile. One could add on the rape, the pregnancy, and the total lack of help or treatment and begin to understand her adult life. Toomer noted that sex abuse victims often become promiscuous. With a ninth-grade education, mental, emotional, and physical disabilities, prostitution seemed virtually the only way for Wuornos to survive.

In that work, she experienced beatings and rapes. She had several times tried to commit suicide.[22] This was the woman who killed Richard Mallory.

Even the state's psychologist found that Wuornos had borderline personality disorder and antisocial personality disorder. He believed she had an impaired capacity and mental disturbance at the time of the crime, but that those factors were "not substantial." The state also brought in a witness, Aileen's brother-uncle Barry Wuornos, who denied any abuse in the family and described their "normal lifestyle."

The prosecution closed the penalty phase with an argument that seemed designed to rebut an insanity defense. But Wuornos had never claimed insanity. Nonetheless, the prosecutor John Tanner told the jury, "The question is whether she knew what she was doing and chose to do it in spite of its wrongness.... [The psychologists] agreed that Aileen Wuornos at the time of the killing, knew right from wrong."[23] It seems Tanner purposely misled or confused the jury into thinking that mitigation required legal insanity rather than involving conditions that could lessen responsibility. He wanted to paint Wuornos as totally responsible for the murder—she planned to get money, she chose her lifestyle. "By an act of her will, he was no more."[24]

Defense attorney Tricia Jenkins pleaded for Wornos's life. She argued that "Lee dealt with her experience with the insight of a damaged, primitive child. In her mind, in her perception, she thought she was in danger; she was threatened. It was the only thing she knew how to do." Perhaps if the jury had actually separated the case of Richard Mallory from the other murders, they might have considered Jenkins's position. As it was, they recommended death by a vote of 12 to 0. They found five aggravating circumstances: previous violent felonies; murder committed during a robbery; murder committed to avoid arrest; murder that was heinous, atrocious, or cruel; and murder that was cold, calculated, and premeditated, without moral or legal justification. The only mitigator—far outweighed by the aggravating circumstances—was her borderline personality disorder.[25] According to one witness, when the judge read her sentence the next day, instead of the traditional statement "May God have mercy on your soul," he said, "May God have mercy on your corpse."[26]

Pleas and Appeals

On March 31, 1992, two months after the Mallory trial, Wuornos pleaded no contest to the murders of Charles Humphreys, Troy Burress, and David Spears. In June of that year she pleaded guilty to the murder of Charles Carskaddon, and in February, 1993, she entered a guilty plea in the Antonio case. She had "fired" the public defenders from her first trial and engaged the services of Steve Glazer, an attorney with no experience in capital cases. A concern at the time and a question in the later appeals was whether Wuornos fully understood the implications of her pleas and whether, in the Carskaddon case, she competently waived her rights to present evidence in mitigation. A secondary question involved why her attorney would advise her to follow such a course of action.

Although the Florida State Supreme Court rejected all her appeals, Wornos's conduct during the Humphreys, Burress, and Spears trial raises serious questions about her competence to plead.[27] It seems her major reason for the no contest plea was to avoid staying in the county jail and to expedite her return to death row at the Broward County Prison. At the hearing, Wuornos made rambling, irrational statements about her desire to die. For example, she said when asked why she wished to plead no contest "Because I love the Lord God. And I just feel that I took a life so it's time for me to go.... So I plead no contest in self-defense and all that jazz because I'm sick of it."[28] Wuornos claimed that the police had created a conspiracy against her. "I am fed up with a great number of the deceptions that have been carried out in these cases ... for ladder climbing, limelighting." She said the police had made up stories about her to sell to movie makers, that they portrayed her as "a man-hating lesbian who only killed to rob or robbed to kill." If that were so, she asked reasonably, why didn't she steal the victims' credit cards or try to sell their cars.[29] In other words, even when she pleaded no contest, she was still arguing that her real motive was self-defense, but that no one would believe her because they were all involved in a conspiracy to sell her out to the media. Her understanding of the implications of her plea and her sometimes incoherent statements to the court surely raise questions about her competence. But those questions were not sufficient either to prevent the sentence of death for the three murders or to substantiate her grounds for appeal.

During the penalty phase of the Humphreys, Burress, and Spears trial, the only mitigation witness Wuornos presented was her new adoptive mother, Arlene Pralle. As if everything about the case were not extraordinary enough, Pralle, a born-again Christian came forward and proclaimed that Jesus had told her to take care of Aileen Wuornos. They initially became acquainted through letters, but when Pralle, having no legal relationship to Wuornos, was denied access to her before and during the Mallory trial, Pralle legally adopted the thirty-six-year-old convict. For a time, Pralle apparently believed that she could save Wornos's life as well as her soul and spent a great deal of time and a fair amount of money on her behalf. Ultimately, their relationship soured while Wuornos was on death row. She seemed to conclude that Pralle had only gotten involved to get notoriety and money for herself. Whatever Pralle may have accomplished in saving Wornos's soul, she did little good in saving her life. Her own testimony was ineffective in persuading the jury to feel sympathy for Wuornos. Even more serious, it was she who introduced Wuornos to Steve Glazer, the attorney who convinced her to plead either no contest or guilty to five murders. There are allegations that he, like Buenoano's and Beets's lawyers, hoped to cash in on the fame of representing a client sentenced to death.[30]

Whatever the exact motive, in June 1992, Wuornos pleaded guilty to the murder of Charles Carskaddon. She complained that unjust pretrial publicity would prevent her from having a fair trial. She told the court that she had killed all her victims in self-defense but pleaded guilty anyway. Despite such contradictory assertions, the court accepted her plea and the State Supreme Court upheld the decision. Her attorney, Glazer, testified that she was competent. "I can represent to this court this woman is not insane. She understands what's going on and she is in full control of her mental faculties." Wuornos added, "I understand everything, and as far as I'm concerned, I'm tired of the re-electorial (sic) scandals of trying to take these cases to court. And I've got three death sentences already that I'm not going to get appealed. I got one that may be appealed, very good appeal, and this one is silly, and I just don't... I know everything. Guilty."[31]

Wuornos had the right to be sentenced by a jury and to present mitigating evidence. She waived those rights, saying she did not care anymore. Although Dr. Harry Krop stated that the defendant was delusional and incompetent to proceed, two state psychologists found that although she suffered from a personality disorder, she could still proceed. During the penalty phase, the State Supreme Court agreed that although her conduct was "profane and disruptive" it was not irrational. Her statements were "rationally organized toward a goal of conveying several impressions: that she was being mistreated by guards, that she could not receive a fair trial, and that she had been unfairly subjected to more trials than male serial killers such as Ted Bundy." This, in the court's opinion, was not delusional, but showed she was capable of "interacting in a meaningful way with the proceedings." As for her refusal to present a case in mitigation, that "constitutes an admission of her belief that no such case exists." The State Supreme Court concluded, in a true Catch-22 ruling, that there was credible evidence that Wuornos suffered from a personality disorder that should be a mitigating factor. However, since she herself conceded that "no case for mitigation exists," the court did not find the failure to consider her personality disorder an error.[32] Thus they agreed that she was mentally ill, but her own unwillingness to offer that mental illness in mitigation relieved the court of its obligation to consider it.

On February 4, 1993, Wuornos pled guilty to the murder of Walter Antonio. She received another death sentence. When that case went forward on appeal, the true failure of her attorney came to light. As the judge discussed the case and came to the end of the colloquy that would determine whether the defendant intelligently and voluntarily entered the plea, Wuornos indicated that Glazer was not the attorney she wished for. At that point, Glazer interjected, "Ms. Wuornos understands that I do not have the capital experience necessary to take her case to trial.... And if this case were to go to trial, I would immediately ask to withdraw because I could not possibly defend her the way she needs to be defended." The judge replied, "Well, all right. I understand," and went no further with that line of inquiry.[33] In the appeal, Wornos's new lawyers pointed out that the defendant had apparently believed that even with a guilty plea, she could have a new trial if new evidence were found. She referred repeatedly to finding proof that the police lied about the Antonio case. Glazer had not explained to her—or had failed to convince her—that she could not ask for a new trial after pleading guilty, that no matter what new evidence she had, the plea agreement was final. "For someone who evidently knew nothing about capital litigation, his advice not only should be suspect in general, it was wrong and misleading specifically [on the point of finality]."[34] At another time in the colloquy, Glazer gave her wrong information about the sentence for armed robbery. She repeated what he said to the court, "Fifteen or thirty, habitual, something like that." The prosecutor felt compelled to intervene and explain that the sentence could be life.[35]

Wornos's appellate lawyers summarized the problem with inadequate assistance of counsel. "What happens, though, in a case like this where a defendant has counsel who apparently does nothing to apprise his client of her defenses but simply acceded to her wish to plead guilty? Was Glazer merely a Dr. Kevorkian of the law, who did what he could to facilitate Wornos's desire to end her life? The law should condemn lawyers who cannot give reasonable advice to their clients as Glazer manifestly could not and did not do here. An attorney does more than simply stand by his client while she bumbles through a plea hearing. Glazer's incompetence fairly shouts from this record."[36]

Wuornos already had one death sentence before she chose Glazer to represent her. But he was responsible for five pleas and five more death sentences. If, as he admitted himself, he was incompetent to take her to trial, what possible motive did he have for wanting to represent her? Whether his interests were financial or simply a desire for personal publicity, certainly his concern was not his client's best interest. His dedication to Wuornos is even more suspect when one takes into account that Glazer admitted on several occasions that he smoked marijuana on the drive to meet his death row client. Lack of experience, lack of preparation, and a clouded mind do not add up to a zealous defense. Even less so when one realizes that Glazer was earning money by brokering deals with filmmakers for Wornos's story.[37]

The Finale

Not long after the failure of the first round of appeals, Aileen Wuornos, like Christina Riggs, decided to stop the process, forego her appeals, and let the state proceed to her execution. With any volunteer for the death penalty, the state must determine whether the person is competent to abandon the appellate process and to proceed to execution. Given Wornos's history of personality disorder, it would not be surprising if confinement on death row caused her mental condition to deteriorate. She complained that prison staff were poisoning her food and that they were infiltrating her thoughts with electric impulses. In a 2001 hearing to determine her sanity, one psychologist found those factors were evidence of paranoid delusions. An FBI analyst, however, believed she was "sane" enough to be executed. He argued that distrust of correctional officers and fears about food were perfectly normal concerns for prisoners, and that the thought monitoring she described might result from actual crackling sounds in an old public address system. He found that Wuornos had given plausible reasons for not choosing to go to court. "She doesn't like it here because of the clothes, because of the shackles. They're uncomfortable. Because of the belt (around her) that if she gets unruly... they can hit her with a jolt or something that she doesn't relish very much."[38] His description does not seem to provide persuasive reasons for a responsible person to give up any chance to stay alive. However, given the courts' minimal standards for competence to stand trial or to forego appeals, it must have been sufficient. She was allowed to drop all appeals in April 2002.

Wornos's execution was set for October 9, 2002. Although the media muddled the issue by referring to her as a serial killer, the actual death sentence was for the murder of Richard Mallory. In the weeks before her execution, a new defense lawyer, Raag Singhal, took over and asked for another competency examination—a request granted by Governor Jeb Bush. In July Wuornos had handwritten a letter to the court claiming that prison guards were trying to harass her to death and drive her to suicide. She said they tainted her food, served her potatoes cooked in dirt and spat and urinated on her meals. She further alleged that staff wanted to rape her. Her lawyer pointed out that either the complaints had merit or Wuornos was delusional. Three psychiatrists appointed to examine Wuornos found that she understood why she was being executed, although one suggested she might not comprehend the finality of the process. District Attorney Tanner who had prosecuted her and whose psychological credentials were questionable said she was lucid and "She knew exactly what she was doing." The governor agreed and let the execution go ahead.[39] Filmmaker Nick Broomfield and writer Christopher Berry-Dee who visited Wuornos in the days before her death said she was "all but insane," that her mind had disintegrated.[40] Her childhood friend Dawn Botkins, the only disinterested person who stayed in touch with Wuornos on death row, wrote a letter every day for eleven years and visited with her on the day before the execution. Wuornos had given Botkins instructions for dealing with her body.

> Please have a smile put on my face. Hair loose and lying relaxed around pillow and shoulders. Also I'd like a cross in my hands, like a small wooden one also a Bible tucked between my arm and rib cage, as my hands are folded holding the cross. Please put a single rose alongside my arm. Coffin—my taste is brown wood one, with light red or white satin exterior design.

She went on to offer suggestions for music to be played "at the wake or any ceremony deal you may have of me. Like a cook-out."[41] Whether or not one concludes Wuornos was delusional on the basis of that letter, her last words leave serious doubt about her lucidity. "I'd just like to say I'm sailing with the rock, and I'll be back like Independence Day, with Jesus June 6. Like the movie, big mother ship and all, I'll be back."[42] The death itself took seventeen minutes from the time Wuornos was injected with lethal chemicals until she was pronounced dead. A reporter for TV news said that before her death Wuornos turned to the witnesses, made a bizarre face "a kind of smile," then rolled her eyes and turned away. She then "shut her eyes and her head jerked backwards ... her mouth seemed to drop open, her eyes opened to slits, and it appeared she was gone."[43] The description suggests that even as she died,

Aileen Wuornos was regarded as an object of curiosity, a "monster," not as a human person experiencing her last moment on earth.

Predictably a relative of one victim commented "It was an easy death. It was a little bit too easy. I think she should have suffered a bit more." And then, oddly, "She was off her rocker."[44]

Mental Illness

The contradiction in that last statement encapsulates key questions with the Wuornos case. If she was "off her rocker" did Wuornos deserve to suffer and to be executed? Is death the appropriate punishment for the mentally ill, regardless of the criminal acts involved? The Supreme Court continues to grapple with the issue of whether it is cruel and unusual punishment for the state to kill people who are recognized as mentally ill but who meet the minimal standard of being aware of the punishment they are about to suffer and why they are about to suffer it. Recently the American Bar Association and the American Psychiatric Association have asked the courts to declare a moratorium on capital punishment for those with severe mental disorders that "significantly impaired" their rational judgment, their ability to assist their lawyers or to make rational decisions about their appeals. A significant percentage of those who abandon the appellate process are seriously mentally ill.[45]

Psychologists repeatedly diagnosed Aileen Wuornos as psychotic and as having a borderline personality disorder. Yet juries sentenced her to death and courts upheld those sentences. According to expert testimony she exhibited marked emotional instability, intense inappropriate anger or inability to control her anger, an extreme need for attention often accompanied by hypersexuality, and a very marked impulsiveness. "In short, she behaved like a three year old."[46] Her first defense attorney, Tricia Jenkins, witnessed her client's intense anger and mood swings. "There were so many breaks in the trial because of it. They'd put her in a holding cell and it would be my responsibility to calm her down. She'd go off in a second, and then she'd be very childlike, affectionate, asking forgiveness. It's something I have a lot of difficulty describing."[47] It is also something juries would have difficulty understanding. Wornos's uncontrollable anger could only serve as further evidence of her guilt.

In a retrospective attempt to diagnose Wornos's mental condition, psychologists Stacey Shipley and Bruce Arrigo examine how she fit the profile for psychopathic antisocial personality disorder (ASPD). They further investigate the connection with attachment theory, arguing that "the quality, frequency, and intensity of childhood bonds that do or do not form with parents or parental surrogates are extremely important to the formation of one's personality structure," including the development of psychopathology.[48] The authors raise the following questions: "Can childhood interactions with primary attachment figures be an important early marker of adulthood behavior and personality development, particularly the onset of ASPD or psychopathic traits? Can the inhibition of early bonding or attachments and abandonment, as well as emotional, sexual, and physical abuse lead to detachment, apathy, or lack of empathy for others? Can hostility and aggression that become part of an individual's internal working model result in preemptive aggression and predatory murder?"[49] Wuornos experienced abandonment by her mother and abuse and neglect from her grandparents who were her adoptive parents. Her biological father was by all accounts a sexual predator who had shown outbreaks of rage toward his wife. Thus, both heredity and especially environment may have contributed to the lack of early bonding. Her grandfather, especially with his harsh and degrading behavior toward Aileen, was a damaging influence. Shipley and Arrigo posit that from these sources, Wuornos learned that she was "wicked, worthless, and hated" by those who should have cared for her; that those who should have loved her hurt her instead; that life was filled with "terror, rejection, and pain," and that others cannot be trusted. To protect herself, she must become hypervigilant.

Those who experience abuse, who see themselves as inherently unlovable and others as threatening, may develop a "grandiose self-view." They imagine themselves as famous and embellish their life story. To compensate for their self-hatred and to disassociate from the painful reality, they construct a reality in which they are significant.

Wornos's early involvement in prostitution is consistent with her experiences. She saw herself as an object of abuse and her body as something to trade as a commodity. The men who employed her services further dehumanized her, and reinforced her grandfather's treatment. Having no positive experiences with males, she responded with anger and hatred, a form of self-protection. Shipley and Arrigo argue that her uncontrolled temper was a result of her "fragile self-worth." She had so little self-esteem, that even the slightest insult could enrage her.[50]

Based on the facts of her life, they conclude that Wornos's personality fell into the severe range of symptoms of attachment disorder. They ranked her as "severe" in eleven of twenty markers: indiscriminately affectionate with strangers; destructive to self, others, and material objects; stealing; lying about

the obvious; no impulse controls; learning lags; lack of cause and effect thinking; lack of conscience; poor peer relationships; history of maltreatment in
first two years of life; and parents exceedingly angry toward the child. With
that attachment disorder score, she was extremely likely to develop ASPD.
Such individuals represent "a serious threat to society, as they are likely to kill
or otherwise seriously harm others, and show no remorse for their actions."[51]

If her early life experiences predisposed her to a pathological personality
disorder, Shipley and Arrigo find that her adult traits supported that predic-
tion. They provide examples that exhibit a majority of the characteristics
associated with pathological ASPD. Wuoros's history includes: a grandiose
sense of self-worth; need for stimulation; pathological lying; manipulative
behavior; lack of remorse; shallow affect (lack of normal emotional response);
callousness, lack of empathy; a parasitic lifestyle; poor behavior controls;
promiscuous sexual relationships; early behavioral problems; lack of realistic
long-term goals; impulsivity; irresponsibility; failure to accept responsibility
for one's actions; juvenile delinquency; criminal versatility.[52] It is worth noting that virtually every one of the factors that are symptoms of her psychosis
may also be interpreted as reasons to condemn her behavior. Poor behavior
control or lack of appropriate emotional response, for example, was seen as
aggravating her guilt and blameworthiness rather than as a manifestation of
mental illness.

Virtually every one of the women examined in this study showed some
characteristics of mental illness and/or mental retardation. The line between
victimization, especially in childhood, and offending in adulthood cannot be
sharply drawn. Rather it is a blurry space where someone who was abused and
neglected by people who were supposed to care for her internalizes the lessons
and wounds of that experience and turns them outward toward someone else.
The criminal justice system in its treatment of these female offenders seems
uniquely unable to grapple with these complexities.

Female Serial Killer

Early in the twentieth century, criminologists Cesar Lombroso and Gina
Ferraro wrote, "As a double exception, the criminal woman is *consequently* a
monster—her wickedness must have been enormous"[53] (italics mine). In their
view, as conformity was the norm, criminality made a person exceptional.
Criminality for women was even more of a rarity. A criminal woman is almost
unimaginable. The second part of their statement is particularly relevant to

the study of Aileen Wuornos. Because she is so unusual, their female criminal is monstrous. And she is defined by individual moral failure (wickedness).

Over and over the press stated that Wuornos was the first woman to fit the FBI's definition of a serial killer. They portrayed her as truly an exception, a freak. At her trial and sentencing hearings, the prosecution wanted juries to see her that way—a serial killer, an abhorrent creature, someone who was definitely "other." Skrapec argues that women serial killers differ from men in their methods, not in their motives. But Wuornos used a gun to kill her victims, so even in that sense she defied female expectations. In Skrapec's view, serial murderers of both sexes always kill out of a "need for a sense of self as an actor; a need for power that has generally arisen out of a forma-tive history in which the individual as a child experienced powerlessness." These individuals feel a "simmering yet pervasive rage" that, if not resolved in healthy ways, leads to violence. But, she finds, because women lack a sense of entitlement to feel anger, they historically turn that rage inward—becoming depressed or developing addictions.[54] Wuornos did all of those things: she was arguably an alcoholic, she exhibited extreme moods, including depression, yet she also turned her anger outward—at the "johns" who incurred her wrath.

Wornos's identity as a prostitute is significant for an analysis of the gen-dered elements of her case. It may be argued that prostitution is the ultimate expression of patriarchal society—a "business" where men have the resources and some women have only their bodies to sell in exchange. Scholars such as Meda Chesney-Lind have repeatedly demonstrated the pattern of girls who escape an abusive home, end up on the streets as runaways, and get involved in prostitution as a survival strategy.[55] Aileen Wuornos followed that pattern with all its attendant dangers. She originally claimed that after too many violent encounters, she struck back. One need not accept all of her hyperbolic claims to believe that she had been raped and beaten by clients—especially living the life she did, getting into their cars and going off to remote spots for sex. Her career was the embodiment of a marginalized woman, powerless in a patriarchal society.

But prosecutors did not want the court to see her that way. Instead they drew the picture of someone who upset the established gender patterns—a gun-toting, celebrity-seeking and power-hungry "femme fatale"—a deadly woman who used sex to create female dominance over men. She inverted the relationship between the client and the prostitute and murdered men when they were most vulnerable.[56] Several of her victims were found nude and wearing only a hat or a pair of socks. They looked ridiculous—the ultimate insult to dominance. Furthermore, when the courts found the killings were "cold, calculated, and premeditated" they did so because they detected a pattern—the victims were all middle-aged men, traveling alone, and murdered in a remote location. But in her appeal, Wuornos noted that "car dates" are usually transacted in remote locations. The clients are usually men who travel alone. Thus, rather than a prearranged plan to target certain victims, Wuornos was simply going about her "business." Her lawyer argued that "to infer that a prostituted woman is setting in motion a prearranged plan because the men who use her and the mechanics of the transactions look much the same day after day is analogous to inferring that a battered woman plots her own abuse by getting married and going home from work every day."[57] Wornos's defense was that "she did what you would do, she defended herself" from sexual assault. But the prosecution and the press reiterated, and juries agreed, Wuornos was "not like you." As a prostitute, she was outside the mainstream and thus forfeited her right to do what others may do when they feel threatened.

If prostitution did not place Aileen Wuornos sufficiently beyond the pale in the public view, her liaison with a lesbian lover surely did. Her sexual orientation also figured prominently into the prosecution's strategy.[58] As in the case of Wanda Jean Allen, the state portrayed Wuornos as the "man" in the relationship with Tyria Moore. The latter was depicted as innocent and dependent, living in fear of Wornos's rage and therefore hesitant to go to the police with her information about the murders. It must have been difficult to wedge the two women into such stereotypes. On the one hand, the prosecution wanted to paint a picture of Wuornos as a femme fatale. On the other hand, they characterized her as the "butch" member of a lesbian relationship. The latter was especially difficult for those acquainted with Tyria Moore. Defense attorney Tricia Jenkins remembered Moore as "aggressive and large. She was the one who'd get violent in bars and start fights."[59]

Finally, Wornos's appearance provided an opportunity for the press and members of the prosecution team to make degrading comments. One attorney for the state believed Wuornos killed all the men for money. "She's so ugly and overweight, even those who patronized her didn't want to pay."[60] Ironically, he felt no need to comment on the appearances of those who had to buy the services of a prostitute. Author Sue Russell never missed a chance to offer an insulting description. Sketching Wornos's appearance in court, Russell says "the defendant looked like some product of a less advanced nation, her uneven teeth veering off unchecked in conflicting directions, her skin rough and blotchy, her dishwater-blond hair in lackluster condition." She talks of "this creature" who "snarled and sneered." In her eyes, Wuornos was to be ridiculed for her poverty and bad teeth and demeaned as a "creature," not a human being.[61] Death penalty defendants are often dehumanized, but it seems especially important that women sentenced to death be degraded and defeminized.

In an amazing interpretation of events, Prosecutor John Tanner was concerned that Wuornos had damaged the good names of Richard Mallory and her grandfather by her accusations of rape and abuse. He interpreted her death sentence in the Mallory case as a vindication. He expressed pleasure that her grandfather and Mallory (previously imprisoned for rape) had their reputations restored.[62] Tanner's comments are the perfect summary of how a patriarchal society interpreted the story of Aileen Wuornos to maintain the status quo. It canonized the men involved who used and abused her and demonized the woman who was both innocent and guilty.

One of the few official voices in the criminal justice system to recognize the complexity of the Wuornos story was Florida Supreme Court Justice Kogan who wrote a concurring opinion in the Mallory appeal. Although he supported the decision to affirm Wornos's death sentence, he acknowledged that there was too little recognition of the problems of "women forced into prostitution at a young age." Those who are forced into prostitution as an escape from an abusive home find "the tragic result that early victimization leads to even greater victimization." A girl who becomes an adult prostitute is labeled a criminal and is often "forced into more crime as the only means of supporting herself. Few escape this vicious cycle."[63] Aileen Wuornos did not.

Endnotes

1. Christopher S. Kudlac, *Public Executions: The Death Penalty and the Media* (Westport, CT: Praeger, 2007), 62.

2. Dorothy Otnow Lewis, *Guilty by Reason of Insanity* (New York: Fawcett Columbine, 1998), 293.

3. Information about the crimes may be found in Dolores Kennedy, *On a Killing Day* (Chicago: Bonus Books, 1992); Sue Russell, *Lethal Intent* (New York: Pinnacle Books, 2002); Aileen Wuornos with Chrisopher Berry-Dee, *Monster: My True Story* (London: John Blake Publishing, 2004) and at www.clarkprosecutor.org

4. Stacey L. Shipley and Bruce A. Arrigo, *The Female Homicide Offender: Serial Murder and the Case of Aileen Wuornos* (Upper Saddle River, New Jersey: Pearson Prentice Hall, 2004), 95.

5. The basic facts of Wornos's life may be found in Kennedy, *On a Killing Day*; Russell, *Lethal Intent*; Wuornos and Berry-Dee, *Monster*; and Shipley and Arrigo, *Female Homicide*

Offender. A very brief summary is included in Kathleen A. O'Shea, *Women and the Death Penalty in the United States, 1900–1998* (Westport, Connecticut: Praeger, 1999).

6. See Kennedy, *On a Killing Day*, Chapter 3, and Shipley and Arrigo, *Female Homicide Offender*, Chapter 8.

7. Quoted in Shipley and Arrigo, *Female Homicide Offender*, 103.

8. Appellant's brief, *Wuornos v. State of Florida*, 19 Fla. Law W. S455 (September 22, 1994).

9. Wuornos and Berry-Dee, *Monster*, 147.

10. Ibid., 152.

11. Ibid., 158.

12. American Civil Liberties Union, American Friends Service Committee, *The Forgotten Population: A Look at Death Row in the United States through the Experiences of Women* (Washington, D.C: 2004), 24.

13. Chimene I. Keitner, "Victim or Vamp? Images of Violent Women in the Criminal Justice System," *Columbia Journal of Gender and Law*, 11 (2002), 59–60.

14. Quoted in Kennedy, *On a Killing Day*, 142–43.

15. Ibid., 210.

16. Keitner, "Victim or Vamp?," 67.

17. *Wuornos v. Florida*, (September 22, 1994).

18. Ibid., and quoted in Kennedy, *On a Killing Day*, 178–86.

19. Appellant's brief and *Wuornos v. Florida* (September 22, 1994).

20. "Serial Killers: A Short History," at www.clarkprosecutor.org

21. Kennedy, *On a Killing Day*, 105.

22. *Wuornos v. Florida* (September 22, 1994).

23. Kennedy, *On a Killing Day*, 220.

24. Ibid.

25. *Wuornos v. Florida* (September 22, 1994).

26. Kennedy, *On a Killing Day*, 228.

27. *Wuornos v. State of Florida*, 644 So 2nd 1012 (October 6, 1994).

28. Ibid.

29. Kennedy, *On a Killing Day*, 249.

30. Ibid., and Russell, *Lethal Intent*. Both books examine the involvement of Arlene Pralle and Steve Glazer in Wornos's story.

31. *Wuornos v. State of Florida*, 676 So 2nd 966 (September 21, 1995).

32. Ibid.

33. *Wuornos v. State of Florida*, 676 So 2nd 972 (May 9, 1996). Appellant's brief.

34. Ibid.

35. Ibid.

36. Ibid.

37. Russell, *Lethal Intent*, 508–09.

38. Ibid., 536.

39. Catherine Wilson, "Aileen Wuornos Says Prison Guards Abusing Her," Associated Press (July 13, 2002); Ron Word, "Florida Executes Female Serial Killer," *St. Petersburg Times*, (October 9, 2002) at www.clarkprosecutor.org

40. Wuornos and Berry-Dee, *Monster*, xiv–xv.

41. Quoted in Paul Lomartire, "Aileen and Dawn: A Sisterhood Haunted by Memories and Madness," *Palm Beach Post* (February 29, 2004).

42. Word, "Florida Executes Female Serial Killer."

43. "Florida Executes Female Serial Killer; Wuornos Declines Final Meal," at www.clark-prosecutor.org

44. Jim Ross, "Execution Evokes a Tide of Memories," *St. Petersburg Times* (October 10, 2002).

45. Ralph Blumenthal, "A Growing Plea for Mercy for the Mentally Ill on Death Row," *New York Times* (November 23, 2006).

46. *Wuornos v. Florida* (May 9, 1996).

47. "Crazy to Kill," *New Times Broward-Palm Beach* (January 22, 2004).

48. Shipley and Arrigo, *Female Homicide Offender*, 66–67.

49. Ibid., 109.

50. Ibid., 109–15.

51. Ibid., 116–19.

52. Ibid., 122–26.

53. Quoted in Keitner, "Victim or Vamp?," 84.

54. Candice Skrapec, "The Female Serial Killer: An Evolving Criminality," in Helen Birch, ed., *Moving Targets: Women, Murder, and Representation* (Berkeley, CA: University of California Press, 1994), 244–45.

55. See, for example, Meda Chesney-Lind and Lisa Pasko, ed., *Girls, Women, and Crime: Selected Readings.* (Thousand Oaks, CA: Sage, 2004).

56. Janice L. Kopec, "Avoiding a Death Sentence in the American Legal System: Get a Woman to Do It," *Washington and Lee School of Law Capital Defense Journal* 15 (Spring 2003), 363.

57. *Wuornos v. Florida* (May 9, 1996).

58. Michael B. Shortnacy, "Guilty and Gay: A Recipe for Execution in American Courtrooms: Sexual Orientation as a Tool for Prosecutorial Misconduct in Death Penalty Cases," *American University Law Review*, 51 (December 2001).

59. "Crazy to Kill."

60. Kennedy, *On a Killing Day*, 222.

61. Russell, *Lethal Intent*, 485–86.

62. Kennedy, *On a Killing Day*, 222.

63. *Wuornos v. Florida* (September 22, 1994).

· 9 ·

PERILOUSLY CLOSE TO
SIMPLE MURDER

Frances Newton

Frances Newton was executed in Texas on September 14, 2005. Newton's case both reprises themes present in the other stories and stands apart from them. The flaws in the criminal justice system that marked most of the death penalties, especially the flaws that go with being poor and female, are present in Newton's case. Yet in contrast to the other defendants described here, it is likely that Frances Newton was innocent of the crimes for which she was put to death. The state relied on dubious physical evidence to link Newton to the murders of her husband and children. Because of her attorney's negligence, that evidence was never subjected to the scrutiny that would have revealed the weaknesses in the prosecution's case. And because of the difficulty of correcting trial errors through the appellate process in Texas, Newton, protesting her innocence to the last, was sent to her death. In *Herrera v. Collins*,[1] the Court held that claims of innocence must be balanced against the justice system's need for finality. In Newton's case, finality won.

Like virtually every other women whose story is recounted in this book, Frances Newton was represented by a shockingly incompetent appointed attorney. Ron Mock, Newton's lawyer, saw twelve of his fifteen capital clients sent to death row. Yet he was for a time the highest-earning court-appointed lawyer in Houston. One might think that after nine or ten losses in capital cases, judges would have stopped appointing him as defense counsel. They must have known also that before coming to court Mock started his days with a visit to Buster's Drinkery, a bar he owned.[2] Nonetheless, the court assigned Mock to Newton. That decision most likely sealed her fate.

Frances Newton shared the experience of other death-sentenced women in the way prosecutors chose to explain the crime of which she was accused. Like Velma Barfield, Marilyn Plantz, Betty Lou Beets, Judias Buenoano, Teresa Lewis, and to some extent Suzanne Basso—all the women accused of killing spouses or male partners—Newton's alleged motive was insurance money. The gendered image that greedy wives murder unsuspecting husbands to get their grasping hands on financial benefits seems to offer an effective route to a successful capital conviction. At some level, juries seem to find it plausible that women kill men for money and that such killings are heinous and atrocious enough to merit a death sentence. In Newton's case, the greed motive was made more shocking by the deaths of her children and by allegations that both she and her husband were involved in infidelities. Frances Newton was prosecuted by Joe Magliolo, the same skilled district attorney who handled Karla Faye Tucker's case. Again he successfully persuaded a jury to lay aside any sympathy for the accused because of her sex and to see her as an embodiment of evil.

Like other men and women put to death in the United States, Frances Newton was processed through a system that seems to value finality over the whole truth. After her appeals were denied in state and federal court, in December 2004, Texas Governor Rick Perry gave Newton a 120-day reprieve to allow for further investigation of the physical evidence used against her. When tests of some evidence proved impossible, rather than acknowledging that Newton's guilt remained in doubt, the state went ahead with the execution. The dissenters in *Herrera v. Collins* wrote that if the state puts an innocent person to death, it comes "perilously close to simple murder."[3] Newton's case stands quite near to that point.

The Crime and the Trial

Houston police were called to an apartment complex on April 7, 1987, at 8:27 PM. There the officers found the bodies of Adrian Newton, seven-year-old Alton Newton, and twenty-one-month-old Farrah Newton. All had been shot. Frances Newton was present at the apartment, along with her cousin, Sondra Nelms, who had placed the 911 call. There were no signs of forced entry or of a struggle.[4] Earlier in the evening, sometime between 7:00 and 7:30 PM, Frances had gone to Sondra's house, visited for a bit, and invited Sondra to return home with her. Before going back to the apartment, Frances removed a blue bag from her car and took it into an abandoned house owned by her parents next door to where Nelms lived. When the two women arrived at Newton's apartment, Adrian appeared to be asleep on the sofa. As she realized that he had been shot, Frances cried out in horror and ran into the bedrooms to find her children had also been shot. According to Sondra Nelms, Newton began to "frantically scream uncontrollably."[5]

Detective Michael Talton responded to the call. After visiting the crime scene, he went with Nelms to the abandoned house and found the bag Newton had left. It contained a Raven Arms .25 automatic, the sort of inexpensive handgun often called a "Saturday Night Special." Later when Talton asked Newton about the gun, she acknowledged that she had taken it from her apartment, put it in the bag, and hidden it because she overheard her husband say he was expecting trouble. Talton submitted the weapon he found for ballistics testing. At trial, he stated that the gun in evidence as the murder weapon was similar to the one he took from the bag. He also testified that Newton admitted to hiding the gun and knapsack.

Newton spent the night at the police station without an arrest. Her hands were tested for gunpowder residue but none was found. The next day, she accompanied Detective Michael Parinello while he searched the apartment where the crimes had occurred. She indicated that she had changed clothes since the previous day, showed Parinello the navy blue skirt and sweater she had worn the day of the shootings. The clothing was folded on top of Newton's dresser. The officer testified that he took the outfit to test it for gunpowder residue. Apparently there were no signs of blood on any of Newton's clothing.

On April 10, Frances and her mother, Ida Nelms, were again asked to come to the police station for questioning. Although the police had received the ballistics reports comparing the gun in the knapsack with the fatal wounds, again Newton was interrogated and released. Sergeant J. J. Freeze who questioned her on the 10th, admitted at trial that he heard the police talking about a second gun. The recovery of a second gun, if ballistics tests showed it to be the murder weapon, would explain why Newton was not arrested at the time. In fact, Frances's father, Bee Henry Nelms, stated that Freeze told him the ballistics analysis did not implicate his daughter.

Frances Newton was not arrested until April 22, more than two weeks after the murders and long after the police had the results of the tests on the guns. Apparently the decision to charge Newton was taken when she and her mother made claims on insurance policies on the lives of Adrian and Farrah Newton. The authorities must have concluded that the "motive," insurance benefits, would explain the crime and explain away the many inconsistencies in the evidence.

Frances and her family believed in her innocence and believed the truth would prevail. They could not foresee how the court's decision to appoint Ron Mock as her attorney would affect the outcome. However, in December 1987, Newton wrote to the judge asking that Mock be removed. She stated that he had not met with her and that he had not talked with any witnesses. The court refused her request without even holding a hearing. By the time her trial began in October 1988, her family had raised enough money to hire private counsel David Eisen and Gerald Fry. The court met to determine whether Newton could replace Mock. Newton also requested a continuance so her new attorneys could prepare for trial.

The clerk of the court produced records showing that Mock had not subpoenaed a single witness. Mock and his co-counsel Catherine Coulter had spoken with Newton only twice and had never spoken to her mother. When Mock was asked why he had not contacted Sondra Nelms, who had been with Newton on the night of the murders, he replied "I tell you I'm a lawyer, I'm not an investigator."[6] Apparently everything he knew about the case consisted of what he found in the prosecution's filings. In the face of Mock's gross failure to prepare, the judge agreed that Fry and Eisen could serve as Newton's counsel. However, he denied the motion for a continuance. Thus Frances Newton faced a Hobson's choice. Her new attorneys were too professional to go to trial without any preparation and decided to withdraw. She was left with Mock, who was perfectly willing to go totally unprepared into a courtroom where a woman's life hung in the balance. The judge allowed the case to go forward.

The prosecution's case consisted of testimony from Detectives Talton and Parinello and Sergeant Freeze about the crime scene, the gun in the knapsack, the search of Newton's apartment, the testing of her clothes, and the ballistics tests.[7] They also called Michael Mouton, the original owner of the knapsack gun. He claimed he had given the gun to his cousin Jerry Frelow, with whom Frances had an affair. She could have, the state claimed, taken the weapon from Frelow's drawer. The prosecutor implied that Frances wanted to get rid of her husband because of her sexual relationship with Frelow. As with a number of the female defendants, Newton was portrayed to the jury as both promiscuous and greedy.

Adrian's brother Sterling Newton next testified for the state. He had been living with Frances and her family at the time of the murders. He claimed to have been at the apartment that evening from sometime between 5:30 and 6:00 until 7:00 or 7:30 and that Frances was there when he left. According to Sondra Nelms, Frances arrived at her house between 7:00 and 7:30. An obvious inconsistency existed. The defense did try to elicit information about Adrian's drug use and his ties to drug dealers from Sterling. In response, the prosecution asked him to identify photographs of the dead children, reminding the jury that if one victim was a drug dealer, the other two were small innocents.

Ramona Bell, a long-time girlfriend of Adrian, who was "dating" him at the time of the crime, claimed he had told her he did not trust Frances. Bell's testimony may have been offered to give Frances an additional motive, jealousy.

Sondra Nelms was called as a witness for the state. Much of the direct examination involved Frances's behavior before the bodies were discovered. Nelms described how Frances kissed all her cousins good-bye that night. Magliolo's questioning seemed designed to create the impression that Newton knew she would not see them again, that she was operating with guilty knowledge. Under cross-examination, however, Nelms said Frances was not behaving strangely before they discovered the bodies and that she became truly hysterical when she found her husband and children murdered. Clearly if the defense had talked with Nelms before the trial, they could have uncovered a number of flaws in the prosecution's time table.

Claudia Chapman, a State Farm Insurance agent, described how Frances Newton had bought car insurance from her in September 1986. In March 1987 Newton took out life insurance policies on herself, with her mother as beneficiary, and on Adrian and Farrah, with Frances as beneficiary. Each policy would pay $50,000.

Prosecutor Magliolo also called the state medical examiner, who discussed the toxicology report showing cocaine in Adrian's system at the time of death; the detective who transported the gun and bullets to the lab; the firearms examiner; and a forensic chemist. Randy Snyder, the supervisor at the Houston Crime Laboratory, stated that he found nitrites consistent with gunpowder at the bottom of the front of Newton's skirt. Those particles could have been left by someone holding a gun between her knee and ankle while shooting it. Or somewhat more logically, they could also have come from fertilizer. Although the chemist admitted the residue could have come from either source, neither the state nor the defense conducted tests to show the actual source of the nitrites.

The defense's case raised a few interesting questions. A competent, well-prepared advocate could easily have created reasonable doubt concerning many points in the prosecution's arguments. Mock missed those opportunities. An independent forensic chemist summoned to identify the material on Newton's skirt actually sounded less than professional. An investigator with the county medical examiner's office explained that spots outside the children's room "might be" blood, and that a hole in the ceiling "might be" caused by a bullet. This was crucial information as no blood had been found on Frances or her clothes. If the murderer had left a blood trail, why were there no traces on her? Unfortunately, Mock did not press this point.

Terrence Lewis, brother of Adrian Newton, changed his testimony while on the witness stand. He had told police on the night of the shootings that his brother was in debt to a drug dealer known as "Charlie." He had further offered to show police where Charlie lived. The police did not follow up on the investigation of the alleged drug connection with Adrian's murder and Terrence Lewis denied he had made such a statement. Officer Frank Pratt of the sherriff's department did testify that Lewis had talked about Charlie. He further testified that the police never followed up on that lead. There was no indication why they made such a decision.

The defense called four character witnesses, whose contributions seemed slight. Barbara Sack, who had taught Frances in a theater class three years earlier stated that the defendant had a good reputation. The prosecutor asked whether Frances had been taught to cry in the class. Perhaps the jury would see her as a consummate actress who fooled everyone with her distress on the night of the murders. Pastor Thomas T. Williams testified that Newton and her children attended the Baptist church regularly. Two neighbors said that Frances was a good mother. The state elicited information from them concerning her extramarital relationships. Thus the defense's attempt to portray Newton's good character was offset by the prosecutor's effort to show her as deceptive and promiscuous.

Frances Newton was the final witness for the defense. According to a reporter for the *Houston Chronicle* she looked "more like a choir member than a woman facing a possible death sentence."[8] Newton described a marriage in which her husband engaged in repeated infidelities, where she was the breadwinner and where Adrian used cocaine and owed money to a drug dealer named Charlie. She had purchased insurance from State Farm because it was better coverage than what was available through her former employer, Popeye's Chicken.[9]

Although her relationship with Adrian was rocky, Frances stated that she had been involved in only one affair, with Jeffrey Ferlow. On the day of the murders, she claimed that after her return from work she and Adrian talked, made love, and decided to reconcile. Frances then showered and changed from her navy blue outfit, leaving it folded on top of her dresser. Adrian got several phone calls which worried Frances. Suspecting the possibility of trouble, she took the gun from the cabinet and hid it in the abandoned house when she picked up Sondra Nelms. Returning home, Frances and Sondra found the bodies of her husband and children. She did not remember much about the rest of the evening, either her reaction or the police interrogation.

The prosecutor focused on the predictable factors. Frances had an affair. Frances hid a gun. Frances took out life insurance. Frances had taken acting classes. Magliolo played the notes that seem to persuade juries to convict female defendants—marital infidelity which calls a woman's morals into question, financial benefits that suggest an unseemly greed, and a practice of deceit that casts doubt on everything the woman said.

Mock's closing did little to vindicate Frances Newton. The beginning is incomprehensible. "Common sense and logic will tell you, or ought to tell you, even if they blow down, we are talking about blow-out and back out when you have a contact when something comes back in the barrel and certainly comes back, number one, on the hands for a metal absorption and certainly some type of powder on some type of garment up here—nothing." Perhaps he was trying to encourage the jury to consider the gunpowder residue. One cannot tell that from the following statement. "They don't have it. And you might have that. Any doubt I tell you that you have and there is a person of an accused, not to state. Mr. Magliolo is a fine fellow but he don't (sic) get points for that. This ain't horseshoes and hand grenades. Getting close don't count, folks." Mock announced that he was representing his client to the best of his ability and continued, "short of good courtroom decorum, good mama raising, and if I have offended anyone, I apologize and ask you to wait until you come out from the deliberation room and beat up on me if you want to." One could only imagine what the jury was thinking of him and of his client.

They returned a guilty verdict after less than two hours of deliberation.

The sentencing phase followed immediately after a motion by the defense arguing that Newton should not be eligible for the death penalty. Their point was that the state could not establish that the defendant would pose a danger in the future. The prosecution offered two witnesses to demonstrate that Newton was a continuing threat and therefore that she should be executed.

Wanda Buckner, a former employer, testified to Newton's "criminal history." In 1985, Frances had stolen $85 from Foley's department store where she worked. Newton was allowed to resign and the incident was not reported to the police. That was the extent of her past lawlessness.

The state then called Dr. Charles Covert, a psychiatrist in private practice. He had never met Frances Newton, never seen her until that moment in court. Yet he was permitted to diagnose her future conduct based on a hypothetical case described by the prosecutor. The hypothetical concerned a 23-year-old married woman in a "stormy relationship," who had "stolen from her employer." Because her husband did not "want her around anymore," she decided to kill him and her children to "wipe out that part of her life and have a new start" without "excess baggage." She wants to be richer so she buys insurance. The prosecutor then described how the hypothetical woman left her children with other people during the day (he failed to mention that she was at work supporting her family). That night while her husband was sleeping she executed him by putting a pistol to his head. She then put a pillow over her son's head and shot him at close range, then "takes her 21-month-old baby and puts her on the floor and holds a pistol eight to twenty inches from her chest and shoots her to death." This hypothetical person then went to a relative's house to create an alibi and "pretended" nothing was wrong. Returning to the apartment, she "pretended" to discover the bodies.

Based on that scenario, the prosecutor asked Dr. Covert whether "there would be a probability that person would commit acts that would constitute violent acts that would constitute a threat to society?" "Yes," responded the doctor.

One could argue that the prosecutor's strategy here was twofold. Dr. Covert's conclusion was completely predictable. He would not have been hired if he did not support the state's position. His opinion, however, went into the record to provide professional support for the future dangerousness element. It seems logical that the prosecutor was reinforcing a particular image, not of a hypothetical individual but of Frances Newton for the jury's benefit. A selfish woman, with a "criminal record," who would calmly execute her sleeping husband and brutally murder her innocent "babies," so she could go off and live a carefree new life without that "baggage." Any resemblance to the real Frances Newton—hardworking, churchgoing, responsible friend, mother, and daughter—was obscured by the "hypothetical" character conjured up by the prosecutor.

Magliolo's closing argument in the sentencing phase reiterated the picture of Frances as hardened criminal and depraved wife and mother.

Newton, he said, "gave up her self-respect in 1985 when she stole from her employer, and what did she steal and I think it is significant—cash money, not shoes, not a dress, not a hat, but cash money." The prosecutor seemed to think Frances would be less blameworthy had she stolen something for herself, rather than money to pay her family's bills. Yet he wanted to make her the destroyer of everything a woman should value, her family. "Think what it tells us about a person who can approach a sleeping spouse, no matter how much you hate her, no matter how much you despise them and stick a gun to that sleeping spouse's head." The prosecutor wanted to create a sense that Newton not only took her husband's life, she took advantage of his weakness, a true role reversal. Of course, the worst role betrayal came if a mother murdered her own children. As Magliolo described, Alton heard his father being shot. " 'Mama, what is going on?' 'Mom, where is dad?' Puts the pillow over his head 'Mom'—boom. She shoots him." The description of Farrah's death was even more heart-rending. "What does it tell us about a person that can pick up or move, or whatever, their own 21-month-old child that they personally bore, sit that baby on the ground…. The baby is looking. There is nothing covering that baby. Whoever shot that baby—and we all knew who it was, you decided who it was and determined from the evidence—look that baby in the eye and what do you suppose that little baby, what is a 21-month old baby think towards its mother. Love. That's all a baby has. That's all a 21-month-old baby knows is love. What does it tell us about a person who could look in that baby's eyes and execute them? Is that person a threat to society? The evidence is clear."

The prosecutor's closing was a masterful argument designed to convince the members of the jury that Frances Newton was not a *real* woman. In his view, she killed a sleeping husband and two "babies." Someone who embodies such a perversion of natural family instincts constitutes a true threat to society and cannot be allowed to stay alive.

Mock attempted to restore some of Newton's virtues by calling relatives, friends, former teachers, and her pastor in response. In fact the defense's total case during the sentencing phase consisted of testimony from those character witnesses, who asserted that they cared about Frances and would write to her and visit her in prison. At the time when her life hung in the balance, Newton's attorney offered virtually nothing to convince the jury to spare her life. On October 25, 1988, the jury returned with a sentence of death.

After the Sentence

Frances Newton would join three other women on Texas' death row in 1989. Karla Faye Tucker, Betty Lou Beets, and Pam Perillo (whose sentence was later commuted to life) prepared for Newton's arrival. They cleaned, made her bed, and bought her a few things from the commissary. Beets was quoted as remarking, "This is upsetting for us for someone else to come here. Not because we didn't want her here personally; we just didn't want anyone else to get a sentence like this. It really hurts."[10]

At the time, the women on death row spent most of the day together crafting the stuffed dolls called Parole Pals. Beets explained "We're moral support for each other. We've all got Christ in our lives. Every night before we go to bed, we hold hands, pray, and give each other a hug. And we thank God for the position we're in, because it could be a lot worse."[11] Frances Newton joined that elite sorority. She would see Tucker and Beets put to death before her. By the time Newton was executed, there were nine women on death row. Of those eleven Texas women (three executed and eight others), five were from Harris County (Houston). The female portion of Texas' death row reflects the national statistics, a disproportionate number of those with capital sentences came from one jurisdiction.

All those sentenced to death were provided with an automatic right to appeal. The purpose is to ensure that any errors in the original trial can be brought to light. The judge who presided over Newton's original trial assigned her appellate counsel. Despite numerous earlier attempts to replace Ron Mock, Judge Charles Hearn assigned him to represent Frances Newton in her appeal. Therefore the judge's refusal to let Newton have the lawyer of her choice at trial would not be raised in the initial appeal. The judge and Mock would have their conduct ratified. They would be insulated from accountability while Newton forfeited the ability to raise those issues later.

As if Mock's performance in Newton's trial had not been bad enough, he surpassed himself at the appellate stage. Appeals are based on errors in the original trial record. Mock did not even request a copy of the trial transcript from the court. Nor did he or his associate Coulter meet once with their client. In November 1988, Newton again tried to replace Mock with an attorney of her choosing. This time she chose to hire Charles Freeman. The judge refused to rule on Newton's petition, effectively leaving her with Mock as her attorney and more importantly, effectively ratifying her death sentence as Mock made only a nominal attempt at appeal.

In addition to Judge Hearn's rulings, Charles Freeman encountered numerous obstacles in his attempt to represent Newton. On several occasions he was refused visitation with his client because he was wearing a Muslin head covering. Other times, dressed the same way, he was allowed in. In 1991, Freeman filed a new appeal citing 37 errors, including the allegations that Newton was denied effective assistance of counsel at both the trial and the appellate stage.[12] In colorful language, he claimed that the appointment of Mock at the appeals stage had contaminated the post-trial proceedings. "The trial court propped up a straw dog to roll over and play dead on Appellant's appeal for her life. The trial court, by and through its straw dog named Mock, precluded Appellant from presenting evidence, making an offer of proof, perfecting a bill of exceptions or otherwise present (sic) a sufficient record attendant to her motions for a new trial." Freeman's brief included dramatic pleas for a reconsideration of his client's case as she ran the "gauntlet of death." "The stark finality of death ought to serve as a reminder of the outright importance of procedural safeguards for accuseds marching ever so slowly, heads hung, along that worn path from indictment to lethal injection to a solemn 'Swing Low Sweet Chariot.' Such procedural safeguards protect weak and lowly accuseds from high and mighty trial courts whose utter recalcitrance thwarts and stifles *meaningful* appellate review."[13] He argued that a reversal would get the lower court's attention. "Betcha that'll insure a heightened sense of procedural safeguards by trial courts presiding over capital felony trials in Texas."[14]

Doubtless Freeman provided Frances Newton with the zealous defense she deserved. However, it was unlikely that his references to "high and mighty" judges would win points with the higher courts. In fact, the Court of Criminal Appeals rejected the appeal in June 1992. They found that Newton had been "ably represented" by Mock who had provided her with a "vigorous defense." They determined that her efforts to replace him were "mere attempts at delay."[15]

Newton filed several additional appeals, including a state application for habeas corpus in 2000.

Habeas Appeals

In September 2000, Newton filed a state habeas appeal that included six points on which she requested relief. First, she argued that the Texas capital law was unconstitutional because it did not provide for the introduction of appropriate mitigating evidence. It has come to light that Frances had suffered psychological abuse from Adrian, including his practice of gloating over his frequent extramarital affairs and threats to infect his wife with a sexually transmitted disease. No provision in the Texas law allowed for the consideration of such facts. Secondly, Newton claimed that the Texas law, contrary to the Supreme Court's ruling in *Furman v. Georgia*, allowed the prosecutor to exercise unfettered discretion. The Harris County District Attorney was able to selectively prosecute capital cases, not because of the characteristics of the crime but because of his own priorities. In addition to challenging the statutory flaws, Newton claimed that she was denied effective assistance of counsel, as her lawyers Mock and Coulter were "functionally absent" from her defense. Among other things, they failed to object when the prosecutor improperly removed African Americans from the jury selection process. Furthermore, lawyers failed to order independent forensics tests although Newton had requested they do so. And, she charged, that because she was stuck with Mock and Coulter in her first appeal, she was denied meaningful appellate review. Her attorneys did no post-trial investigation to uncover errors in her original trial. The Court of Criminal Appeals affirmed the trial court's findings and denied relief.[16]

Newton then attempted to take her appeals to federal court. Because she began that process after the Antiterrorism and Effective Death Penalty Act (AEDPA) became effective in 1996, the courts would not consider her case unless she was able to obtain a Certificate of Appealability (COA). To receive a COA, a petitioner was required to make "a substantial showing of the denial of a constitutional right." Further, the person trying to appeal had to demonstrate that "reasonable jurists" would find the lower court's rulings on her constitutional claims "debatable or wrong." Thus Newton had to overcome a two-pronged obstacle before the United States Court of Appeals would consider her case. She had to show that she was denied a constitutional right and that judges would find the decisions of the lower courts either unreasonable or wrong. AEDPA also ordered the federal courts to show deference to the ruling of the state courts. Thus by the time Newton's case got to the Court of Appeals, the bar for achieving review was set very high indeed. To make matters more difficult for her, the Fifth Circuit Court, where her case was argued, has been especially unwilling to reconsider death penalty pleadings.

Thus it came as no surprise when that court denied Newton's request for a COA and let the earlier decisions stand. They rejected her first claim that she had been denied effective assistance of counsel when the trial court refused her motion for a continuance so she could be represented by the lawyers her family had hired. Incredibly, the court ruled that the failure to grant a continuance did not harm Newton's defense. They noted that the attorneys she wished to hire did not specify the length of time they needed to prepare for trial. As eighteen months had passed between the time Newton was indicted and the start of her trial, apparently the appellate court believed any delay would undermine the justice process. They seemed to imply that if Newton had really wanted to employ counsel, she should have done so sooner. That position assumes not that it took Newton's family eighteen months to gather funds to pay lawyers, but that they were simply dragging their feet for ulterior motives. It is hard to imagine that the court had much empathy for a poor African American family with no discretionary funds to pay attorneys' fees.

Newton's second constitutional claim concerned the "special issues" in the Texas law that determined future dangerousness. She claimed that the sentencing process offered no mechanism for the jury to consider her mitigating evidence: her youth, a philandering husband, his drug addiction, her cooperation with the police, her religiousness, and her family's poverty. The appellate court held that Newton could have brought forth all of those factors under the "future dangerousness" issue. In other words, when the state said she would be a danger because she once stole $85 and because a paid psychologist agreed with a hypothetical example, she could respond that she was not dangerous based on the factors listed above. Therefore, they found her jury had not been deprived of the opportunity to consider mitigating evidence.

The Fifth Circuit denied Newton's appeal on May 20, 2004. Two months later, a Houston judge set her execution date for the following December 1.

Several revealing *Houston Chronicle* articles covered the proceedings. Both focused on the role of Ron Mock in Newton's case and noted that his work had been the focus of her "complaints" since the outset. The paper mentioned that Mock had frequently been accused of doing "shoddy work on capital cases" and that he had admitted to filing no motions, speaking to no witnesses, and submitting no list of witnesses. Mock blamed those failings on his "busy schedule." Various attorneys who had represented Newton during appeals commented on her inadequate counsel. "She's had bad representation at every stage of the process. That's partly how she got where she is today," said Kenneth Williams who had handled her federal habeas case. David Eisen, who would have replaced Mock had the trial court granted a continuance called Newton's sentence "a real travesty." Eisen was shocked that Newton never got a new trial. "I thought it was a clear case of ineffective assistance of counsel."

Those who had prosecuted Frances Newton disagreed. Assistant District Attorney Roe Wilson made the amazing statement, "Ron Mock did a lot of these death penalty cases.... He did a good job of them. If you go back and look at the fact of this case, he did a more than adequate job."[17] Thus until the end, the state could maintain that an attorney who did not meet with his client, file any motions, call any witnesses, or do any investigation was *more than adequate*. One can only conjecture how much less he could have done to be merely adequate.

Reprieve

After Frances Newton was given an execution date, executive clemency became the only real possibility of saving her life. In Texas, executive clemency is a rare phenomenon indeed.

Lawyers for the Texas Innocence Network, David Dow and John LaGrappe filed the petition seeking a 120-day reprieve on November 8, 2004. Three weeks before Newton's scheduled death, the petition argued that she was actually innocent of the murder of Adrian, Alton, and Farrah Newton and that the reprieve would allow her new attorneys to carry out further investigations. The major claims in the filing asserted that the ballistics analysis connecting the murder weapon to Newton may have been flawed. Tests on Frances Newton's hands showed she had not fired a gun. No blood stains were found on Newton or on her clothes, although there was evidence of blood spatter in the apartment. Nor were there indications that the apartment or anyone in it had undertaken a clean-up. If Newton killed her family, what happened to the blood? Doubts about the forensic evidence were reasonable particularly since a 2003 audit of the Houston Police Department crime laboratory showed serious defects in its operations. Yet the circumstantial case against Newton was bolstered by material from that crime lab.

Other problems with the state's prosecution of Newton involved the timetable. Testimony of witnesses, if analyzed, suggested that she would have had no more than 20 minutes to shoot her husband and children, clean up herself and her home, compose herself, and drive to her cousin's house where she appeared perfectly calm. Additionally, the petition argued that the police made no effort to investigate whether the murders were drug related, despite Adrian's history and the tips about Charlie the drug dealer.[18]

At the end of November, the Texas Board of Pardons and Paroles recommended and Governor Rick Perry agreed, that Frances Newton would be granted a 120-day reprieve so that her case could be reopened. Covering all his bases, Perry stated that he saw "no evidence of innocence," but that the delay in executing Newton would allow for the use of new technology to re-test the gun allegedly used in the murders and to conduct further tests on the nitrates found on the skirt. The Harris County district attorney stated that he was "very disappointed" at the reprieve but went on to say "it doesn't make any difference to me if she is executed today or in 120 days." Apparently killing Frances Newton was his goal; the change in timing was only a "disap-pointment." Bill White, the mayor of Houston, showed a bit more concern for justice. He wrote in a letter to the governor, "as a supporter of capital punishment, I believe it is absolutely necessary that there are legal safeguards that would remove any question or doubts that an innocent person may be executed."[19] It is hard to argue that a person should be executed when there were doubts about guilt or innocence, but that is precisely what happened to Frances Newton.

After the December 2004 reprieve further ballistics tests were conducted on the gun police claimed was the same one found in the abandoned house. Once again, it was shown to be the murder weapon. However, they were unable to do additional tests to determine whether Frances Newton's skirt was exposed to fertilizer or to gunpowder residue. When the state conducted its original analysis of the nitrites, it effectively destroyed the skirt. In other words, they cut out a piece of the fabric, tested it to find it contained nitrites without determining the source of the nitrites, and ruined the material. After Newton's original trial, the skirt was placed in the same box with the victims' clothes, cross-contaminating all the physical evidence. Thus in 2004–05, the director of the Crime Laboratory at the Texas Department of Public Safety refused to test the skirt any more. "In my professional opinion," he wrote, "I would consider retesting the clothing to be of no value due to the destruc-tive nature of the original tests and unknown handling and storage of the evidence."[20]

Lacking proof of Newton's innocence, the 120-day reprieve expired, and the state set a new execution date for September 14, 2005. Her attor-neys could only make a last-ditch effort to reopen the case based on three claims: Newton was actually innocent and would never have been con-victed if she had a competent attorney; no jury would have found "future dangerousness" if she had adequate counsel; and the state should not be allowed to execute someone after they had destroyed potentially exculpa-tory evidence.

The articulation of these arguments summarizes the significant problems with Newton's case.

Final Pleas

For Newton to make a successful habeas corpus argument in Texas courts she had to persuade them that constitutional violations had led to her conviction and sentence. Two points related to the failures of her trial attorney. If Mock had not been "constitutionally ineffective," no rational juror would have found her guilty beyond a reasonable doubt nor would any rational juror have found the special issue, future dangerousness, applicable to Newton. The third constitutional claim concerned the denial of due process that resulted from the state's destruction of the only physical evidence that connected Newton to the crime.

The United States Supreme Court had defined the meaning of ineffective assistance of counsel in *Strickland v. Washington.*[21] In 2003, they found that failure of an attorney in a capital case to conduct investigations or to make a reasonable decision that investigations were unnecessary constituted ineffective assistance.[22] Given those rulings, it seemed inarguable that Newton's case was prejudiced by Mock's failures. It is most likely that Frances Newton was not guilty of the murders. Mock's performance was responsible for the jury's inability to see that the state had not proved her guilt beyond a reasonable doubt. The prosecution argued that Newton had a motive, insurance money, and opportunity, access to the gun she hid in the abandoned house. Mock should have raised numerous questions about that simple story. He should have done what any competent defense attorney would do, subjected the state's theory to "rigorous adversarial testing."[23]

There were numerous problems with the insurance money motive. Policies covered Adrian and Farrah Newton. There was no policy on Alton Newton. If Frances killed her husband and daughter for payoffs of $50,000 each, did she kill Alton for free? The state never addressed this question and neither did Mock. Claudia Chapman, the insurance agent for State Farm, testified that she sold the policies to Frances Newton. It was Chapman who persuaded Newton to buy the life insurance. Newton had come in to buy car insurance. In contrast to the state's allegation that she bought the policies as part of a plot to relieve herself of the "baggage" of husband and children, there was another explanation. Three months before Newton bought the life insurance, three of her cousins had died in a house fire. They were uninsured and their families had no money to bury them. Mock could have raised these points to undermine the state's theory of motive. The fires were written up in the *Houston Chronicle*. He might have placed that information before the jury had he bothered to do the most cursory investigation. Surely that motive for buying insurance might be more consistent with the character of the loving mother everyone who knew her found Frances Newton to be.

Mock further failed to challenge the possibility that Newton had time to do all that the prosecution had claimed. A simple timeline, bolstered by testimony from the state's own witnesses, would have shown that Newton had at most twenty minutes to kill her family, clean up the apartment, remove all traces of blood from herself and her clothing, remove any evidence from her car, and compose herself before driving to her cousin's house. In fact, an examination of the timeline would show that Sterling Newton, Adrian's brother, was the last person known to be alone with the victims. Furthermore, a neighbor told investigating officers on the night of the shooting that he heard a gunshot at 7:30 PM. Frances was definitely not present at that time. The police had that information. It was in the reports available to Mock. He never mentioned nor called the neighbor. If a disinterested witness heard a shot at 7:30 and Frances Newton was somewhere else at 7:30, would the jury have grounds for reasonable doubt of her guilt?

In addition, Mock was woefully inadequate in challenging the state's claim that the nitrites on the hem of Newton's skirt proved she had committed the murders. Would a reasonable jury believe that someone held a gun at her ankle three times, to shoot three different people, and shot perfectly each time from that awkward position? She would have had to hold the gun at her hem, put her leg up on the sofa next to Adrian's head and fire. Why did Mock not pursue this bizarre scenario? The only nitrites were found on the skirt—not a speck on Newton's sweater. Nor was there even a trace of gunshot residue on her hands.

There were two other possible explanations for the nitrites on Newton's skirt. Farrah had spent the day with Newton's uncle who used fertilizer containing nitrites in his garden. Farrah had been playing in the garden. Might her mother have picked up the child and the fertilizer from the child's shoes gotten on the bottom of the mother's skirt? Surely that is a more plausible picture than a murderer killing people with a gun held at ankle height. Newton claimed she had changed out of the navy blue outfit before leaving the apartment. A second possible explanation for the residue on the skirt is that the actual shooter fired over the clothes while they were folded on Newton's dresser.

The skirt was the only piece of evidence linking Frances Newton to the scene of the crime. Yet her attorney did not ask that it be tested to find out if the nitrites came from fertilizer or from gunpowder. He essentially let the state win that argument. Nor did he object to the use of a test that destroyed the clothing and made additional examination of it impossible.

The lack of any blood whatsoever on Frances Newton or her clothes should have raised serious questions. Police reports of the crime scene describe blood trails from the living room to the bedrooms. It would seem that when the killer shot Adrian Newton in the head, execution style, he or she would have been splattered with blood and brain matter and trailed those into the children's rooms. Likewise the murder weapon would have been covered in blood. Why did the police find no blood on Newton or on the gun in the abandoned house? She could not have washed up and gotten rid of all the traces, as the police report showed the bathroom shower and the kitchen sink of the apartment had not been used. Here again, Mock did not present his client's case. His inept questioning failed to get the evidence of the blood trail into the record. Newton's appeal notes, "This is a failure of defense counsel of monumental proportions."[24]

There are additional difficulties with the gun as evidence. The police tested the gun found in the abandoned house the day after the crime. They could easily connect it to Frances Newton, based on her own testimony and that of Sondra Nelms. Yet they did not arrest Newton until two weeks later. A possible explanation is that they found a second weapon which was not linked to her in any way. Sergeant Freeze admitted he heard about a second gun. If the police found two guns, both cheap and readily available Raven Arms .25s, possibly the second gun fired the fatal shots. If the murder weapon was not the gun Frances Newton admitted to hiding, in plain view of Sondra Nelms, it would explain why the police waited two weeks to arrest her. That theory is also consistent with the other physical evidence—the lack of blood and gunpowder residue on Newton.

Sondra Nelms testified for the prosecution at Newton's trial. Yet she had information that, had Mock interviewed her, would have undermined the state's case. In an affidavit she provided a picture of Frances Newton that did not come out in court. Nelms described that on the way from her house to Newton's apartment, they stopped off to pick up a necklace Frances had bought for Adrian. She had explained to Nelms that they were trying to work out a reconciliation. She was able to report on Newton's shock and horror at the crime scene and to explain, as one who knew Frances well, that her reaction was not feigned. Nelms also clarified that Alfonso Harrison called the Newton apartment just as she and Frances arrived. He was put on hold because the two women had just discovered three dead bodies. Nelms led the police to the gun in the abandoned house. After such cooperation with their investigation, it is unlikely that she would be untruthful about Newton's other behavior on the night of the murders. But because Mock never talked with Nelms prior to trial, he did not ask the questions that would place his client in a favorable light.

Finally, a day after the murders the Harris County Sheriff's Department received an anonymous phone call that reported seeing a red pickup truck, driven by a black male approximately 30-years-old, outside the Newton apartment the night of the crime. The caller provided a license plate number. The call was recorded. Neither the police nor Mock ever followed up on the lead.

Nor did either side pursue the possibility of a drug-related connection to the murders. Not only did Terrence Lewis tell the police about Charlie, he provided an address. Frances Newton's father gave them the same information. An inmate in the Harris County jail swore that he shared a cell with a man who claimed credit for the murders. The informant, Darrell Chiles, said his cellmate was working for a drug dealer and went to Newton's house to collect a debt from Adrian.

Newton's trial attorney failed to ask questions, and he overlooked evidence that would vindicate her. The jury did not hear a great many things that created more than a reasonable doubt about Frances Newton's guilt. They did not know those things because her "notoriously incompetent attorney" did not do his job. Mock's co-counsel "unequivocally stated that Frances Newton did not receive effective representation at trial." A juror told Newton's attorneys that Mock was asleep during most of the trial. Taken altogether, it seemed clear that Frances Newton was denied her constitutional right to counsel and that her lawyer's offenses had prejudiced the outcome. The layperson might well ask, what could be a greater denial of fundamental rights than to punish an innocent person—by death—because of her attorney's callous failure to provide a defense?

The second point in Newton's 2005 habeas appeal argues that in the sentencing phase no reasonable jury would have voted for death except for Mock's ineffectiveness in challenging the prosecution's arguments. The critical factor in a Texas capital case is "future dangerousness." For Newton, the major evidence was the testimony of Dr. Charles Covert, based on his response to the state's hypothetical. The jury apparently believed that a mental health professional could, without even seeing or talking to a subject, predict future conduct.

Newton's appellate attorneys pointed to scholarly research that showed such predictions were wrong 95% of the time. The state used unreliable evidence to establish that Newton met the requirement for execution. Not only was the type of testimony inherently flawed, Frances Newton's own record since her trial showed the information to be false in her individual case. During the entire period of her incarceration, Newton did not commit one single violent act.

The third and final claim was that because the state—whether intentionally or not—destroyed the evidence that could have established Newton's innocence, it should not be allowed to proceed with her execution. The condemned woman was prevented from ever testing the skirt that could show her conviction was unreliable. In effect, she was denied the opportunity to use contemporary technology to challenge the questionable interpretation of ambiguous evidence. Her attorneys asked the Texas courts to rule that in capital cases due process is violated when the state destroys exculpatory evidence that it used to convict, even if the evidence is destroyed inadvertently. The United States Supreme Court had often held that "death is different," that because of the irreversible consequences due process requires a higher degree of reliability in capital proceedings. The habeas petition argued in summary that the case against Frances Newton was wrong as to motive; that it was flawed as to opportunity, based on doubt about the murder weapon; and that there were unanswerable questions about the nitrites on her clothes. Thus her conviction and sentence were "unreliable," or not to be trusted and her execution should be stayed.

On August 24, 2005, the Texas Court of Criminal Appeals denied the appeal. Most comments on the ruling focused on a statement by the court that it would not matter whether the police had recovered one gun or a thousand guns if the revolver Newton put in the abandoned house was the murder weapon. Of course, that was Newton's point. There were questions about whether the abandoned-house gun was the murder weapon. This issue was raised again in a new habeas petition filed on August 25.

Newton's attorneys learned that Roe Wilson, Assistant District Attorney for Harris County, had given an interview on a Dutch television station that referred to the existence of a second gun. At first, Wilson denied the statement but Newton's counsel obtained a copy of the videotape in which she said "the police recovered a gun from the apartment that belonged to the husband."[25] Records indicated that Adrian Newton had purchased a Raven Arms .25, the same make and model as the gun in the abandoned house. A second gun, with no link to Frances Newton, was favorable evidence that had not been shared with the defense. Although there were rumors of several guns at the time of trial, Wilson's statement seemed to confirm that fact. A second gun raised questions not only about the state's violation of procedural rules but about Newton's innocence. No one had recorded the serial number of the gun at the abandoned house. At trial, Officer Talton had testified that the gun in evidence was "similar to" the one he found there. If there were at least two Raven Arms .25s in the hands of the police, and there were questions about which was which, who could be sure that the murder weapon was the one Frances Newton hid?

When Roe Wilson was faced with the videotape of her TV interview, she claimed she "misspoke," that she meant to say the police found ammunition at Newton's apartment. David Dow, Newton's attorney, remarked that he did not see how a prosecutor could confuse a gun with ammunition.[26]

Nonetheless, the Texas courts, the Supreme Court, and the Board of Pardons and Paroles rejected Newton's last appeals. She was executed by lethal injection on September 14, 2005. Newton's family witnessed her execution, holding hands, weeping, and consoling one another. Reporters managed to find Tamika Craft-Demming, a cousin of Adrian Newton, who gave them the requisite sound bite advocating retribution. She wanted Frances to apologize. "Justice to me was not served. If we saw some kind of apology, that would have been justice." Sobbing loudly in the death chamber, Craft-Demming said she cried for the kids, "not one tear for Frances."[27] Adrian Newton's parents, on the other hand, had believed Frances innocent and supported her throughout.

The More Things Change, the More They Remain the Same

Despite the profound questions concerning her innocence, Frances Newton's story resembles the other cases chronicled in this book. As one article noted, it was "painfully unexceptional.... one in a long line of Texas death row cases in which the prosecutions were sloppy or dishonest, the defenses incompetent or negligent, and the constitutional guarantee of a fair trial was honored only in name."[28] Indeed the elements in Newton's case were common not only in Texas, but in Oklahoma, Arkansas, Alabama, Florida, North Carolina, and Virginia. Newton may have had the worst defense attorney, but almost every other woman sent to death row was inadequately represented. The failure of the court system to live up to its promise that all defendants will be provided with competent counsel reflects the persistent class biases that affect criminal justice in general and capital punishment in particular. Frances Newton did not live in poverty, but her working-class status priced her out of the market for a good private attorney. Because her family was unable to hire counsel to replace the appalling Ron Mock until the last minute before her trial, Newton paid dearly—with her life.

As discussed above, Mock not only did not prepare for Newton's trial, he blithely admitted his lack of concern to the judge who appointed—and reappointed—him. Although Judge Hearn found no fault with him, and Roe Wilson claimed that Mock had provided Frances Newton with a "more than adequate defense,"[29] Mock was eventually brought before the State Bar five times to face disciplinary charges for professional misconduct. He was fined and suspended several times. Most recently he was banned from the practice of law until the end of 2007.[30]

Whether or not the prosecution was "sloppy or dishonest," it is true that they had a weak case against Frances Newton and an even weaker argument for the death penalty based on future dangerousness. They played upon the "unwomanliness" of the crime—killing a husband and children, the ultimate failure of gendered expectations. Newton's brief extramarital affair was another factor that could have diminished sympathy for her. And they successfully portrayed her as greedy, a characteristic that seems infallibly to be persuasive with juries. But there are things about the prosecution of Newton's case that remain puzzling. Nationwide and in Texas it is rare that prosecutors seek the death penalty when both the victim and the defendant are African American. This is especially unusual when there is evidence of a drug-related murder. Why did Harris County go after Frances Newton? Could it have been an ill-conceived attempt to demonstrate a lack of bias in prosecution, an attempt to make a show of concern for black victims?

At best, Newton's case was characterized by careless forensic work. At worst, potentially exculpatory evidence was intentionally mishandled or destroyed. The Houston crime lab was repeatedly accused of shoddy investigations. Even police in Houston expressed distrust in the lab's findings. Yet the paltry physical evidence against Newton was supported by that lab's analysis.

The police did not follow up on a number of obvious leads, most importantly the information about Charlie the drug dealer. They also failed to pursue the information from the anonymous caller who reported a strange vehicle outside the apartment and even provided a license number. Nor is there any indication they looked at the inmate who allegedly confessed his involvement in the murders to his cellmate. Once they had chosen Frances Newton as their prime suspect, all other possibilities were ignored.

The tragedy—the real possibility that Frances Newton was innocent—is what sets this case apart from the other thirteen executed women. Texas courts and federal courts were less able, due to legislative restraints such as AEDPA, or unwilling, in a conservative political climate, to look critically at the serious defects with her conviction and sentence. Given the question of innocence, why, when she was finally executed, was there so little attention to her death, especially when compared to the case of Karla Faye Tucker seven years earlier? Like Tucker and a number of other executed women, Newton was a practicing Christian. In her case, the religious commitment was consistent throughout her life, not a post-conviction conversion. Yet none of the big names in the evangelical pantheon pleaded on television for her life. Some commentators attribute the relative lack of interest in Frances Newton to her race and the tendency of Americans not to care when an African American is put to death.[31] Perhaps many of those who might have spoken out for her were distracted by the aftermath of Hurricane Katrina, which had struck just weeks before. And perhaps the media had little space left to share for her story when they were busy covering the disaster of other lost and ruined lives on the Gulf Coast.[32]

Endnotes

1. *Herrera v. Collins*, 506 U.S. 390 (1993).
2. Richard Dieter, *With Justice for Few: The Growing Crisis in Death Penalty Representation* (Washington, DC: The Death Penalty Information Center, 1995).
3. *Herrera v. Collins*, 506 U.S. 390 (1995).
4. The basic facts of the crime are covered in the trial transcripts and in the appellate pleadings and opinions. See for example, *State of Texas v. Frances Elaine Newton*, 263rd District (1988); *Newton v. Dretke*, 371 F. 3d 250 (5th Cir, May 20, 2004); Application for Postconviction Writ of Habeas Corpus and Motion for Stay of Execution, 2005.
5. Application for Habeas Corpus.
6. Ibid.
7. Information about Newton's trial is taken mostly from the trial transcripts, *Texas v. Newton* (1988).
8. John Makeig, "Wife Admits Hiding Gun, Denies Killing Mate, Two Children," *Houston Chronicle*, October 22, 1988.
9. *Texas v. Newton.*
10. Christy Hoppe, "Four Condemned Women Share Life on Death Row," *Dallas Morning News*, July 9, 1989.

11. Ibid.
12. *Newton v. Texas*, No. 70770, Appellant's Brief, 1991.
13. Ibid. Italics included in original.
14. Ibid.
15. *Newton v. State*, No. 70770, 1992 WL 175742 (Tex. Crim. App. 1992).
16. *Ex Parte Newton*, (Tex. Crim. App. December 6, 2000).
17. Andrew Tilghman, "Woman Awaits Execution Date," *Houston Chronicle* (July 7, 2004); Andrew Tilghman, "Woman's Execution Scheduled for Dec. 1," *Houston Chronicle* (July 8, 2004).
18. Andrew Tilghman, "Condemned Woman Files Clemency Petition," *Houston Chronicle* (November 11, 2004); Texas Death Penalty/Legal Concern: Frances Elaine Newton (November 19, 2004) at www.amnesty.org
19. Ralph Blumenthal, "Condemned Woman Given Reprieve in Texas," *New York Times* (December 2, 2004).
20. Quoted in Application for Postconviction Writ of Habeas Corpus and Motion for Stay of Execution, filed in the 263rd Judicial District Court of Harris County, Texas and in the Court of Criminal Appeals of Texas, July 28, 2005.
21. *Strickland v. Washington*, 466 U.S. 668 (1984).
22. *Wiggins v. Smith* 539 U.S. 510 (2003).
23. The details of issues that raise questions about Newton's guilt and the constitutionality of her conviction are taken from Application for Postconviction Writ of Habeas Corpus, July 28, 2005.
24. Ibid.
25. Quoted in Application for Postconviction Writ of Habeas Corpus, August 25, 2005.
26. Ralph Blumenthal, "Report of Second Gun Is Used in Defense of a Texas Woman Facing Death," *New York Times*, August 25, 2005.
27. Michael Graczyk, "Woman Executed for Slayings of Husband, Children in Texas," at www.news.findlaw.com
28. Jordan Smith, "Without Evidence: Executing Frances Newton," *The Austin Chronicle* (September 9, 2005).
29. Tilghman, "Woman Awaits Execution Date."
30. Smith, "Without Evidence."
31. Dave Lindorff, "Sacrificial Murder in Texas: Frances Newton Died for Bush's Sins," *Counterpunch* (September 15, 2005) at www.counterpunch.org
32. Ibid.

·10·

NOT THE "TRIGGERMAN"

Teresa Lewis

In the middle of the night on October 30, 2002, two men entered the mobile home near Danville, Virginia, where Teresa and Julian Lewis lived. Julian's son, Charles, who was on leave from his Army Reserve unit, was also in the house. One of the intruders shot Julian five or six times with a shotgun loaded with birdshot. The other murdered Charles (C.J.), also firing numerous shotgun blasts. The deaths were the final result of a plot concocted by the shooters, Matthew Shallenberger and Rodney Fuller, and Teresa Lewis, the wife and stepmother of the victims. Three people plotted the murders. Two men were killed. Two men were the killers. All three pled guilty and were sentenced by the same judge. Two received life sentences. One person was executed for the crime—Teresa Lewis, the conspirator who never touched a gun and who killed no one. Why?

Teresa Wilson grew up poor in Danville, Virginia, burdened by a repressive home environment and mental disabilities. She attended six different schools before the seventh grade and dropped out of school altogether after her sophomore year in high school. Over the next fourteen years, she held forty-nine low-paying and generally unskilled jobs. She apparently found it difficult to get to work regularly.[1] At 16, Lewis left home and married, gave birth to a daughter Christie, and divorced shortly after. Teresa became her ailing mother's primary caregiver, cooking and cleaning for her parents, bathing and attending to her mother. Friends later testified that Teresa was not an organized person, that, although compassionate and caring and capable of running errands and performing household chores, she "had difficulty planning beyond the next day." Others noted that she was unable to balance a checkbook.[2] Her former mother-in-law, Marie Bean, described Teresa as "not right."[3]

However, in 2000 Teresa took a job at Dan River Mills and there she met and began a relationship with a supervisor, Julian Lewis, a recent widower.[4] Lewis and Teresa moved in together and married a few months later. After the annual plant closing in the summer of 2000, Teresa did not return to work. She had several gynecological surgeries and later became dependent upon prescription painkillers. Early the following year, Julian's elder son, Jason was killed in an automobile accident. A member of the Navy, Jason had a life insurance policy for approximately $200,000. As primary beneficiary of his son's policy, Julian received the money and used it to purchase several acres of land and a mobile home in Pittsylvania County. He and Teresa were living there at the time of the murders. Julian's younger son, C.J., was a member of the National Guard. He was called to active duty in August 2002. Anticipating his military service, C.J. bought a $250,000 life insurance policy. He named his father as primary beneficiary and his new stepmother, Teresa, as secondary beneficiary.

Sometime in the fall of 2002, Teresa Lewis, 33 years old at the time, met Matthew Shallenberger, a 19-year-old who was recently discharged from the U.S. Army. In the checkout line at the local Wal-Mart, they apparently struck up a conversation and exchanged phone numbers.[5] Shallenberger reportedly told a friend that Teresa was "just what I was looking for: some ugly bitch who married her husband for the money and I knew I could get her to fall head over heals (sic) for me."[6] And so she did. Lewis visited Shallenberger often. She gave him gifts and money and sent him flowers. Meanwhile, Shallenberger was involved with several other women at the same time. When Teresa told him that her husband was abusive, Shallenberger proposed that they kill Julian, take his money, and run off together. He later admitted to deceiving Teresa in the hopes of getting some cash so he could pursue his ambition of moving to New York and becoming a hit man for the Mafia.[7]

The talk of killing Julian for his money escalated when Teresa became eligible to inherit the proceeds of C.J.'s life insurance if both he and his father died. The co-conspirators first developed a plan to waylay and kill Julian on his way home from work and then to murder C.J. when he came home for his father's funeral. Shallenberger enlisted his roommate Rodney Fuller, a young African American man, to assist in the killings. Court documents allege that Teresa put on a "lingerie show," presumably to encourage the potential killers. There were also accusations that she brought along her teen-aged daughter to have sex with Fuller, presumably as another enticement to carry out the plot. These sordid details were an essential part of the state's case against Lewis, emotionally charged evidence of her general lewdness. On October 23, Teresa withdrew $1200 from the bank (presumably from her joint account with her husband) and gave it to Shallenberger and Fuller to buy guns. Their plan to follow Julian's car, stop and shoot him, and make the crime look like a random robbery was foiled when another car got between Lewis's and the would-be murderers. Their next ploy called for Shallenberger and Fuller to enter the Lewis residence when everyone was asleep, kill Julian and C.J. who was home on leave, and make it look like a violent home invasion. Teresa would, apparently, be responsible for leaving the door unlocked and for providing a convincing story to the police.[8]

As in the case of Marilyn Kay Plantz (Chapter Six), a woman of limited intellectual capability, smitten with a younger manipulative man, assisted in the brutal murder of her defenseless spouse. Neither woman took a life but each allowed herself to be a participant in a violent homicide. In both cases, courts determined that the accomplice was more responsible than the killer based to a large extent on her sexual conduct, her infidelity, her failure to grieve adequately, and her alleged greed. But at least Marilyn Plantz had a full trial.

About a month after the crime, a grand jury in Pittsylvania County indicted Teresa Lewis on multiple counts: capital murder for hire of both Julian and C.J. Lewis; conspiracy to commit capital murder; robbery; the use of firearms to commit murder; and the use of firearms to commit robbery. At the advice of her court-appointed attorneys, Thomas Blaylock and David Furrow, Lewis agreed to plead guilty to all counts. Dr. Barbara Haskins, a court-appointed psychiatrist, found that Lewis pled "voluntarily, intelligently, and knowingly." She also stated that Lewis had an IQ of 72, "in the borderline range of mental retardation." [9]

Teresa Lewis was persuaded by her court-appointed attorneys to plead guilty to murder for hire (the only offense where a non-triggerman is eligible for the death penalty in Virginia) and to take her chances before a judge rather than a jury. Thus instead of a full-fledged capital trial, Lewis had only a sentencing hearing at which the state put on its evidence to demonstrate that the circumstances of her crime merited the death penalty and the defense argued that mitigating factors should result in a life sentence without the possibility of parole. It was an extremely risky strategy and Teresa Lewis paid with her life.

All three defendants, Lewis, Fuller, and Shallenberger ended up pleading guilty. As John Grisham wrote, "Fuller's lawyers were quick off the mark." They made a deal, he took a guilty plea and agreed to testify against the others in return for a sentence of life without the possibility of parole.[10] Shallenberger went to trial, but entered a guilty plea in the middle of his trial. He also received life without parole. Lewis's lawyers encouraged her to plead guilty. They apparently believed that because she was a woman, because she had assisted the police in finding the killers, and because the actual triggermen had received life sentences, her chances of avoiding death were good.[11] They were wrong of course, and her case tragically illustrates the dangers of pleading guilty in a capital case without a plea bargain. When Lewis went before Judge Charles Strauss for her sentencing hearing, the narrative of the case came directly from the prosecution's arguments.[12] As she had agreed to the charges, the judge had little reason to question the state's facts. Her attorneys made no effort to suggest any motivations for her actions other than those offered by the Commonwealth's Attorney. They offered no alternative narrative, only a half-hearted plea to spare her life.

The Commonwealth's Case

When Shallenberger and Fuller arrived at the Lewis home on October 30, 2002, they found the door unlocked and the family members in bed. As planned, Teresa left her room. Shallenberger entered and shot Julian six or seven times, while Fuller went to the other bedroom and shot C.J. several times. After the shooting stopped, Teresa took $300 from Julian's wallet and divided it between the two men. When they left the trailer with their weapons and money, Teresa apparently smoked cigarettes, drank some iced tea, called a friend to report the alleged robbery, and finally, after about 45 minutes, she called the police.

According to the version of events put forth by the prosecution and agreed to by Teresa Lewis when she accepted a guilty plea, the local police dispatcher received a call at 3:55 AM.[13] After some difficulty locating the residence, police arrived about 25 minutes later and found Teresa Lewis standing in the doorway, talking on a cell phone. Asked about her emotional condition at the time he arrived, the deputy described her as "very calm."[14] When he entered the trailer home, the officer heard slow moans and a male voice saying, "Baby, baby, baby, baby." He found Julian Lewis in a fetal position on the floor of the bedroom and saw shotgun shells strewn around him. Before his last breath, Lewis said "My wife knows who did this to me."[15] The deputies then found the body of C.J. Lewis in the other bedroom. Under questioning from Commonwealth's Attorney David Grimes, the officer stated that while they checked on the two victims, Teresa was sitting on a loveseat in the living area, talking on the phone. She asked the officer for her cigarettes and a glass of iced tea. Again, he used the word "calm" to describe her emotional condition.[16] He claimed to hear her telling someone on the phone that she had told C.J. not to leave the back door open. During the time Teresa was in the living room, she did not inquire about the condition of Julian or C.J. Lewis. Later when the officer told her Julian was dead, she slumped over but he did not see her face and could not tell whether she was distressed or not. Clearly while questioning this officer on the witness stand, the prosecutor was attempting to draw for the judge a picture of Teresa's lack of grief and her cold demeanor.

The second deputy called to testify repeated the exact same description of Teresa's emotional condition. "She appeared to be very calm," he said.[17] And again, noting that she had asked for her medication, he used the expression, "very, very calm."[18] Lewis's defense attorneys made no effort to ask the deputies to explain her "calm" state, nor did they mention that perhaps her medication could have affected her demeanor. They allowed the description of a woman unmoved by her husband's death to be the image implanted on the judge's mind at the very outset of the sentencing hearing.

The third prosecution witness, Investigator J.T. Barrett from the Sheriff's Department, had arrived at the Lewis mobile home approximately an hour later. Asked about Lewis's emotional state, he answered "She appeared to be calm."[19] Barrett took a statement from Teresa Lewis in which he noted the seemingly irrelevant detail that she had "a lot of rings on her fingers." He also noticed some black ink on her hands which, according to Lewis, came from a magic marker she used to write a note on her husband's lunch bag. The note said "I love you. I hope you have a good day. I miss you when you're gone!" It was accompanied by a smiley face.[20] The investigator asked Lewis what had happened on the evening before the shooting. She claimed that she and Julian had prayed together before going to bed. "We prayed because we had been fussing a couple of days, just fussing, fussing."[21] Teresa stated that both she and Julian wanted their marriage to work out. Asked whether she tried to go to Julian's aid after he was shot, Teresa said she did not hear him calling for her and that she was afraid to enter the room. When the investigator mentioned that Julian claimed she knew who shot him, Teresa's answer was incoherent. "He's the one that wanted his own self shot."[22] Finally, she claimed that C.J. had told her how lucky his father was. "I wish I had a wife like you, to treat him (sic) as good as you do, and if C.J. was living he could tell you that."[23] Finally, Teresa told the investigator that she had hidden in the bathroom during the shooting and even posed for a photograph crouched across from the shower stall. In cross-examining Investigator Barrett, the defense attorney did not try to challenge the descriptions of Lewis's "calm" demeanor or her alleged account of events. Instead, he acknowledged that she had lied to Barrett, but emphasized that later she had helped to lead him to Matthew Shallenberger and Rodney Fuller. The prosecutor took the opportunity to reinforce for the judge the fact that Teresa had lied in her initial statements.

Other witnesses called by the prosecution included the Medical Examiner who explained that Julian and C.J. were shot multiple times with bird shot. The small pellets killed C.J. almost immediately but caused Julian to suffer a drawn out and painful death resulting from the loss of blood. The court was provided with extensive details about the wounds inflicted upon the two victims, the level of pain they would have suffered, and the possibility that Julian might have survived if help had arrived sooner. At this point, then, the prosecution had created a version of the crime for the judge—two brutal murders during which at least one of the victims experienced a great deal of suffering, a callous woman who delayed summoning help and who seemed unmoved by the deaths of her husband and stepson, and who, in addition, had intentionally lied to the police. The next part of the picture involved the state's portrayal of a motive that lay behind the murders.

Lieutenant Michael Booker, an officer of the National Guard battalion in which C.J. served added another dimension to the state's story. He provided an account of conversations with Teresa Lewis in which she had, without provocation, denied involvement in the murders of her husband and stepson and asked about the payout on C.J.'s insurance policy. Less than a week later, she again contacted the Army to inquire about the insurance money and to remind Booker that she was the secondary beneficiary. She reportedly told the lieutenant that C.J.'s sister Kathy could have all of his effects "as long as I get the money."[24] Oddly, the defense's only question for this witness was whether he knew that Teresa had confessed to the crime. Her lawyers made no effort to minimize the image of her as greedy and money hungry.

Julian's supervisor at Dan River Mills, Mike Campbell, added to the prosecution's effort to show Teresa's heartlessness. First, he testified that Julian never brought his lunch in a paper bag but always in a cooler. Thus it seemed that Teresa had created the lunch bag with the love note and the smiley face in an attempt to mislead investigators about her attitude toward her husband and her activities around the time of his death. Secondly, Campbell told the court that on the very day Julian was killed, Teresa asked for his paycheck. The next day when he went to the Lewis home to offer his condolences, Teresa told him about her plans to buy a new car and to sell the trailer so she could move away. Both Lieutenant Booker and Campbell provided the financial motive for the murders—Teresa Lewis had wanted money. She apparently imagined a lifestyle beyond what Julian had provided.

A few days after the murders, on November 7, Vic Ingram, an investigator for the Pittsylvania County Sheriff's Department, conducted a videotaped interview with Teresa lasting more than six hours. He informed her of her rights and asked that she write out an account of what happened on October 30. During that interview, Lewis changed her story dramatically. She told the investigator that the shooter had not been a masked robber, but Matt Shallenberger. She provided information about his home address and assisted police in locating both Shallenberger and Rodney Fuller. The prosecution offered Lewis's confession as an illustration of her participation in the plot to kill Julian and C.J. and a desperate effort to save herself. Her attorneys would try, unsuccessfully, to argue that Teresa's cooperation with the police investigation should count in her favor.

Julian Lewis's daughter Kathy and her husband were called to provide victim impact evidence and to add to the picture of the avaricious, unfeeling woman the state was constructing. Larry Clifton, the son-in-law, told the court what fine people Julian and C.J. were. He especially emphasized the loss his 9-year-old son Christopher felt when his uncle and grandfather were killed. The boy's life "revolved around" those men. He "constantly" asked to see "Papa." The boy could not understand what happened or why his beloved relatives had been taken. Clifton testified that Teresa had thrown Kathy into a faint by telling her of the alleged home invasion that killed her father. He also described Teresa's behavior at the funeral home when the family made plans to bury the men. Again, Teresa regaled them with the story of the intruders, but she also bragged about the insurance money she would inherit. Based on her anticipated windfall, Teresa said that price was no object when it came to the funeral arrangements.

Kathy Lewis Clifton took up the story and provided more victim impact evidence. She told of her father's career in the military and of his devotion to her mother who suffered a long fatal illness. Soon after his wife's death, Julian met Teresa Lewis. Teresa moved into the house Kathy shared with her father while Kathy was in the hospital—not a propitious start for Teresa's relationship with his daughter. A few months later, Julian and Teresa were married. Shortly thereafter, the elder Lewis son, Jason was killed in a car accident. Kathy related how her father, as Jason's beneficiary, had spent much of the insurance money on "one of the biggest single wide trailers you can buy and five and a half acres of land...whatever else happened to the money I have no idea."[25] The groundwork was laid to see Teresa as a woman who used men to get the money and the things she wanted. Kathy also described Teresa on the day of Julian's funeral, telling how Teresa had her nails done and wore a beautiful new suit. She offered to sell Kathy the trailer where her father had been murdered.

Perhaps the most emotional part of Kathy's statement came when she showed the judge pictures of her father and her "baby brother C.J." and read a letter she had written to the court. "My daddy will never take Christopher fishing again. He won't be there for Christopher's first ball game or take pride in him when he graduates. There won't be any more Christmases with Dad or C.J. They will never be able to be hugged or touched."[26] She continued with many other examples of how her life would be poorer without them and described how she and her family were victims. Kathy ended her testimony with a speech saying "to everyone here, don't take your loved ones for granted." It is not clear whom she might have been addressing, other than the judge, when she talked of giving love freely. The defense attorneys opted not to cross-examine Kathy Clifton.

After the state had concluded its presentation of evidence intended to persuade Judge Strauss to sentence Teresa Lewis to death, the defense had the opportunity to bring witnesses who would provide mitigating evidence—reasons why Teresa Lewis should not be executed. They offered the testimony of a probation officer who said that Teresa had been compliant with the terms of her probation after her conviction for forgery of a prescription. She had never been violent and had showed up for meetings. However, the prosecutor was able to extract from this witness that, although probationers were supposed to be employed or seeking employment, Teresa had not done so.

Next the chief deputy of the Roanoke City Jail testified that Teresa was a cooperative prisoner. Then a longtime friend stated that he had never known her to be violent. Finally, the defense explained to the judge that Teresa's father, brother, and sister would be glad to testify that they loved her and did not want to see her die. "But your honor, we don't see the need to call them. The Court's used to that kind of testimony."[27] Thus the judge was presented with hours of testimony designed to establish the appropriateness of the death penalty for Teresa's Lewis and with only the most perfunctory attempt to argue that her life should be spared. Perhaps the defense relied on their ability to persuade the judge that the aggravating factors themselves were not applicable in this case.

The Aggravating Factors

Under Virginia law, a murder becomes eligible for the death penalty based on any or all of the statutory aggravating factors. The state will try to prove beyond a reasonable doubt that the accused poses a continuing threat to society (future dangerousness) and/or that the crime itself was deemed to be "wantonly vile."[28] A determination of future dangerousness is typically based on the prior criminal history of the defendant. If he or she has been convicted of violent crimes in the past, the prosecution might argue that such a pattern would continue. "Vileness," on the other hand, is a more subjective consideration. It may include torture, evidence of depravity of mind, or aggravated battery. However, a sentencing body (jury or judge) could determine that mitigating factors outweighed the aggravators, even if aggravating circumstances are present. Among items that might be considered in mitigation are the defendant's state of mind and mental capacity at the time of the crime and her lack of criminal history.[29] Breslow notes that the sentencing phase of a capital trial in Virginia essentially involves rendering a moral judgment. But whereas in a typical jury trial, twelve people must be unanimous and agree that the aggravating factors outweigh the mitigating factors, in a bench trial "only one person undertakes the moral balancing."[30] Such a procedure allows for the moral calculus of a single individual to determine life or death. Lewis's lawyers told a reporter, "We didn't feel like the judge would give her the death sentence."[31] But their feelings were incorrect. The way Commonwealth's Attorney Grimes described Teresa's role in the murders fit perfectly into the judge's definition of "vileness." Her failures as a wife, her sexual improprieties, and her desire for money and material things must have been well synchronized with Strauss's moral compass. While the judge sentenced the two shooters to life in prison, he saw no place for mercy in meting out the ultimate punishment to Teresa Lewis.

The prosecutor attempted to make the case that both future dangerousness and vileness merited death in this case. Although he agreed that Lewis had only been convicted of one earlier non-violent offense, Grimes referred repeatedly to unspecified "unadjudicated conduct" that might prove her propensity for violence. He even alleged that she could have had gunpowder residue on her hands, suggesting that her role in her husband's death was more violent than the evidence proved. But Grimes put most of his effort into establishing the vileness aggravator. As there was no evidence of torture, nor was Teresa herself involved in aggravated battery, the aggravating factor would have to be "depravity of mind and moral turpitude greater than ordinary malice."[32] The state approached that element by citing a number of factors. Grimes noted that Teresa was present before, during, and after the horrific deaths, that her "moral debasement" was greater than the men she hired because she knew the victims intimately. He claimed that she purposely stalled for time before calling for help and that she called 911 from the bathroom so the dispatcher would not hear the sounds of her dying husband. Earlier, the prosecutor alleged, Teresa "set up" her husband and son by having a quiet evening at home, making them "completely unaware of the savagery that awaited them." The two "young men" who did the shooting were doing her bidding, "she used two young men as weapons."[33]

Teresa Lewis, he said, was "one of the rare few who meets all the requirements of law [to be eligible for death] and just as importantly deserves to die for what she did." To establish her unworthiness to remain alive, Grimes found a grand plan. He noted that "her entire existence of her entire life is not very productive." He claimed that every choice she made was selfish, "whatever works for Teresa's benefit." She "hones (sic) in" on Julian so she no longer had to work.[34] She took advantage of a vulnerable man who had recently lost the wife he had cared for just to avoid having to support herself. When Julian received the insurance money from his elder son, "one can only imagine the mixture of emotions that ran through Teresa Lewis when that money started rolling in." Besides the "new mobile home, a piece of land in the country," she used Julian's money "for fixing herself up, looking attractive, taking care of her jewelry, lots of jewelry, a flashy red car."[35] Julian loved her, the prosecutor stated, but he did not know "that whatever there was in her chest beating was not a heart, not a human heart."[36]

Grimes piled on the negatives—Teresa saw C.J.'s insurance as another chance to satisfy her greed, she "came home with a new boyfriend, Matthew Shallenberger," there was a sexual relationship but "we don't know everything that occurred there by a long shot." However, he claimed, we do know that she did not value the sexual part of her relationship with her husband and that she used sex to "seal the deal" with Shallenberger. All in all, the state wanted the judge to see Teresa as "a woman whose sense of right and wrong doesn't match up with anything civilized." Why, the prosecutor exclaims, Teresa does not even have custody of her daughter "for reasons we don't know," but she used the daughter as a sexual lure to get Fuller involved in the plot and then also tried to use her daughter as part of her alibi.

On the night of the murders, while her husband was awake and conscious, although fatally wounded, what did she do? Here Grimes found "the definition of vileness." She may purposely have given the police dispatcher incomplete directions to the house and delayed their arrival. She fixed the fake lunch bag with the smiley face, and she looked at her rings and jewelry and counted her bracelets. (Apparently the basis for this version of events was Barrett's comment that she was wearing a lot of rings.) She also smoked cigarettes and drank iced tea. (Here her smoking is meant to suggest a weakness in her character.) "Obviously this is a person who smokes and obviously she's not going to go without for long if she can."[37]

And the prosecutor even made Lewis's guilty plea further evidence of her bad character. She is not taking responsibility, he says, but simply calculating what is in her best interest. He alleges that she thinks that people, "and particularly men," will believe anything she tells them. She misled Julian, she persuaded Shallenberger and Fuller to do her bidding, and she actually tried to fool the police. Even when she confessed, "there's not a hint of anything like human emotion for the people that she killed or had killed." Her confession and guilty plea were calculated to "avoid the penalty that she's entitled to."[38]

The peroration continued as Grimes defined vileness as "a woman who will stop at nothing to satisfy her own needs." She had no thought for Julian or C.J. or for Kathy or her son. He argued that she deserved two death sentences—or perhaps more as she was also responsible for ruining the lives of Fuller, Shallenberger, and her daughter. "This never would have happened but for her."[39]

Thus the state made its case for vileness—Teresa Lewis was the instigator and initiator of the murders. Her motive was greed, enhanced by her laziness and unwillingness to work for the things she wanted. She deceived her husband and stepson. She used sex to lure the "young" Shallenberger and Fuller into her web of evil. Her "calmness" after the crime showed how heartless she was. In fact, Grimes tried several times to make the case that Lewis was not even human. Surely all of those evil deeds and failures of character were enough to add up to a moral judgment of vileness—beyond a reasonable doubt.

Having advised Teresa Lewis to plead guilty and to agree to being sentenced by a judge, it was surely her attorneys' responsibility to make the strongest possible case for mitigation, to refute the picture of her the prosecution had drawn. It does not seem unfair to describe their efforts as halfhearted, even pitiful. The first argument, offered by Furrow, contended that the only precedents in Virginia for sentencing someone to death for hiring a killer (and not being the actual triggerman) occurred when the court found "a bunch of future dangerousness."[40] He distinguished Teresa from those cases by noting that she had accepted responsibility and cooperated with the police, and he argued that a death sentence for her would be disproportionate compared to the prior cases. He then went on to point out that the judge had sentenced Rodney Fuller, an actual shooter in this case, to life in prison. Again, the issue of proportionality seemed relevant.

Blaylock continued the defendant's case by reminding the judge that Lewis had taken a calculated risk by pleading guilty and that in the federal system "you get points for that."[41] She had no criminal history; she was not violent; she was cooperative, and she showed remorse. What is remarkable in both defense arguments is a total lack of effort to contradict the evil picture painted by Grimes. Neither lawyer made an attempt to refute the version of an oversexed, greedy, heartless, "inhuman" architect of the murders. But in his closing, the prosecutor returned to his themes—the complete absence of human emotion shown by a woman who would manipulate men into killing members of her family, a "mastermind" of crime who will do anything to get what she wants. Compared to the bland and colorless statements made by the defense team, the state left the judge with a dramatic version of events in which Teresa Lewis, the conductor, orchestrated the crime.

Finally Lewis herself had the opportunity to make a statement in her own behalf. She asked the judge to spare her life, she asked for forgiveness, and she expressed a willingness to testify against Shallenberger. Following her remarks, the judge ruled that the state had not made the case for future dangerousness beyond a reasonable doubt. Thus he based his sentencing decision only on the issue of vileness. There he considered "moral turpitude and psychical debasement," points that had been at the heart of the prosecution's argument. As support for those factors, Judge Strauss mentioned Lewis's coldness, her greed, and her sexual activities. He commented on Lewis's lack of concern for the surviving family members. He seemed especially offended by her ruse with the lunch bag. The crime, he stated, "fits the definition of the outrageous or wantonly vile, horrible act." For her role in the crime, he considered her "the head of the serpent."[42] Thus on June 2, 2003, Teresa Lewis became the first woman sentenced to death in Virginia since capital punishment was rein-stated. She was only the second woman in a century to face execution there.

Before the Pittsylvania County Court finished with Teresa Lewis's case her attorneys returned to ask for consideration of several motions. They asked the judge to clarify which of the three elements of vileness (torture, aggravated battery, or depravity of mind) he had considered in reaching her sentence. When the judge replied that he had relied on aggravated battery and depravity of mind in reaching his sentence, the defense did not object. This would become an important issue later in the appeal process. During this hearing, Judge Strauss also expressed his opinion that Lewis's conduct was "more egre-gious" than Shallenberger's. It was that conclusion that most clearly illustrates the gendered nature of the decision that ended Teresa Lewis's life. Her failure to fulfill her role as a decent, faithful, modest wife was deemed worse than killing a man in cold blood for money.

The Appeal Process

Virginia is one of the least likely places in the nation to have a death sentence overturned. Whereas the national rate for reversing death sentences is 41%, in Virginia it is less than 10%.[43] The 2002 report by the Joint Legislative Audit and Review Committee (JLARC) noted that in the mandatory direct review of capital cases the Virginia Supreme Court had affirmed 93% of capital cases since 1977. In the process of affirming those sentences, the court rejected 83% of all claims of trial error. Also in these reviews, although comparison among capital cases was required, not one single application of capital punishment was found to be disproportionate. As the JLARC report indicates, "the Virginia Supreme Court appears to have narrowly applied the statutes defining proportionality review in Virginia."[44] The prospects for a reversal of a death sentence become even more remote as many claims are rejected on the basis of procedural default. If an attorney fails to raise an issue in the initial phases of the process, the odds are great that such a claim would be considered defaulted and therefore ineligi-ble for consideration during later stages of the review process. These elements of the Virginia process had a strong effect on the outcome of Teresa Lewis's case. Indeed, they helped to determine that she would be executed in 2010. The statistics were against her. In Virginia, 70% of those who receive a death sentence are actually put to death. The national rate is 15%.[45]

The Supreme Court of Virginia in its initial mandatory review of Lewis's case in 2004 affirmed her conviction and sentence. Lewis first challenged her sentence on the grounds of proportionality. The issue of gender was "like an elephant in the room" as in no other case with a female accomplice had a woman been sentenced to death in Virginia.[46] Throughout the sentencing process the prosecutor and the judge drew attention to Lewis as a woman and treated that fact as a de facto aggravator. The judge repeatedly referred to her as a "wife and mother," roles only a woman could fill. The consistent emphasis on her "coldness" surely had a gendered meaning. Showing a lack of warmth is seldom regarded as a serious vice in a man. And of course there were the many references to Lewis who, allegedly, "lured men and her juvenile daughter into [her] web of deceit and sex and greed and murder."[47] The images of the "black widow" and the "head of the serpent" were surely gendered. Additionally the judge and the prosecutor referred often to the idea that Lewis was motivated by greed. It is hard to see that as a particular quality of her behavior when Shallenberger and Fuller committed the murders only for whatever payment they expected to receive. And yet, it seems that in the eyes of the court, they were unfortunate dupes who fell into the web of the temptress. Gender clearly played a role in the way Teresa Lewis was judged—compared to other cases in Virginia and compared to her co-conspirators. Yet the State Supreme Court said the issue could not be considered. "All criminal statutes in the Commonwealth must be applied without respect to gender," they said. Lewis's claim was "an invitation to apply Virginia's capital murder statutes in a discriminatory fashion based on gender."[48] Graham believes that raising the gender issue "allowed the court to sidestep a real comparison of Lewis with other defendants." She argues that focusing on the notion that her punishment was disproportionate because of her lack of criminal history and her cooperation with the police would have been more fruitful than raising the gender claim.[49] Nonetheless, given the many gendered comments from all participants in the trial, including the defense attorneys, it is hard to see why that issue should not have been raised on appeal. The Supreme Court's reaction was simply disingenuous.

Other matters of proportionality involved comparing Lewis's sentence to other non-triggermen who were not sentenced to death. As Crawford comments, the court's review of such cases was cursory and actually often contradicted their ruling. For example, in *Clark v. Commonwealth*, cited by the court but not explained, it was the gunman who was sentenced to death.[50] Further, the Virginia State Supreme Court said it could not compare Lewis's sentence with that of Shallenberger and Fuller. It then cited cases where no comparisons were allowed. Those, however, were cases where co-defendants were convicted of different offenses. In this case, all three were convicted of the same offense, only the sentences were different.[51] There was also the issue of proportionality concerning the vileness aggravator. Lewis's lawyers argued that Virginia courts had never upheld a death sentence when "vileness" consisted only in hiring someone to kill. Here the court chose not to look at any cases where a defendant had gotten a life sentence, but surely those were the ones where the circumstances were most similar to Lewis's. As Graham commented, "*Lewis* seems to stand for the proposition that if the crime is especially bad, then the court can ignore its mandate to compare crimes and definitions and deny that a death sentence is disproportionate without comparing it to an appropriate set of similar cases."[52] And finally, there was the definition of "vileness," which potentially could include torture, depravity of mind, or aggravated battery. Judge Strauss claimed that he found vileness beyond a reasonable doubt based on *both* aggravated battery and depravity of mind. But the aggravated battery was committed by Shallenberger and Fuller, not by Lewis. In other words, it was not an eligible aggravator in her case. After the 2004 denial of relief, Lewis next undertook collateral review.

In June of 2007, that Virginia Supreme Court ruled against her on every point raised in her petition for a writ of habeas corpus.[53] She claimed that she had been denied effective assistance of counsel for several reasons. Her attorneys had failed to conduct an adequate investigation of mitigating evidence and to present mitigation during her sentencing hearing. She also challenged the efficacy of their advice that she plead guilty. In judging the adequacy of counsel, courts apply the two-pronged *Strickland* standard. To be found inadequate, the attorney's behavior must fall below an objective standard of reasonableness. In other words, he or she must make decisions or follow strategies that a reasonable lawyer would not. Secondly, the defendant must be able to demonstrate that he or she was harmed by the attorney's conduct. In other words, the defendant must show that the outcome would have been different, had the attorney proceeded differently. In a capital case, this usually means that the defendant must be able to prove she would not have been sentenced to death had her lawyer followed a different strategy. The standard is extremely difficult to meet as proof of a different outcome is generally purely a matter of speculation.

Lewis's habeas petition included the claim that her attorneys failed to investigate and present mitigating evidence (her mental disability and her addiction to prescription drugs), their advice to Lewis to plead guilty, their failure to advise her that even with a guilty plea she retained the right to be sentenced by a jury and to have a jury determine the existence of aggravating factors.

Was Teresa Lewis mentally disabled? Did she meet the requirements for "mental retardation" as defined in Virginia? According to Dr. Leigh D. Hagen, the psychologist hired by the state, Lewis's IQ was 70. He determined, however, that she was not putting forth her best effort and that the test "underestimated" her actual IQ. He cited her "adaptive functioning." She had attended to her parents' needs, never failed a grade in school (although she dropped out at 16), and was never terminated from a job (although she held 49 jobs in fourteen years). He further noted that she was able to keep "cosmetic appointments" in preparation for her court appearances and that she wrote many letters while incarcerated. All of these factors led Hagen to conclude that Lewis had the ability to plan the murders and to attempt to profit from them.[54]

Conversely, a psychologist retained by the defense found that Lewis had an "intellect equivalent to that of a 12- or 13-year-old child." He concluded that she did not have the "mental ability to autonomously initiate or lead the planning and execution of the murders." Although the court's opinion stated that "Other witnesses described Lewis' abilities to plan, lead, and implement various activities," in fact all of the other testimony highlighted the deficiencies in Lewis's intellectual skills.

Dr. Elinor McCance-Katz testified that Lewis suffered from an addiction to prescription drugs, that she exhibited impulsivity (consistent with her inability to plan ahead), and had a dependent personality disorder. Others indicated that Lewis had a strong desire to please and consistently sought the attention of men, that she allowed men to "take advantage of her." Several psychologists stated that Lewis suffered from dependent personality disorder and that she had difficulty initiating projects. Dr. Hagan, the state's psychologist, disagreed.

The issue in the habeas hearing was whether her trial counsel should have raised these issues of mental capability and psychological disorders as mitigating factors at the sentencing hearing. Blaylock, one of her defense attorneys, said he thought raising these issues would have been unsuccessful at trial.

Further witnesses addressed the matter of Lewis's addiction to prescription drugs. Her gynecologist stated that he recognized her addiction shortly before the crime, he recommended that she seek help and refused to prescribe any additional medication. However, in 2002, four doctors were simultaneously prescribing pain medicine for Lewis. Her records showed that she also took relaxants, sedatives, and antidepressants. According to Dr. McCance-Katz, Lewis was severely addicted to pain medication and to alcohol. Her intake of various substances may well have made her seem "uncaring" at the time of the murders.[55] Dr. Hagan, the state psychologist, disagreed.

Lewis's attorney Blaylock indicated his reasons for not mentioning her drug addiction. He had "never seen success with people using [the excuse that] I was taking drugs voluntarily and there I should be excused for committing murder."[56] Of course had he raised the issue in those terms, he was guaranteed not to succeed. In fact, that statement by Blaylock seems quite revealing of his low opinion of his client. Such contempt would hardly lead to a zealous defense.

As for the advice that Lewis plead guilty without a plea bargain in place, her attorneys argued that they had written her a letter advising her to plead guilty and had later discussed the decision with her. Both contended that Lewis "understood everything counsel explained to her."

Was her counsel's performance deficient in not presenting evidence in mitigation? Did it prejudice the outcome against her? The Virginia Supreme Court found that it did not. Why not? Because the aggravating evidence (her extensive planning, her recruitment of the killers, her arranged sexual activities, her payment to the killers, her assisting their entry into the house, her motivation—greed, her failure to call the police) were sufficient to warrant a death sentence. Of course the presentation of mitigating evidence (mental retardation, dependent personality disorder, drug addiction) would call the state's characterization of the crime into question. All of the aggravators depended on an assumption of her cognitive ability and her emotional normality. If those matters were challenged, then the whole argument for depravity of mind falls apart. The court justified the reasonableness of her attorneys' performance, and therefore they accepted her sentence based on her "carefully calculated conduct." All of the expert evidence, except that provided by the state's psychologist, ran counter to that version of events. Nonetheless, the court concluded that Lewis was not prejudiced by her lawyers' conduct.

In a separate order released on the same day, the Virginia Supreme Court also addressed the issue of whether Lewis's lawyers were remiss in not informing her that even though she pled guilty, based on several decisions of the U.S. Supreme Court, she was entitled to be sentenced by a jury rather than by a judge.[57] Furthermore, her attorney should have objected when the judge failed to tell her that she had the right to jury sentencing. The Virginia Supreme Court denied this claim, saying that even if the attorneys failed to inform her of her constitutional rights, Lewis had not been "harmed" by this oversight. Somehow the court was certain that even if she had been sentenced by a jury, the result would have been the same. Further, the court invoked the doctrine of procedural default. Because Lewis's attorney had not in the direct review raised the issue of whether sentencing by a judge was unconstitutional, the issue could not be raised in a habeas petition. In other words, if her earlier lawyers were not competent enough to object, the defendant forfeited the right to challenge their competence for not objecting. Procedural default truly binds a defendant into a Catch-22 situation where she is prohibited from making a claim because she was denied adequate assistance of counsel.

The issue of sentencing a defendant who pleads guilty in a capital case is a serious one. Although Virginia law specifies that in the case of a guilty plea to a capital offense, a judge will "hear and determine the case without the intervention of a jury."[58] Breslow notes that a guilty plea may have procedural and moral benefits to a defendant, but those benefits will not be realized if she forfeits her constitutional rights. In this case, Lewis unknowingly gave up the right to have a jury determine whether the state had proved her eligibility for death beyond a reasonable doubt. The unanimity required when the twelve people on a jury render a death sentence is a protection against prejudice and requires the balancing of mitigating and aggravating factors that should go into such a decision.[59] For Teresa Lewis, the entire moral judgment was placed in the hands of Judge Strauss. Lewis was unaware that she had any alternative.

Teresa Lewis's habeas petition reached the United States Court of Appeals for the Fourth Circuit in 2010.[60] They affirmed her conviction and sentence. As the Fourth Circuit recounted the facts of Lewis's case, they placed emphasis on the same issues that had been so persuasive to Judge Strauss and the Virginia Supreme Court. As Crawford notes, gender biases were "lurking" throughout the opinion, as the court used the same language that pervaded the prior decisions.[61] The first paragraph mentions that Teresa quit working when she married Julian. The holding reiterates the sordid account of her relationship with Shallenberger. He was "11 years her junior." She "performed a lingerie show" for Shallenberger and Fuller. Her daughter had sex with Fuller. After the murders, Lewis "did not appear to the officers to be upset." She drew a smiley face on the lunch bag. At the funeral, she said that "money was no object." She reportedly went to the hairdresser before the funeral. The medical examiner testified that Julian Lewis had been alive for approximately 45 minutes after the shooting, but Teresa had waited to call 911.[62] All in all, the appellate court accepted the version of events that not only placed Teresa in the most unfavorable light but a version that emphasized her failure to behave as a decent and respectable woman. Instead, they saw her as she was portrayed—as self-centered, promiscuous, and hard hearted.

The Fourth Circuit accepted the contention of her court appointed lawyers that they "became convinced" that Lewis would fare better before Judge Strauss than before a jury and that their advice to plead guilty without a plea bargain was reasonable. Finally they agreed that the trial court was correct in applying the vileness aggravator because Teresa Lewis was the "mastermind of these gruesome crimes." She "showed no emotion or remorse."

The major issue before the Fourth Circuit, however, was whether Lewis's attorneys provided adequate assistance under the *Strickland* standard. They had failed to raise the issue of Lewis's mental capacity, her prescription drug addiction, and her dependent personality disorder as part of the case in mitigation because, they claimed, raising those issues was "unnecessary and potentially harmful." The attorneys saw the addiction and personality disorder not as illnesses but as "excuses." The Fourth Circuit said the lawyers' position was "reasonable." Further, they noted that the evidence of Lewis's disability was contested (by the state's psychologist) and that because she killed "her two relatives solely for monetary gain," the aggravating factors were beyond dispute. Shallenberger and Fuller, on the other hand, had never met the victims, they were "substantially younger than the more experienced and knowledgeable Lewis." The court mentioned sexual favors and Lewis's daughter on virtually every page of the opinion. Rather than an analysis of the lawyers' performance, the opinion seems at times to be an additional condemnation of Lewis's character.

As federal courts almost always defer to state rules about procedural default, it is not surprising that the Fourth Circuit found that Lewis had defaulted on the issue of the constitutionality of the Virginia sentencing scheme when a capital defendant pleads guilty. The appellate court also found the advice that Lewis plead guilty to be a reasonable decision on the part of her attorneys. They believed that if a jury heard the evidence that Lewis's minor daughter had sex with "an adult black male" while her mother was nearby it would "have a horrible effect on the jury both among white [s] and blacks, men and women." Thus, the Fourth Circuit affirmed the denial of habeas relief. After this decision, Lewis's only hope of avoiding execution would be a grant of clemency from Governor Bob McDonnell.

New Evidence and Clemency

From the time of her trial, Lewis was incarcerated in a segregation cell at the women's prison, the Fluvanna Correctional Center. She was prohibited from contact with anyone, presumably because she was dangerous. However, Lynn Litchfield, the prison chaplain, told another story. On the day Teresa arrived in blue scrubs and chains, she appeared "meek, almost pliant." She did not appear to be the remorseless killer, the "mastermind" portrayed by the state and not challenged by her lawyers. She was "slow and overeager to please," "an easy mark for a con."[63] For the next six years, the chaplain communicated with Lewis through a small slot in the metal door of her cell. Sometimes Litchfield sat in a chair or squatted on the concrete floor to talk with Lewis or give her communion. The chaplain found the visits "unbearable," as she had become convinced that Teresa Lewis did not deserve to die.[64]

As Crawford states, three men—the Pittsylvania County Commonwealth's Attorney David Grimes, Judge Charles J. Strauss, and Governor Robert McDonnell—were "representatives of the court system and of the clemency process through which a defendant sentenced to die must traverse for the slim, rare shot at reversal, operated amidst laws that teeter dangerously close to a punishment that is cruel and unusual for its arbitrariness."[65] As clemency remained the only possible way for Teresa Lewis to escape death by lethal injection, new evidence came to light uncovered by the law firm who represented her during the last stages. Because of the procedural default policy, new evidence could not be introduced into court and placed before a jury, it could only be provided to the governor as an argument for clemency. The major new evidence was Shallenberger's admission that he had been the mastermind behind the murders. "Teresa was in love with me," he told an investigator. "She was very eager to please me. She was also not very smart." Fuller supported this account, placing the blame squarely on his fellow shooter.[66] According to one version, Shallenberger wanted the money from Julian's death and the experience of murder so he could go to New York to become a hit man for the Mafia.[67] Shallenberger wrote from prison that the only reason he had sex with Teresa was "to get her to fall in love with me so she would give me the insurance money." This time he claimed that he would use the money to buy drugs cheaply and begin a career as a dealer in New York. His relationship with Lewis "was just part of what had to be done to get the money."[68] Author John Grisham described Shallenberger as "intelligent and manipulative."[69] If the governor was willing to consider this information, then the whole rationale for sentencing Teresa Lewis to death would be undermined. Grimes and Judge Strauss had determined that Lewis was the mastermind, the "head of the serpent." They had based the determination that the crime met the standard of "vileness" on the depravity of mind that they claimed led her to organize the murders. If the whole plot had been Shallenberger's idea, then Teresa's actions did not meet the standard for vileness, and she could not be put to death. This is the major issue that McDonnell was asked to consider as he contemplated clemency.

The executive's power to order conditional clemency (a reduced sentence) is based on two elements—correcting mistakes or showing mercy. Governor McDonnell had stated that he would grant clemency "only when there is substantial evidence of extraordinary circumstances to warrant it."[70] The process required that the inmate provide the governor with background information and reasons for the altered sentence. Then, behind closed doors and without any formal process, he would make his decision. The lack of accountability in the clemency process was one issue addressed in the 2000 JLARC report. The legislature recommended that the governor make a public report of the decision-making process, including the factors he had considered in rendering his ruling.[71] However, as in many other states, the procedure in Virginia remains shrouded in secrecy.

The petition for clemency sent to McDonnell was 270 pages long and included 29 exhibits. More than 7300 people from around the United States, from Europe, even from Iran, wrote to the governor asking that Lewis's sentence be commuted. Many argued, in addition to the new evidence challenging the grounds of her punishment, that Lewis was a changed woman. Along with the chaplain at the women's prison, numerous letter writers told the governor that Teresa would help other prisoners if she were allowed to live.[72] Chaplain Litchfield wrote that "It would be hard to count the number of women who, either in church or in writing, have expressed their gratitude for Teresa's impact in their lives."[73]

In response to all of these pleas, McDonnell issued a brief statement denying clemency. It was less than one full page in length. He pulled a few facts from the court record and made no mention of new evidence.[74] No one knows whether he even read the petition or if he was aware of the issues raised.

Nothing further stood in the way of Teresa Lewis's appointment with lethal injection on September 23, 2010. An observer stated that Lewis "appeared fearful" when she came into the death chamber where fourteen prison officials and members of the victims' family watched. She was bound to the gurney with heavy leather straps. Her last words were "I want Kathy to know that I love her and I'm very sorry." As the drug "cocktail" was released, her feet bobbed a few times. Then while her spiritual advisor Reverend Julie Perry sobbed, Teresa Lewis died.[75] Her lawyer during the appellate process, Jim Rocap, said, "Tonight the death machine exterminated the beautiful, child-like, and loving spirit of Teresa Lewis."[76]

As press reports noted each time the United States carries out an execution, especially the execution of a woman, it means "strenuously bad public relations for an increasingly unpopular facet of the American justice system." Lewis's execution drew worldwide attention to the fact that the United States is "on the roll call of countries with the less than salubrious distinction" of putting its citizens to death.[77]

The death of Teresa Lewis also highlighted the internal failures and arbitrariness of America's death penalty system. As Victor Streib pointed out in his work on women sentenced to death, their stories "illustrate the differential impact of factors such as ... mental deficiency, confessions, and physical demeanor at trial." Such extralegal factors help to explain why these few women are selected for death and so many others involved in murder are not.[78]

Not Unique

Teresa Lewis's story bears striking resemblances to others recounted in this book. Like Velma Barfield and Karla Faye Tucker, she became a model prisoner who ministered to others. Like all the other women sentenced to death, Lewis was blamed for her moral failures as a woman. Such behavior became part of the state's case against her and was treated as incriminating and aggravating evidence.

Most vividly, Lewis's case parallels that of Marilyn Kay Plantz. Both were executed for their participation in the killing of a husband. Plantz had an IQ of 76; Lewis's was several points lower. Plantz allegedly conspired with two younger men, one black, one white. So did Lewis. In both cases, the apparent motive was the husband's insurance money. Plantz did not assist with the killing but cleaned up after the assailants. She seemed uncaring. Lewis was condemned for being "very calm." In both cases, one or more of the actual killers received a life sentence for cooperating with the investigation. The killers claimed that Plantz had "lured" them into the crime with promises of sex and money. The state drew a similar picture of Lewis, the temptress. Plantz's attorney was inexperienced and underfunded and inadequate. He failed to find out about her low level of mental functioning or her history of abuse. When those factors came to light they were ignored because of procedural default. Lewis's case was eerily similar.

Women who are singled out for execution go to their deaths at least as much for the way they have offended the public sense of gender propriety as for their actual involvement in crime. Teresa Lewis and Marilyn Plantz are powerful examples.

Endnotes

1. Testimony of Deborah T. Gray, *Lewis v. Warden*, 645 S.E. 2d 492 (Va. 2007).
2. Ibid.
3. Lawrence Hammack, "Teresa Lewis to be Executed by Lethal Injection," *Roanoke Times* (September 12, 2010).
4. Much of the factual information about the events in Teresa Lewis's life and her relationship with Julian Lewis is included in the transcripts of her sentencing hearing *Commonwealth v. Lewis*, (Va. Cir. June 2, 2003, and June 3, 2003). Additional accounts are found in the subsequent opinions of the appellate courts, *Lewis v. Commonwealth* 593 S.E. 2d 220 (Va. 2004), *Lewis v. Warden*, 645 S.E. 2d 492 (Va. 2007) and *Lewis v. Wheeler*, 609 F. 3d (4th Cir. 2010).
5. *Commonwealth v. Lewis*.
6. Ibid.
7. Ibid.
8. Ibid.
9. Tamara L. Graham, "Lewis v. Commonwealth," *Capital Defense Journal* 17:1, (2004), 230.
10. John Grisham, "Teresa Lewis Didn't Pull the Trigger: Why Is She on Death Row?" *Washington Post* (September 22, 2010).
11. Sarah Breslow, "Pleading Guilty to Death: Protecting the Capital Defendant's Sixth Amendment Right to a Jury Sentencing after Entering a Guilty Plea," *Cornell Law Review* 98 (2012–2013) 1247–48.
12. Graham, "Lewis v. Commonwealth," 241.
13. The account of events at the time of the crime, unless otherwise noted, is taken from the transcript of Lewis's sentencing hearing, *Commonwealth v. Lewis*.
14. Ibid., 119.
15. Ibid., 121.
16. Ibid., 122.
17. Ibid., 126.
18. Ibid., 128.
19. Ibid., 135.
20. Ibid., 138.
21. Ibid., 139.
22. Ibid., 143.
23. Ibid.

24. Ibid., 170.
25. Ibid., 206.
26. Ibid., 214.
27. Ibid., 241.
28. Joint Legislative Audit and Review Commission of the Virginia General Assembly, *Review of Virginia's System of Capital Punishment* (Richmond: Commonwealth of Virginia, 2002), 10. Hereinafter JLARC.
29. Ibid.
30. Breslow, "Pleading Guilty to Death," 1253.
31. Hammack, "Teresa Lewis to Be Executed."
32. *Commonwealth v. Lewis*, 222.
33. Ibid., 229.
34. Ibid., 247.
35. Ibid., 248.
36. Ibid., 249.
37. Ibid., 256.
38. Ibid., 260.
39. Ibid., 264.
40. Ibid., 267.
41. Ibid., 271.
42. Ibid., 283.
43. Richard C. Dieter, *Struck by Lightning: The Continuing Arbitrariness of the Death Penalty Thirty-Five Years after its Reinstatement in 1976* (Washington, DC: Death Penalty Information Center, 2011), 8.
44. JLARC, *Virginia's System of Capital Punishment*, IV.
45. Dieter, *Struck by Lightning*, 9.
46. Melanie Crawford, "A Losing Battle with the 'Machinery of Death': The Flaws of Virginia's Death Penalty Laws and Clemency Process Highlighted by the Fate of Teresa Lewis," *Widener Law Review* 18 (2012), 88.
47. Ibid.
48. Graham, "Lewis v. Commonwealth," 232.
49. Ibid., 235–36.
50. Crawford, "Losing Battle," 91–92.
51. Graham, "Lewis v. Commonwealth," 237–38.
52. Ibid., 236. Crawford, "Losing Battle," 93.
53. *Lewis v Warden*, 645 S.E. 2nd, (2007). Part I.
54. Ibid.
55. Ibid.
56. Ibid.
57. *Lewis v. Warden*, 645 S.E. 2nd, (2007), Part II.
58. Quoted in Crawford, "Losing Battle," 78.
59. Breslow, "Pleading Guilty to Death," 1264–69.
60. *Lewis v. Wheeler*. The summary of the opinion is taken from the text itself. No page numbers are included.

61. Crawford, "Losing Battle," 89–90.

62. *Lewis v. Wheeler*.

63. Lynn Litchfield, "Unfit for Execution," *Newsweek* (August 27, 2010).

64. Ibid.

65. Crawford, "Losing Battle," 83.

66. Hammack, "Teresa Lewis to Be Executed."

67. Virginians for Alternatives to the Death Penalty, "Virginia Set to Execute Woman with 72 IQ as Mastermind," (August 2010) at www.vadp.org

68. Melissa Scott Sinclair, "Blood Sisters: Virginia Prepares to Execute Only the Second Woman Sentenced to Death in a Century," *Style Weekly* (September 15, 2010).

69. Grisham, "Teresa Lewis Didn't Pull the Trigger."

70. Quoted in Crawford, "Losing Battle," 82.

71. JLARC, "Virginia's System of Capital Punishment."

72. Litchfield, "Unfit for Execution," "Teresa Lewis Executed by Virginia amid International Outcry," *Daily Mail Online* (September 26, 2010) at www.dailymail.co.uk

73. Hammack, "Teresa Lewis to Be Executed."

74. Crawford, "Losing Battle," 95.

75. "Teresa Lewis Executed amid International Outcry."

76. "A Woman Dies," *America*, (November 1, 2010), 5.

77. "The Cruel and Unusual Punishment of Teresa Lewis," *Chicago Press Release* (August 22, 2010).

78. Deborah W. Denno, "How Many Lives Has Victor Streib Saved? A Tribute," *Ohio Northern University Law Review* 38 (2011–1012), 415.

·11·

#500 AND #510

Kimberly Mccarthy and Suzanne Basso

Kimberly McCarthy: Number 500

When Kimberly Lagayle McCarthy was executed by lethal injection on July 26, 2013, she became the five hundredth person to be put to death in Texas since the reinstatement of the death penalty. Much of the attention to her execution focused on the number 500, as commentators noted that Texas was responsible for more than one third of state-imposed deaths in the modern period. Carrying out McCarthy's death sentence also marked Texas as the state which executed over one third of the women put to death since *Furman v. Georgia*.

McCarthy was African American. Her victim was white and female. The crime occurred in the Dallas area, one of the most active death-penalty jurisdictions in the country. Those factors made McCarthy's case a likely candidate for capital punishment. On the other hand, it differed from many of the other crimes that sent women to death row in that McCarthy was found guilty of murdering Dorothy Booth in the course of a robbery. Although Booth was a neighbor and acquainted with McCarthy, the crime stands apart from many discussed in this book as it did not involve an intimate. In a sense, the robbery and murder were more like crimes committed by men than by women, especially as the motive was related to drugs. The incident apparently grew out of

McCarthy's need for money to buy crack cocaine. McCarthy's story is unusual also because her first conviction and sentence were reversed by the Texas Court of Criminal Appeals (TCCA). She was, however, retried and again sentenced to death. The second time, there were no reversals.

The Crime and the First Trial

Dorothy Booth, a retired psychology professor, was murdered in her home on July 21, 1997.[1] McCarthy had contacted Booth asking to visit, ostensibly to borrow some sugar. Instead, she "stabbed Mrs. Booth five times, hit her in the face with a candelabrum, cut off her left ring finger in order to take her diamond ring, and nearly severed her left little finger as well."[2] Almost every account of the crime mentions the removal of Booth's finger, an especially callous and brutal act. This gruesome image would follow McCarthy through her trial to her death, much like Karla Faye Tucker's comment about experiencing an orgasm became indelibly associated with her offense. After killing Booth, McCarthy allegedly returned to her home where she washed the murder weapon and put it away in her kitchen. Taking Booth's purse, credit cards, and the stolen ring, she drove off in the victim's Mercedes and headed for places where drugs were available. McCarthy pawned the ring for a few hundred dollars, bought some drugs, and used the credit cards at least four times for groceries and at gas stations during the next day. She was caught using the credit cards at a liquor store, where she was also carrying Booth's driver's license.[3]

McCarthy was arrested on July 24, three days after the murder. Police found a 10-inch butcher knife in her home. Although the knife had been washed, subsequent forensics tests found traces of Booth's blood under the handle.[4] The murder weapon, the fact that McCarthy had several of the victim's possessions, and the trail to the crack house seemed to clearly identify her as the killer. After she was taken into custody, Sergeant Patrick Stallings of the Lancaster Police Department tried to interview McCarthy. However after agreeing to talk to the officer, she asked for an attorney and stated that she did not wish to talk further. That interview was terminated, although apparently McCarthy was not assigned an attorney. A few days later Detective Dwayne Bishop of the Dallas Police Department telephoned Stallings stating that McCarthy's husband had asked Bishop to talk with her at the jail. Stallings faxed Bishop several pages of notes and, according to his testimony, reminded the detective that the suspect had invoked her right to an attorney. Nonetheless, Bishop visited McCarthy, read her Miranda rights, and took a statement from her. He claimed that he did not threaten or coerce her nor did he promise anything in return for her cooperation. He did not mention her earlier request for an attorney or ask if one had been appointed. McCarthy made a statement to Bishop providing her version of the crime.[5] That statement became a significant part of the state's case against her at her first trial.

McCarthy was tried in November 1998 for the capital murder of Dorothy Booth. She was convicted by a Dallas jury and, as the jury found special circumstances making her death-eligible, the judge sentenced her to death. On hearing her mandatory direct appeal, the Texas Court of Criminal Appeals made the rare decision to reverse the lower court.[6] The grounds for reversal involved her alleged confession. The TCCA found that the police had interrogated McCarthy and taken a statement from her after she had asked for an attorney. At trial, McCarthy's court-appointed counsel asked that her statement be suppressed as it was elicited after she had asked for a lawyer. However, the trial judge allowed the confession to be admitted, and it became part of both the state's case in chief and their arguments in favor of a death sentence. On appeal the TCCA found that the statement was inadmissible because McCarthy had clearly asked for a lawyer prior to Bishop's questioning. They further found that the error of admitting the confession had harmed the defendant. The prosecution had used it to discredit her version of events as the confession ran counter to the evidence. Thus McCarthy was presented to the jury as lying to protect herself. The statement was further used by the prosecution to portray McCarthy as unrepentant, cruel, and greedy. All of those qualities seem to make defendants, especially women, more worthy of death in the eyes of juries. The jury was also informed by the prosecution that after making and signing the statement, McCarthy told Detective Bishop that it was a lie, but that she would tell the truth in exchange for one rock of cocaine. While the prosecutor discredited much of the factual material in the confession, he reminded the jury that it did show that the defendant had motive, means, and opportunity to kill Booth. Thus the TCCA found that the statement, although not the only evidence leading to McCarthy's conviction and sentence, did contribute to the verdict. As they noted, "A confession is likely to leave an indelible impact on a jury."[7] They ordered that McCarthy must receive a new trial. What was included in this contested statement?

In her "confession," McCarthy claimed that on the night of the murder, two dealers "Kilo" and "J.C." brought drugs to her house. When they ran out of drugs, the two men wanted McCarthy to get money to buy more. In response to their verbal abuse, she agreed to call Dorothy Booth and ask to borrow some sugar. Supposedly Kilo and J.C. had the idea to rob Booth once McCarthy got into her house. She claimed the two men killed Booth, took her purse and money while she was told to wait in the car. According to McCarthy, while the men were picking up some drugs, she drove off in the car and went to get "dope" from someone called "Smiley." Later, after those drugs ran out, she claimed to have found the credit cards and Booth's diamond ring in the purse. She stated that an unknown woman had gone with her to pawn some of Booth's possessions and had used the credit cards.

The "confession" was full of details, many of them implausible. The police never found Kilo or J.C. They did find Booth's driver's license and credit cards in McCarthy's possession when she was arrested. They also located Smiley, who testified that McCarthy was driving the victim's car on the day after the murder. Likewise, Booth's daughter testified that "the black lady who lived across the alley" (McCarthy) had called her mother in the middle of the night on other occasions to borrow money. Booth's caller ID showed two such phone calls in the early hours on the morning she was killed. Along with the DNA evidence of the victim's blood on the knife in McCarthy's kitchen, the state had ample proof of her involvement in the crime. They used the alleged confession to provide the jury with confirmation of her bad character. The assumption that it contributed to the guilty verdict in her first trial seems well founded.

Further Proceedings

McCarthy was retried in Dallas County. On October 29, 2002, she was again found guilty and sentenced to death. This time the TCCA affirmed the lower court's decision. All of her subsequent appeals were denied by both state and federal courts. In several stages of the case, McCarthy was represented by the same court-appointed attorney, Brad Loller, who had represented her in the first trial. During jury selection, the prosecution used peremptory strikes to remove four of five non-white individuals left in the pool at the time they were individually questioned. Only one African American man remained on the actual jury. McCarthy's attorney did not object to the state's removal of the black members of the jury pool, even though the Dallas courts had a history of discrimination in jury selection.[8]

The state's description of the crime was similar to the 1998 trial. The DNA evidence of the blood on the murder weapon found in McCarthy's kitchen seemed to be quite persuasive.[9] There were no other suspects, given that the defendant's earlier statement had been discredited. McCarthy's behavior after the crime seemed to confirm her guilt and the heinousness of the offense. "Witnesses who saw [her] at the 'crack house' on the morning after the murder testified that she was calm, did not appear to be on drugs, and was dressed for work."[10]

Once McCarthy had again been found guilty, the state argued that she deserved the death penalty based primarily on her "future dangerousness." As in other cases (including Velma Barfield, Aileen Wuornos, and Judias Buenoano), the prosecution made the claim that "collateral offenses," crimes for which the defendant had been charged but not tried or convicted, stood as proof that she had a history of violence and that she was a threat to the community. Here the state told the jury that McCarthy had murdered two other elderly women, one a friend of her mother and the other a distant relative. They too had been robbed of their purses and credit cards after being beaten and stabbed. Although those murders had been committed fourteen years earlier in 1988, McCarthy had only been "linked" to them a decade later, after Booth was killed.[11] She denied involvement, but the jury was allowed to consider those crimes. In addition they were shown photos of the bodies of those two women. The jury also heard that McCarthy had broken some rules while in prison. She refused to turn over a razor to a guard after showering and she apparently threatened another inmate. In response, the defense claimed that she only committed crimes because of her addiction to crack cocaine and her need for money to support the addiction. But clearly the jury heard sufficient evidence to support a finding of future dangerousness. The TCCA agreed. "Based upon the brutal and calculated nature of appellant's conduct in committing the instant offense, the two extraneous murders in which appellant used her position of trust with the elderly victims to gain entry into their homes, the brutal nature of those offenses, and other bad acts, including violating prison rules" it was reasonable to conclude beyond a reasonable doubt that she would remain a continuing threat to society.[12] It is interesting that the appellate court held that the jury was able to conclude "beyond a reasonable doubt" that McCarthy was dangerous when the state had not proved her guilt in the earlier murders beyond a reasonable doubt. They had only asserted that she was guilty but had not met any legal standard of proof.

McCarthy's direct appeal to the TCCA in 2004 was denied. Not only did the appellate court uphold the future dangerousness finding, they found that she did not suffer any other violations of her constitutional rights. When she filed for a writ of habeas corpus in state court, the TCCA denied her motion without a hearing in 2007. She then filed a habeas petition in federal court. In that case, decided in 2011, there were nine grounds for appeal. Several of McCarthy's points focused on ineffective assistance of counsel at her trial.[13] Other issues involved the constitutionality of the Texas death penalty statute. The latter claims, although suggestive, tend to be ignored by the federal courts who reason that such matters have already been decided.

One ineffective assistance of counsel claim argued that McCarthy's attorney had failed to object when the victim's daughter, Donna Aldred, was allowed to remain in the courtroom after she had testified. Although the TCCA had rejected that point on procedural default grounds, stating that it should have been raised on direct appeal rather than in a habeas proceeding, the federal district court disagreed and chose to judge the issue on its merits. The result was the same, as they found that McCarthy's attorney was not deficient in his failure to object to Aldred's presence in the courtroom even though she broke down and had to be removed after looking at the medical examiner's photos of her mother's body. They considered the impact of Aldred's presence and reaction upon the jury and determined that McCarthy was not harmed under the *Strickland* standard. Her attorney's conduct was not sufficiently deficient to affect the outcome of the trial.

McCarthy had also challenged her attorney's competence based on his failure to introduce her "confession" into evidence in the second trial. The argument was that the statement portrayed McCarthy as a participant in the robbery but not as a murderer. However, lower courts had found that the statement was inadmissible, and her attorney "should not be faulted for failing to take a useless action."[14] Besides, the federal court concluded, the statement would only have painted a terrible picture of McCarthy as "an unrepentant liar and [it would have] set out her cruel and greedy motive for killing her elderly neighbor."[15] Had the "confession" been admitted, it would not have improved McCarthy's prospects for a different verdict or sentence. She also made a claim that her appellate counsel had been inadequate for failing to raise appropriate issues in her direct appeal. However, she was not able to cite what the appropriate grounds should have been. Therefore the allegations that her attorneys had been inadequate at her trial and in the earlier appeals were denied. What is truly remarkable is that up until this point, none of McCarthy's lawyers had raised questions about the racial makeup of her jury.

With respect to the Texas death penalty law, McCarthy argued that the state should be required to prove the absence of mitigating circumstances beyond a reasonable doubt. The federal court denied this claim and noted that the state had proved aggravating circumstances (the murder occurred in the course of a robbery) beyond a reasonable doubt. Thus McCarthy's petition for a writ of habeas corpus was denied. She was not granted a Certificate of Appealability (COA), which would have sent her case back to the lower court for review. Instead, she appealed the district court's decision to the Fifth Circuit Court of Appeals. Their decision was handed down on July 11, 2012.

They, too, denied the COA.[16] Again, McCarthy claimed that her counsel had failed to represent her adequately when he neglected to introduce her statement to police and when he did not object to the presence of Booth's daughter in the courtroom. Using the *Strickland* standard, the Fifth Circuit held that her attorney was employing "sound trial strategy" when he chose not to include her "confession" as part of the defense case. They noted that after representing her at her first trial and successful appeal to the TCCA, her lawyer knew that the statement could harm McCarthy. As to ineffective assistance for not objecting to the presence of Aldred in the court, the judges found that here, too, his actions were "not unreasonable." Thus McCarthy's execution seemed inevitable, as it appeared that only the U.S. Supreme Court or the Texas Board of Pardons and Paroles could avert her death which was set for January 29, 2013. Two things occurred to delay but not to alter that outcome.

The Final Efforts

In January 2013, shortly before she was due to be executed, McCarthy was appointed a new attorney, Maurie Levin, an experienced capital defense advocate. Levin was able to win a stay of execution to finally raise the claim that McCarthy had been denied a fair trial due to the racial makeup of the jury. A second stay was granted in April 2013 because the Texas Legislature was considering bills that might have provided relief for defendants who could make credible claims that racial bias had affected the outcome of their trials.[17] During those months that McCarthy remained alive, Levin developed the strongest argument against her execution—namely, that her trial attorney had been ineffective for not challenging the jury-selection process.

In her final set of appeals, McCarthy's case focused on the conduct of her trial lawyer and her earlier appellate counsel who had failed to raise the issue of whether the defendant had been denied her Fourteenth Amendment right to equal protection of the law and her Sixth Amendment right to an impartial jury. As the habeas pleadings noted, Dallas County where McCarthy was sentenced was "infamous for its exclusion of African Americans from criminal juries."[18] In her case, only four non-white citizens made it to voir dire, the stage where they were questioned individually by the prosecution and defense attorneys. The state excused three of those four potential jurors using peremptory challenges. In other words, the prosecutor did not need to provide any reason or explanation for their exclusion. However, at that point the defense should have raised a *Batson* challenge.[19] Under that procedure, if the defense can make a prima facie case that individuals are being excused for racial reasons, the prosecution is required to provide a rationale other than race to explain their exclusion. The judge will then decide whether or not to accept that justification. Although *Batson* challenges are not a foolproof way to eliminate racial bias in jury selection, they do force prosecutors to explain their decisions. Even more important, if a defense attorney makes such a move at trial, the issue would be preserved to be considered on appeal. Strangely, in McCarthy's case, neither her original lawyer nor the lawyers earlier in her appeal process had raised the issue. Thus in the final habeas appeals, her attorney had not only to demonstrate racial bias in the jury selection but also to overcome the matter of procedural default—trying to raise matters that had not been considered in the earlier appeals. She had to associate the bias claim with an ineffective assistance of counsel claim and hope that the courts would not invoke procedural default.

It was significant to the argument for habeas relief that the trial had taken place in Dallas County where the "capital system [was] riddled with prejudice."[20] Prosecutors there often used "disparate questioning," asking white and non-white potential jurors different things. The strategy was an attempt to get minority jurors excused for cause, most likely on the grounds that they were not sufficiently willing to vote for a death sentence. Also in Dallas, not only were murders with white victims more likely to draw capital charges, but juries were likely to hear "expert testimony" that African Americans were more prone to be dangerous in the future. In McCarthy's case, future dangerousness based on the accusation that she had committed two non-adjudicated murders was a decisive factor in the jury's decision to sentence her to death. All of these factors, which had been amply demonstrated in earlier Dallas County cases, should have alerted McCarthy's trial attorney and her earlier appellate attorneys to pursue the issue of racial bias. Instead, her "trial counsel was patently deficient" and her state habeas attorney "filed a petition essentially devoid of cognizable claims. But for trial and habeas counsel's deficient performance, Ms. McCarthy would have obtained a new trial devoid of racial prejudice."[21]

It is inexplicable that her earlier attorneys failed even to mention issues of race, given long-standing patterns of discrimination not only in Dallas County but in Texas's capital punishment system as a whole. "The ubiquity of this history is such that trial counsel had to have been [aware] of it, and was thus all the more deficient in failing to object to the prosecution's actions in Ms. McCarthy's case."[22] Not only should a competent defense attorney have known of the history of prejudicial jury selection in Dallas, he could easily have found out that the prosecutors in McCarthy's case were the products of a "culture of discrimination" in the district attorney's office.

The argument that McCarthy's trial was tainted by racial bias would seem to be strong enough to pass the *Strickland* test. The *Strickland* standard requires that for an attorney's behavior to be unconstitutionally inadequate it must not be part of a reasonable trial strategy, and it must actually cause harm to the defendant's case. Clearly prosecutorial conduct that denied a fair trial due to racial discrimination should not pass the *Strickland* test. However, the other barrier to McCarthy's claim was the matter of procedural default. Here her attorney, Maurie Levin, believed a Supreme Court decision handed down only weeks before McCarthy's scheduled execution might overcome that hurdle.

In *Trevino v. Thaler*[23] the Supreme Court addressed the very issue of whether a defendant whose trial and habeas counsel were both deficient could raise a claim that otherwise would have been procedurally defaulted. In other words, if, through no fault of her own, a person going through a capital procedure was not only denied adequate counsel at trial but was also denied adequate assistance of counsel during the state habeas phase, he or she could later in federal court raise issues those incompetent lawyers failed to raise. The argument in McCarthy's case was that the TCCA should fix the problem and not open the door for federal intervention. But just in case the Texas Court was not willing to address McCarthy's claims in light of *Trevino*, Levin also filed a habeas petition in federal court.

The TCCA essentially rejected these arguments entirely. Refusing to consider that the Supreme Court said that *Trevino* was retroactive, the TCCA declined to stay her execution. In fact they held that McCarthy was asking them to "treat initial state habeas counsel's ineffectiveness as an *excuse* to reach her claim of ineffective assistance of trial counsel."[24] And, perhaps even more remarkably, the TCCA found there was no evidence that McCarthy had been harmed by her attorney's failure to raise a *Batson* challenge.

With no avenues left to stay her execution other than an appeal to Governor Rick Perry for a 30-day delay, it seemed inevitable that on

June 26, 2013, Kimberly McCarthy would become the 500th person to be executed in Texas during the post-*Furman* era. Perry, a staunch advocate of capital punishment, presided over 261 of the 500 modern Texas executions, more state-sponsored deaths than any other governor in American history. The chances of his support for McCarthy's case were nonexistent.

On the day of McCarthy's execution, protestors gathered at the Huntsville prison to draw attention both to her death and to the relentless use of capital punishment in Texas. About one hundred demonstrators chanted "Harris County says death row. We say hell no! Perry says death row. We say hell no!" Clergyman Peter Johnson from Dallas said "The death penalty is not only economically stupid. It says something about our moral fiber…. The solution to murder cannot be murder." Another protestor noted that capital punishment was a part of the violent American culture, "our love of guns, our love of violence. I think each person, even McCarthy, has value and worth." Pro-death penalty demonstrators commented "It's an eye for an eye."[25] Donna Aldred, the daughter of the victim, read a statement indicating that she expected the execution to bring some closure. "After waiting sixteen years, the finality of today's events have (sic) allowed me to say goodbye to my mother. Although I am grateful to see justice served, nothing will ever fill the holes we have in our hearts."[26]

Texas inmates are no longer provided with a special last meal. The legislature in 2011 ordered that they must be served the same food as the general population, apparently because some condemned men ordered meals that were considered too lavish. McCarthy was given oatmeal, fruit, and chicken sandwiches about seventeen hours before her execution. After that she spent her final day reading, meeting with her spiritual advisor and the prison chaplain, and visiting with her ex-husband.[27]

During her time on death row, McCarthy had earned a certificate from Crossroad Bible Institute, a nonprofit prison ministry. She had received high marks from her instructors during her period of discipleship. The program involved an opportunity for inmates to engage in independent serious Bible study under the direction of a trained instructor. Just before the execution, the Institute issued a statement, "Pray for Kimberly and her family during this difficult time. Also pray that justice will be equitably and compassionately served throughout the country."[28]

Observers noted that McCarthy was pronounced dead about twenty minutes after she was given a single lethal dose of pentobarbital.[29] McCarthy's last words were "This is not a loss. This is a win. You know where I'm going. I'm going to be home with Jesus. Keep the faith. I love you all."[30] Her attorney had described her as "a very spiritual person. She believes what's meant to be is meant to be, and it's all in God's hands."[31] But, Levin also noted, McCarthy's execution was "an emblem of Texas' 500th execution, something all Texans should be ashamed of."[32]

Race as an Issue

Kimberly McCarthy's case exemplified a number of themes that characterize the administration of capital punishment in Texas. First of all, it typified the situation where the race of the victim influenced the decision to seek the death penalty and the likelihood of a capital sentence. Overall 80% of capital cases involve a white victim, while only 49% of all those murdered are white. In other words, murders of whites are more likely to lead to capital charges. This disparity may suggest that prosecutors select cases with white victims as more winnable.[33] Baldus and Woodworth agreed that prosecutorial discretion was the most common explanation for the overrepresentation of capital cases with white victims. They found that the race of the victim had an effect on capital sentencing in Texas. Between 1976 and 2002, even though less than half of all murder victims were white, 79% of those executed had, like Kimberly McCarthy, murdered a white person.[34]

Most obviously, McCarthy's case raised the ongoing issue of racial bias in the selection of juries. In all death penalty states, a jury in a capital trial must be "death qualified." They must, based on the estimation of the prosecutor, be willing to confer a sentence of death, should the defendant be found guilty and meet the requirements for capital punishment. Generally this means that a juror must be ready to vote for death if the aggravating circumstances outweigh the mitigating circumstances. The Supreme Court has allowed the rejection of potential jurors who express general opposition to capital punishment, but those whose position is more ambiguous often become targets of dispute between the prosecution and the defense. In other words, there is no simple formula to decide how firm a prospective juror's support of the death penalty must be before he or she is judged to be "death qualified." Furthermore, the process of death qualification may implant in jurors' minds the idea that the defendant is definitely guilty. As former Justice John Paul Stevens stated, the prolonged questioning of veniremen [potential jurors] about their ability to impose the death penalty "creates an atmosphere in which jurors are likely to assume that their primary task is to determine the appropriate punishment for a presumptively guilty defendant."[35] They assume that the prosecutor would not be asking for the death penalty if the defendant were not obviously guilty.

Because polls consistently show that support for capital punishment is lower among African Americans and women, the process of death qualification will inevitably exclude more members of those groups. In addition, studies of jurors who meet the standard of support for capital punishment show they are more likely to favor the prosecution, more likely to convict, and more likely to believe that if the death penalty is on the table, the defendant must be guilty. A study done at the University of Texas in 2004 found that death penalty supporters were more fearful of freeing the guilty than of convicting the innocent.[36] Thus even if the jury-selection process is not characterized by intentional racial bias, it is likely that fewer minorities will be seated in capital trials and that defendants will face jurors already predisposed to convict and sentence them.

Although many minority jurors who express insufficient support for capital punishment may be eliminated for cause, there is even more concern when prosecutors intentionally use their peremptory challenges to remove African Americans from the jury pool. A frequently quoted series published in the Dallas Morning News uncovered a pattern of prosecutorial attempts to exclude minorities from juries. The practice went back at least to the 1930s when a black college president was thrown headfirst down the Dallas courthouse steps for asserting his right to be considered for jury duty.[37] In 1969, an assistant district attorney advised his fellow prosecutors to remove freethinkers, the physically disabled and the overweight as well as racial minorities from juries. In fact, his policy was characterized in a headline as "Women, Gimps, Blacks, Hippies Need Not Apply."[38] In the mid-1980s, prosecutors were still using the same controversial 1969 selection manual which proclaimed that minorities did not make good jurors because they sympathized with defendants. It further suggested that the prosecution did not want fair jurors but "strong, biased, and sometimes hypercritical individuals who believe defendants are different from them in kind rather than degree."[39] Such advice, almost an invitation to select (white) jurors who were unlike the (black) defendant, led to the exclusion of nine out of ten African Americans through peremptory challenges. Blacks were excused at five times the rate of whites and twice as often as Hispanics. And lest the racially based jury selection might be thought to be a relic of the twentieth century, in one 2005 Dallas case, the prosecution struck an African American man for having "gold teeth and wearing gold necklaces." Also in 2005, studies showed that blacks were still being dismissed twice as often as whites from juries. When the answer to whether they or someone close to them had a bad experience with the criminal justice system was "yes," 39% of whites and 100% of blacks were dismissed.[40]

Such systematic exclusion of African Americans from juries violates the rights of both the prospective jurors and the defendants. One group is deprived of the constitutional right to equal protection; the other is deprived of the impartial jury guaranteed in the Sixth Amendment. The combination of death qualification and the racially biased use of peremptory challenges meant that many defendants would not have a jury that represented a cross-section of the community to decide whether they lived or were put to death.

The Supreme Court addressed the racial use of peremptory challenges in Dallas in their 2005 decision, *Miller-El v. Dretke* in which they upheld Miller-El's claim that he was denied a fair trial based on the improper exclusion of blacks from the jury in his capital trial.[41] Like McCarthy, Miller-El was tried in Dallas, and, as in her case, the prosecution used peremptory challenges to remove all but one of the qualified blacks from the jury. The difference was that Miller-El's attorney objected to the state's actions. Although the trial court upheld the prosecution, the Supreme Court ultimately found that Miller-El's constitutional rights were violated and indeed that "the very integrity of the courts is jeopardized."[42] The Court looked not only at the percentage of blacks who were excluded from the jury but also looked at the explanations the state gave for eliminating them. The justices found that several African Americans were excused when whites who answered questions in a similar way were seated on the jury. Furthermore, they noted that in Miller-El's trial, the prosecutor "shuffled" the jury several times. In other words, the district attorney used a long-standing Texas technique of moving prospective jurors around to different seats when black prospects got to the front of the line, rearranging the order in which they would be questioned. "The Dallas County District Attorney's Office had, by its own admission, used this process to manipulate the racial composition of the jury in the past."[43] No racially neutral reason was offered to explain the shuffling. In addition, in Miller-El's trial, as in McCarthy's, the prosecution asked black potential jurors different questions than they asked white potential jurors. In some instances, these questions were designed to elicit responses unfavorable to capital punishment from blacks. Based on all of these factors, the Supreme Court concluded, "We know that for decades ... prosecutors in the Dallas County office had followed a specific policy of systematically excluding blacks from juries."[44] For that reason, they overturned Miller-El's sentence.

McGonigle and Timms state that the judicial community differs about the impact of the exclusion of minorities on sentencing, but no one can deny that such practices affect the appearance of justice. A predominantly white court-room determining the fate of a black defendant who is accused of harming a white victim looks like a persistent version of "white man's justice."[45] But several commentators note that the prosecution alone is not to blame for the makeup of juries. Defense attorneys and judges often fail to object to the practice of racial exclusion.[46] That is what happened to Kimberly McCarthy. The neglect by her lawyer in not raising a claim of racial discrimination when her jury was selected foreclosed the possibility of challenging that violation at a later time.

In addition, the outcome of McCarthy's trial was surely influenced by the introduction of her alleged past crimes as "evidence" that she would be a threat to society in the future. This notion of future dangerousness as a significant factor in determining capital sentencing is unique to Texas. Other states do not use it as a way to determine who will be put to death. As the American Bar Association found in its 2013 assessment of the Texas capital system, the estimation of future dangerousness opens the way for junk science, speculation, and racial bias. They note that "only after deciding unanimously that 'there is a probability that the defendant would commit criminal acts of violence that would constitute a continuing threat to society' will the jury consider whether any evidence in mitigation supports a sentence less than death." The issue of the defendant's future dangerousness is placed "at the center of the jury's punishment decision."[47] And, as the ABA points out, the terms that are used to describe future dangerousness have no precise definition and are not explained to the jury. Thus they are left to decide the meaning of "probability," "criminal acts of violence," and "society." The state has often used highly questionable evidence and the testimony of unreliable "experts" to support their arguments. And, at the same time that prosecutors make wide-ranging claims of future dangerousness to juries as an argument for why the defendant should not live, jurors typically do not receive an explanation of how to weigh mitigating evidence.[48] Sixty-eight percent of Texas capital jurors interviewed believed that death was *required* if the defendant would be dangerous in the future.[49] The allegation that McCarthy would be a continu-ing threat (based to a great extent on "linking" her to the two murders never proven) made before a racially unrepresentative jury certainly raises questions about the process by which she was sentenced to death.

The responsibility for challenging the prosecution's tactics, witnesses, their narrative of the crime, and for exposing junk science and the flaws in arguments about future dangerousness lies with defense lawyers. Kimberly McCarthy, whose lawyer failed dismally to raise questions about the jury selection process, was doubly disadvantaged when his incompetence combined with the state's interpretation of procedural default made it impossible for the issue to be brought up on appeal. However, her experience was not unique, and certainly not in Texas where one in four capital defendants are assigned a lawyer who has been reprimanded, or is on probation, suspended, or even been banned from practicing by the state bar.[50]

The 2013 assessment by the American Bar Association raised a number of points about the effectiveness of capital representation in Texas. They found that the state, at best, complied only partially with the ABA's standards for defense services. In 2007, Texas established the Regional Public Defender for Capital Cases (RPDO), and in 2009 it established the Office of Capital Writs (OCW). Both were created to provide lawyers with capital expertise to represent indigent defendants—the RPDO at trial and the OCW during habeas proceedings. This system was an improvement over the earlier situation, where defense attorneys were appointed from lists maintained by the local trial courts.[51] Texas was notorious for providing inadequate counsel, as in the case of Frances Newton whose lawyer appeared drunk in court or Betty Lou Beets, whose lawyer attempted to profit from her death sentence. However, the RPDO has not solved the problem in the most active death penalty jurisdictions (Dallas County and Harris County), where attorneys are still appointed by the trial judge. These lawyers are chosen from the list of supposedly qualified counsel. However, there are no state wide criteria for these "qualifications" and the appointments are left up to the elected judges. The only standard that seems to be followed is that these attorneys have experience in capital cases. However, as in the case of Ron Mock who represented Frances Newton, experience may mean that the attorney has seen the majority of his clients sent to death row.[52] Clearly the mere fact of serving on a capital case may provide a dubious sort of experience.

There are other problems with the Texas system of providing counsel for indigent defendants. Although the accused may be assigned two attorneys at trial, only one of them needs to have capital experience. No particular training is required, and no agency monitors defense attorneys to ascertain whether they have pursued continuing education to keep up with developments in capital litigation. There are few, if any, consequences for the incompetent or corrupt attorney. As the ABA report states, [although] "the ill effects of the system remain well-documented," even so "no formal mechanism exists for lodging complaints against attorneys providing representation in capital cases short of alleging professional misconduct."[53] The case of Kimberly McCarthy is a clear example of an instance where a court-appointed attorney unaccountably failed to raise a significant issue at trial (the jury selection process) and because of his error, the matter was defaulted and never considered by any court. But the lawyer did not pay the price, the client paid the price of his ineptitude, and she paid with her life. The ABA seems to conclude that as long as elected judges continue to appoint counsel (especially in the jurisdictions with the most capital cases), the process will be "influenced by factors irrelevant to ensuring effective representation."[54]

Compensation for court-appointed attorneys presents other problems. There are caps on the fees an attorney may receive, and attorneys are compensated more generously for in-court than out-of-court services. This policy may have the effect of limiting the time spent in adequate preparation for a capital trial, or it may encourage an attorney to bring a case to trial, where his or her fee will be higher, rather than negotiating a plea agreement. And, most unfortunately, "qualified counsel may opt not to represent capital defendants out of concerns that their considerable efforts will not be fairly compensated."[55]

Judges also must approve funds that the defense uses for investigations, expert witnesses, and mitigation specialists in the jurisdictions where attorneys are selected from the lists. A judge may deny funding for these services, if he or she so chooses. At the very least, "such a responsibility unnecessarily complicates the judge's role as neutral arbiter, as well as invites uneven treatment in capital cases."[56] We will see that the judge's unwillingness to allow funds for an investigation into Suzanne Basso's mental health had an impact on her case. And yet, such judicial decisions seem impervious to review.

The connection between electing judges and the handling of capital cases is clear in the ABA's analysis. They note that the selection of judges is often connected with the nominee's views on capital punishment and that re-election may depend on the handling of capital cases. Implicit is the notion that judges will avoid actions that might be characterized as too helpful to the defendant. The report states that in addition to judges' decisions possibly being influenced by electoral pressures, the existing process "ignores the larger interests of justice and fairness, focuses narrowly on the issue of capital punishment, and undermines society's confidence that individuals in court are guaranteed a fair hearing."[57]

When the Supreme Court ruled in Powell v. Alabama and Gideon v. Wainwright[58] that indigent defendants had a constitutional right to adequate counsel, they talked of a level playing field and fundamental fairness. Yet it seems that the reality of the Texas scheme for providing attorneys to indigent capital defendants falls far short of providing such assistance to many who face the possibility of a sentence of death. Indeed, the loopholes in the system seem to make a mockery of the adversarial process.

Odd features of the Texas capital system would also play a role in the story of the most recent execution of a female inmate. Suzanne Basso was put to death in Huntsville, Texas, on February 5, 2014.

Number 510: Suzanne Basso

Suzanne Basso's story may be the most bizarre of the fourteen cases included in this book.[59] Certainly the murder for which she was put to death was extraordinarily gruesome and sadistic. Her own life, as reported in the media and court documents, is almost too strange and horrible to believe. But even in this case, there are questions of due process, of gender as a factor, and of the deficiencies of the Texas capital system.

Louis "Buddy" Musso, the murder victim, was a 59-year-old mentally disabled man who had met Basso at a church carnival in New Jersey in 1997.[60] About a year later, he boarded a bus and travelled to the Houston area, apparently with the expectation of marrying Basso. Between his arrival in Texas and his death on August 25, 1998, Musso was abused and exploited unmercifully by Basso, her son, and other associates. Although most sources allege that the motive for this behavior was a $65,000 life insurance policy on Musso with Basso as the beneficiary, such an explanation does not account for the cruelty and apparent sadism that characterized the treatment of the victim. If life insurance was the motive, Musso could have been killed without torture. But all accounts of the crime emphasize the repeated beatings, woundings, and humiliation inflicted on Musso. The viciousness of mistreating a defenseless and disabled person deprived the perpetrators, and especially Suzanne Basso, the alleged "mastermind," of any persuasive arguments against the harshest punishment possible. And yet, the very outrageousness of the crime, added to the many extraordinary elements in Basso's life, reflect the major question that arises in her case—whether she suffered from severe mental illness.

Susan Margaret Burns Peek (O'Malley) Basso was born in Schenectady, New York in 1954.[61] She was the youngest of three girls in a family of eight children. She grew up in a family characterized by drunkenness and abuse. Like Judias Buenoano, Karla Faye Tucker, and Aileen Wuornos, Basso was involved in delinquent behavior as a teenager. She landed in a Catholic reform school, where she did receive a high school education. The parallels between Basso's adolescence and that of Karla Faye Tucker and Aileen Wuornos are worth noting. The three women who were executed for the most violent offenses also shared experience of dysfunctional homes, an early intro-duction to deviant behavior, and teenaged delinquency. Like Velma Barfield, Basso married young, probably to escape a miserable and abusive home life. With her husband James Peek, a Marine, Basso gave birth to two children before the age of twenty. According to the testimony of both her son and daughter, the Peek home was marked by sexual deviance, promiscuity, and instability. The family moved from North Carolina to Texas and back to North Carolina, usually on the edge of financial disaster. Ultimately James Peek was convicted and sent to prison for sexually abusing his own daughter and taking indecent liberties with a child. Upon his release, the family moved together to Houston. The mere fact that he resumed life with the children he had abused speaks to the chaotic life within their home. In the early 1990s, in an apparent effort to make a fresh start, Basso changed the family name to O'Malley and immersed them in a fictitious Irish heritage.[62] Even so the family dysfunction continued after they had moved to Texas. Apparently the son, James, tried to inform authorities of the abusive conditions in his home, but no one from child services followed up on his complaints.[63]

While still legally married to Peek, Suzanne met Carmine Basso, the owner of a security firm near Houston. A courtship followed, including an engagement announcement that appeared in the *Houston Chronicle* in 1995. As Buenoano had done, Basso created a grandiose and fictitious identity for herself. The prospective bride was identified as "Suzanne Margaret Anne Cassandra Lynn Theresa Marie Mary Veronica Sue Burns-Standlinskowlski," one of twelve children and an heiress to an oil fortune in Nova Scotia. Assert-ing that she had been educated at St. Anne's Institute in Yorkshire, England, Suzanne claimed to have been both a gymnast and a former nun. Carmine Basso was described in the notice as a winner of the Congressional Medal of Honor during the Vietnam War. When the *Chronicle* did not receive the $1372 due for the announcement, they withdrew it, to look into "possible inaccuracies."[64] There was no finishing school, no oil fortune, and no Medal of Honor. The whole situation was certainly irregular. Some sources state that Suzanne and Carmine Basso never married because she was not divorced from Peek. In any case, they claimed to be husband and wife, and she used his name for the remainder of her life. However, in May 1997, shortly before she met

Buddy Musso, Suzanne Basso called the Houston police to report that Carmine was missing. When police checked the office at the security firm, they found his body. He had apparently died of natural causes, "erosion of the esophagus due to the regurgitation of stomach acid," related to malnutrition.[65] The police found human waste in the trash cans and surmised that Carmine Basso had been living in the office where there was no restroom. Perhaps the most puzzling element of the story is why someone whose business was "security" did not simply leave the office or phone for help. Although later accounts of Suzanne Basso's story indicate suspicions that she was implicated in Carmine's death, no investigation ever substantiated her involvement. Nonetheless, the episode further supports the notion of Basso as "an odd woman with a wild imagination and a murderous streak."[66]

Basso's entire life story provides a wealth of evidence that Suzanne Peek Basso suffered from mental illness and a variety of delusions. Her behavior after the murder of Buddy Musso and during her trial continued to manifest that tendency.

The Legal Proceedings

On August 28, 1998, a jogger found the battered body of Buddy Musso where it had been dumped near a roadway in Galena Park in Houston. He was wearing clean clothes, which showed no bloodstains, although Musso had been badly beaten and had hundreds of bruises. Investigators concluded that he had been killed elsewhere and that his body had been moved to the site in the park.[67] The night before the body was found, Basso phoned several people expressing concern about his whereabouts. She also reported Musso missing to the police. She claimed to think he had left town with "a little Mexican lady" he met at a laundromat. That story quickly fell apart when Basso and her son were questioned. James O'Malley, the son, told police that "We killed Buddy." Basso admitted that she had driven the body to the park in the trunk of her friend Bernice Ahrens's car. Ahrens, her son Craig and daughter Hope and Hope's fiancé Terence Singleton were all implicated in the beating death of Musso and had disposed of incriminating evidence, including Musso's bloody clothes, in a dumpster.[68] All six suspects were charged with capital murder for "murdering Musso during the course of kidnapping or attempting to kidnap him, and for remuneration or the promise of remuneration in the form of insurance proceeds."[69] But although all six individuals were charged with capital murder, the state sought the death penalty only for Basso. She, in the eyes of the Harris County District Attorney, was the ringleader and the mastermind who somehow controlled the behavior of all the other participants. One source notes that all the participants were "egged on by the evil and avaricious Basso."[70]

James O'Malley had a low IQ, and, according to some reports, he lived a fantasy life as a special operations soldier, including wearing military regalia even to bed. He admitted to beating Musso and kicking him with steel-toed boots. It is likely that O'Malley struck the fatal blow although that remained undetermined.[71] However, O'Malley claimed that he participated in the lengthy torture of Musso because his mother told him to do so and he was afraid of her. The jury sentenced him to life in prison. Likewise Singleton, Bernice, and Craig Ahrens were also convicted of capital murder for their parts in the brutal killing. Singleton was sentenced to life in prison. Bernice was given an 80-year sentence, and Craig received 60 years.[72] Why all these adults, who had no relationship to Basso, became accomplices in this crime never became clear. It remains a mystery why they would be obedient to her orders to engage in inhumane cruelty unless they freely chose to participate. Yet Basso, as the alleged ringleader, was definitely the major target of the prosecution.

Whatever the distribution of blame for the treatment of Buddy Musso, the last accomplice, Hope Ahrens, testified against Basso in exchange for a 20-year sentence. Hope asserted that Basso ordered O'Malley to beat and kick Musso, and that Basso herself hit the victim with a bat, a belt, and a vacuum cleaner. According to Hope, the 350-pound Basso also jumped on Musso and pummeled him. At some point on the day Musso was killed, Basso left and went to work, but the others continued with the beatings and did not leave the apartment or use the phone during her absence. Allegedly Basso had told O'Malley to watch them. Again, it seems curious that four large adults were held in thrall by the absent Basso and her son. Any rationale for their actions—continuously brutalizing a helpless man because Suzanne told them to do so—defies logical explanations. Nonetheless, the jury seemed to buy that version of events, and Basso was sentenced to death by lethal injection on September 1, 1999.

The Issue of Competence

The Texas Court of Criminal Appeals heard and denied Basso's mandatory direct appeal. They affirmed her conviction on January 3, 2003.[73] Basso had raised a number of issues on appeal—some, like the unreliability of determining future dangerousness, were familiar matters in Texas capital cases. Others relating to the defendant's mental competence were particular to Basso's appeal.

The usual method of determining future dangerousness—one of the factors Texas law uses to determine whether a defendant will be sentenced to death—is consideration of past convictions for violent crimes. Basso had no prior convictions and thus challenged the basis for the jury's decision that she posed a threat of future dangerousness. However, the TCCA found that in her case, the circumstances of the offense itself were sufficient to determine Basso's potential behavior. They noted that she had "directed" O'Malley to assault Musso and cited her "authoritative role" in the murder. The TCCA found that the testimony of Basso's daughter and son-in-law that she had physically and sexually abused her children and "her highly manipulative" character meant that "appellant probably would be a continuing threat to society."[74] As the ABA stated in their review of the Texas capital system, the terms used to determine future dangerousness are so broad that "a death sentence would be deemed warranted in virtually every capital murder case." Further, they pointed out that the whole concept of future dangerousness is based on questionable science.[75] Nonetheless, Texas courts uphold such determinations, as they did in Basso's case.

A number of points of appeal referred to both the process and the substance of Basso's mental competency. Among other things she claimed to have been involuntarily medicated during her trial, and she alleged that the medication had prevented her from properly assisting in her own defense. The TCCA rejected this point, contending that Basso herself had requested that she be given Atavan (an anti-anxiety drug), along with the Zoloft (an anti-depressant) and Trazadone (for insomnia) prescribed by a state psychiatrist. If her medicine made her less able to participate in her trial, she was at fault for not informing her attorney about what she was taking. Of course, if the medication itself fogged her mind, she might not realize that she was not assisting fully in her defense. Such a contradiction apparently did not bother the TCCA.

During the period of slightly more than a year between her arrest and her trial, Basso lost almost 200 pounds. She had gone from morbidly obese to average size. In court, she sat in a wheelchair. The prosecution contended that she "feigned illness" and "cried wolf" and that state physicians were unable to find any specific disorder that accounted for her condition. They claimed that she was "faking" and "malingering." One commentator described her changed appearance and demeanor as a "ploy." He noted "This murderous and manipulative freak of nature even attempted to extract misplaced sympathy from the jury by appearing in a wheelchair at her trial after having shed an enormous 200 pounds in an attempt to look frail."[76] The defense asked for medical experts and testing to find out the cause of her disabilities and her extraordinary weight loss, perhaps to determine whether or not Basso had been physically capable of carrying out Musso's murder. Essentially the TCCA ruled that Basso had no right to such expert assistance and that the trial court had legitimately refused her request.[77] Her request for additional experts to provide information about false confessions and mitigation issues was also denied by the trial court and upheld by the TCCA. As the ABA noted in its report, the fact that trial judges can determine whether or not funds are available for defense experts complicates the judge's ability to be neutral and "invites uneven treatment in capital cases."[78]

As in many capital appeals, Basso claimed that her court-appointed attorney had been ineffective, in part because he had failed to secure other additional medical testing. The TCCA did not find her attorney's performance deficient in this regard. In fact, they cited Basso's refusal to cooperate with some state doctors who had been assigned to identify the cause and extent of her medical conditions. It is certainly possible that Basso's physical problems and her mental condition were related, that she resisted the state's efforts at diagnosis for reasons connected with side effects of her medication or with her delusions. In any event, there would never be a full investigation into her physical or mental disabilities. The courts found that due process did not require such an inquiry, and most seemed satisfied to assume that her condition was simply a pretense she devised to help her cause.

Several other issues concerning the competency of the defendant were raised in the direct appeal. During jury selection, the prosecutor had indicated that finding Basso not competent to stand trial would delay the proceedings and perhaps prevent a trial altogether. Because her attorney did not object every time the state made such comments, Basso forfeited her right to raise the issue of the prosecutor's remarks later in her appeal. Finally there was the matter of whether one of the psychologists who evaluated Basso had found that she had an actual mental disorder or whether she was malingering. For some reason the state found that question irrelevant and the court sustained their objection. It is not clear why the existence of an actual mental illness would be considered not relevant to the guilt of the defendant.[79]

The ABA report on the Texas capital system listed a number of concerns about the process by which Texas courts determine the competence of those on charged with capital crimes. As the ABA notes, "mental illness can affect every stage of a capital trial," from the person's competence to stand trial, as a defense for a murder charge, and as a "centerpiece of the mitigation case."[80] Texas does not require that juries be informed that mental illness is a mitigating not an aggravating factor, nor are they informed that evidence of mental illness should not be an issue in considering future dangerousness. This concern is amplified because Texas courts often rely on "unqualified experts" to prove that a defendant is a future danger to society. Additionally, the ABA contends that because Texas has a very narrowly defined insanity defense, "persons suffering from severe disorders such as schizophrenia are still eligible for capital punishment, even if their actions were based on delusions caused by their illness."[81] It seems clear that Suzanne Basso did not have a real opportunity to raise the matter of mental illness based on her long history of delusionary behavior. Her attorney may not have fully understood her condition, and the courts who heard her case seemed to equate mental illness with feigning mental illness. In reference to Basso's claims of physical disability and mental illness, the district attorney who prosecuted her said "It was challenging but I saw her for who she was. I was determined I was not going to let her get away with it."[82] She was, in the view of the state, "an evil and unscrupulous confidence trickster."[83]

The final issue related to Basso's mental condition was whether she met the definition of competence to be executed. The Supreme Court has ruled in *Ford v. Wainwright* that the Eighth Amendment's ban on cruel and unusual punishment prohibits the execution of the insane.[84] They concluded that putting to death someone who did not understand the reasons or the implications of the execution would serve neither the purpose of deterrence nor the goal of retribution. They also held in *Panetti v. Quarterman*, a Texas case, that there must be appropriate procedures for determining competence at the time when execution is imminent.[85] Some would argue, however, that the standard for sufficient mental competence to be executed is fairly low, especially in Texas and that the procedure for determining competence may be one-sided in favor of the state.

Only days before Basso's execution, the U.S. District Court ruled that her rights under *Ford* and *Panetti* had been observed. The Fifth Circuit Court of Appeals upheld that decision. In November 2013, Basso had an evidentiary hearing to establish her sanity. She was assisted by counsel. The federal court determined that hearing provided sufficient due process. As to the substance of Basso's claim, corrections officers testified that her behavior in prison had been "normal" and that she had carried on lucid conversations. One officer expressed the opinion that Basso claimed to hear voices but that "she never acted as if she actually heard voices."[86] The prison physician denied that Basso had ever reported any auditory or visual hallucinations. Her conversations with him had been "rational." Basso's spiritual advisor, a Catholic nun, stated that Basso had reported delusional facts to her, and that Basso had claimed some of her health problems resulted from a beating by police. The nun's testimony was considered unpersuasive as it was based on "self-serving information provided by Basso."[87] The crucial evidence about Basso's sanity came from two doctors, Mark Moeller, a psychiatrist, and Walter Quijano, a clinical psychologist, who noted symptoms of mental illness but concluded that Basso was competent to be executed. Both had interviewed Basso a few months before her scheduled execution. At the evidentiary hearing Quijano testified that Basso's performance on IQ tests was inconsistent and saw this as Basso's attempt to manipulate the testing. Although Basso claimed that she could not remember her capital murder trial and that she could not understand the rudiments of the competency hearing, these claims were found "not credible" based on her history of malingering. A key question was whether Basso's competence was "synthetic." Was she competent only because she was medicated? Dr. Quijano thought so, arguing that if Basso were taken off her medication she would become psychotic and possibly incompetent. Dr. Moeller disagreed, stating that Basso's medications treated her "mood disorders," not delusional disorders. He claimed that "she understands both the fact of the impending execution and the reasons for it, including her own involvement in and responsibility for the murder."[88] The court found Moeller's opinion more convincing and determined that Basso was competent to be executed.

The ABA found the procedures for determining competence for execution in Texas to be inadequate. The law that determines fitness to be put to death requires that the condemned person show substantial evidence of incompetency before his or her own experts will be appointed to argue in his or her behalf. Such a process "effectively require[s] the inmate to prove s/he suffers from a mental disorder before being granted resources to investigate that disorder."[89] In other words, the testimony about competency will come from state-appointed experts, as in Basso's case where the TCCA adopted the findings of those experts verbatim. Furthermore, the Texas statutory definition of competence is not fully compliant with the definition developed by the US

Supreme Court which requires that an inmate have a *rational* understanding of the reasons why she has been sentenced to death.[90] In Texas, the statute does not include the word "rational" and does not mandate an examination as to whether the inmate has suffered from delusional thinking. However, the TCCA held that Basso's "allegations of delusional thinking" had been considered but that these reported delusions were rejected because of her "history of malingering and engaging in attention-seeking behavior," including "falsifying psychiatric and physical symptoms."[91] The federal courts agreed and thus on February 4, 2014, the US Court of Appeals for the Fifth Circuit found neither incompetence nor constitutional violations. They therefore refused Basso's motion for a stay of execution.[92] She was put to death by lethal injection the next day. Basso was the fifth woman and the 510th person to be executed in Texas since the reinstatement of the death penalty.

It is difficult to understand Suzanne Basso's story without some attempt to determine an explanation for her involvement in the murder of Buddy Musso and for her history of cruel and irrational behavior. Robert Weisberg has offered some ideas about the relationship between psychopathology or antisocial personality (ASP) and capital punishment. Those who suffer from ASP, a mental disease recognized by the American Psychological Association, show a reckless indifference to human life as Basso did. That trait is often a tool the prosecution uses to condemn the individual and certainly to predict her future dangerousness. Yet if ASP is a disease, if the brains of those who are so afflicted differ from "normal" brains, how can the same moral judgments be applied to them? Specifically how does psychopathology affect responsibility for criminal behavior? Is such a person more or less fit to be executed?[93]

Suzanne Basso's crime was horrific. There is little evidence that she was ever diagnosed with a severe mental illness or brain disorder. Rather she seemed to self-medicate and to be treated for the symptoms. Should she have been executed if her actions stemmed from a sickness rather than from viciousness? Would society be better or worse off if Suzanne Basso had spent the rest of her life in a secure mental health facility? Those questions remain unanswered.

Gender as an Issue

The ways in which gender had an impact on the cases of Kimberly McCarthy and Suzanne Basso echo themes found in the other stories of executed women. For both women the motive—described as greed—was treated as an aggravator. In addition, both were accused of lacking remorse and both were portrayed as schemers, instigators, totally free agents, and "masterminds." As all of these qualities contradict notions of appropriate female behavior, they serve to multiply the elements of guilt and heinousness associated with their crimes. In Basso's case, her unorthodox sexual history and her promiscuity as well as her failures as a mother contributed to the portrayal of her future dangerousness. As little evidence of her mental illness was allowed in court, there was almost nothing to offer in mitigation. Finally the press made much of Basso's weight at the time of the crime. Although obesity is not a legal aggravator, as in the case of Christina Riggs, stereotypes that associate excess weight with character flaws such as laziness and self-indulgence surely played a part in the descriptions of Suzanne Basso. Consider the following comment, "Standing only five feet two inches tall and weighing in at a massive 365 pounds, the porcine Basso was built for the world of gridiron football."[94] In Basso's case, her weight at the time of the crime seemed an added factor in depriving her of her identity as a woman.

Kimberly McCarthy was most remembered for cutting off the finger of her victim. That heartless act was coupled with the unproven accusations that McCarthy had killed two other elderly women. Those murders were presented as part of the state's argument that McCarthy deserved the death penalty. As a home health care worker, McCarthy had allegedly "used her position of trust with the elderly victims to gain entry into their homes."[95] Instead of acting as a nurse, as the state portrayed McCarthy she had betrayed her nurturing role and defied womanly expectations.

Like the other "wretched sisters," McCarthy and Basso not only committed violent crimes, they failed to behave in conformity with expectations of them as women.

Endnotes

1. Descriptions of the crime, unless otherwise noted, are taken from state and federal court opinions. See *McCarthy v. State*, 65 S.W. 3d 47 (Tex. Crim. App 2001); *McCarthy v. State*, 2004 WL 3099230 (Tex. Crim. App. 2004); *McCarthy v. Thaler* (2011) WL 1754199; *McCarthy v. Thaler* 483 Fed. App. 898 (5th Cir. 2012).
2. *McCarthy v. Thaler* (2011).
3. Robert Wilonsky, "Found Guilty Twice of Murdering Neighbor in '97. Dallas County Woman on Death Row Has Appeal Tossed" (July 11, 2012) at DallasNews.com
4. Ibid.
5. *McCarthy v. State*, 65 S.W. 3d 47 (Tex.Crim.App. 2001).

6. Ibid.
7. Ibid.
8. Application for Post-conviction Writ of Habeas Corpus, Ex Parte Kimberly McCarthy, June 20, 2013.
9. "Female Gets Death Sentence, Again," *Dallas Morning News* (November 1, 2002).
10. *McCarthy v. State*, 2004 WL 3099230 (Tex. Crim. App. 2004).
11. The press typically stated that McCarthy was "linked" to these murders. The vague terminology implies her involvement, but the state never proved it in a court of law.
12. *McCarthy v. State* (2004).
13. *McCarthy v. Thaler* (2011).
14. Ibid.
15. Ibid.
16. *McCarthy v. Thaler*, 843 Fed. App. 898 (5th Cir. 2012).
17. David Carson, "Kimberly McCarthy," Texas Execution Information Center at txexecutions.org
18. Application for Post-conviction Writ of Habeas Corpus, Ex Parte Kimberly McCarthy, June 20, 2013.
19. *Batson v. Kentucky*, 476 U.S. 79 (1986).
20. Application for Post-conviction Writ of Habeas Corpus, Ex Parte Kimberly McCarthy, June 20, 2013.
21. Ibid.
22. Ibid.
23. *Trevino v. Thaler*, 133 U.S. 1911 (2013).
24. *Ex Parte Kimberly Lagayle McCarthy*, No. WR-50-360-04 (Tex. Crim. App, June 24, 2013). Italics added.
25. Allan Turner, "Dallas Woman Becomes Texas' 500th Execution," *Houston Chronicle* (June 27, 2013).
26. Cody Stark, "Woman Executed for 1997 Slaying." *Huntsville Item* (June 27, 2013).
27. Turner, "Dallas Woman Becomes Texas' 500th Execution."
28. Stoyan Zaimov, "Crossroad Bible Institute Graduate to Be 500th Inmate Executed in Texas" (June 25, 2013) at global.christianpost.com
29. Michael Graczyk, "Kimberly McCarthy Executed: Texas Carries out 500th Execution," *Associated Press*, (June 26, 2013).
30. Stark, "Woman Executed for 1997 Slaying."
31. Maurie Levin quoted in Ed Pilkington, "Texas Poised to Execute 500th Prisoner as Lawyers Fight to Save Her Life," *The Guardian* (June 20, 2013).
32. Jennifer Emily, "Kimberly McCarthy Put to Death in Texas' 500th Modern Execution," DallasNews.com (June 26, 2013).
33. Richard C. Dieter, *Blind Justice: Juries Deciding Life and Death with Only Half the Truth* (Washington, DC: The Death Penalty Information Center, 2005), 12.
34. David C. Baldus and George Woodworth, "Race Discrimination and the Legitimacy of Capital Punishment: Reflections on the Interaction of Fact and Perception," *DePaul Law Review* 53 (2004), 1426.
35. Quoted in *Blind Justice*, 6.

36. Ibid., 5.

37. Steve McGonigle and Ed Timms, "Race Bias Pervades Jury Selection," *Dallas Morning News* (March 6, 1986).

38. Ibid.

39. Ibid.

40. E. Earl Parson and Monique McLaughlin, "Citizenship in Name Only: The Coloring of Democracy While Redefining Rights, Liberties, and Self-Determination for the 21st Century," *Columbia Journal of Race and Law*, 3: 1 (2013), 109. *Blind Justice*, 3.

41. *Miller-El v. Dretke*, 545 U.S. 231 (2005).

42. Ibid.

43. Ibid.

44. Ibid.

45. McGonigle and Timms, "Race Bias."

46. Ibid., Dieter, *Blind Justice*.

47. American Bar Association, *Texas Capital Punishment Assessment Report: An Analysis of Texas Death Penalty Laws* (American Bar Association, 2013), xxxix. Hereinafter ABA, *Texas Capital Punishment*.

48. Ibid., xl.

49. Ibid.

50. Dieter, *Blind Justice*, 15.

51. ABA, *Texas Capital Punishment*, xxix–xxx.

52. Ron Mock who represented Frances Newton was suspended by the Texas Bar Association in 2004. He had served as counsel for 19 capital defendants. Sixteen of them were sent to death row.

53. ABA, *Texas Capital Punishment*, xxxi.

54. Ibid., xxx.

55. Ibid., xxxi.

56. Ibid., xxxii.

57. Ibid., xli.

58. *Powell v. Alabama*, 287 U.S. 45 (1932). *Gideon v. Wainwright*, 372 U.S. 335 (1963).

59. Information on the Basso case comes largely from published sources and the appellate cases available online. At this writing, the Texas State Archives have not yet processed the case files. Nor are the governor's capital case files available to researchers. Thus there are gaps and questions about both Basso's past and the conduct of the legal proceedings in her case.

60. Accounts of the basic facts of the case seem fairly consistent. They can be found in the appellate cases, *Basso v. State*, No. 73672 (Tex. Crim. App. Jan. 15, 2003), *Basso v. State*, No. 7702 (Tex. Crim. App. Feb. 3, 2014).

61. Information about Basso's early life comes from David Carson, "Suzanne Basso," *Texas Execution Information Center* at www.txexecutions.org., David Krajicek, "Suzanne Basso," at www.crimelibrary.com, and "Suzanne Basso," at www.murderpedia.com. I have included only items that appear in several sources.

62. Krajicek, "Suzanne Basso."

63. Ibid.

64. Carson, "Suzanne Basso."
65. Ibid.
66. Mike Tolson, "Appeals Run Out for Harris County Woman on Death Row," *Houston Chronicle* (October 4, 2010).
67. *Basso v. State* (2003).
68. Ibid., Attorney General of Texas. "Suzanne Basso Scheduled for Execution" (February 3, 2014), at www.texasattorneygeneral.gov
69. Attorney General of Texas, "Suzanne Basso."
70. Christopher Berry-Dee and Tony Brown, *Dead Men Walking: True Stories of the Most Evil Men and Women on Death Row* (London: John Blake, 2008), 9.
71. Krajicek, "Suzanne Basso."
72. Carson, "Suzanne Basso."
73. *Basso v. State* (2003).
74. Ibid.
75. ABA, *Texas Capital Punishment*, xxxix–xl.
76. Berry-Dee and Brown, *Dead Men Walking*, 12.
77. *Basso v. State* (2003).
78. ABA, *Texas Capital Punishment*, xxxii.
79. *Basso v. State* (2003).
80. ABA, *Texas Capital Punishment*, xlvii.
81. Ibid., xlix.
82. Carson, "Suzanne Basso."
83. Berry-Dee and Brown, *Dead Men Walking*, 12.
84. *Ford v. Wainwright*, 477 U.S. 399 (1986).
85. *Panetti v. Quarterman*, 551 U.S. 930 (2007).
86. *Basso v. Stephens*, No. 14-70005 Fed. App. (5th Cir., February 4, 2014).
87. Ibid.
88. Ibid.
89. ABA, *Texas Capital Punishment*, xlix.
90. Ibid., 443.
91. *Basso v. Stephens* (February 3, 2014).
92. Ibid.
93. Robert Weisberg, "The Unlucky Psychopath as Death Penalty Prototype," *Who Deserves to Die: The Executable Subject*. Austin Sarat and Karl Shoemaker, eds. (Amherst and Boston: University of Massachusetts Press, 2011).
94. Berry-Dee and Brown, *Dead Men Walking*, 5.
95. *McCarthy v. State* (2004).

·12·

LESSONS FROM *WRETCHED SISTERS*

We return to the major question that began this book. Why these few? After giving each case detailed attention, is it possible to state that Velma Barfield, Karla Faye Tucker, Betty Lou Beets, Wanda Jean Allen, Marilyn Plantz, Lois Nadean Smith, Christina Riggs, Judias Buenoano, Lynda Block, Aileen Wuornos, Frances Newton, Teresa Lewis, Kimberly McCarthy, and Suzanne Basso were the "worst of the worst?" Were they criminals whose offenses were so heinous and whose responsibility was so clear that the world has become better since their deaths? If not, how do we explain that they were singled out for execution?

The Decision to Prosecute

The first stage of the process that puts certain offenders on the road to the death chamber is the prosecutor's decision to charge them with a capital offense. Since *Gregg v. Georgia*[1] the states with capital punishment have listed specific aggravating factors in their criminal laws. Prosecutors must work within those guidelines. However, as discussed earlier, the aggravating factors often include such vague descriptors as "heinous, atrocious, or cruel" allowing the state a great deal of latitude. Is it possible that some crimes are more heinous, more atrocious, or crueler when committed by a woman? Are they worse if the victim is a man? So it would seem. There are no statistics telling how many of the men executed since 1977 killed family members or intimate partners. But Department of Justice data reveal that women in prison for homicide were almost twice as likely to have killed an intimate than were men incarcerated for homicide.[2] Of the fourteen executed women, eight (57%) killed an intimate. The image of an Evil Woman wreaking domestic havoc—the bad mother or the untrustworthy wife—seems powerful as an aggravating factor. All of the family-member victims except Riggs' and Newton's infant daughters and Allen's partner were male. Perhaps prosecutors do not specifically think "Women killing men upsets the patriarchal system," when they decide to ask for a capital sentence. Nonetheless, the pattern seems clear—and the patriarchal system seems secure—when juries are told they must protect society from women who threaten the natural order of things when they are greedy, or promiscuous, or selfish, or aggressive, or all of those things. Even the most passive, ineffectual women like Marilyn Plantz, Betty Lou Beets, or Teresa Lewis were portrayed as "masterminds" plotting against their unwary male victims. It may be that these images are so deeply embedded in the culture that prosecutors invoke them unconsciously. Or it may be that district attorneys anticipate that those tropes will be effective and use them intentionally. In any event, one can see gendered assumptions and gendered perceptions at work in the selection of these cases and in the portrayal of these defendants for capital prosecution. Arguably, the sex of the defendant and the sex of the victim did make a difference.

Unbiased Juries?

The Constitution provides that in criminal trials the defendant has the right to a trial by an impartial jury. The structure and practice of the death penalty system call that promise into question.

In 2005, the Death Penalty Information Center (DPIC) issued a report called "Blind Justice" detailing problems with jury selection and with the information jurors have available when they are asked to make decisions regarding the life or death of a defendant.[3] Several points raised in that report echo difficulties discussed in the preceding chapters. The DPIC notes the requirement that jurors in capital trials must be "death qualified," eliminating those with conscientious scruples against the death penalty, and, one might argue, failing to provide a real cross-section of the community. More

African Americans and women than white males oppose the death penalty. Those groups are likely to be disproportionately excluded. Likewise, the DPIC states, and numerous studies support the claim that death-qualified jurors are likely to be more pro-prosecution and more likely to convict than those who are excluded. As Justice John Paul Stevens said in 2005, "In case after case many days are spent conducting voir dire examinations in which prosecutors engage in prolonged questioning to determine whether the venire person has moral or religious scruples that would impair her ability to impose the death penalty. Preoccupation with that issue creates an atmosphere in which jurors are likely to assume that their primary task is to determine the penalty for a presumptively guilty defendant."[4]

Justice Stevens' point has support in the trial transcripts reviewed for this book. Although some states do not allow access to the voir dire portion of the transcripts in order to protect the anonymity of jurors, where that information was available, many prospective jurors seemed to work from a presumption of guilt rather than a presumption of innocence. Many also seemed to assume that if the person was guilty the death penalty was mandatory. And a great many potential and actual jurors seemed to have difficulty with the notion of aggravating and mitigating factors. Yet these men and women were required not only to determine past guilt or innocence but to foresee what was to come and to make a prophecy about "future dangerousness." On the basis of that forecast, they determined whether a defendant should be put to death.

How are jurors supposed to deal with the confusing direction that they should not let the sex of the defendant influence them? The statement both calls attention to the defendant's sex and tells the prospective jurors not to notice that it is a woman sitting before them. At Velma Barfield's trial the prosecutor asked women in the jury pool, "Would the sex of the defendant influence you? Would you try her just like a man?" The correct answers were "no" and "yes." One of the potential jurors in Barfield's case stated, "I would try her just like a person." That was not enough "equality" for the prosecutor. The panelist was excused. If the defendant is a man, do prosecutors ask "Would you try him just like a woman?" Formal equality would demand that query.

Defendants are supposedly promised impartial juries chosen without racial bias. Yet it requires a capable defense attorney—and it should require an unbiased judge—to ensure that jury selection does not unfairly eliminate minority jurors. In the case of Kimberly McCarthy, her attorney unaccountably failed to challenge the jury selection process and she lost the opportunity to raise the issue on appeal.

Once they have been seated, juries rely on lawyers for the prosecution and for the defense to provide the information they need to reach an accurate verdict and an appropriate sentence. Here there are faults on both sides. Where prosecutors, as indicated above, might use gendered stereotypes to condemn a defendant in the jurors' eyes, defense attorneys often erred by omission, especially in the presentation of mitigating evidence.

Inadequate and Unethical Defense

Almost every chapter in this book contains a horror story of incompetent, inexperienced, negligent, or corrupt attorneys at trial stage. With the exception of Christina Riggs's lawyer hired by her family and Lynda Lyon who defended herself, the women facing death were stuck with appallingly bad defense lawyers. Their failures ran the gamut from Velma Barfield's inexperienced court-appointed attorney, to the Oklahoma lawyers who were denied funds for investigation and psychological testing, to the venal individuals who tried to make a personal profit from selling the stories of Betty Lou Beets, Judias Buenoano, and Aileen Wuornos to Teresa Lewis's lawyers telling her to plead guilty without a plea bargain in place. Frances Newton's lawyer may have been the worst of all, as he treated his probably innocent client with contempt.

The bifurcated trial is meant to afford special protections against the arbitrary and capricious use of the death penalty. During the sentencing phase, the defense is offered the opportunity to humanize the accused person, to make her, if not sympathetic, at least a fully human being by describing the circumstances of her life. But because those attorneys failed to present crucial information about their clients during the sentencing phase, juries could not take into consideration that a defendant may have been the victim of abuse, that she was mentally retarded, that she suffered from mental illness or addiction. Instead, lacking an alternative picture of the defendant, juries were left with a one-dimensional "monster," "black widow," promiscuous, acquisitive, grasping wife, or unnatural mother. All of those images served to exaggerate the gulf between the woman on trial and social expectations for female behavior.

A report by the Texas Defender Service (TDS) called *Lethal Indifference* explains that the problem of incompetent attorneys does not end with the trial.[5] The TDS found that attorneys representing defendants in post-conviction appeals often did no investigation, provided no new information outside the trial record, raised the wrong kind of claims, or raised claims that had previously been rejected. Even if a defendant finds a good lawyer to represent her after conviction, the options for correcting errors made by her original lawyer are limited. A claim of ineffective assistance must meet the *Strickland* standard. The convicted woman must prove that her lawyer's actions were unreasonable and that his behavior is responsible for the outcome of her trial. Appellate courts seldom hold an attorney accountable, no matter how egregious his failures. They are simply "harmless errors." And even a substantial claim, if not raised in timely fashion, will run up against the barrier of procedural default.

All of these women were poor or working class. They were stuck with the only lawyers available to them. Except for the attorney who represented Christina Riggs, none of them showed they made an effort to see their clients as complex human beings, as women with a life history that antedated the crime. There were many errors—of strategy, of fact, and of omission. Many were not harmless.

The Political Context

In several cases, politics contributed to the executions in obvious ways. Governor Jim Hunt, running for the Senate, denied Velma Barfield's request for clemency to demonstrate that he was as pro-death penalty as his opponent, Jesse Helms. Hunt lost anyway. Preparing for the 2000 presidential campaign, George Bush calculated that he could risk an affront to his evangelical supporters in exchange for enhancing his tough image when he denied Karla Faye Tucker's petition. Commenting on the deaths of Tucker and Betty Lou Beets, Bush asserted that because the sex of the killer did not matter to the victim, it did not matter to him. It was a perfect statement of formal equality, so perfect that Governor Rick Perry repeated the same sentiments when Frances Newton was executed.

In the enthusiasm for tough punishments, governors have generally decided that only claims of actual innocence—and in Newton's case even that was not enough— deserve clemency. Governors apparently fear that any mercy toward a convicted woman would result in a charge of favoritism based on sex. Fear of that criticism leads politicians to ignore the reality that men's and women's lives are different and to refuse to consider that equal protection is not the same as identical punishment.

Finality

The electric chair or a lethal injection was the final event in the lives of these fourteen women. Each of them arrived at that place after a hard life. Some had lived with years of abuse. Some had been victims of sexual assault as young girls. Most of them were addicts—prescription drugs and alcohol were the most popular self-medication. Where family history is known, only Frances Newton was raised in a loving, stable home. The others had experienced rejection and abandonment from parents, relatives, or peers. Most of the women suffered from some form of mental illness at the time of the crime. Yet the states of North Carolina, Texas, Oklahoma, Arkansas, Alabama, Florida, and Virginia set in motion a process that took on a life of its own and culminated in their deaths. We have traced those processes in these pages.

Justice Thurgood Marshall wrote that if people were *fully informed* about the death penalty, they would find it "shocking, unjust, and unacceptable."[6] We have seen how these fourteen stories unfolded, how exaggerating gendered fears and stereotypes contributed to their conclusions, how class combined with gender and sometimes with race to affect their outcomes. We have noted many failures of due process. For some people, it may be that those flaws are an acceptable price to pay for retribution. For others, especially considering the likelihood of a wrongful conviction, the fourteen wretched sisters demonstrate that capital punishment is "shocking, unjust, and unacceptable."

Endnotes

1. *Gregg v. Geogia*, 428 U.S. 153 (1976).
2. American Civil Liberties Union, *The Forgotten Population: A Look at Death Row in the United States through the Experiences of Women.* Washington, DC: 2004, 9.
3. Deiter, Richard C., *Blind Justice: Juries Deciding Life and Death with Only Half the Truth.* Washington, DC: Death Penalty Information Center, 2005.
4. Quoted in Ibid., 6.
5. Texas Defender Service, *Lethal Indifference: The Fatal Combination of Incompetent Attorneys and Unaccountable Courts in Texas Death Penalty Appeals.* Houston: 2002.
6. *Furman v. Georgia*, 408 U.S. 238 (1972).

BIBLIOGRAPHY

Acker, James R., Robert M. Bohm, and Charles S. Lanier, eds. *America's Experiment with Capital Punishment: Reflections on the Past, Present, and Future of the Ultimate Penal Sanction* Durham, NC: Carolina Academic Press, 1998.

Alfieri, Anthony V. "Mitigation, Mercy, and Delay: The Moral Politics of Death Penalty Abolitionists." *Harvard Civil Rights-Civil Liberties Law Review* 31 (Summer 1996): 325–352.

American Bar Association.*Texas Capital Punishment Assessment Report: An Analysis of Texas Death Penalty Laws, Procedures, and Practices*. American Bar Association, 2013.

American Civil Liberties Union, American Friends Service Committee. *The Forgotten Population: A Look at Death Row in the United States through the Experiences of Women*. Washington, DC: 2004.

Amnesty International. "Old Habits Die Hard: The Death Penalty in Oklahoma." (April 26, 2001) [Available online at www.amnesty.org/library]

Anderson, Chris, and Sharon McGehee. *Bodies of Evidence: The Shocking True Story of Judias-Buenoano: Florida's Serial Murderess*. Secaucus, NJ: St. Martin's Press, 1991.

Attorney General of Texas. "Suzanne Basso Scheduled for Execution." February 3, 2013. wwwtexasattorneygeneral.gov

Atwell, Mary Welek. *Equal Protection of the Law? Gender and Justice in the United States*. New York: Peter Lang, 2002.

Baldus, David C., and George Woodworth. "Race Discrimination and the Legitimacy of Capital Punishment: Reflections on the Interaction of Fact and Perception." *DePaul Law Review* 53 (2004): 1411–1496.

Barfield, Velma. *Woman on Death Row*. Nashville, TN: Thomas Nelson, 1985.

Berlow, Alan. "The Texas Clemency Memos." *The Atlantic Monthly* (July/August 2003).

Berry-Dee, Christopher, and Tony Brown. *Dead Men Walking: True Stories of the Most Evil Men and Women on Death Row*. London: John Blake, 2008.

Birch, Helen, ed. *Moving Targets: Women, Murder, and Representation*. Berkeley, CA: University of California Press, 1994.

Bledsoe, Jerry. *Death Sentence: The True Story of Velma Barfield's Life, Crimes, and Execution*. New York: Dutton, 1998.

Bloom, Barbara, ed. *Gendered Justice: Addressing Female Offenders*. Durham, NC: Carolina Academic Press, 2003.

Breslow, Sarah. "Pleading Guilty to Death: Protecting the Capital Defendant's Sixth Amendment Right to a Jury Sentencing after Entering a Guilty Plea." *Cornell Law Review* 98 (2012–2013): 1245–1270.

Burnett, Cathleen. *Justice Denied: Clemency Appeals in Death Penalty Cases*. Boston: Northeastern University Press, 2002.

Butterfield, Fox. "Governor Bush on Crime: Bush's Law and Order Adds Up to Tough and Popular." *New York Times* (August 18, 1999).

Campos, Carlos. "We're Human, Just Like Anybody Else." *Atlanta Journal-Constitution* (July 18, 2004).

Carlson, Tucker. "Devil May Care." *Talk*. (September 1999).

Carroll, Jenny E. "Images of Women and Capital Sentencing among Female Offenders: Exploring the Outer Limits of the Eighth Amendment and Articulated Theories of Justice." *Texas Law Review* 75 (May 1997): 1413–1452.

Chancer, Lynn. *High Profile Crimes: When Legal Cases Become Social Causes*. Chicago: University of Chicago Press, 2005.

Chesney-Lind, Meda, and Lisa Pasko, eds. *Girls, Women, and Crime: Selected Readings*. Thousand Oaks, CA: Sage, 2004.

Crawford, Melanie. "A Losing Battle with the 'Machinery of Death': The Flaws of Virginia's Death Penalty Laws and Clemency Process Highlighted by the Fate of Teresa Lewis." *Widener Law Review* 18 (2012): 71–98.

Crocker, Phyllis L. "Is the Death Penalty Good for Women?" *Buffalo Criminal Law Review* 4 (2001): 917–965.

"The Cruel and Unusual Punishment of Teresa Lewis." *Chicago Press Release*. (August 22, 2010).

Denno, Deborah W. "How Many Lives Has Victor Streib Saved? A Tribute." *Ohio Northern University Law Review* 38 (2011–2012): 413–416.

———. "Is Electrocution an Unconstitutional Method of Execution? The Engineering of Death over the Century." *William and Mary Law Review* 35 (Winter 1994): 551–693.

Dieter, Richard C. *Blind Justice: Juries Deciding Life and Death with Only Half the Truth*. Washington, DC: Death Penalty Information Center, 2005.

———. *With Justice for Few: The Growing Crisis in Death Penalty Representation*. Washington, DC: Death Penalty Information Center, 1995.

———. *Struck by Lightning: The Continuing Arbitrariness of the Death Penalty Thirty-Five Years after Its Reinstatement in 1976*. Washington, D.C.: Death Penalty Information Center, 2011.

Dow, David R. *Executed on a Technicality: Lethal Injustice on America's Death Row.* Boston: Beacon Press, 2005.

Eckholm, Erik. "Woman on Death Row Runs out of Appeals." *New York Times* (September 21, 2010).

Fuhrman, Mark. *Death and Justice: An Exposé of Oklahoma's Death Row Machine.* New York: HarperCollins, 2003.

Furio, Jennifer. *Letters from Prison: Voices of Women Murderers.* New York: Algora Publishing, 2001.

Giardano, Peggy C., and Sharon Mohler Rockwell. "Differential Association and Female Crime." In *Of Crime and Criminality: The Use of Theory in Everyday Life*, edited by Sally Simpson. Thousand Oaks, CA: Pine Forge Press, 2000.

Gillespie, L. Kay. *Dancehall Ladies: Executed Women of the Twentieth Century.* Lanham, MD: University Press of America, 2000.

Glaeser, Edward L., and Bruce Sacerdote. "Sentencing in Homicide Cases and the Role of Vengeance." *Journal of Legal Studies* 32 (January 2003): 362–382.

Graham, Tamara L. "*Lewis v. Commonwealth* 593 S.E. 2nd 220." *Capital Defense Journal* 17:1 (2004): 229–241.

Grisham, John. "Teresa Lewis Didn't Pull the Trigger. Why Is She on Death Row?" *Washington Post* (September 12, 2010).

Haines, Max. "Deadly Betrayal: Suburban Housewife Led a Sordid Double Life." *Daily Oklahoman* (October 15, 1996).

Hammack, Lawrence. "Teresa Lewis to Be Executed by Lethal Injection." *Roanoke Times* (September 12, 2010).

Harris, Keith, and Darral Cheatwood. *The Geography of Execution: The Capital Punishment Quagmire in America.* Lanham, MD: Rowman and Littlefield, 1997.

Herbert, Bob. "Death Penalty Dilemma." *New York Times* (February 1, 1998).

Hoffman, Jim. "Execution in Texas: Legal Debate, Seeking Clemency in a Labyrinth That Varies by State." *New York Times* (February 4, 1998).

Howarth, Joan W. "Deciding to Kill: Revealing the Gender in the Task Handed to Capital Juries." *Wisconsin Law Review* (July/August 1994): 1345–1424.

——. "Executing White Masculinities: Learning from Karla Faye Tucker." *Oregon Law Review* 81 (Spring 2002): 183–230.

Ingle, Joseph B. *Last Rights: Thirteen Fatal Encounters with the States' Justice.* Nashville, TN: Abingdon Press, 1990.

Jackson, Jesse L., Sr., Jesse L. Jackson, Jr., and Bruce Shapiro. *Legal Lynching: The Death Penalty and America's Future.* New York: The New Press, 2001.

Joint Legislative Audit and Review Commission of the Virginia General Assembly. *Review of Virginia's System of Capital Punishment.* Richmond: Commonwealth of Virginia, 2002.

Jones, Ann. *Women Who Kill.* Boston: Beacon Press, 1996.

Katz, Rebecca S. "Explaining Girls' and Women's Crime and Desistance in the Context of Their Victimization." In *Girls, Women, and Crime: Selected Readings*, edited by Meda Chesney-Lind and Lisa Pasko. Thousand Oaks: CA: Sage, 2004.

Kaufman-Osborn, Timothy V. *From Noose to Needle: Capital Punishment and the Late Liberal State.* Ann Arbor: University of Michigan Press, 2002.

Kay, Judith W. *Murdering Myths: The Story behind the Death Penalty.* Lanham, MD: Rowman and Littlefield, 2005.

Keitner, Chimene I. "Victim or Vamp? Images of Violent Women in the Criminal Justice System." *Columbia Journal of Gender and Law* 11 (2002): 38–87.

Kelleher, Michael D., and C. L. Kelleher. *Murder Most Rare: The Female Serial Killer.* Westport, CT: Dell, 1998.

Kendall, Kathleen, and Shoshana Pollack. "Cognitive Behaviorism in Women's Prisons: A Critical Analysis of Therapeutic Assumptions and Practices." In *Gendered Justice: Addressing Female Offenders,* edited by Barbara Bloom. Durham, NC: Carolina Academic Press, 2003.

Kennedy, Dolores. *On a Killing Day.* Chicago: Bonus Books, 1992.

Kobil, Daniel T. "How to Grant Clemency in Unforgiving Times." *Capital University Law Review* 31 (2003): 219–241.

Kohler, Kathryn. "Women on Death Row: A Chilling Sign of the Times." *Cleveland Plain Dealer* (May 26, 1993).

Kopec, Janice L. "Avoiding a Death Sentence in the American Legal System: Get a Woman to Do It." *Washington and Lee School of Law Capital Defense Journal* 15 (Spring 2003): 353–382.

Krajicek, David. "Suzanne Busso and the Murder of Louis 'Buddy' Musso," at www.crimelibrary.com

Kudlac, Christopher S. *Public Executions: The Death Penalty and the Media.* Westport, CT: Praeger, 2007.

Lamb, Sharon. "The Psychology of Condemnation: Underlying Emotions and Their Symbolic Expressions in Condemning." *Brooklyn Law Review* 68 (2002–03): 929–958.

Lardner, George. "Executive Clemency and the American System of Justice: The Role of the Press in the Clemency Process." *Capital University Law Review* 31 (2003): 179–184.

Leonard, Elizabeth Dermody. "Stages of Gendered Disadvantage in the Lives of Convicted Battered Women." In *Gendered Justice: Addressing Female Offenders,* edited by Barbara Bloom. Durham, NC: Carolina Academic Press, 2003.

Lewis, Dorothy Otnow. *Guilty by Reason of Insanity.* New York: Fawcett Columbine, 1998.

Litchfield, Lynn. "Unfit for Execution." *Newsweek* (August 27, 2010).

Long, Walter C. "Karla Faye Tucker: A Case for Restorative Justice." *American Journal of Criminal Law* 27 (1999–2000): 117–127.

Lowry, Beverly. *Crossed Over: A Murder, a Memoir.* New York: Vintage Books, 2003.

Margulis, Joseph. "Memories of an Execution." *Law and Inequality* 20 (Winter 2002): 125–129.

Martin, Earl F. "Masking the Evil of Capital Punishment." *Virginia Journal of Social Policy and Law* 10 (Winter 2002): 179–230.

McCoy, Tana, Patti Ross Salinas, and W. Wesley Johnson. "The Execution of Karla Faye Tucker: An Examination of the Attitudes and Motivations." *Justice Professional* 12:2 (September 1999): 209–222.

Mogul, Joey L. "Equality: The Dykier, the Butcher, the Better: The State's Use of Homophobia and Sexism to Execute Women in the United States." *New York City Law Review* 8:2 (Fall 2005), 473–494.

Nagel, Ilene H., and John Hagen. "Gender and Crime: Offense Patterns and Criminal Court Sanctions." *Crime and Justice* 4 (1983): 91–144.

Oberman, Margaret. "A Brief History of Infanticide and the Law." In *Infanticide: Psychological and Legal Perspectives on Mothers Who Kill*, edited by Margaret G. Spinelli. Washington, DC: American Psychiatric Publishing, 2003.

——. "Mothers Who Kill: Coming to Terms with Modern American Infanticide." *American Criminal Law Review* 34 (Fall 1996): 1–110.

Ogle, Robbin S., Daniel Maier-Katkin, and Thomas J. Bernard. "A Theory of Homicidal Behavior among Women." *Criminology* 33:2 (1995): 173–193.

O'Neil, Melinda E. "The Gender Gap Argument: Exploring the Disparity of Sentencing Women to Death." *New England Journal of Criminal and Civil Confinement* 25 (Winter 1999): 213–244.

O'Shea, Kathleen A. *Women and the Death Penalty in the United States, 1900–1998*. Westport, CT: Praeger, 1999.

Owen, Barbara. "Differences with a Distinction: Women Offenders and Criminal Justice Practice." In *Gendered Justice: Addressing Female Offenders*, edited by Barbara Bloom. Durham, NC: Carolina Academic Press, 2003.

Pence, Irene. *Buried Memories: The Chilling True Story of Betty Lou Beets, the Texas Black Widow*. New York: Pinnacle Books, 2001.

Prejean, Helen. *The Death of Innocents: An Eyewitness Account of Wrongful Executions*. New York: Random House, 2005.

Price, Barbara Raffel, and Natalie J. Sokoloff, eds. *The Criminal Justice System and Women: Offenders, Prisoners, Victims, and Workers*. New York: McGraw-Hill, 2004.

Rapaport, Elizabeth. "Capital Murder and the Domestic Discount: A Study of Capital Domestic Murder in the Post-*Furman* Era." *Southern Methodist University Law Review* 49 (July/August 1996): 1507–1548.

——. "The Death Penalty and Gender Discrimination." *Law and Society Review*. 25:2 (1991): 367–383.

——. "Equality of the Damned: The Execution of Women on the Cusp of the 21st Century." *Ohio Northern University Law Review* 26 (2000): 581–600.

——. "Some Questions about Gender and the Death Penalty." *Golden Gate University Law Review* 20 (1990): 501–566.

——. "Staying Alive: Executive Clemency, Equal Protection, and the Politics of Gender in Women's Capital Cases." *Buffalo Criminal Law Review* 4 (2001): 967–1007.

Renzetti, Claire M., and Lynne Goodstein, eds. *Women, Crime, and Criminal Justice: Original Feminist Readings*. Los Angeles: Roxbury, 2001.

Robertson, Pat. "Sparing Cain: Executive Clemency in Capital Cases: The Importance of an 'Escape Valve' for Mercy." *Capital University Law Review* 28 (2000): 579–583.

——. "Religion's Role in the Administration of the Death Penalty." *William and Mary Bill of Rights Journal*, 9 (December 2000): 215–222.

Rosenburg, Irene Meeker, and Yale L. Rosenburg. "Lone Star Liberal Musings on 'an Eye for an Eye' and the Death Penalty." *Utah Law Review* (1998): 505–541.

Russell, Sue. *Lethal Intent*. New York: Pinnacle Books, 2002.

Salvacci, Jessica. "Femininity and the Electric Chair: Equal Protection Challenge to Texas's Death Penalty Statute." *Boston College Third World Law Journal* 31 (2011): 405–437.

Sarat, Austin. *Mercy on Trial: What It Means to Stop an Execution.* Princeton, NJ: Princeton University Press, 2005.

Schmall, Lorraine. "Forgiving Guin Garcia: Women, the Death Penalty, and Commutation." *Wisconsin Women's Law Journal* 11 (Fall 1996): 283–326.

Schneider, Elizabeth M. *Battered Women and Feminist Lawmaking.* New Haven, CT: Yale University Press, 2000.

Schulberg, Daniel E. "Feature: The Execution of Females." *Orange County Lawyer* 42 (July 2000): 25–32.

Shipley, Stacey L., and Bruce A. Arrigo. *The Female Homicide Offender: Serial Murder and the Case of Aileen Wuornos.* Upper Saddle River, NJ: Pearson Prentice Hall, 2004.

Shipman, Marlin. *"The Penalty Is Death:" U.S. Newspaper Coverage of Women's Executions.* Columbia, MO: University of Missouri Press, 2002.

Shortnacy, Michael B. "Guilty and Gay, A Recipe for Execution in American Courtrooms: Sexual Orientation as a Tool for Prosecutorial Misconduct in Death Penalty Cases." *American University Law Review* 51 (December 2001): 309–365.

Simons, Michael A. "Born Again on Death Row: Retribution, Remorse, and Religion." *The Catholic Lawyer* 43 (Fall 2004): 311–337.

Sinclair, Melissa Scott. "Blood Sisters: Virginia Prepares to Execute Only the Second Woman Sentenced to Death in a Century: The Echoing Stories of Virginia Christian and Teresa Lewis." *Style Weekly* (September 15, 2010).

Skrapec, Candice. "The Female Serial Killer: An Evolving Criminality." In *Moving Targets: Women, Murder, and Representation,* edited by Helen Birch. Berkeley, CA: University of California Press, 1994.

Spinelli, Margaret G., ed. *Infanticide: Psychological and Legal Perspectives.* Washington, DC: American Psychiatric Publishing, 2003.

Steffensmeier, Darrell, and Lisa Broidy. "Explaining Female Offending." In *Women, Crime, and Criminal Justice: Original Feminist Readings,* edited by Claire Renzetti and Lynne Goldstein. Los Angeles: Roxbury, 2001.

Steffensmeier, Darrell, and Jennifer Schwartz. "Contemporary Explanations of Women's Crime." In *The Criminal Justice System and Women: Offenders, Prisoners, Victims, and Workers,* edited by Barbara Raffel Price and Natalie J. Sokoloff. New York: McGraw-Hill, 2004.

Streib, Victor. "Death Penalty for Battered Women." *Florida State University Law Review* 20 (Summer 1992): 163–195.

——. "Death Penalty for Lesbians." *National Journal for Sexual Orientation Law* 1 (1994): 105–126.

——. *Death Penalty in a Nutshell.* St. Paul, MN: Thompson-West, 2003.

——. "Gendering the Death Penalty: Countering Sex Bias in a Masculine Sanctuary." *Ohio State Law Journal* 63 (2002): 433–472.

——, and Lynn Somitz. "Executing Female Juveniles."*Connecticut Law Review* 22 (1989–90): 3–59.

Strom, Linda. *Karla Faye Tucker Set Free: Life and Faith on Death Row*. Colorado Springs, CO: Water Brook Press, 2000.

"Teresa Lewis Executed," *Daily Mail Online* (September 26, 2010) www.dailymail.co.uk

Texas Coalition to Abolish the Death Penalty. *Texas Death Penalty Developments in 2013: The Year in Review*. Austin, TX: TCADP, 2014.

Texas Defender Service. *Lethal Indifference: The Fatal Combination of Incompetent Attorneys and Unaccountable Courts in Texas Death Penalty Appeals*. Houston, TX: 2002.

Texas Execution Information Center. "Suzanne Basso." www.txexecutions.reports

Tolson, Mike. "Appeals Run out for Harris County Woman on Death Row." *Houston Chronicle* (October 4, 2010).

———. "A Deadly Distinction." *Houston Chronicle* (February 5, 2001).

Vandiver, Margaret. "The Impact of the Death Penalty on Families of Victims and Condemned Prisoners." In *America's Experiment with Capital Punishment: Reflections on the Past, Present, and Future of the Ultimate Penal Sanction*, edited by James R. Acker, Robert M. Bohm, and Charles S. Lanier. Durham, NC: Carolina Academic Press, 1998.

Verhovek, Sam Howe. "The Nation: AK-47s, Battery Acid: Dead Woman Waiting: Who's Who on Death Row." *New York Times* (February 8, 1998).

———. "Execution in Texas: The Overview." *New York Times* (February 4, 1990).

———. "Karla Tucker Is Now Gone, but Several Debates Linger." *New York Times* (February 5, 1998).

———. "Near Death, Tucker Gave Suggestions to the Prison." *New York Times* (February 8, 1998).

Virginians for Alternatives to the Death Penalty. "Virginia to Execute Woman with 72 IQ" (August 2010) at www.vadp.org

"When the Murderer Is a Woman." *New York Times* (January 31, 1998).

Williamson, Allen R. "Clemency in Texas—A Question of Mercy?" *Texas Wesleyan Law Review* 6 (Fall 1999): 131–150.

Wilson, Nanci Koser. "Gendered Interaction in Criminal Homicide." In *Homicide: The Victim/ Offender Connection*, edited by Anna Victoria Wilson. Cincinnati, OH: Anderson, 1993.

"A Woman Dies," *America* (November 1, 2010).

Wuornos, Aileen, with Christopher Berry-Dee. *Monster: My True Story*. London: John Blake, 2004.

Yardley, Jim. "Bush and the Death Penalty: Texas Busy Death Chamber Helps Define Bush's Tenure." *New York Times* (January 7, 2000).

———. "Texas Board Denies Clemency for Woman, 62, on Death Row." *New York Times* (February 23, 2000).